FAIRY TAIL

45

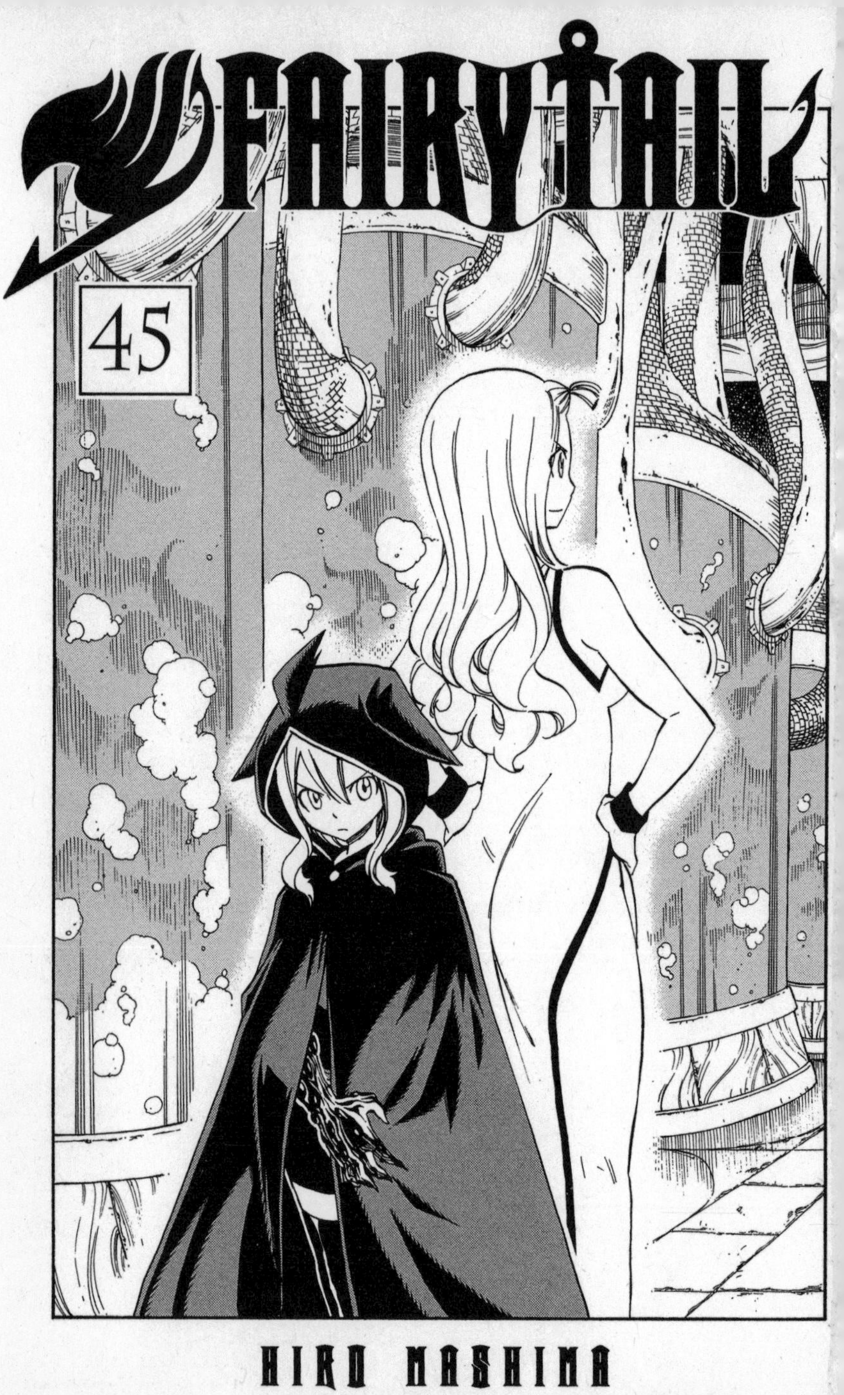

HIRO MASHIMA

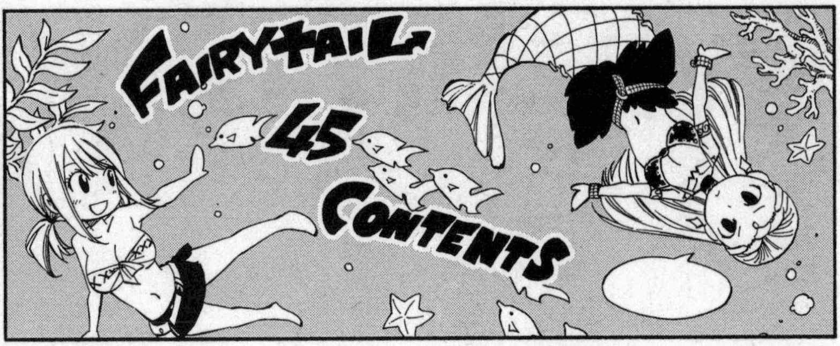
FAIRY TAIL
45
CONTENTS

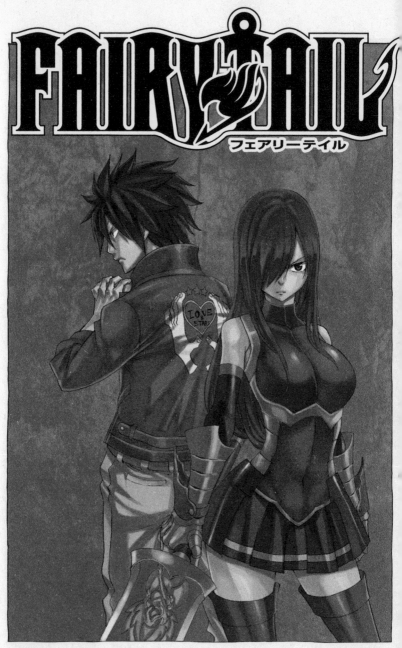

Chapter 379: Tartaros Arc, Part 3: Underworld King

FAIRY TAIL
フェアリーテイル

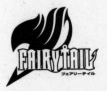

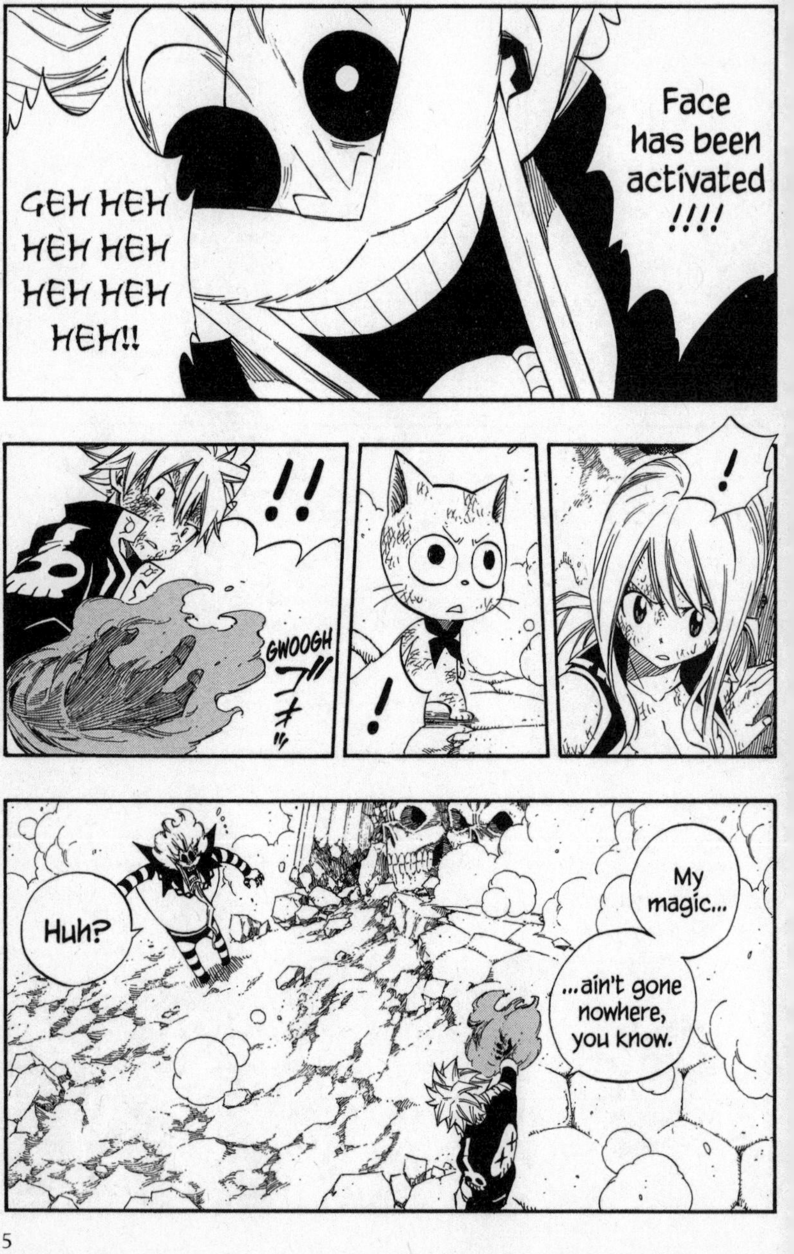
Face has been activated !!!!
GEH HEH HEH HEH HEH HEH HEH!!
!
!
!!
GWOOGH
My magic...
...ain't gone nowhere, you know.
Huh?

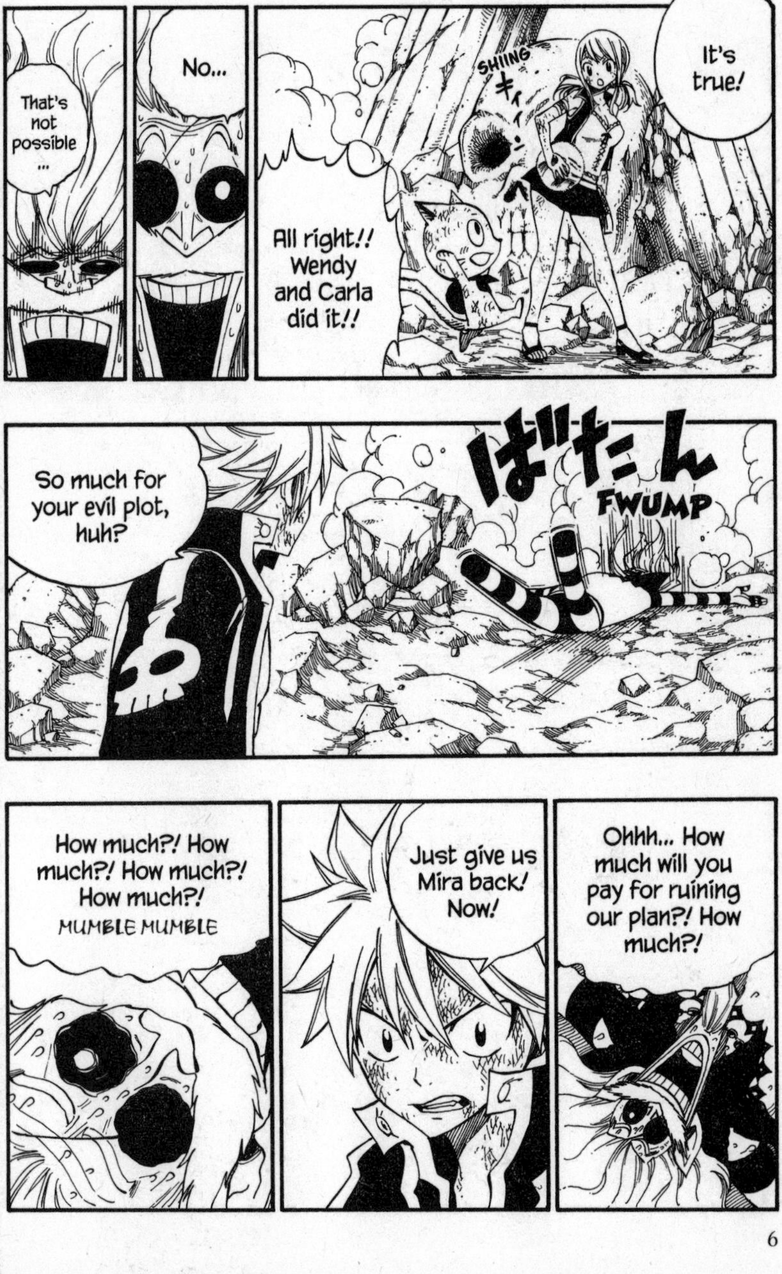

It's true!
SHIING
キィィ
All right!! Wendy and Carla did it!!
No...
That's not possible ...
ばたん
FWUMP
So much for your evil plot, huh?
Ohhh... How much will you pay for ruining our plan?! How much?!
Just give us Mira back! Now!
How much?! How much?! How much?! How much?!
MUMBLE MUMBLE

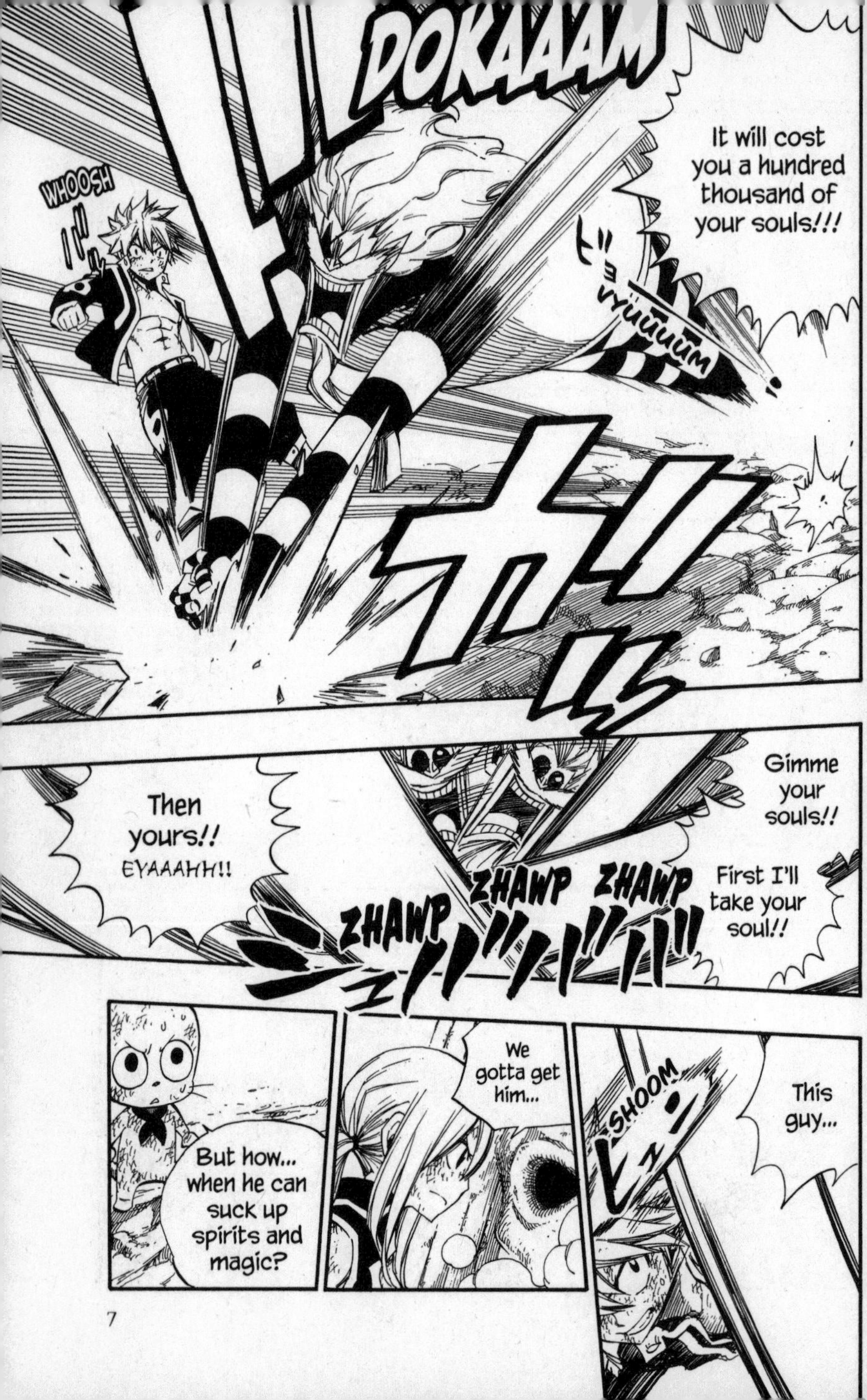
It will cost you a hundred thousand of your souls!!!
DOKAAAM
VYUUUUUM
WHOOSH
Gimme your souls!!
First I'll take your soul!!
ZHAWP
ZHAWP
ZHAWP
Then yours!!
EYAAAHH!!
This guy...
SHOOM
We gotta get him...
But how... when he can suck up spirits and magic?

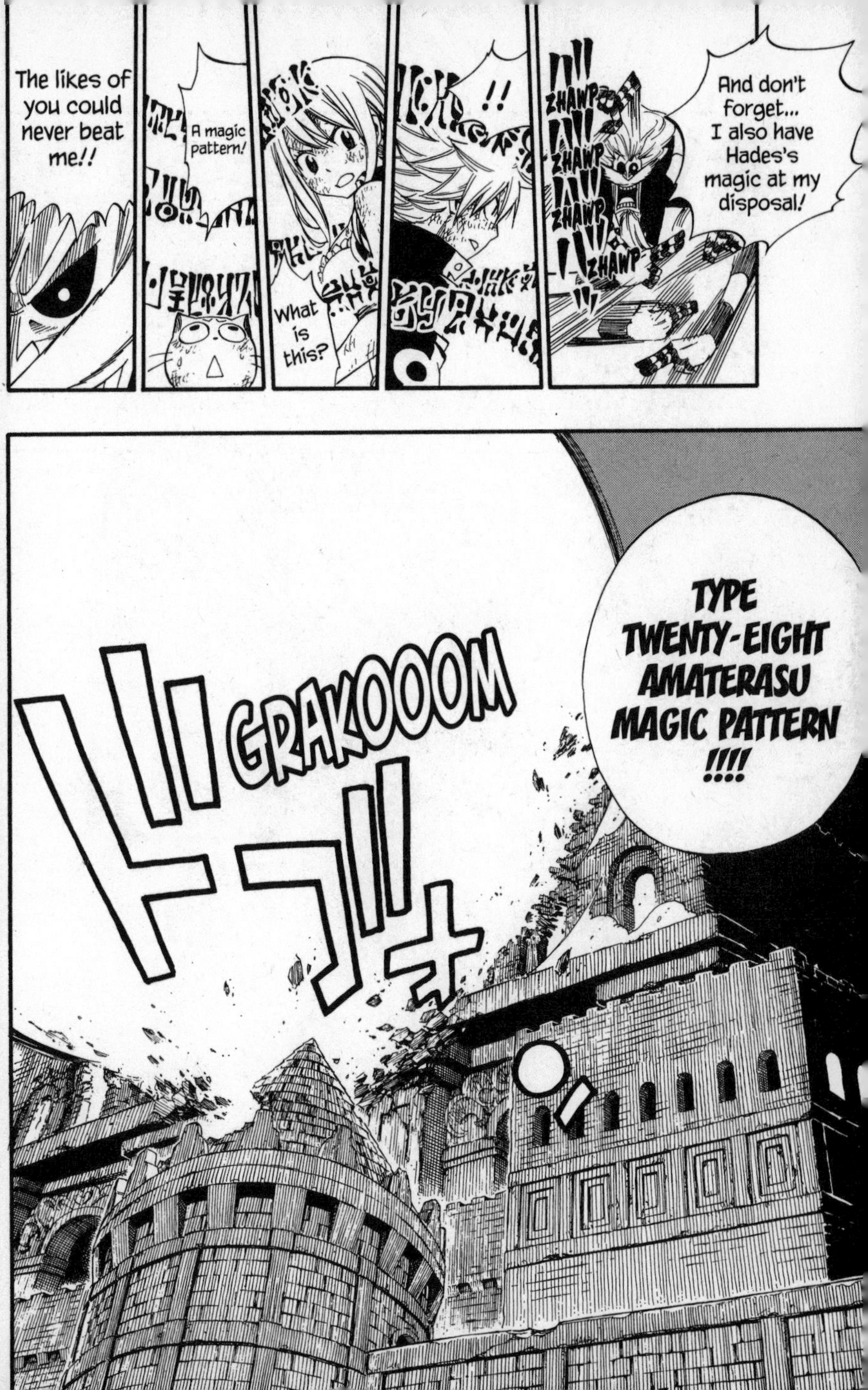
And don't forget... I also have Hades's magic at my disposal!
ZHAWP
ZHAWP
ZHAWP
ZHAWP
!!
What is this?
A magic pattern!
The likes of you could never beat me!!
TYPE TWENTY-EIGHT AMATERASU MAGIC PATTERN!!!!
GRAKOOOM

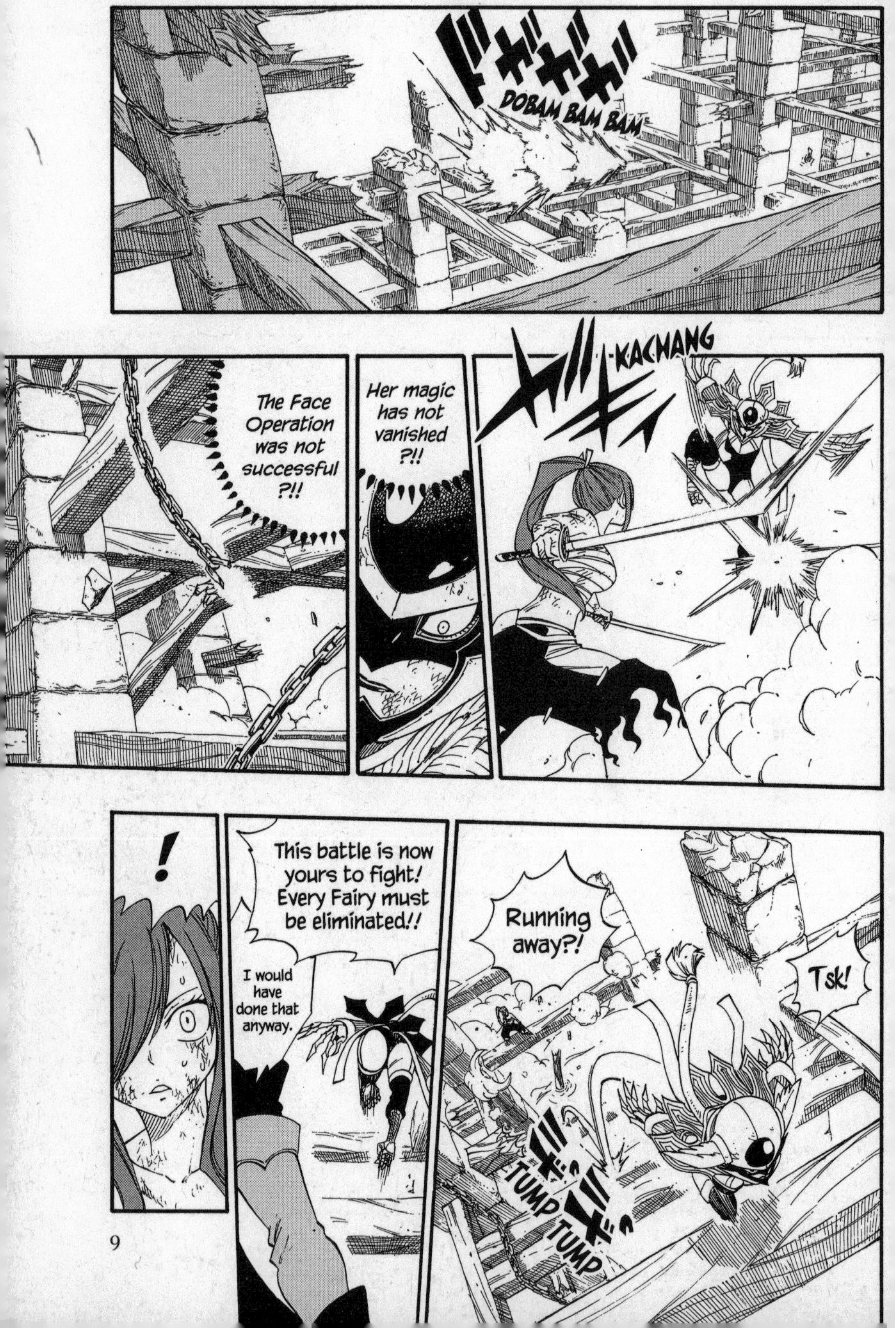
DOBAM BAM BAM
KACHANG
Her magic has not vanished ?!!
The Face Operation was not successful ?!!
Running away?!
Tsk!
TUMP TUMP
This battle is now yours to fight! Every Fairy must be eliminated!!
I would have done that anyway.
!

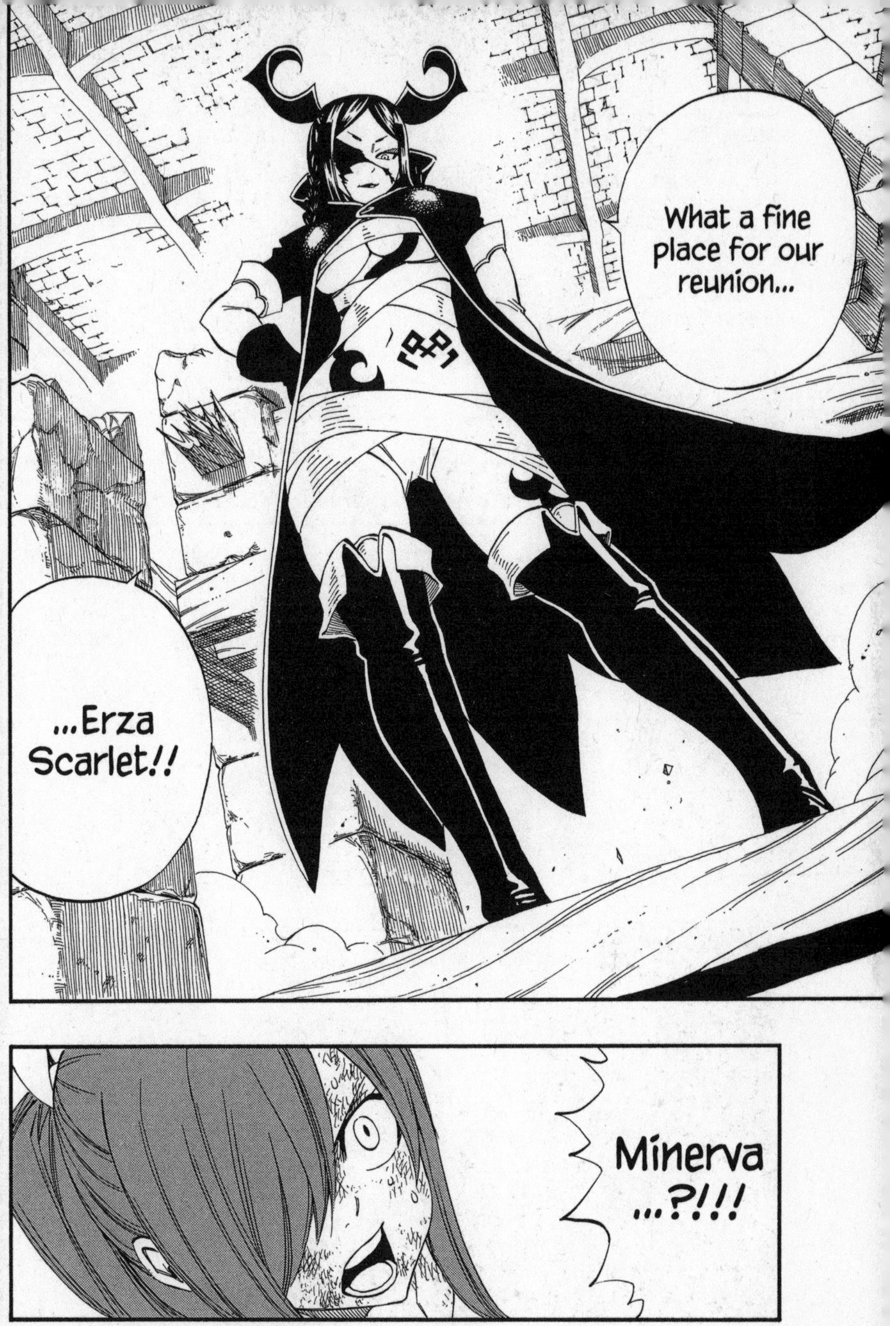
What a fine place for our reunion...
...Erza Scarlet!!
Minerva ...?!!!

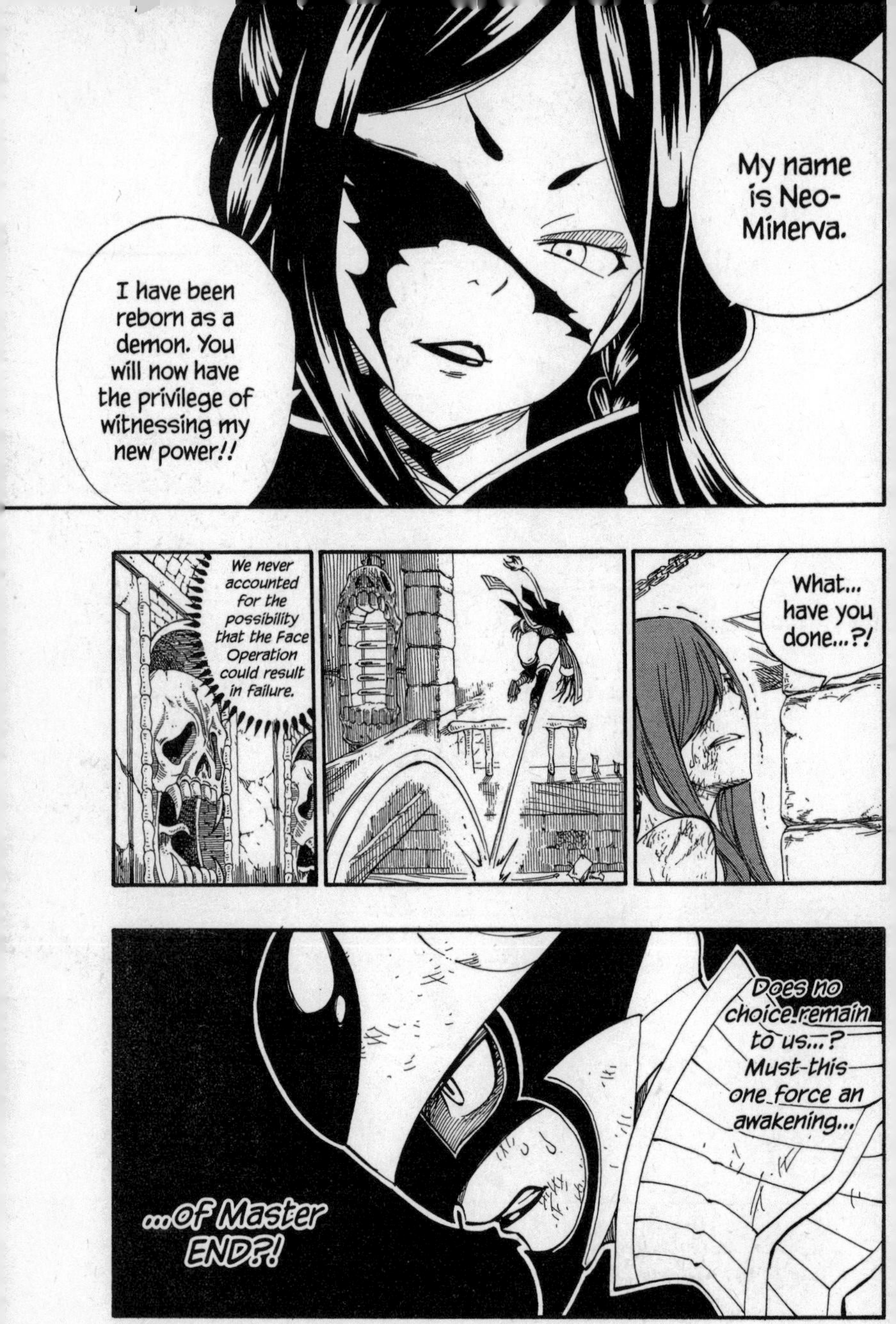
My name is Neo-Minerva.
I have been reborn as a demon. You will now have the privilege of witnessing my new power!!
What... have you done...?!
We never accounted for the possibility that the Face Operation could result in failure.
Does no choice remain to us...? Must this one force an awakening...
...of Master END?!

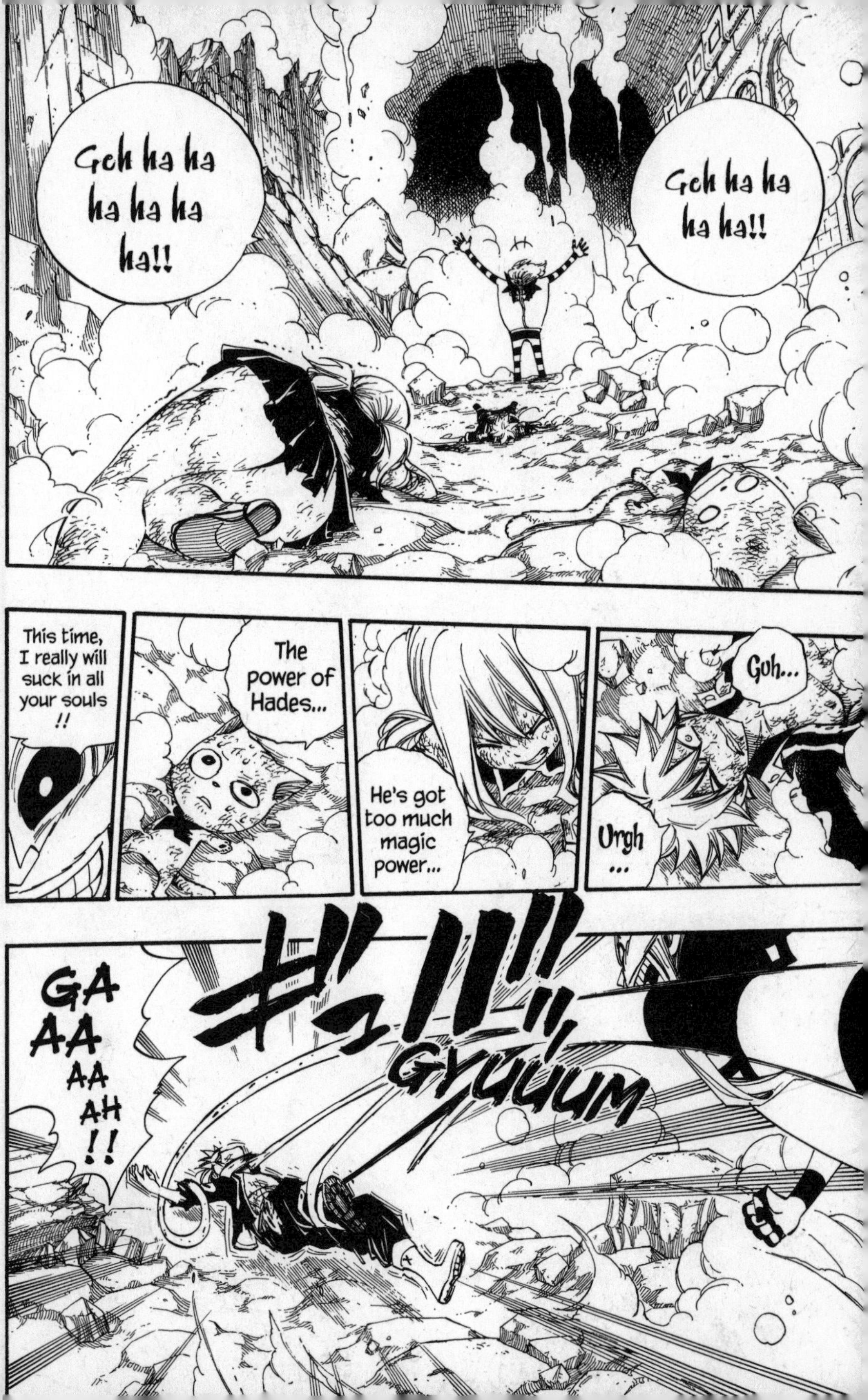
Geh ha ha ha ha!!
Geh ha ha ha ha ha ha!!
Guh...
Urgh ...
He's got too much magic power...
The power of Hades...
This time, I really will suck in all your souls !!
Gyuuum
GAAAAAAH!!

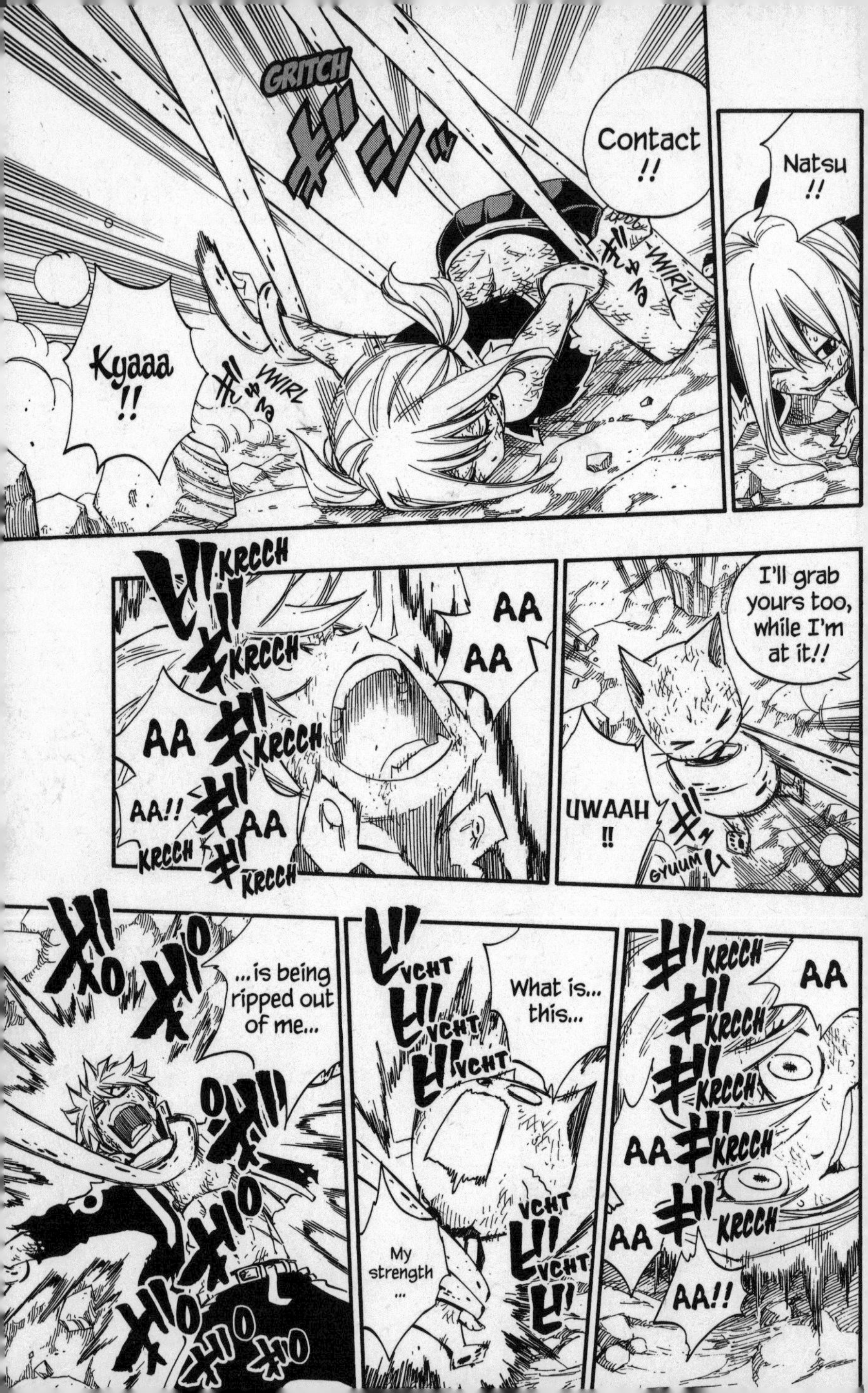
Natsu!!
Contact!!
GRITCH
SWIRL
Kyaaa!!
SWIRL
I'll grab yours too, while I'm at it!!
UWAAH!!
GYUUM
KRCCH
AA
AA
KRCCH
AA
KRCCH
AA!!
AA
KRCCH
KRCCH
AA
KRCCH
KRCCH
KRCCH
AA
AA
KRCCH
AA!!
What is... this...
VCHT
VCHT
VCHT
VCHT
VCHT
My strength...
...is being ripped out of me...

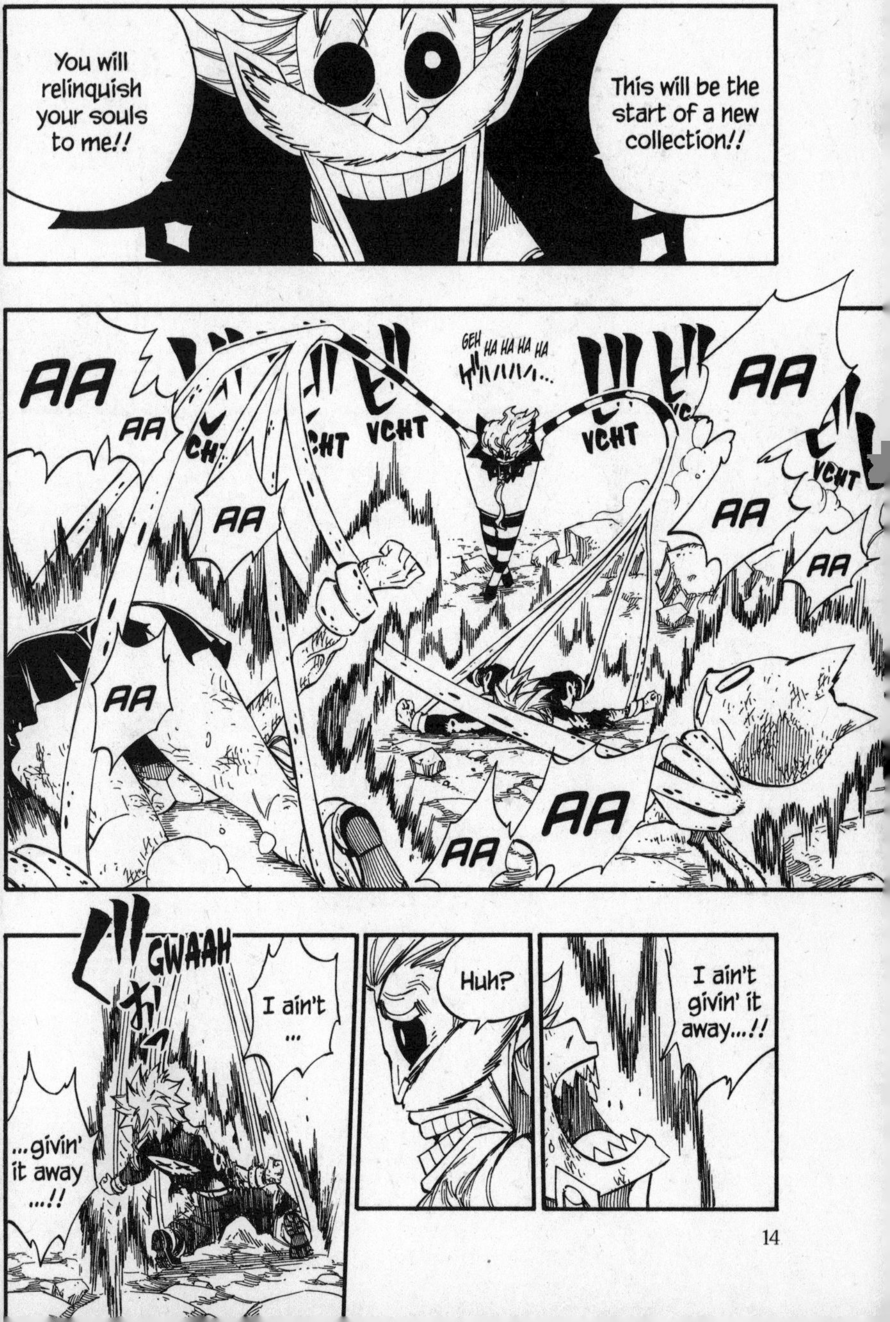
This will be the start of a new collection!!
You will relinquish your souls to me!!
AA
VCHT
AA
AA
VCHT
GEH HA HA HA HA...
VCHT
VCHT
AA
AA
AA
AA
AA
AA
I ain't givin' it away...!!
Huh?
GWAAH
I ain't ...
...givin' it away ...!!

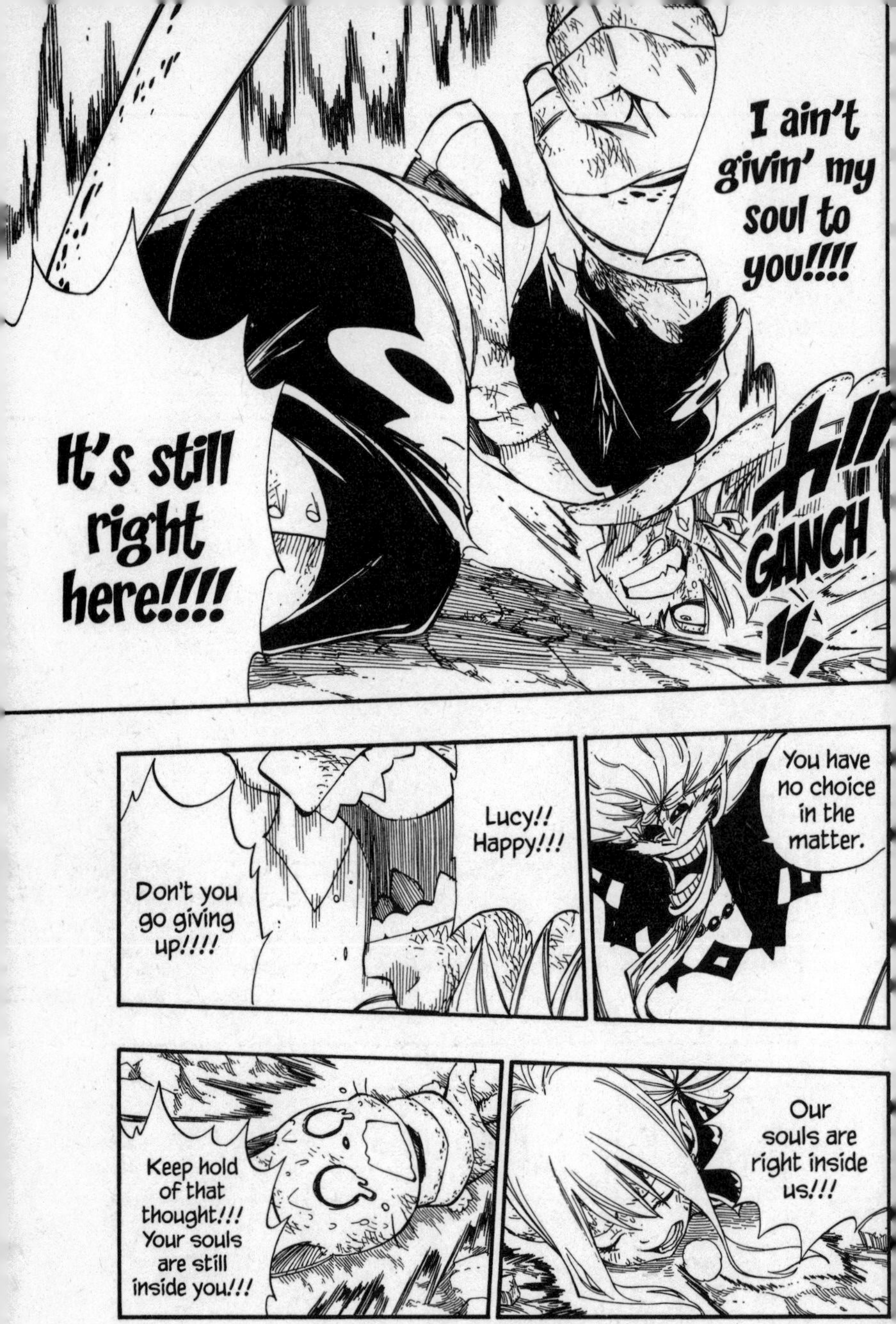
I ain't givin' my soul to you!!!!
GANCH
It's still right here!!!!
You have no choice in the matter.
Lucy!! Happy!!!
Don't you go giving up!!!!
Our souls are right inside us!!!
Keep hold of that thought!!! Your souls are still inside you!!!

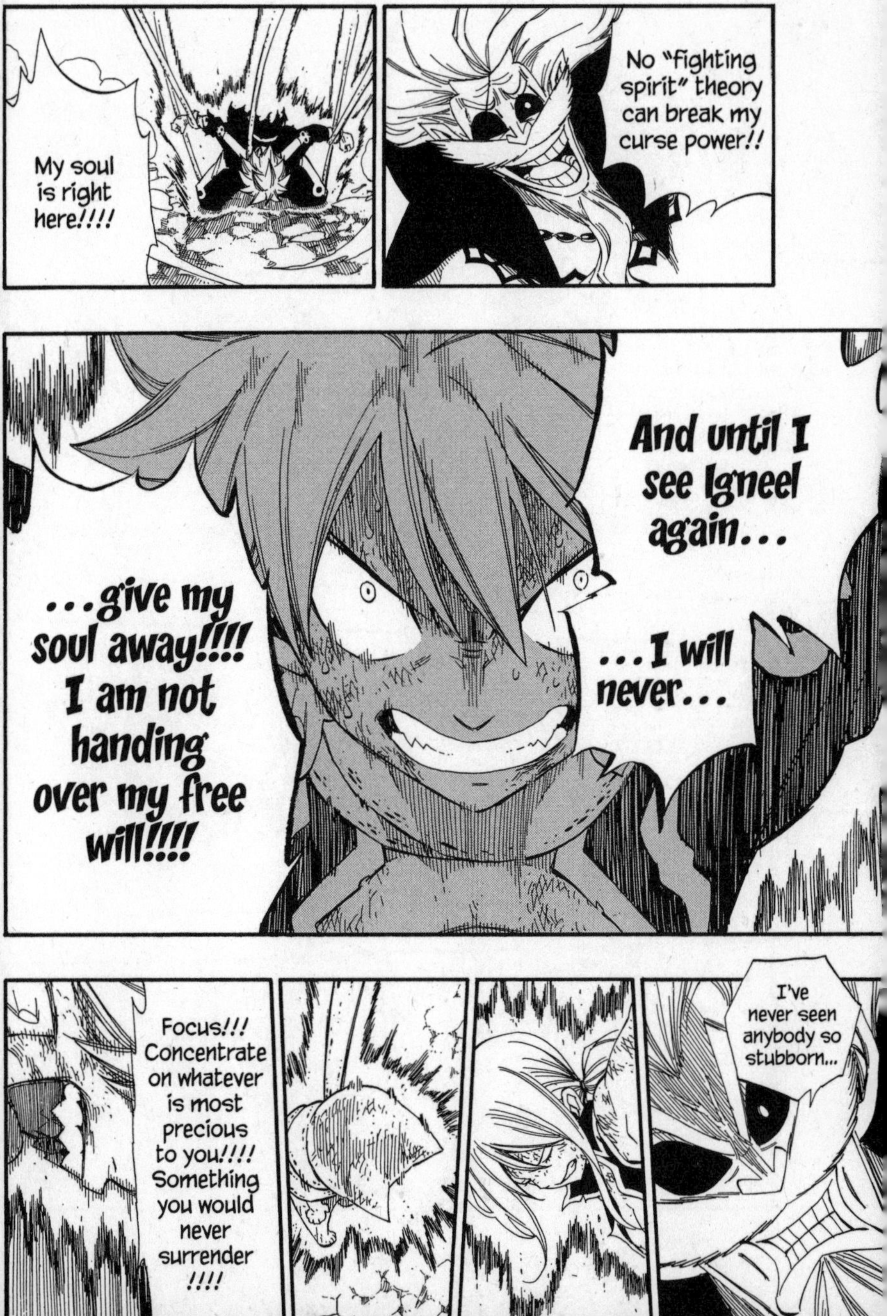
No "fighting spirit" theory can break my curse power!!
My soul is right here!!!!
And until I see Igneel again...
...I will never...
...give my soul away!!!! I am not handing over my free will!!!!
I've never seen anybody so stubborn...
Focus!!! Concentrate on whatever is most precious to you!!!! Something you would never surrender !!!!

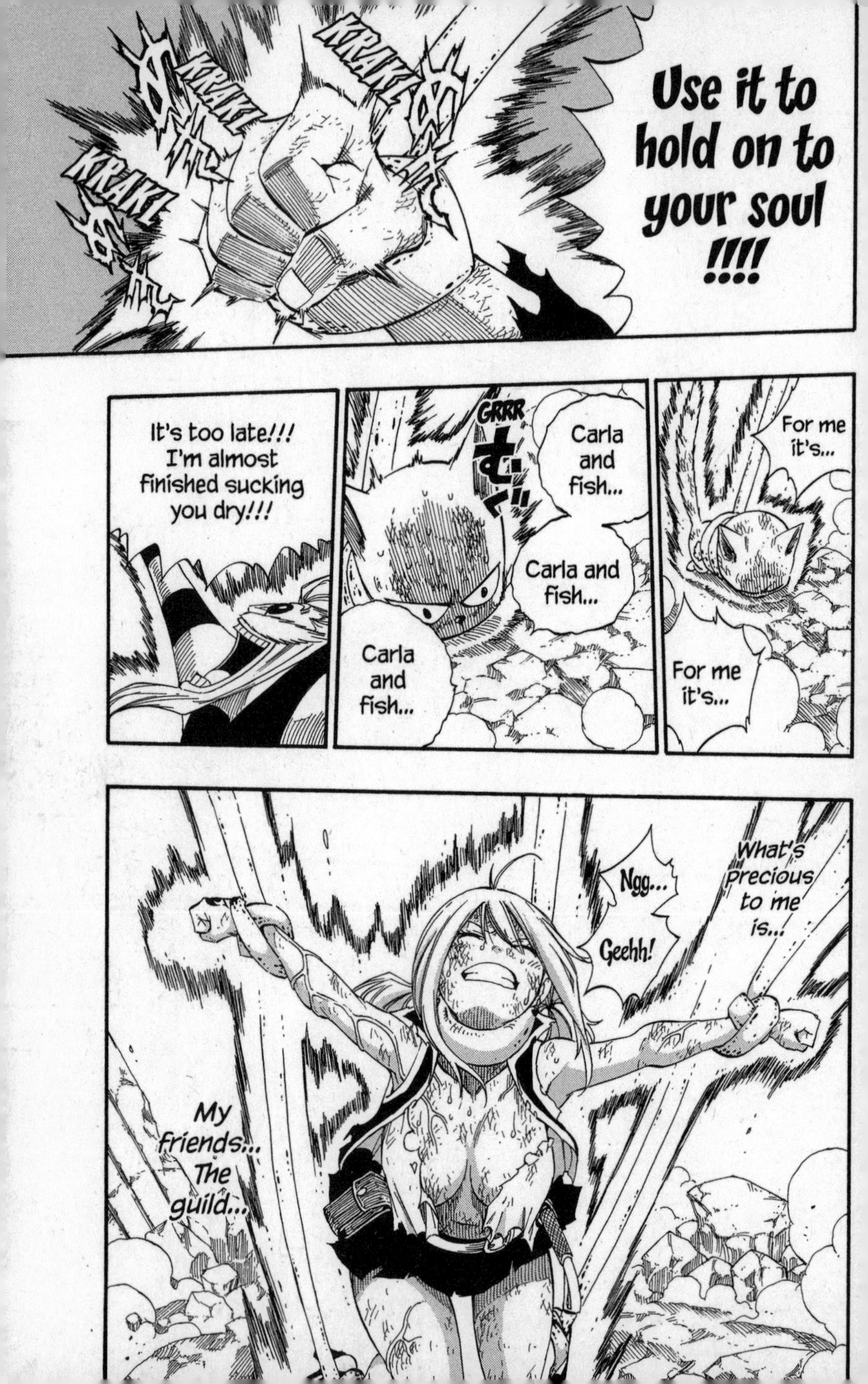
Use it to hold on to your soul!!!!
KRAK!
KRAK!
KRAK!
For me it's...
For me it's...
GRRR
Carla and fish...
Carla and fish...
Carla and fish...
It's too late!!! I'm almost finished sucking you dry!!!
What's precious to me is...
Ngg...
Geehh!
My friends... The guild...

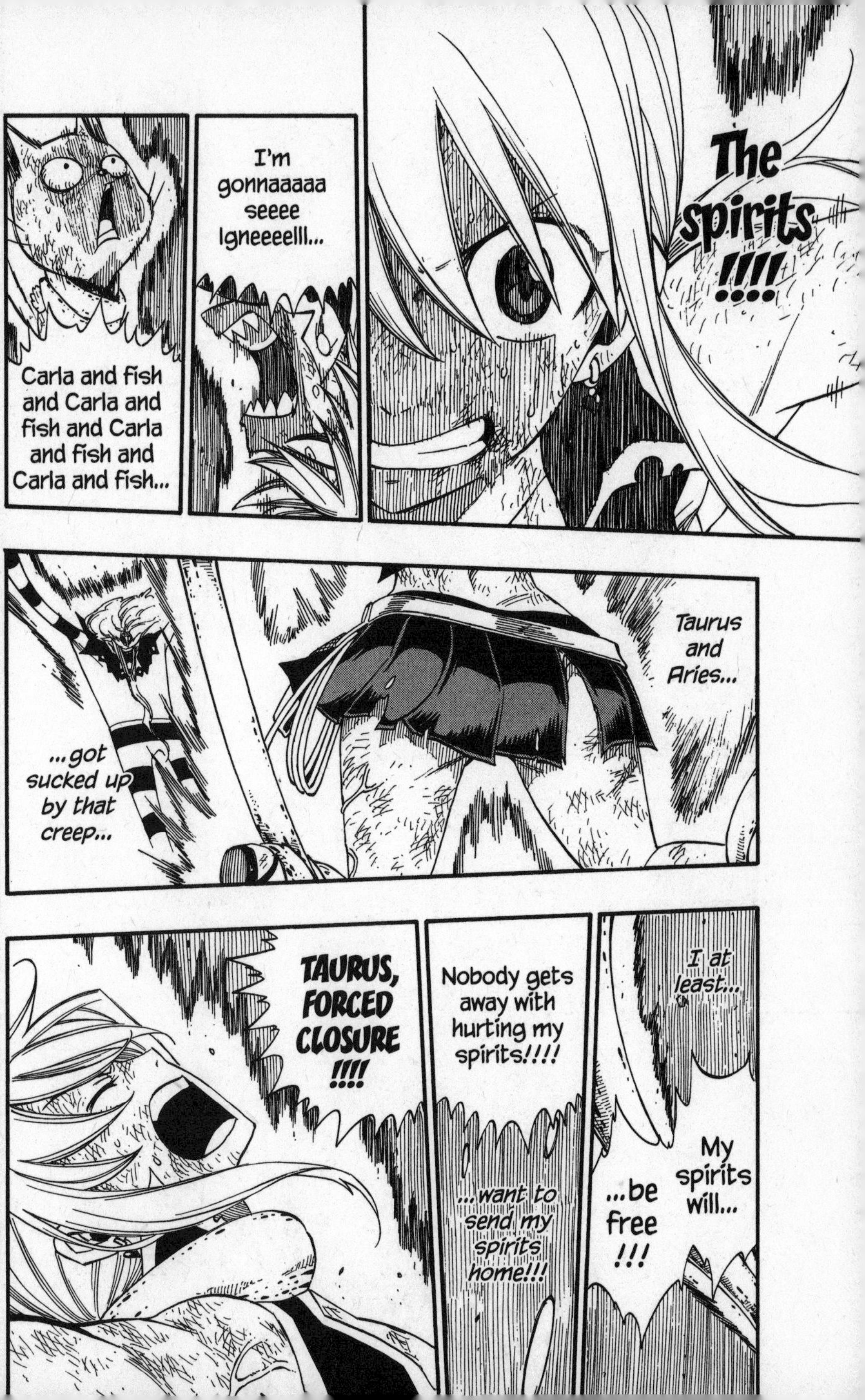
The spirits!!!!
I'm gonnaaaaa seeee Igneeeelll...
Carla and fish and Carla and fish and Carla and fish and Carla and fish...
Taurus and Aries...
...got sucked up by that creep...
I at least...
My spirits will...
...be free!!!
Nobody gets away with hurting my spirits!!!!
...want to send my spirits home!!!
TAURUS, FORCED CLOSURE!!!!

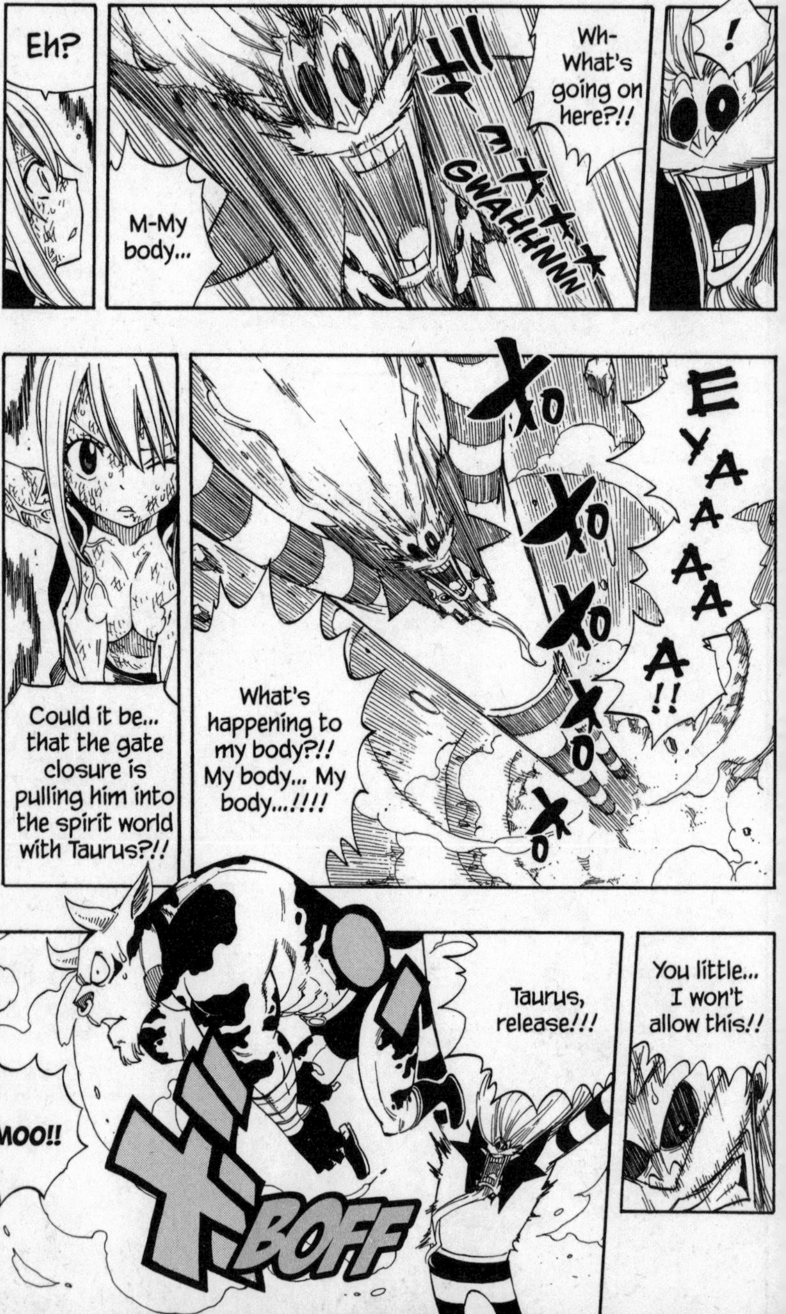
!
Wh- What's going on here?!!
GWAHHNNN
M-My body...
Eh?
EYAAAAA!!
What's happening to my body?!! My body... My body...!!!!
Could it be... that the gate closure is pulling him into the spirit world with Taurus?!!
You little... I won't allow this!!
Taurus, release!!!
NMOO!!
BOFF

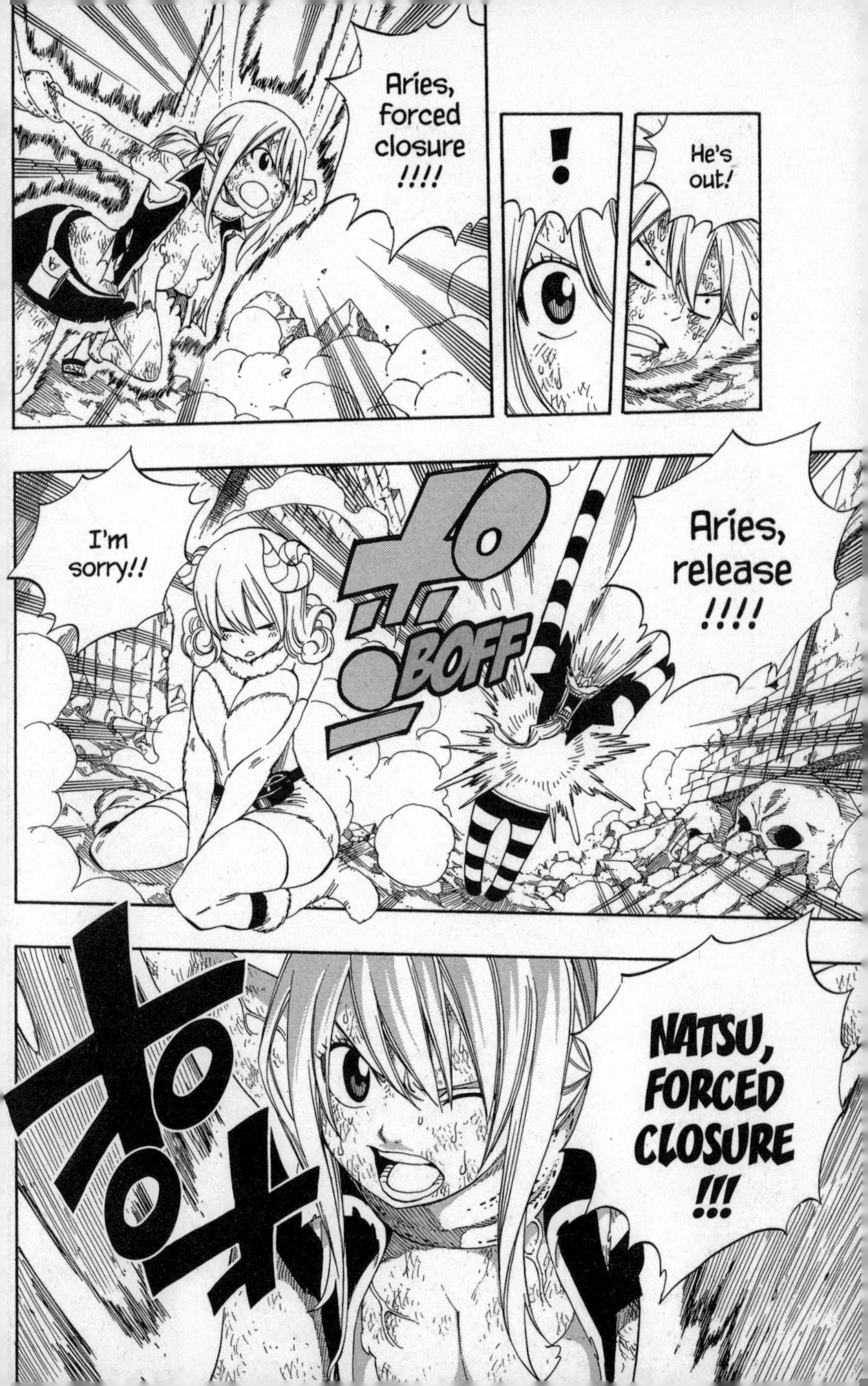
He's out!
!
Aries, forced closure !!!!
Aries, release !!!!
BOFF
I'm sorry!!
NATSU, FORCED CLOSURE !!!

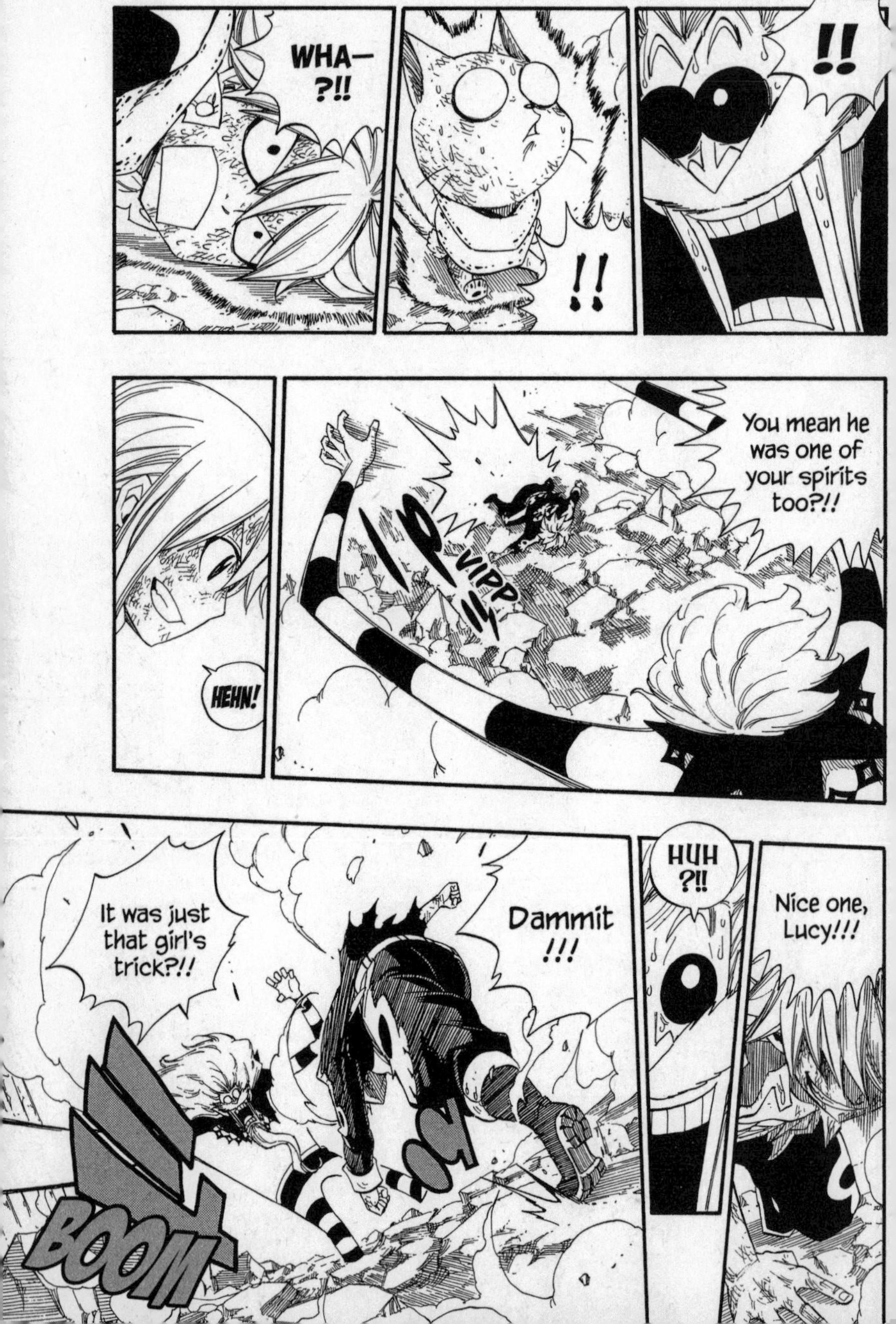
!!
!!
WHA—?!!
You mean he was one of your spirits too?!!
VIPP
HEHN!
Nice one, Lucy!!!
HUH ?!!
Dammit !!!
It was just that girl's trick?!!
BOOM

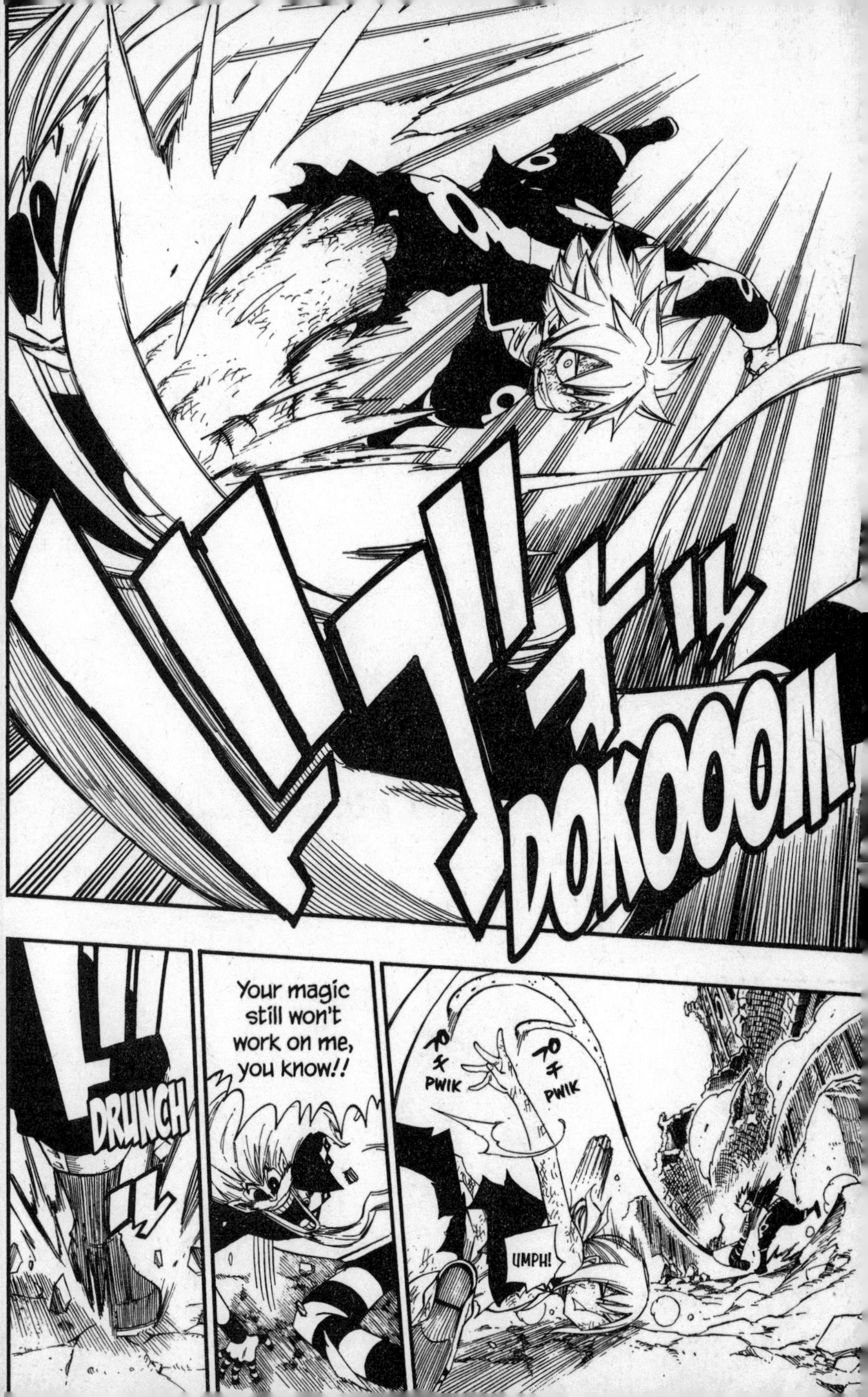
DOKOOOM
PWIK
PWIK
UMPH!
Your magic still won't work on me, you know!!
DRUNCH

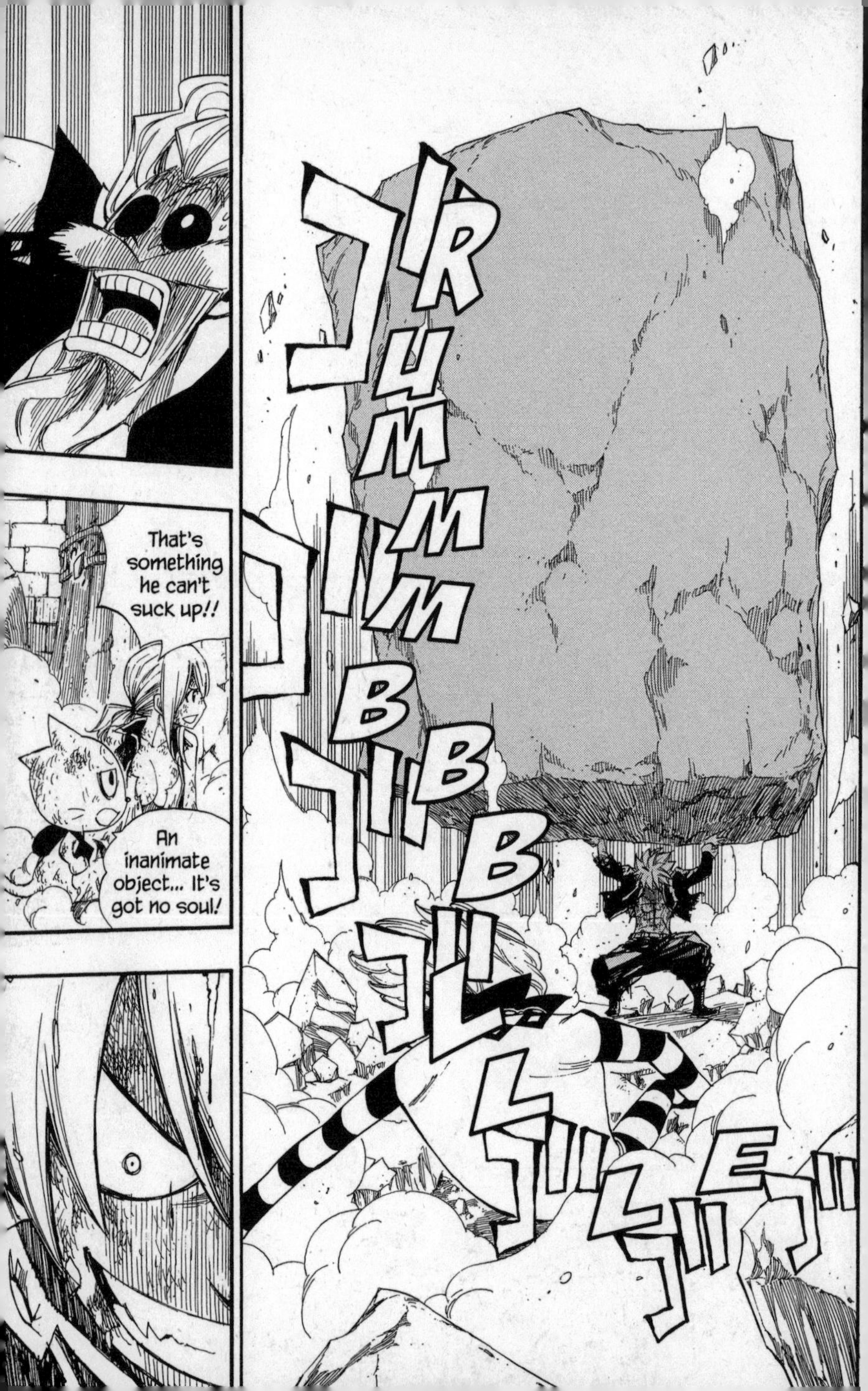
RUMMMBBBLLE
That's something he can't suck up!!
An inanimate object... It's got no soul!

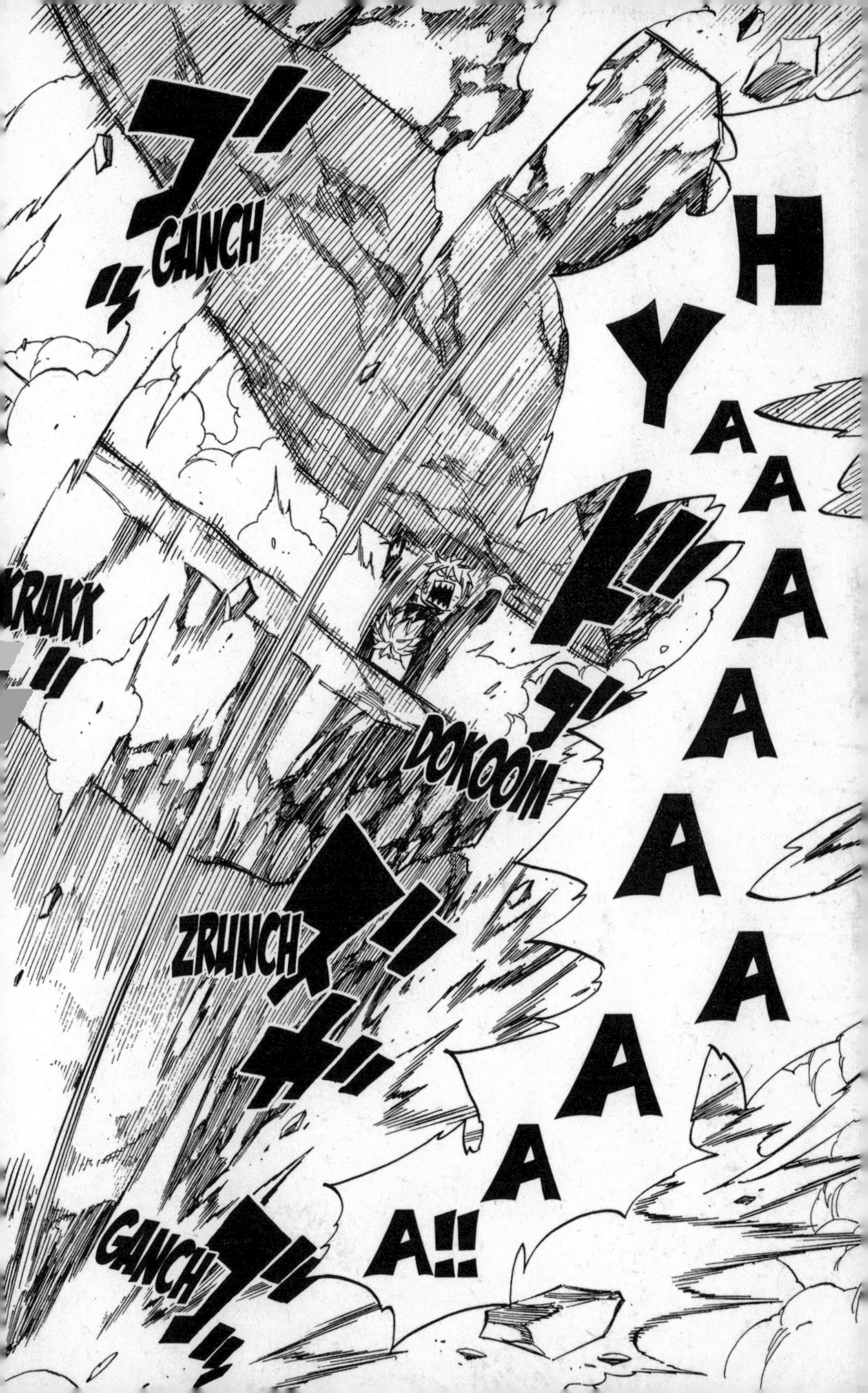
HYAAAAAAAAA!!
GANCH
KRAKK
DOKOOM
ZRUNCH
GANCH

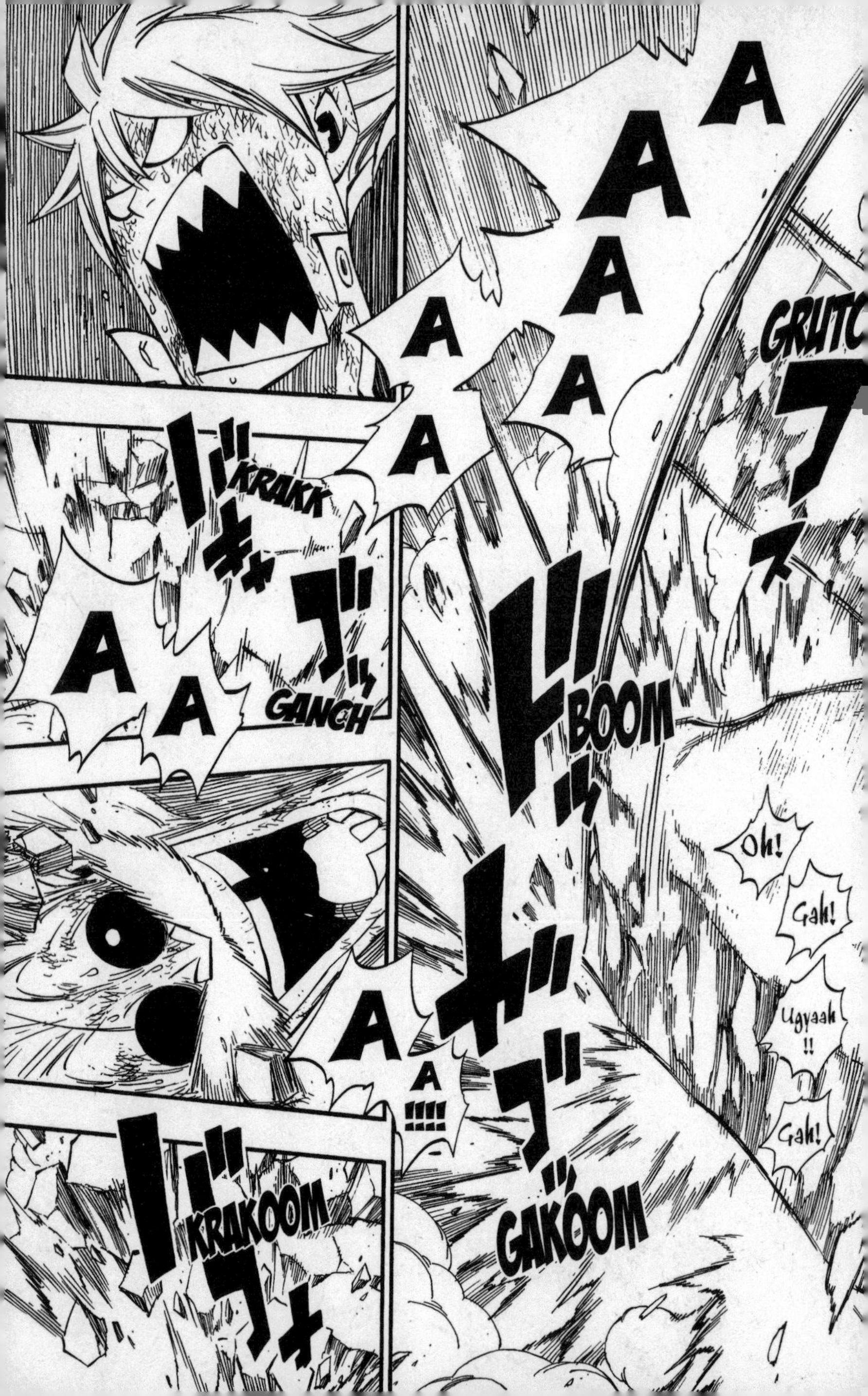
A
A
A
A
A
A
A
GRUTC
BOOM
Oh!
Gah!
Ugyaah!!
Gah!
A
A!!!!
GAKOOM
KRAKK
A
A
GANCH
KRAKOOM

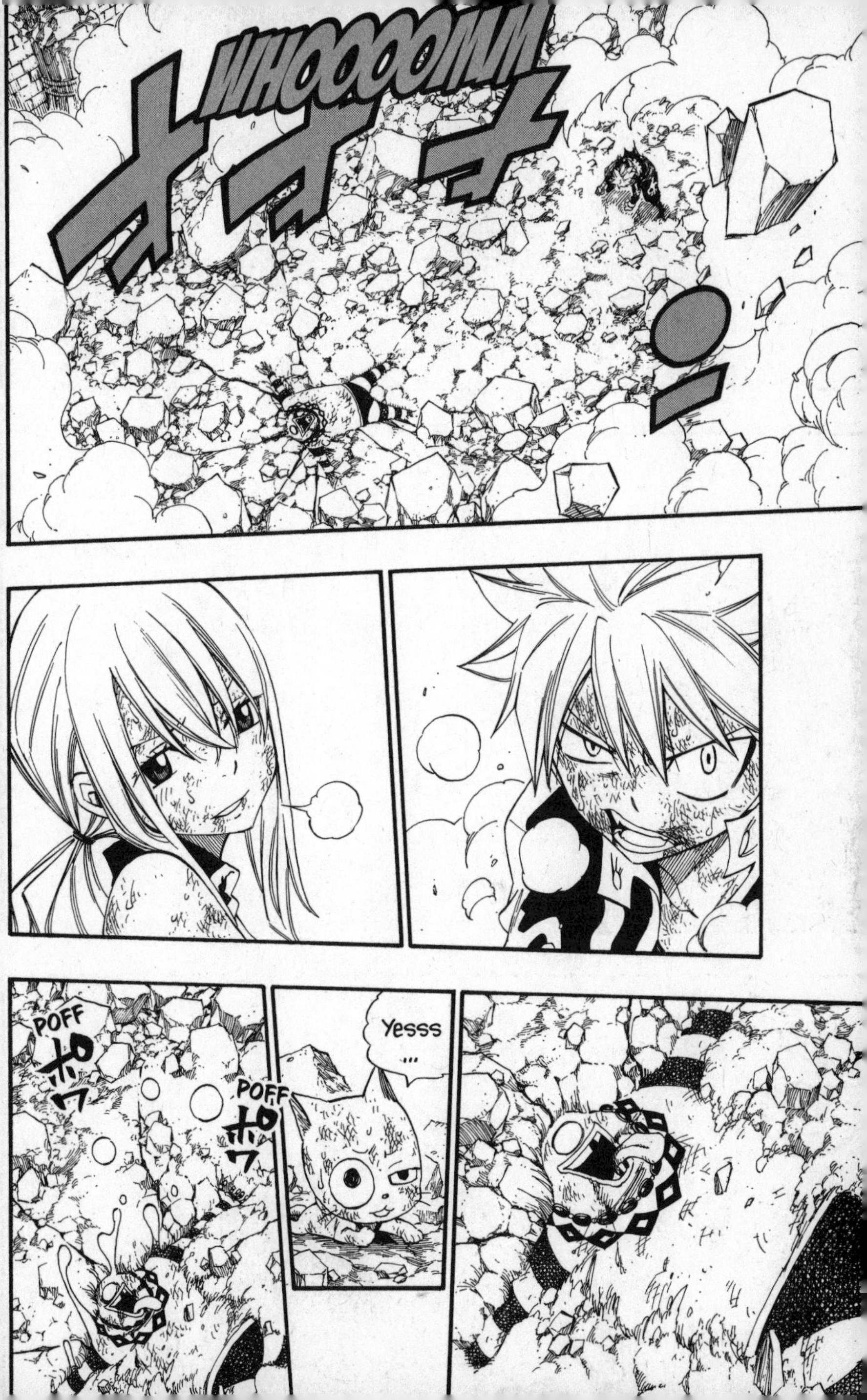
WHOOOOMM
オオオ
Yesss
...
POFF
ポワ
POFF
ポワ

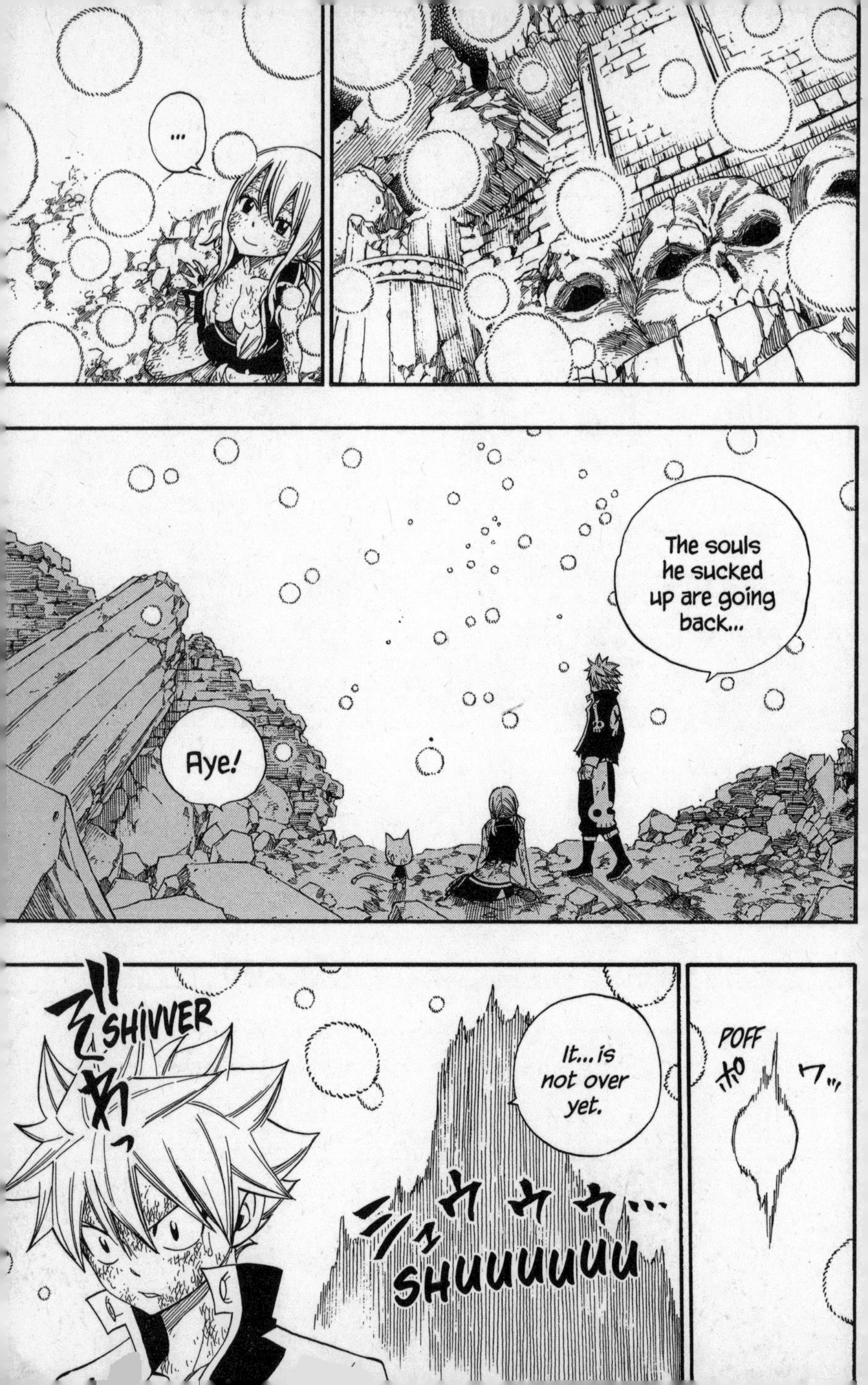
...
The souls he sucked up are going back...
Aye!
POFF
ポワ…
It...is not over yet.
シュウウウ…
SHUUUUUU
SHIVVER
ぞわっ!!

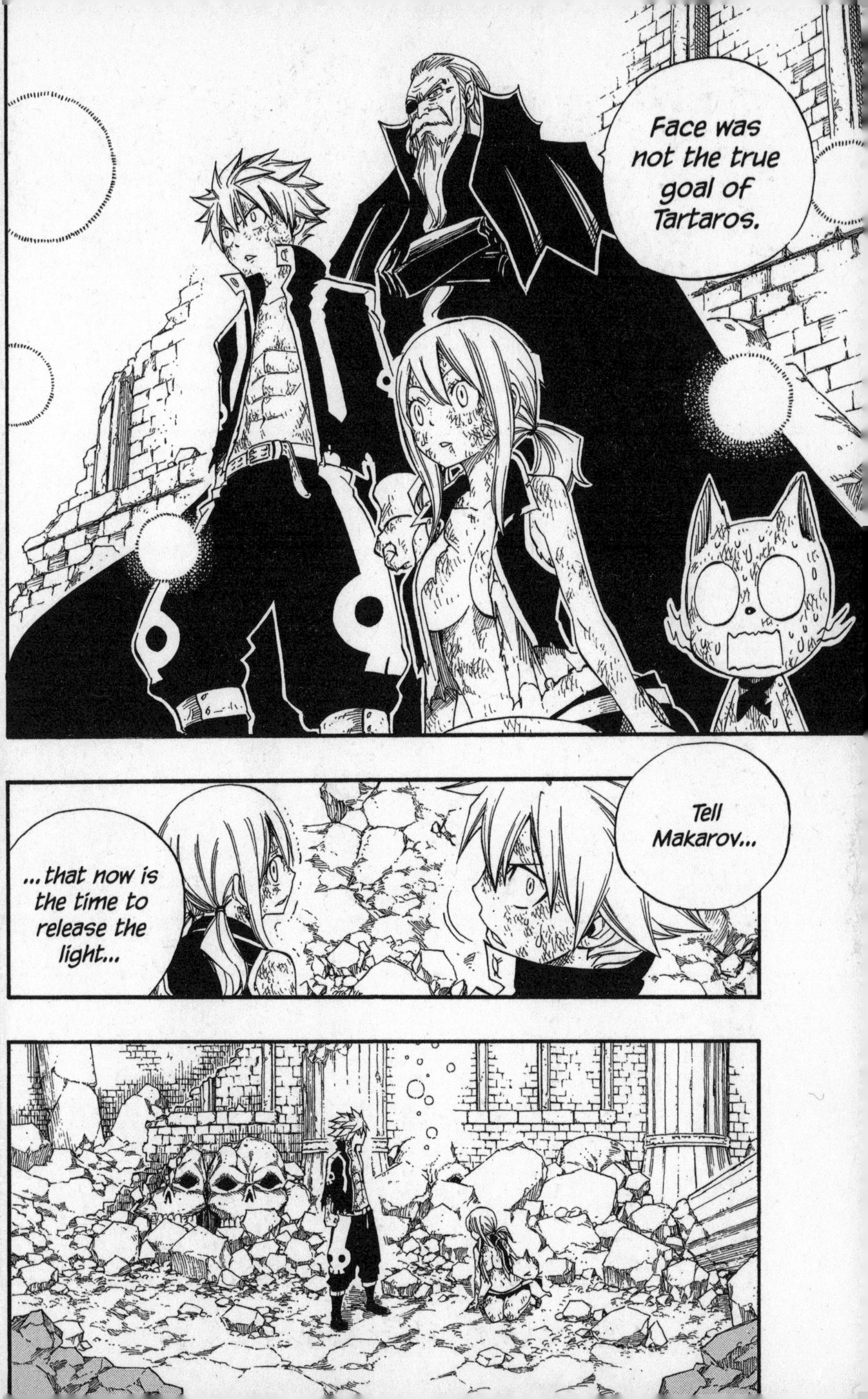
Face was not the true goal of Tartaros.
Tell Makarov...
...that now is the time to release the light...

FAIRY TAIL

フェアリーテイル

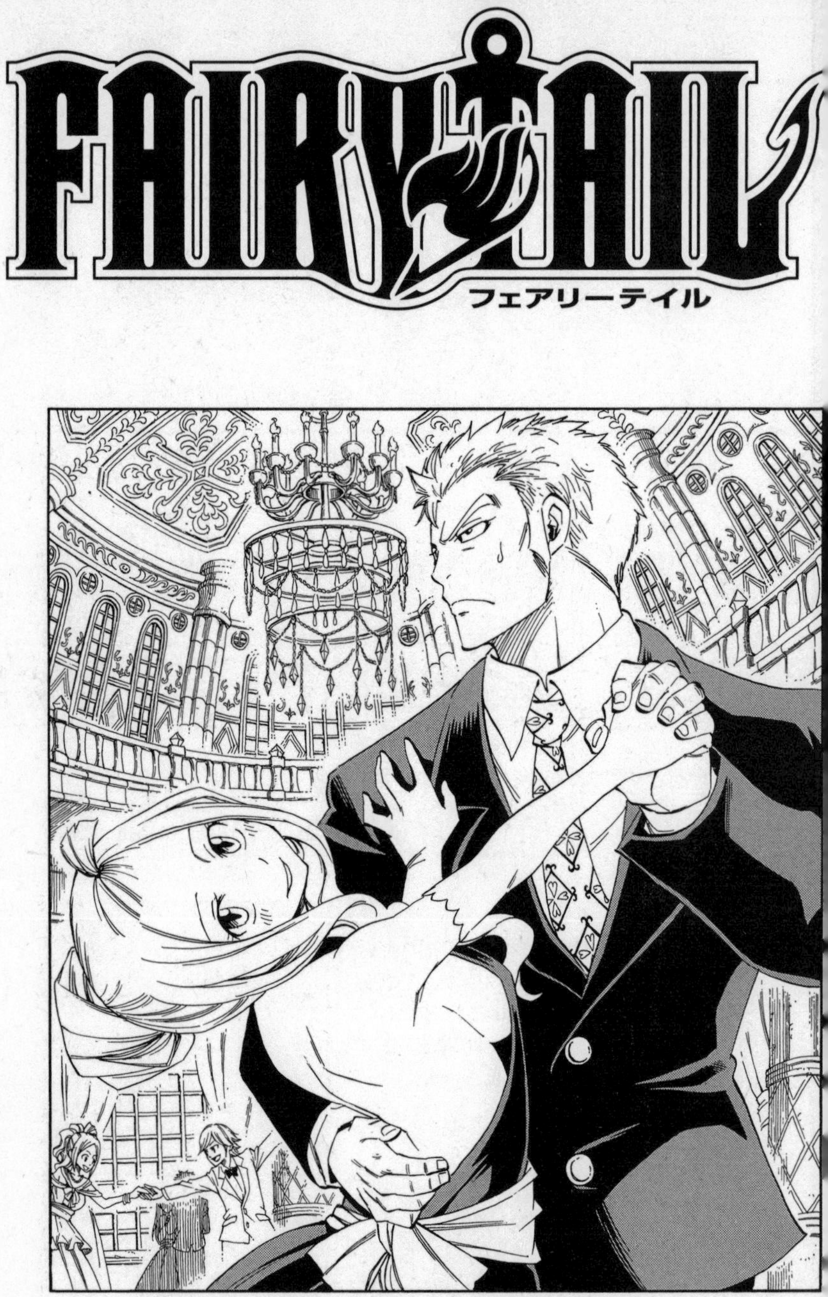

Chapter 380: Hell's Core

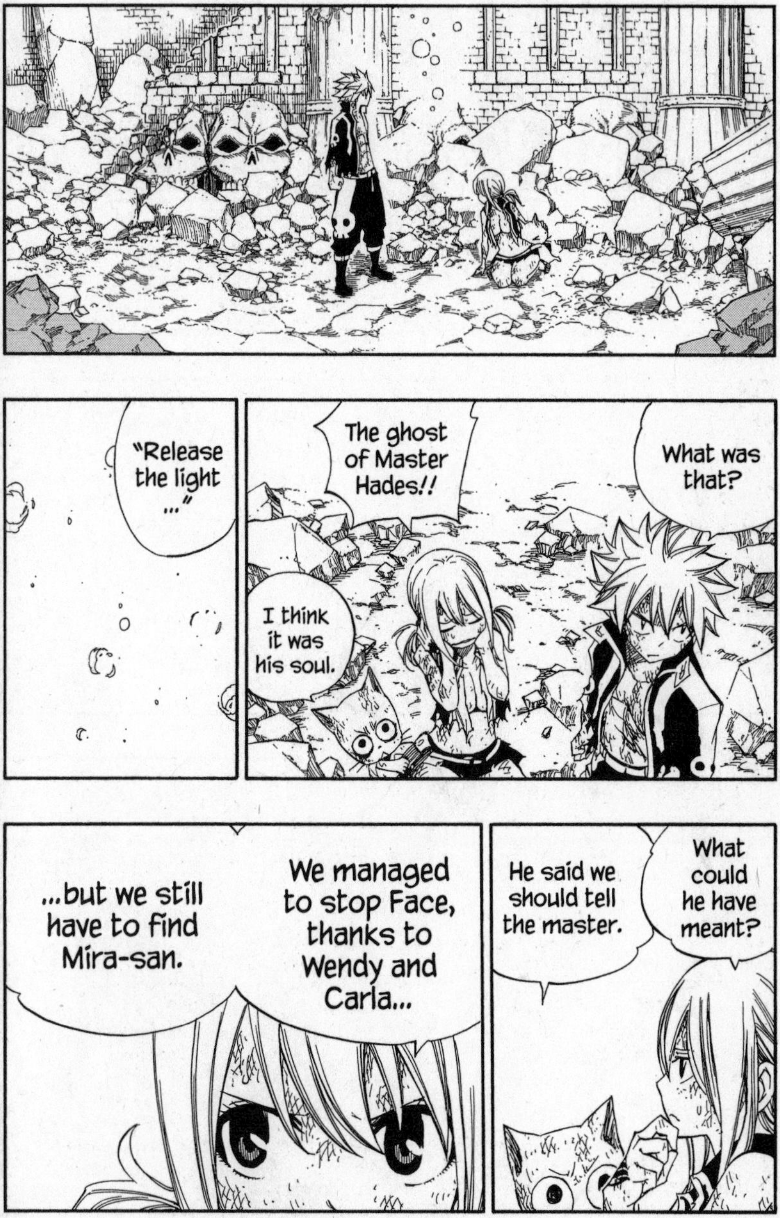
What was that?
The ghost of Master Hades!!
I think it was his soul.
"Release the light ..."
What could he have meant?
He said we should tell the master.
We managed to stop Face, thanks to Wendy and Carla...
...but we still have to find Mira-san.

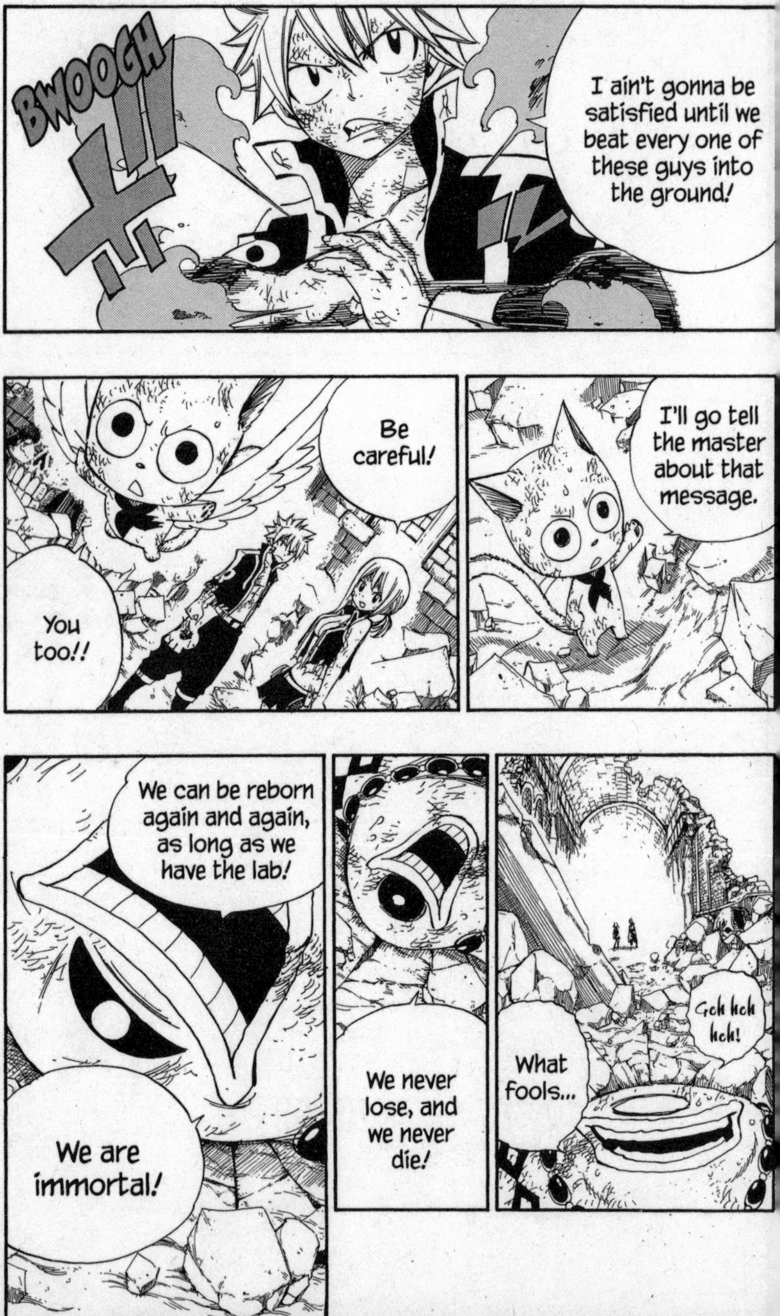
I ain't gonna be satisfied until we beat every one of these guys into the ground!
BWOOGH
I'll go tell the master about that message.
Be careful!
You too!!
Geh heh heh!
What fools...
We never lose, and we never die!
We can be reborn again and again, as long as we have the lab!
We are immortal!

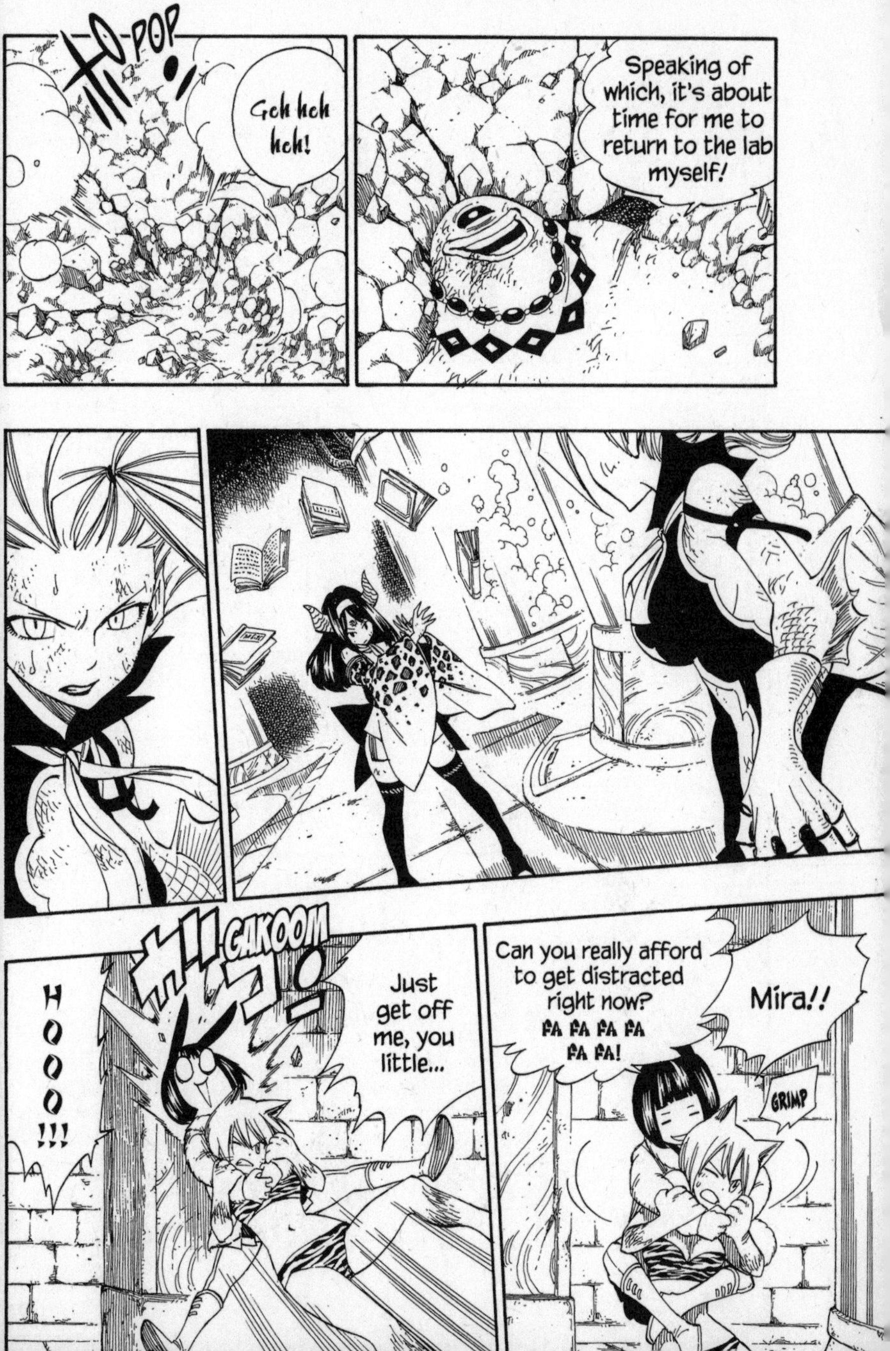
Speaking of which, it's about time for me to return to the lab myself!
POP
Geh heh heh!
Mira!!
Can you really afford to get distracted right now? FA FA FA FA FA FA!
GRIMP
GAKOOM
Just get off me, you little...
HOOOO!!!

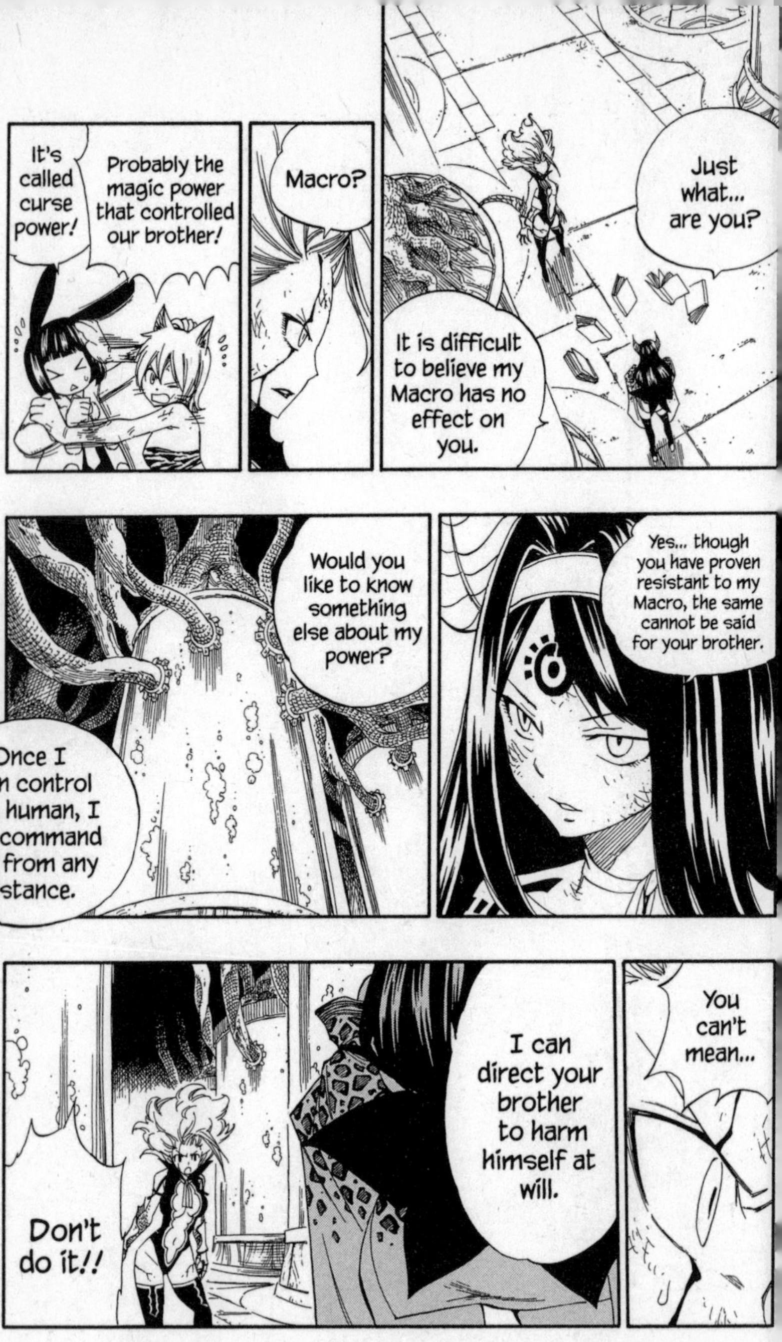
Just what... are you?
It is difficult to believe my Macro has no effect on you.
Macro?
Probably the magic power that controlled our brother!
It's called curse power!
Yes... though you have proven resistant to my Macro, the same cannot be said for your brother.
Would you like to know something else about my power?
Once I gain control of a human, I can command him from any distance.
You can't mean...
I can direct your brother to harm himself at will.
Don't do it!!

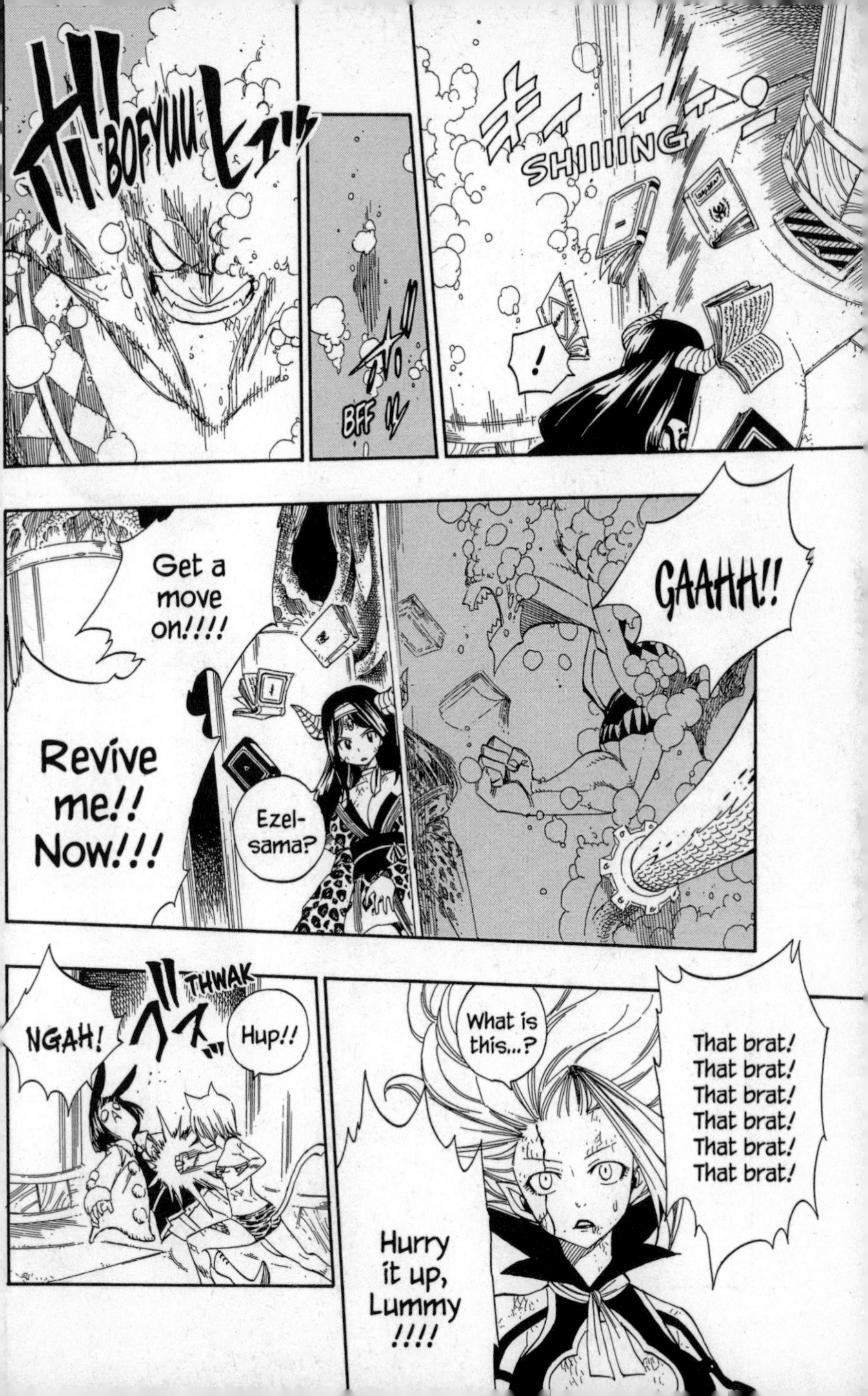
SHIIIING
!
BFF
HI BOFYUU
GAAHH!!
Get a move on!!!!
Ezel-sama?
Revive me!! Now!!!
That brat! That brat! That brat! That brat! That brat! That brat!
What is this...?
Hurry it up, Lummy!!!!
THWAK
Hup!!
NGAH!

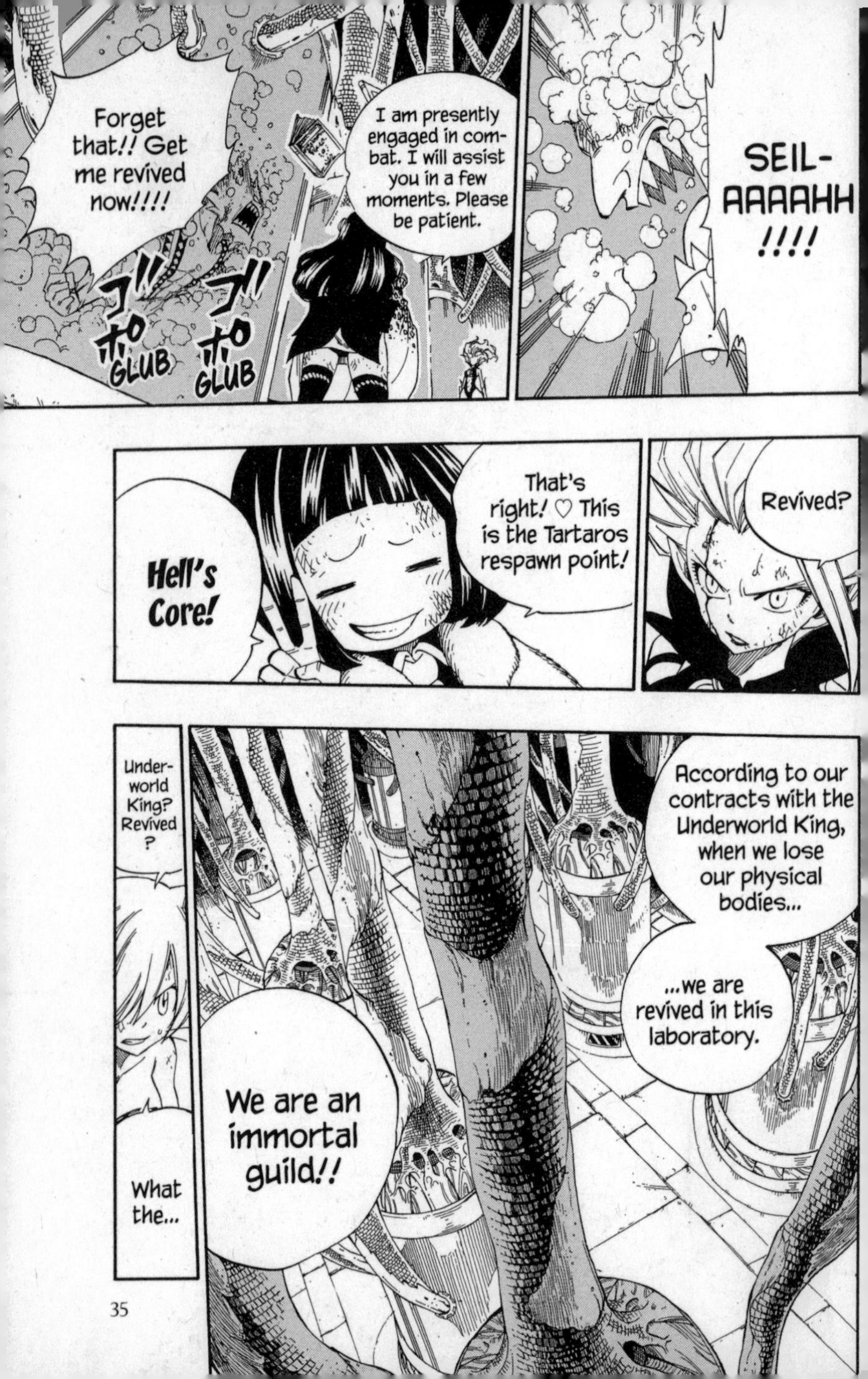

SEIL-AAAAHH!!!!
Forget that!! Get me revived now!!!!
I am presently engaged in combat. I will assist you in a few moments. Please be patient.
GLUB
GLUB
Revived?
That's right! ♡ This is the Tartaros respawn point!
Hell's Core!
According to our contracts with the Underworld King, when we lose our physical bodies...
...we are revived in this laboratory.
We are an immortal guild!!
Underworld King? Revived?
What the...

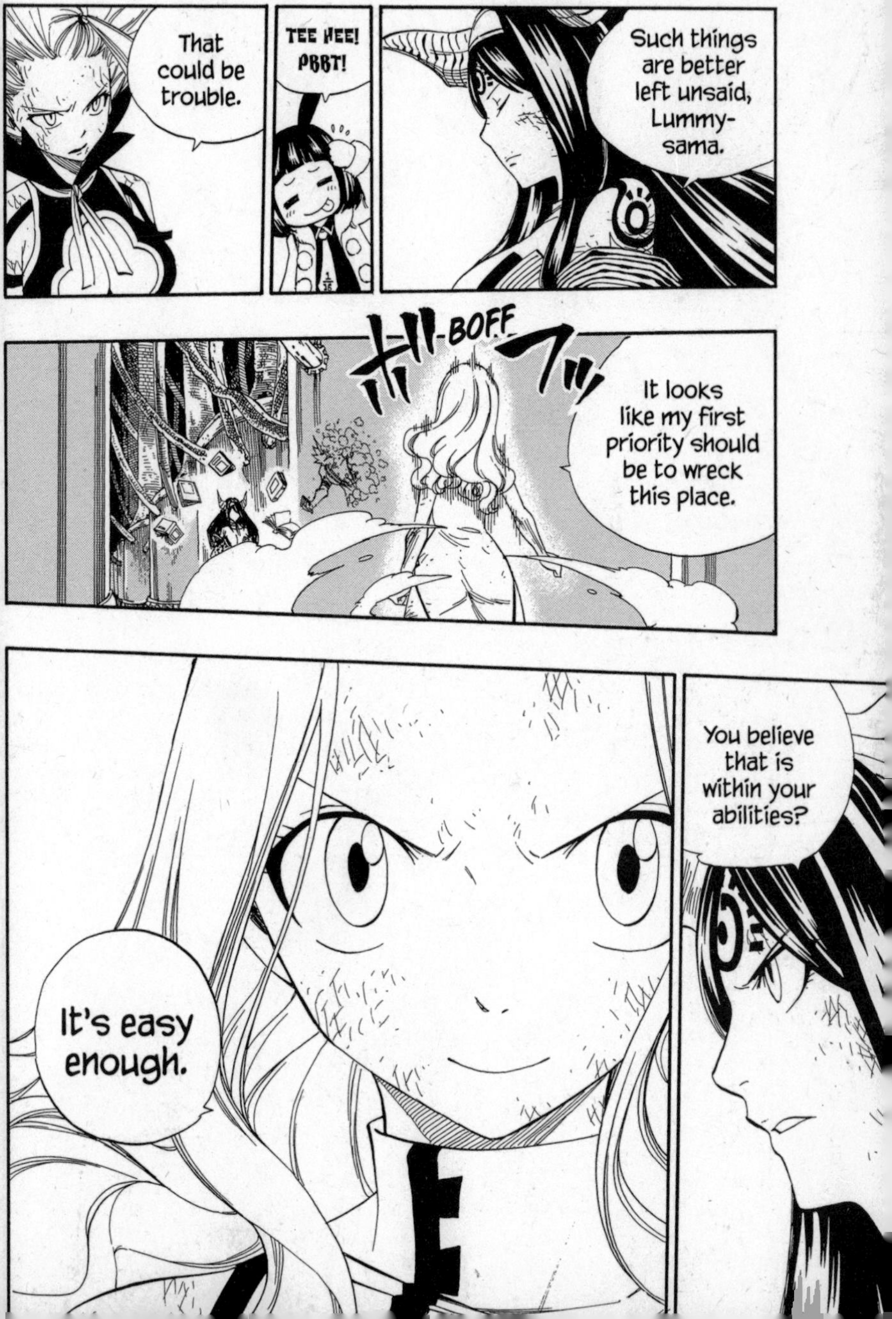
Such things are better left unsaid, Lummy-sama.
TEE HEE! PBBT!
That could be trouble.
BOFF
It looks like my first priority should be to wreck this place.
You believe that is within your abilities?
It's easy enough.

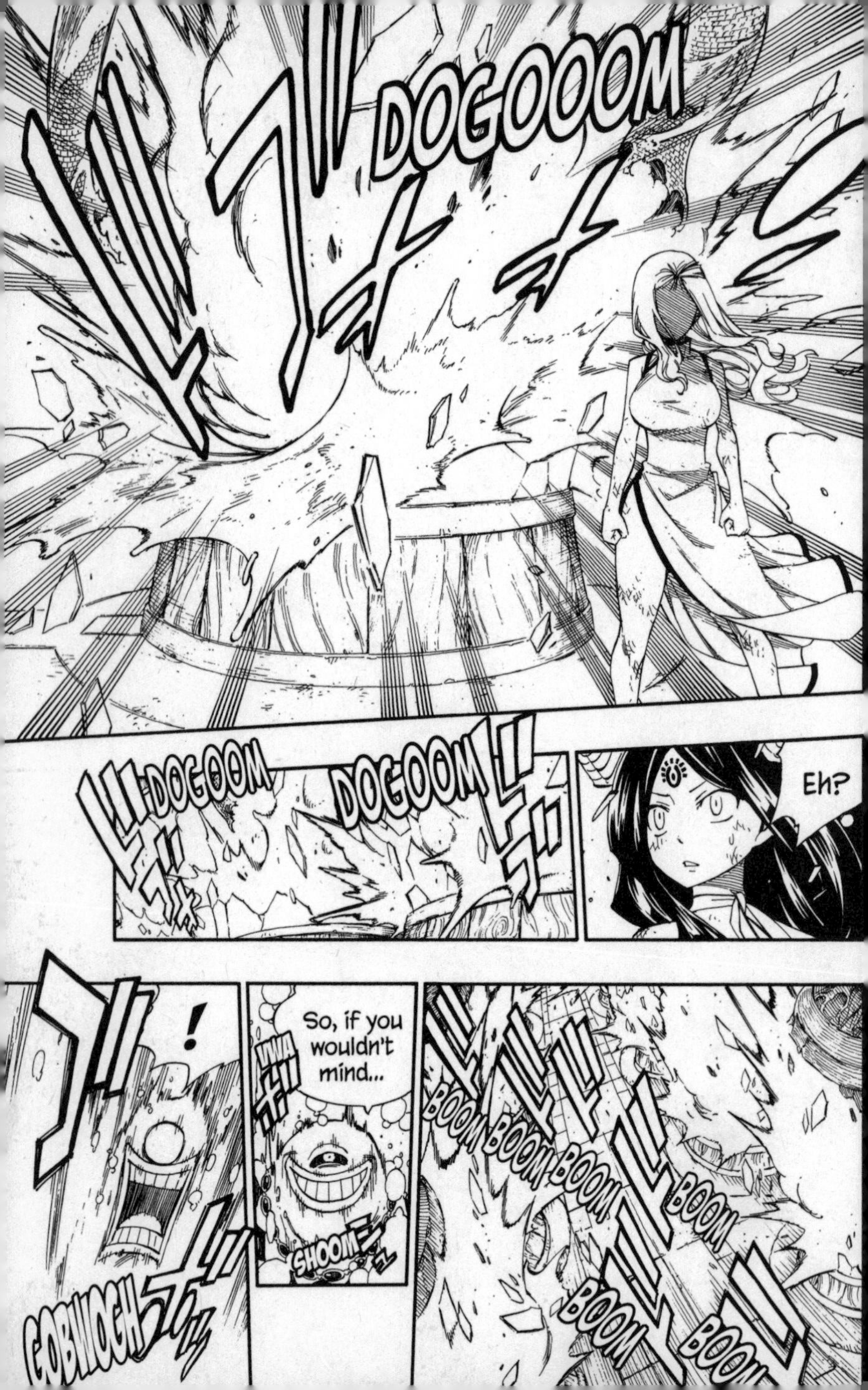
DOGOOOM
Eh?
DOGOOM
DOGOOM
BOOM BOOM BOOM BOOM BOOM BOOM
So, if you wouldn't mind...
VWA
SHOOM
!
GOBWOOCH

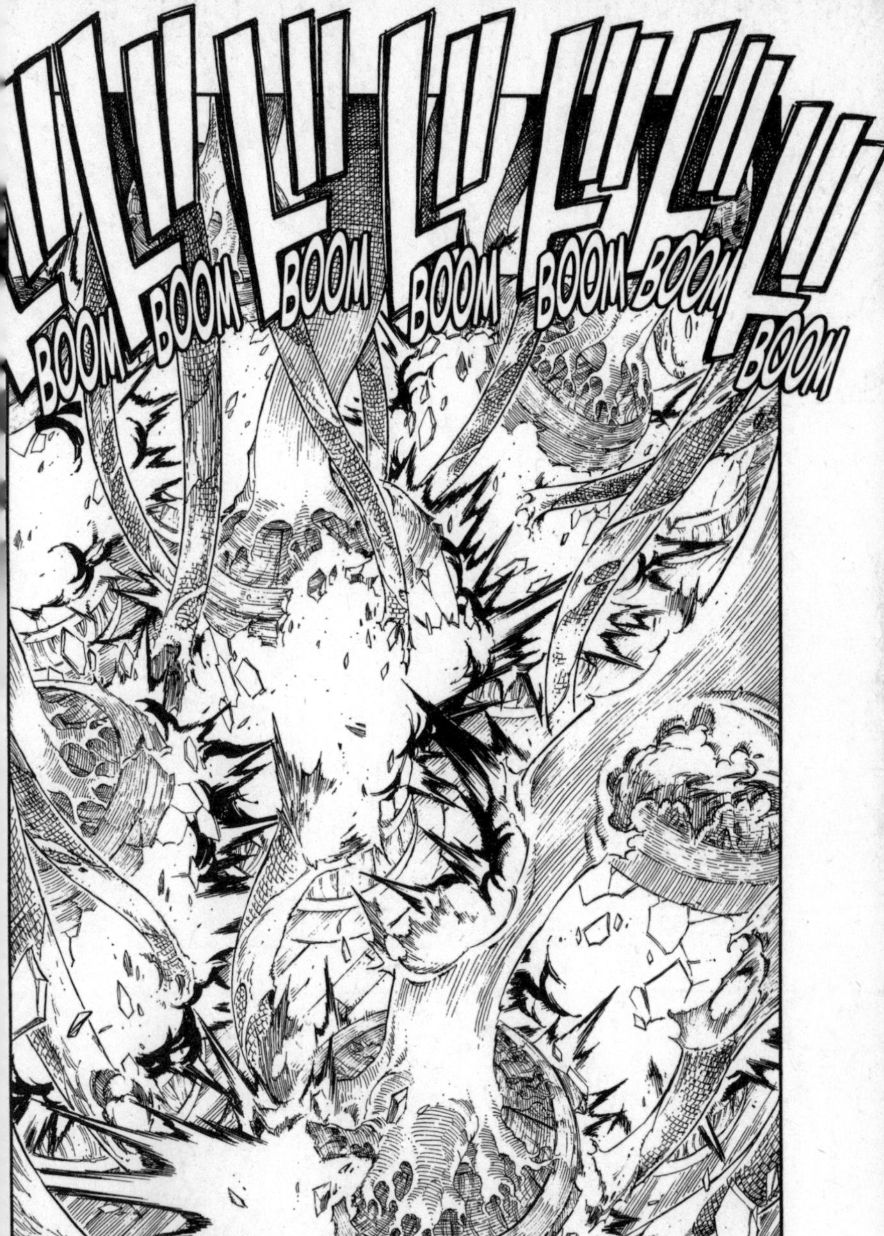
BOOM
BOOM
BOOM
BOOM
BOOM
BOOM
BOOM

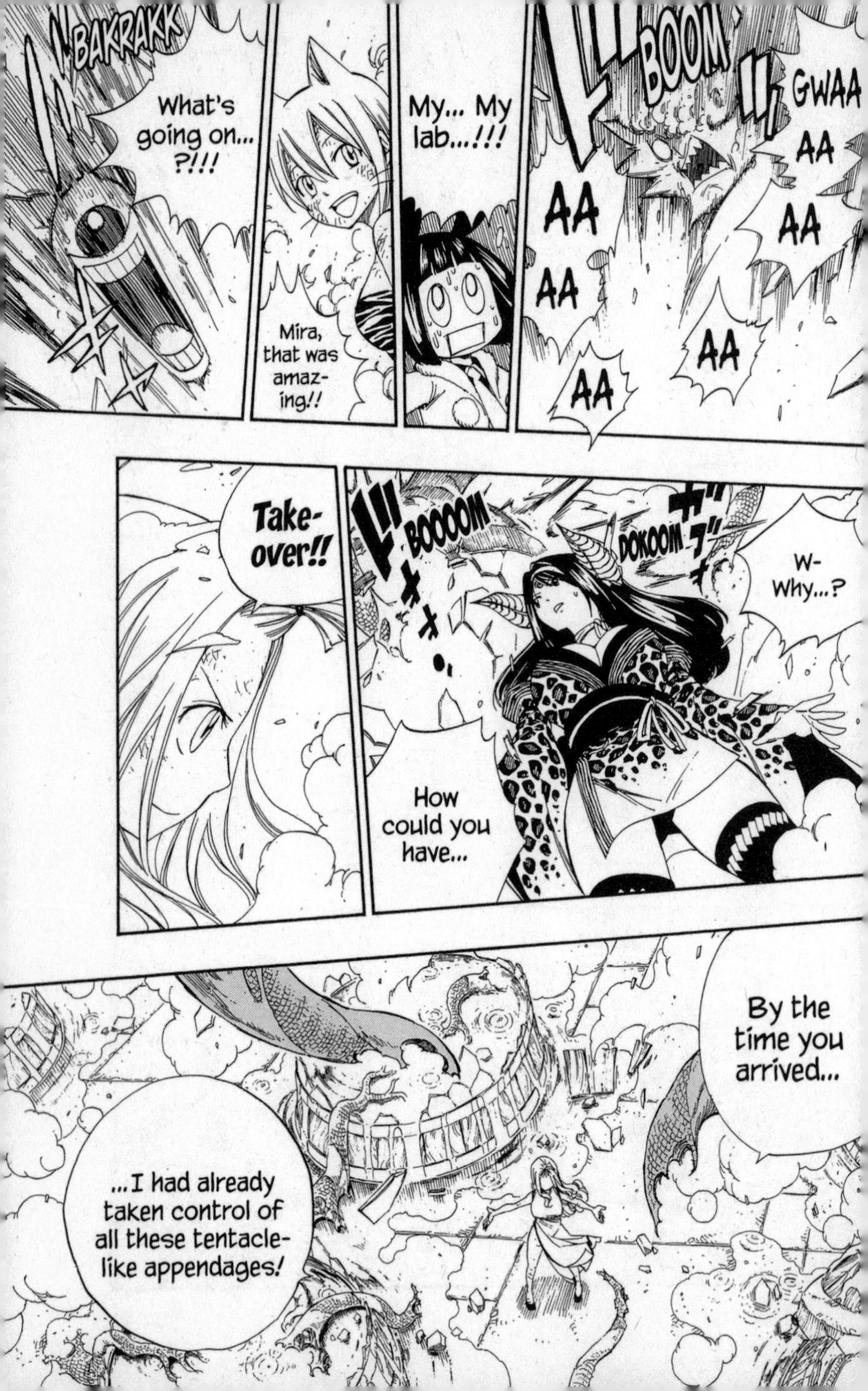
BOOM
GWAAAAAAAAAAAAAA
My... My lab...!!!
Mira, that was amaz-ing!!
BAKRAKK
What's going on...?!!!
DOKOOM
W-Why...?
BOOOOM
How could you have...
Take-over!!
By the time you arrived...
...I had already taken control of all these tentacle-like appendages!

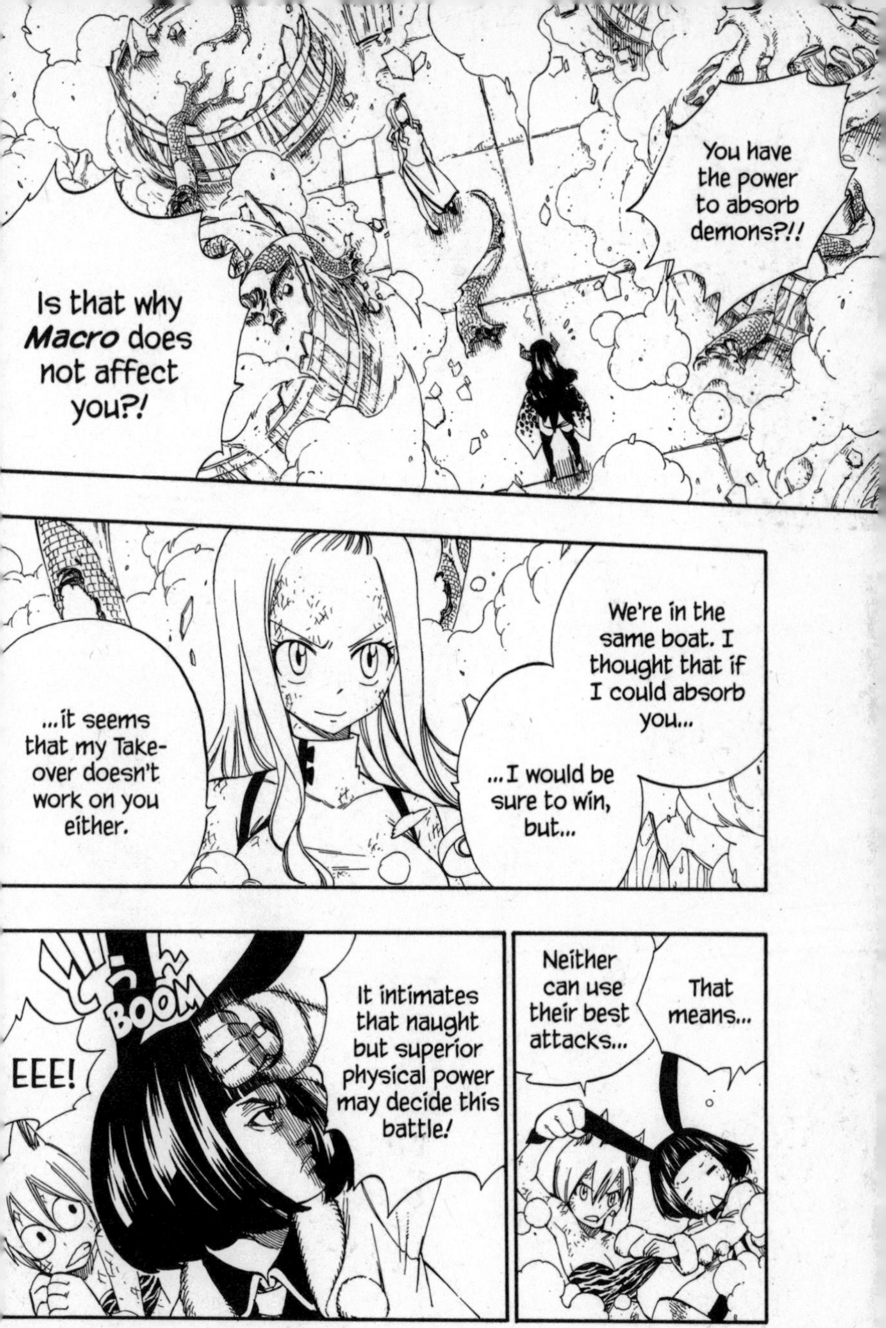
You have the power to absorb demons?!!
Is that why *Macro* does not affect you?!
We're in the same boat. I thought that if I could absorb you...
...I would be sure to win, but...
...it seems that my Take-over doesn't work on you either.
That means...
Neither can use their best attacks...
It intimates that naught but superior physical power may decide this battle!
BOOM
EEE!

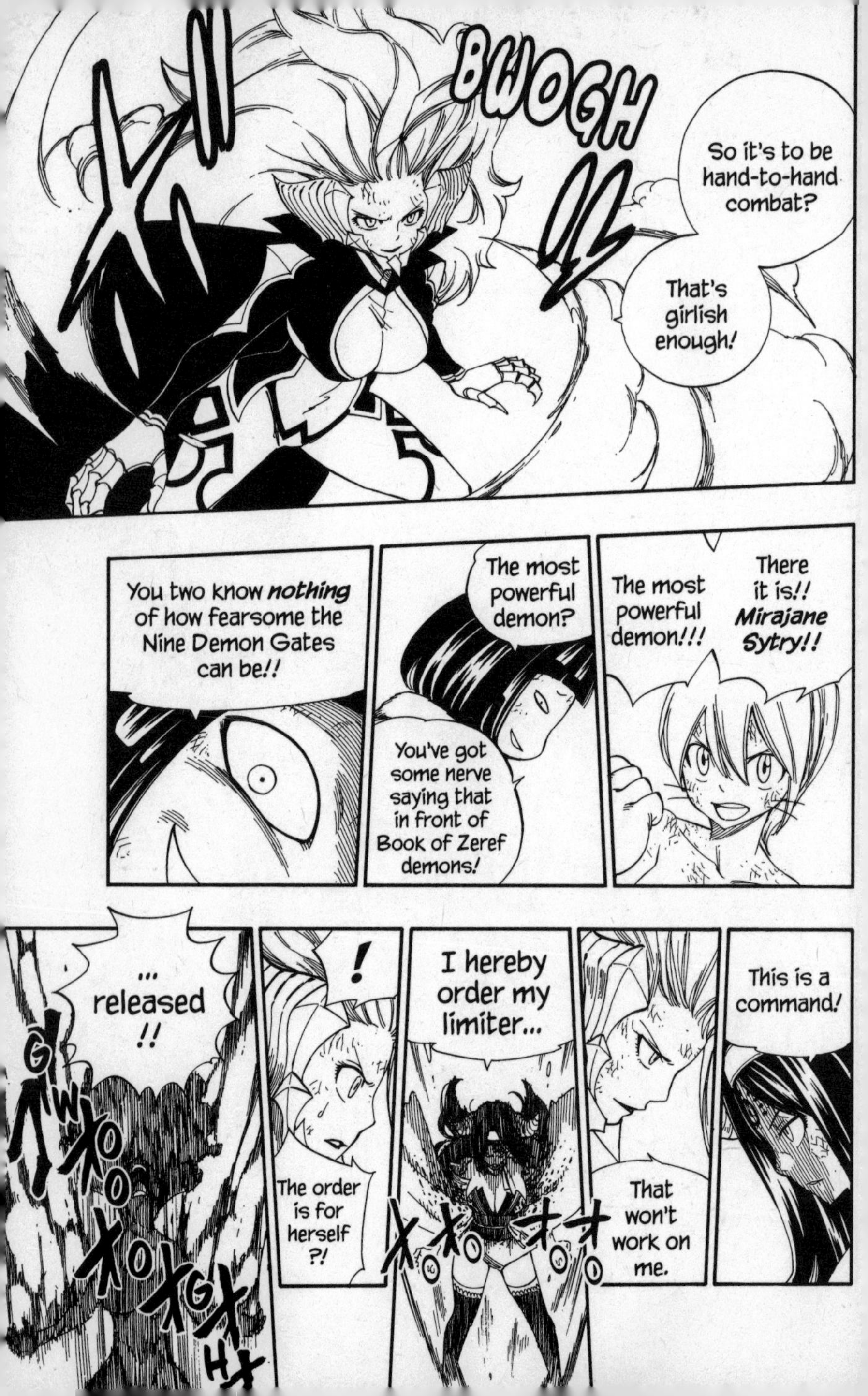
BWOGH
So it's to be hand-to-hand combat?
That's girlish enough!
There it is!! *Mirajane Sytry!!*
The most powerful demon!!!
The most powerful demon?
You've got some nerve saying that in front of Book of Zeref demons!
You two know *nothing* of how fearsome the Nine Demon Gates can be!!
This is a command!
That won't work on me.
I hereby order my limiter...
!
The order is for herself?!
... released!!

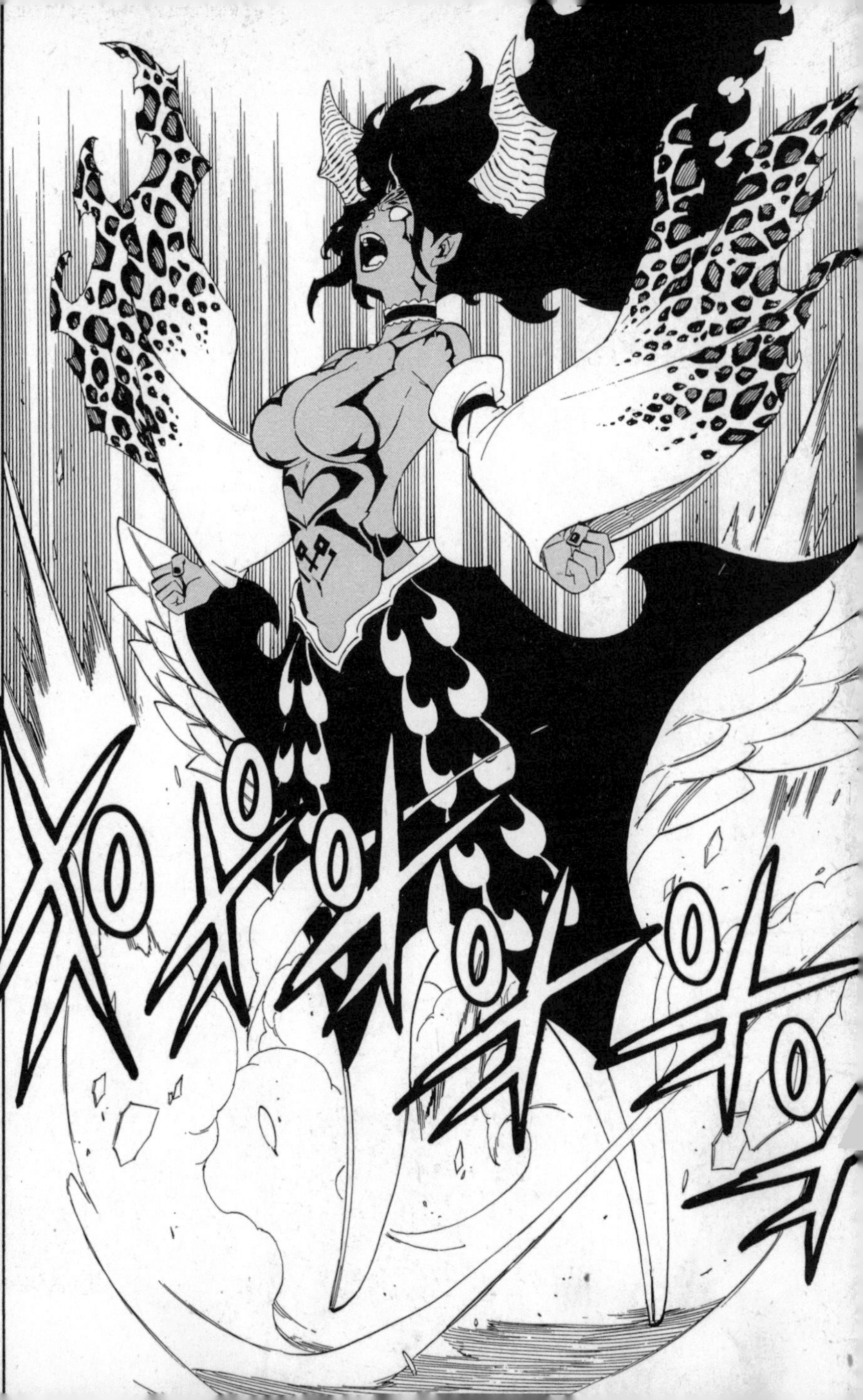

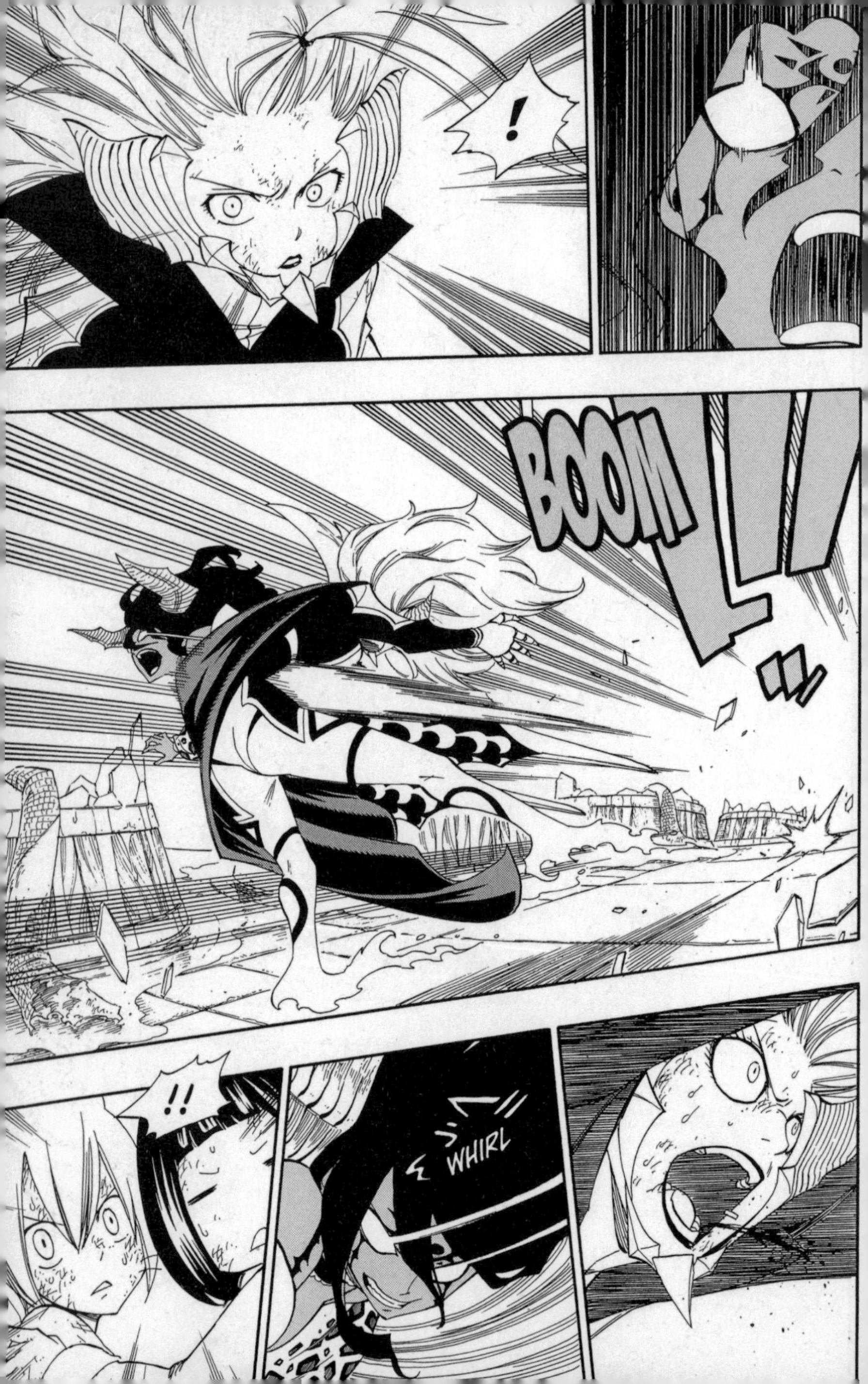
!
BOOM!!
WHIRL
!!

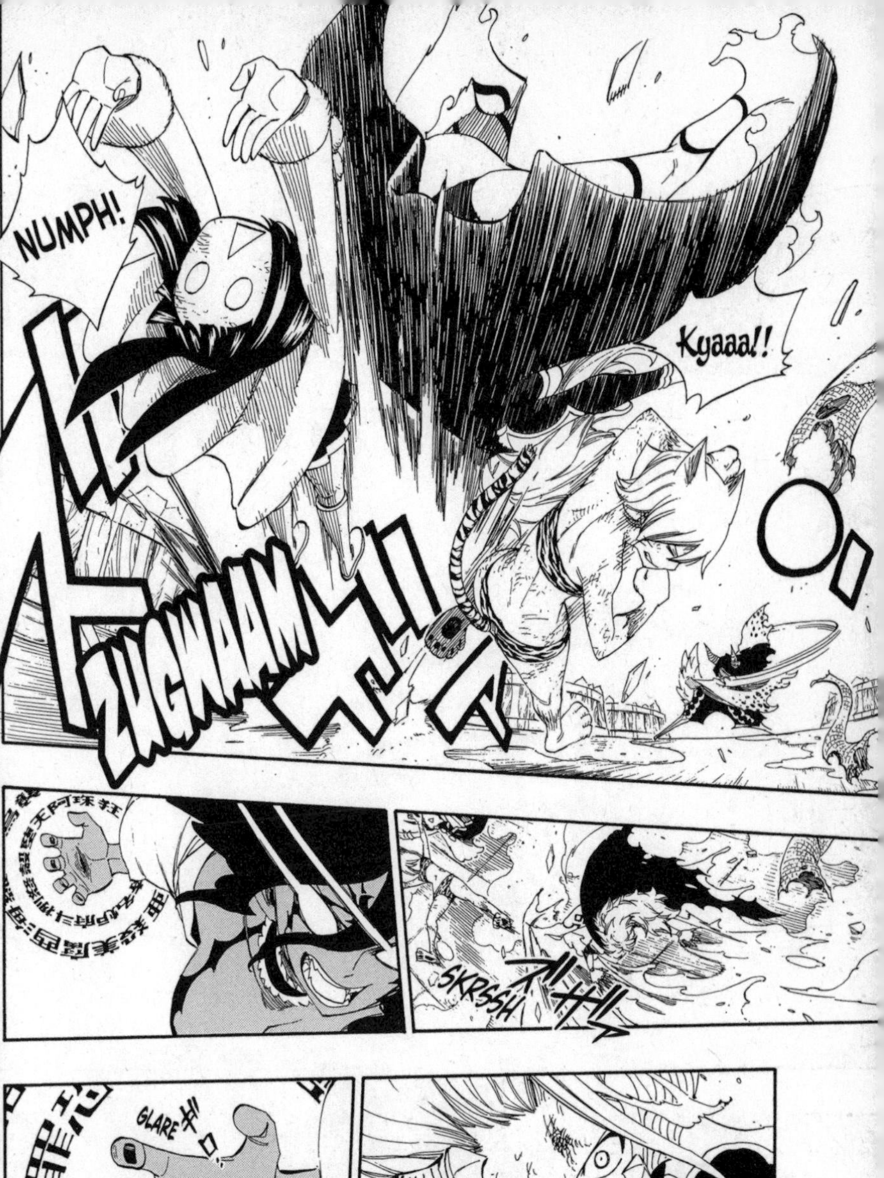
Kyaaa!!
NUMPH!
ZUGWAAM!!
SKRSSH
GLARE

Surrounding Seilah's hand are kanji, but they do not form words. They are simply symbols in a magic pattern. The kanji's meanings are concepts like "murder," "beauty," "rot," "sea," and other primal-seeming terms.

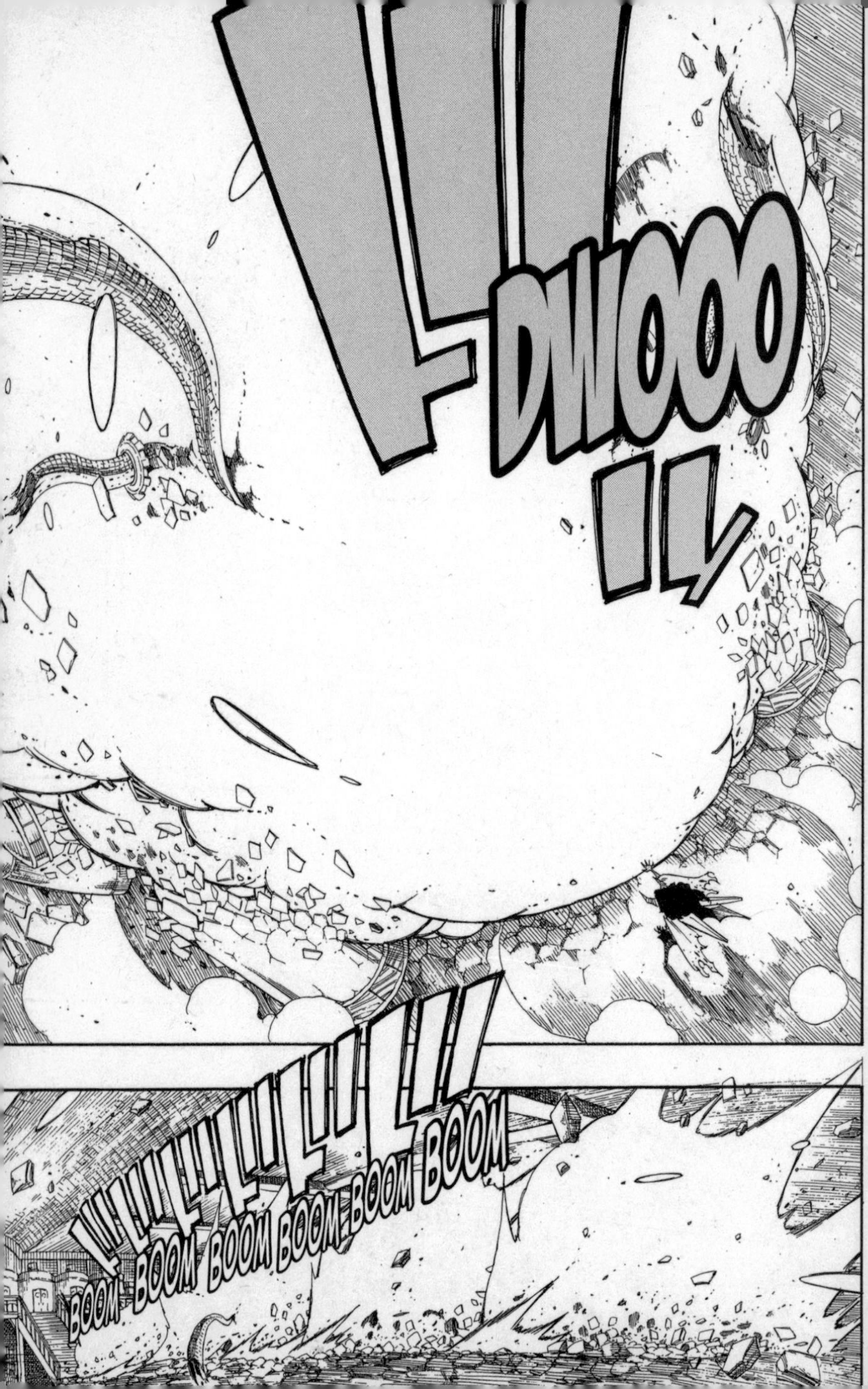
DWOOO
BOOM BOOM BOOM BOOM BOOM BOOM

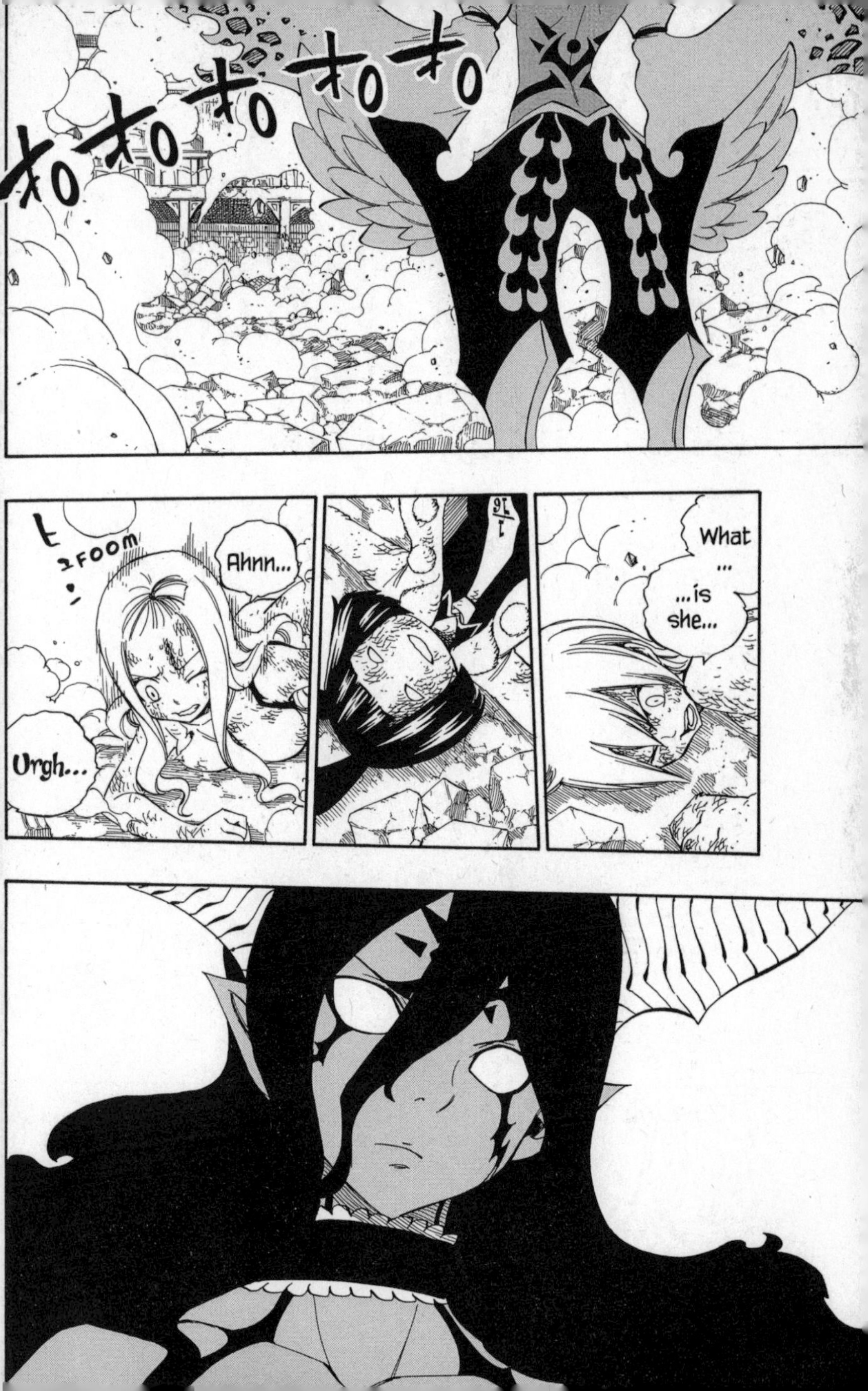
What ... ...is she...
Ahnn...
FOOM
Urgh...

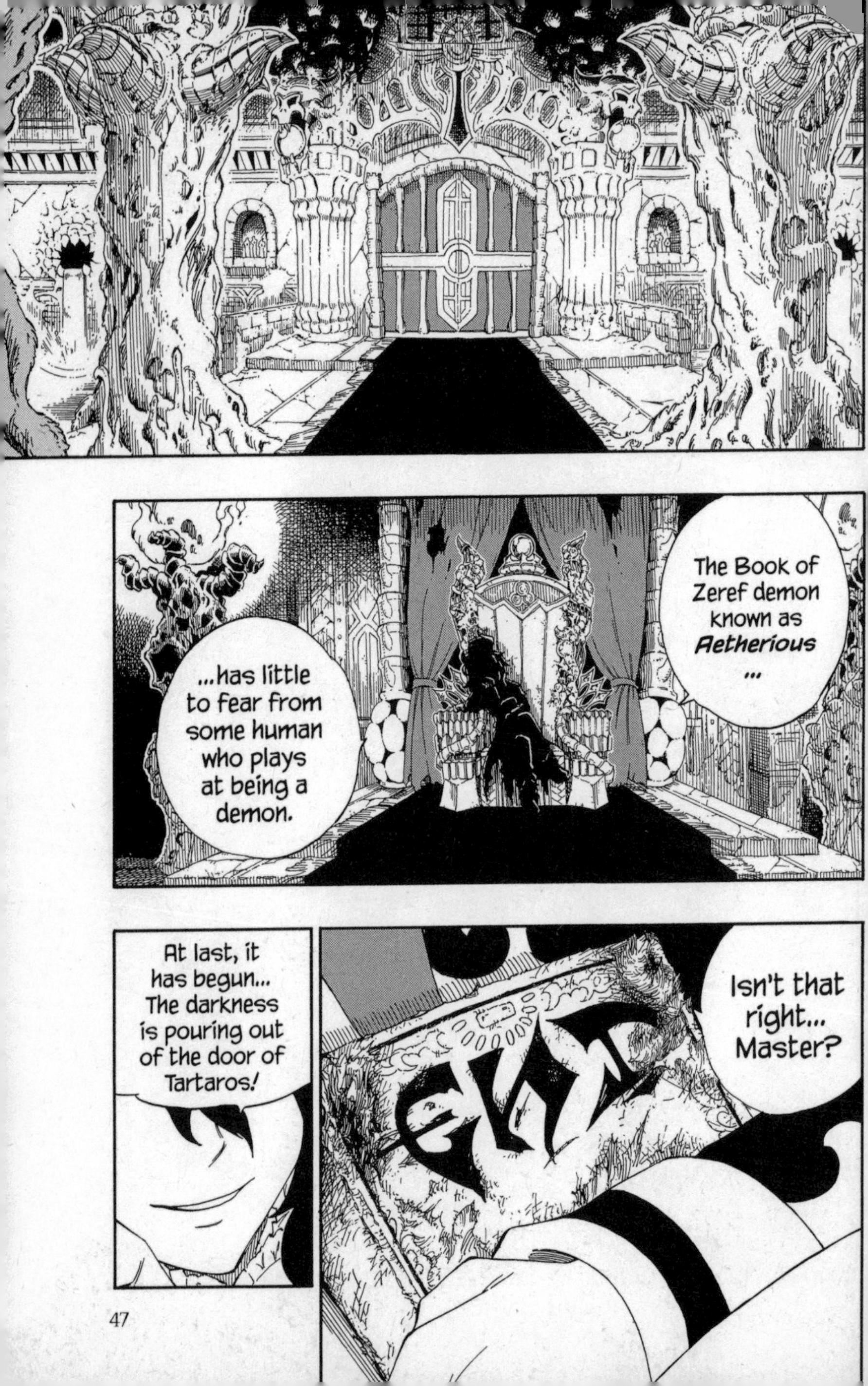
The Book of Zeref demon known as *Aetherious* ...
...has little to fear from some human who plays at being a demon.
Isn't that right... Master?
At last, it has begun... The darkness is pouring out of the door of Tartaros!

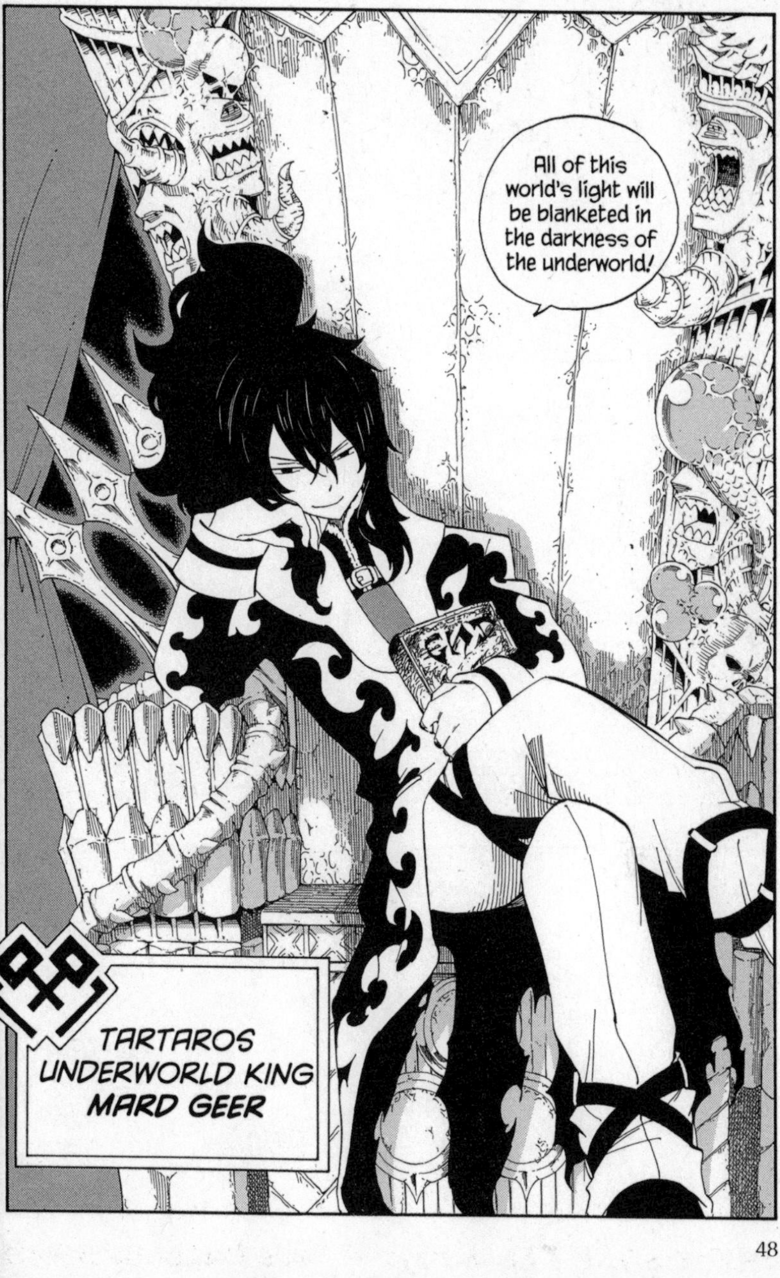
All of this world's light will be blanketed in the darkness of the underworld!
TARTAROS UNDERWORLD KING MARD GEER

FAIRY TAIL

フェアリーテイル

MENU

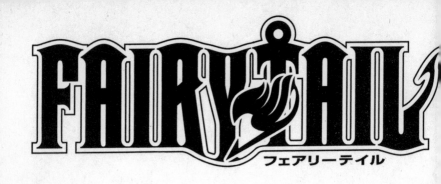

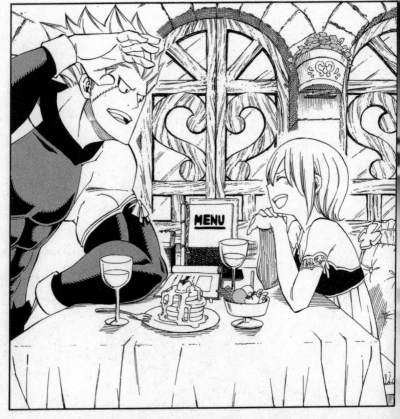

Chapter 381: The House Where Demons Dwell

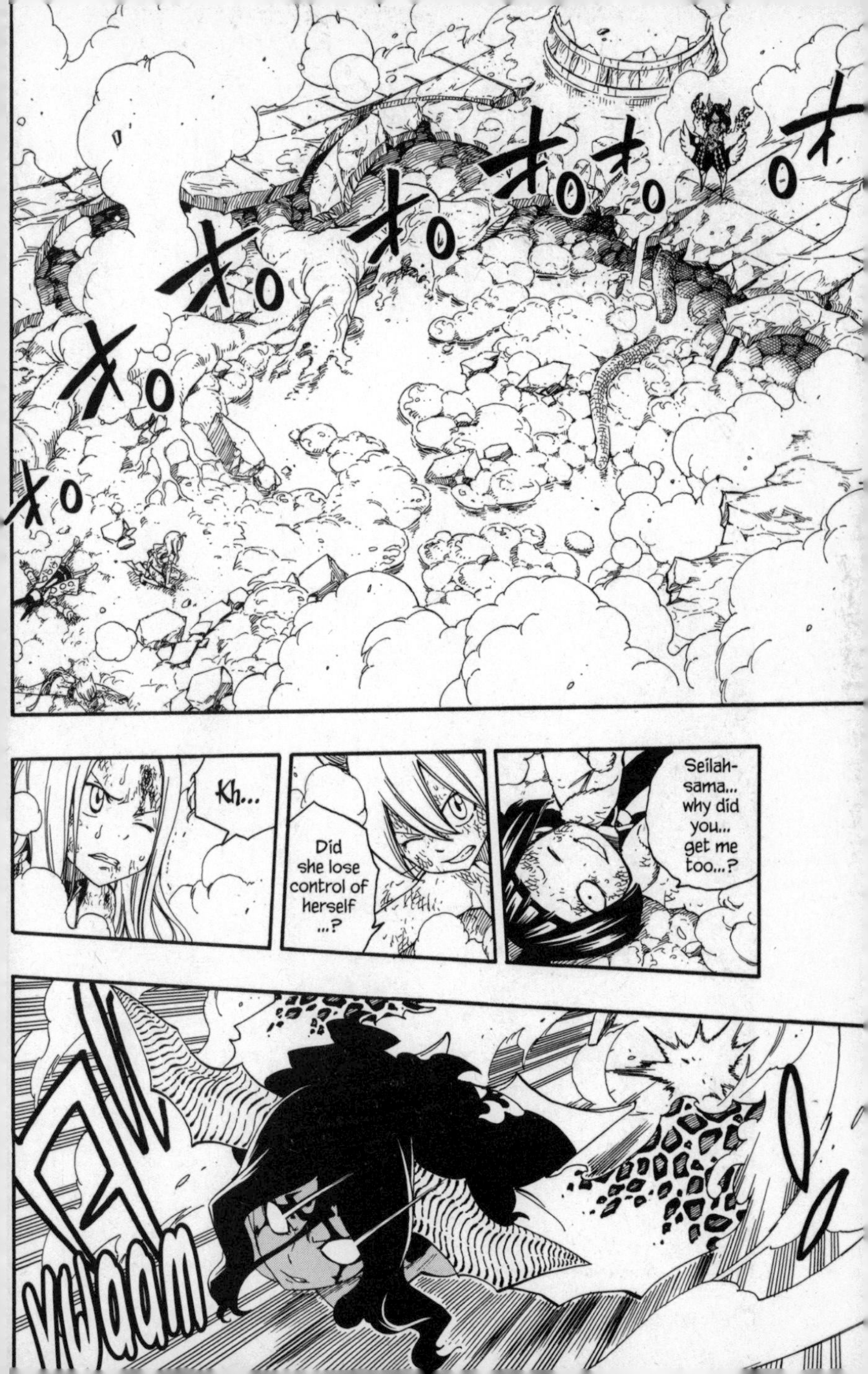

オォオォオォオォオォオォオォ
Seilah-sama... why did you... get me too...?
Did she lose control of herself ...?
Kh...

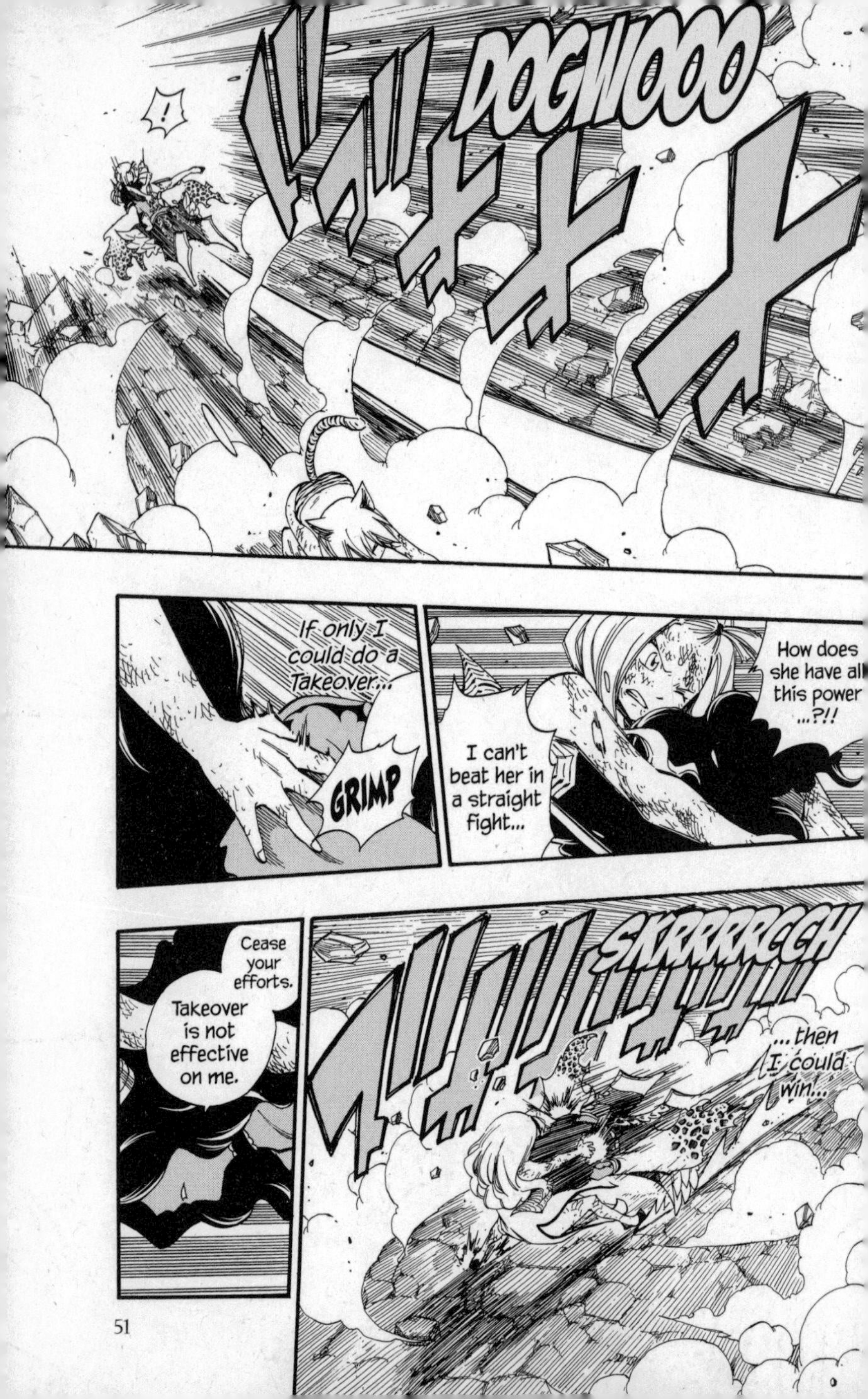
DOGWOOO
!
How does she have all this power ...?!!
I can't beat her in a straight fight...
If only I could do a Takeover...
GRIMP
SKRRRRRGCH
...then I could win...
Cease your efforts.
Takeover is not effective on me.

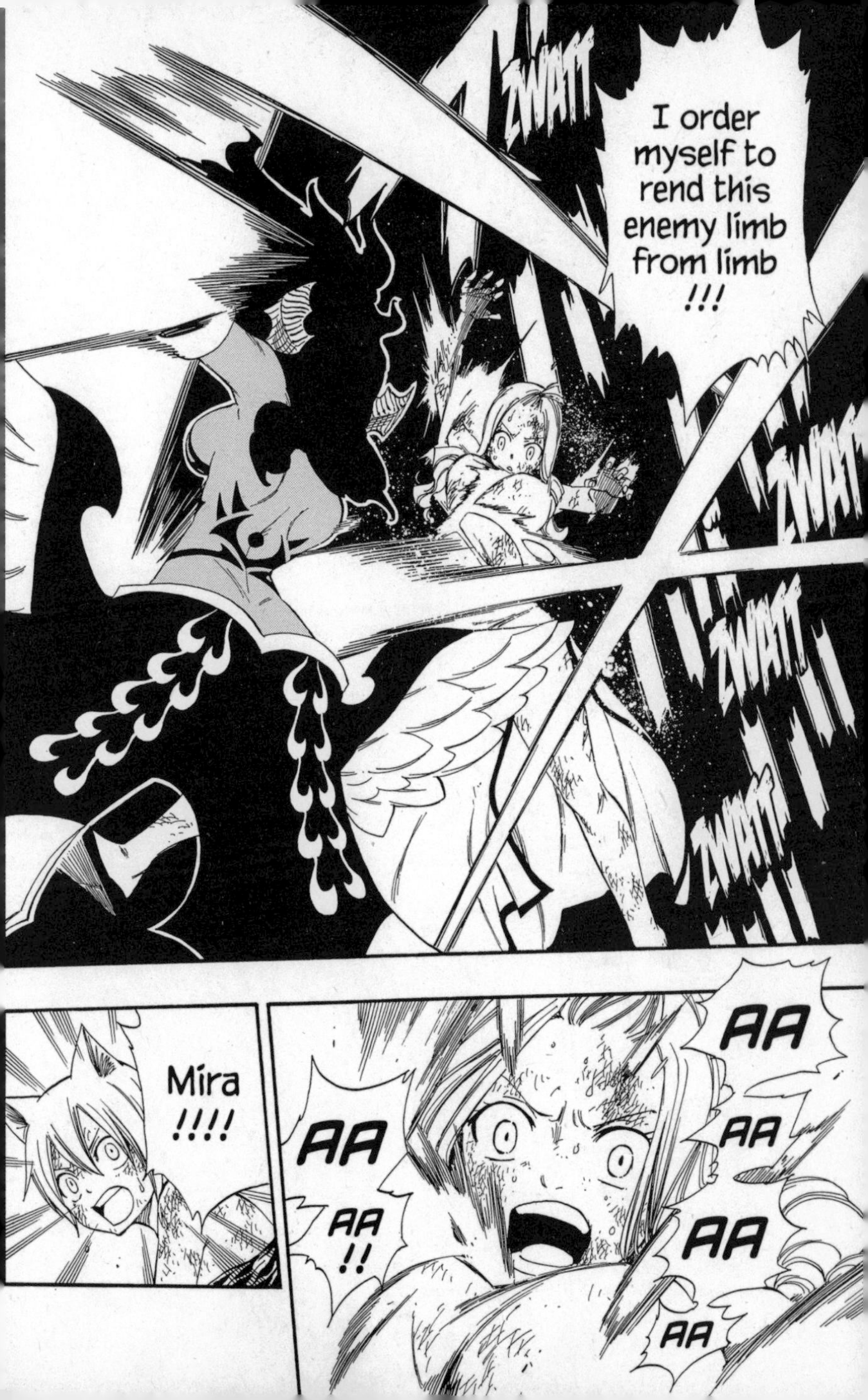

ZWATT
I order myself to rend this enemy limb from limb !!!
ZWATT
ZWATT
ZWATT
AA
AA
AA
AA
AA !!
AA
Mira !!!!

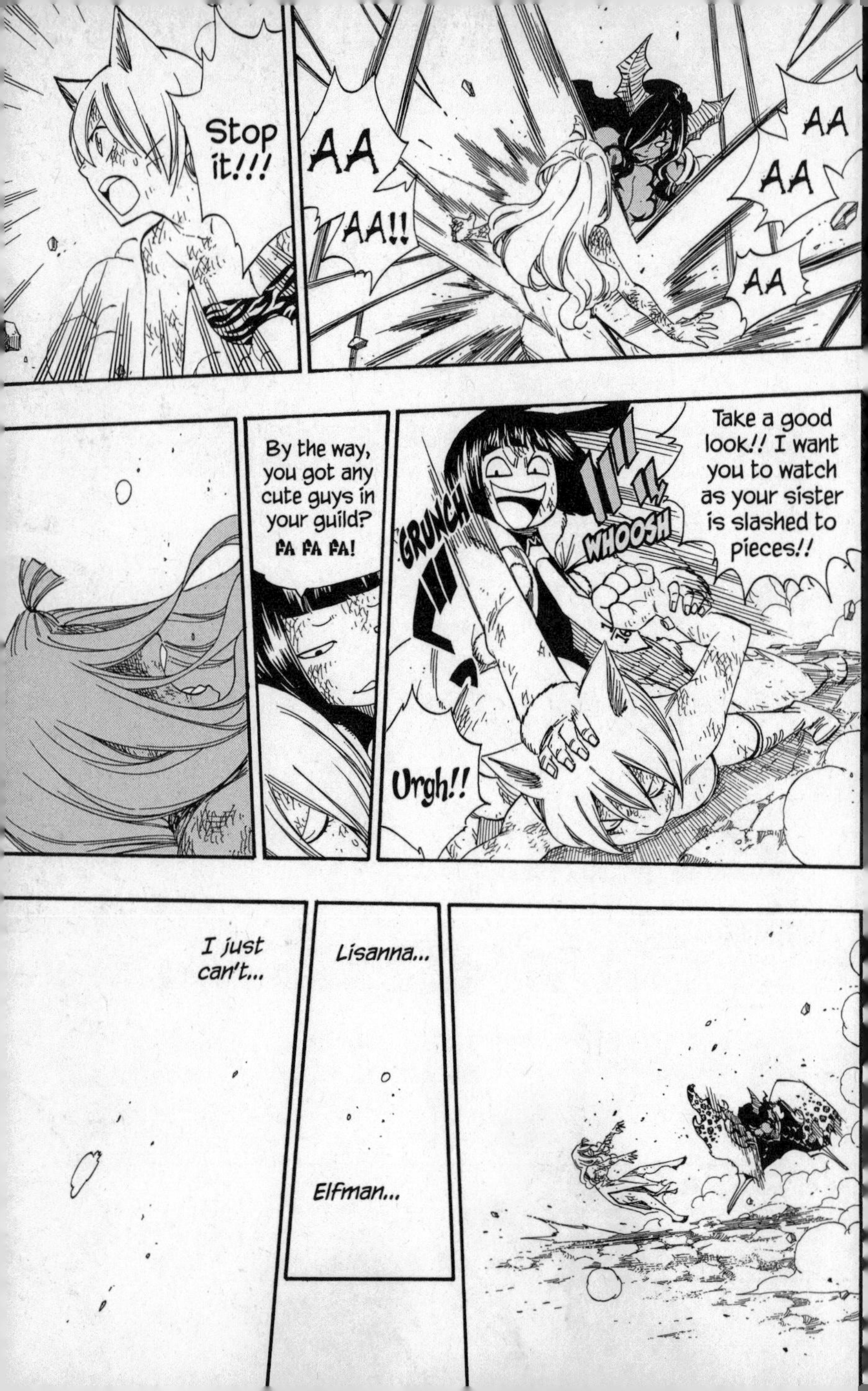
AA
AA
AA
AA
AA!!
Stop it!!!
Take a good look!! I want you to watch as your sister is slashed to pieces!!
WHOOSH
GRUNCH
Urgh!!
By the way, you got any cute guys in your guild?
FA FA FA!
Lisanna...
Elfman...
I just can't...

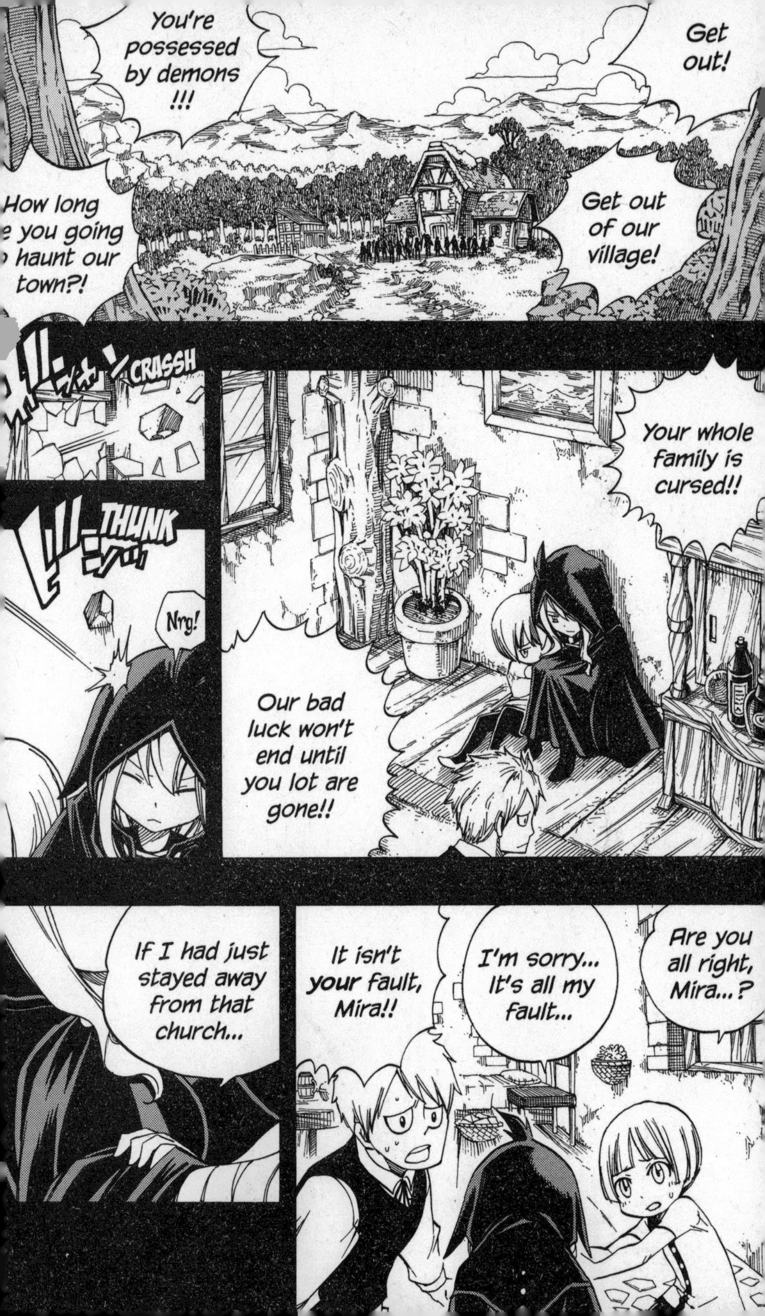
Get out!
Get out of our village!
You're possessed by demons!!!
How long you going haunt our town?!
Your whole family is cursed!!
Our bad luck won't end until you lot are gone!!
CRASSH
THUNK
Nrg!
Are you all right, Mira...?
I'm sorry... It's all my fault...
It isn't **your** fault, Mira!!
If I had just stayed away from that church...

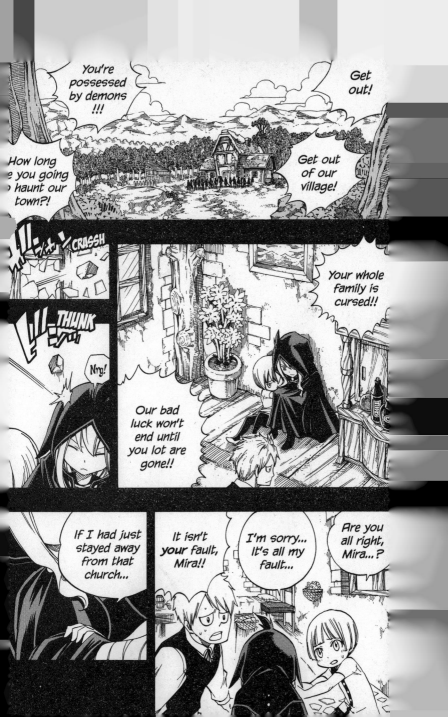

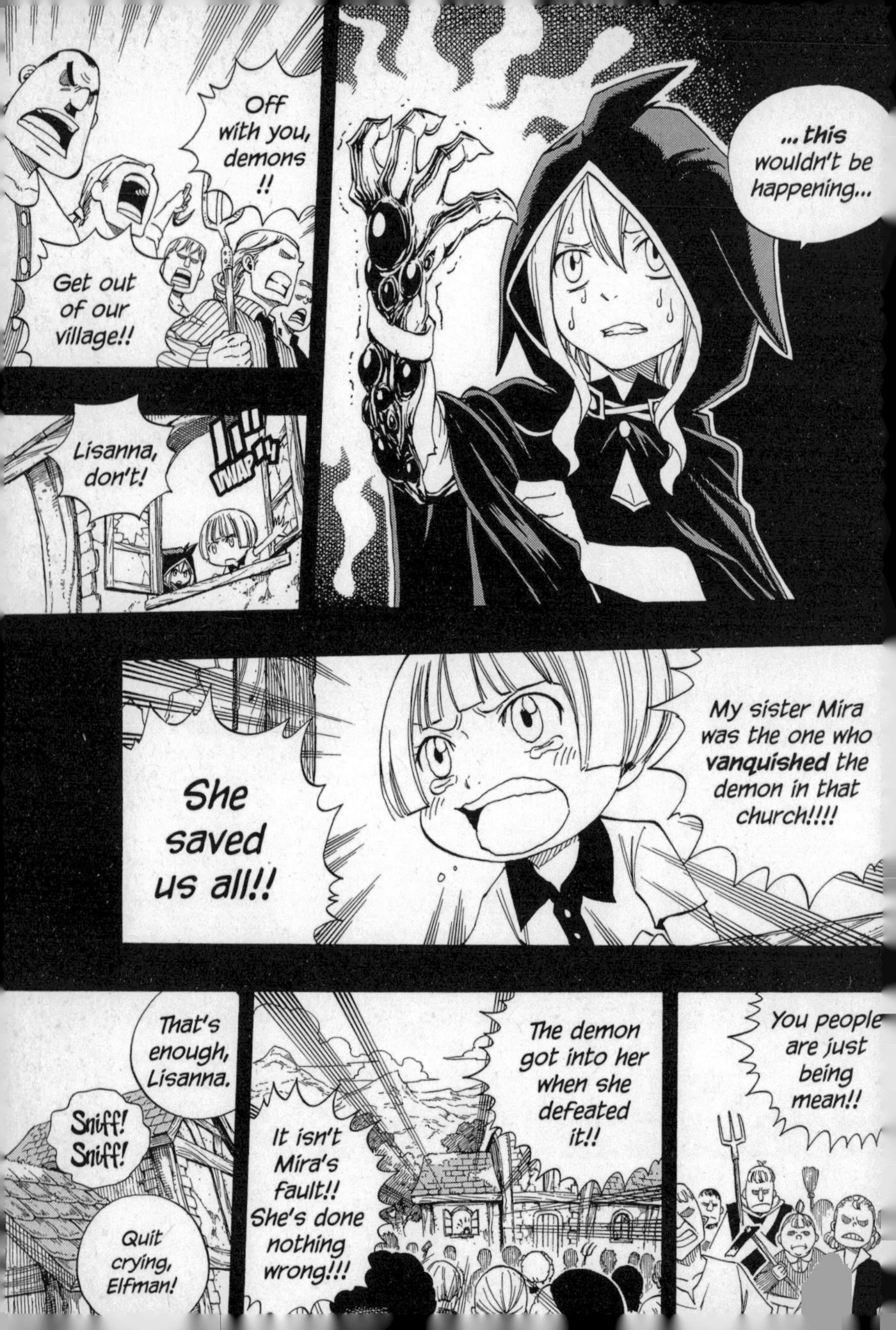

...this wouldn't be happening...
Off with you, demons!!
Get out of our village!!
Lisanna, don't!
My sister Mira was the one who vanquished the demon in that church!!!!
She saved us all!!
You people are just being mean!!
The demon got into her when she defeated it!!
It isn't Mira's fault!! She's done nothing wrong!!!
That's enough, Lisanna.
Sniff! Sniff!
Quit crying, Elfman!

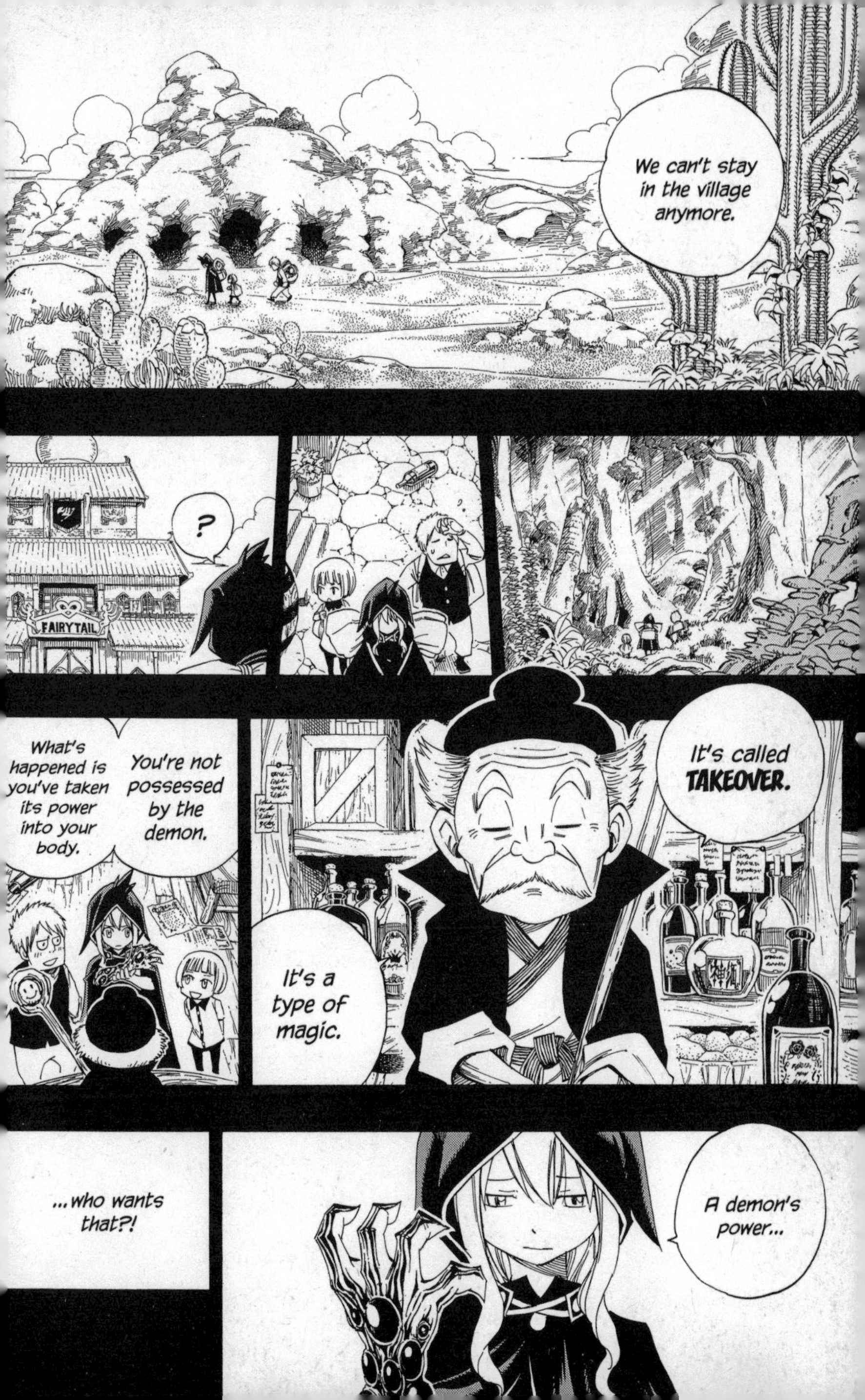
We can't stay in the village anymore.
FAIRYTAIL
?
It's called TAKEOVER.
It's a type of magic.
You're not possessed by the demon.
What's happened is you've taken its power into your body.
A demon's power...
...who wants that?!

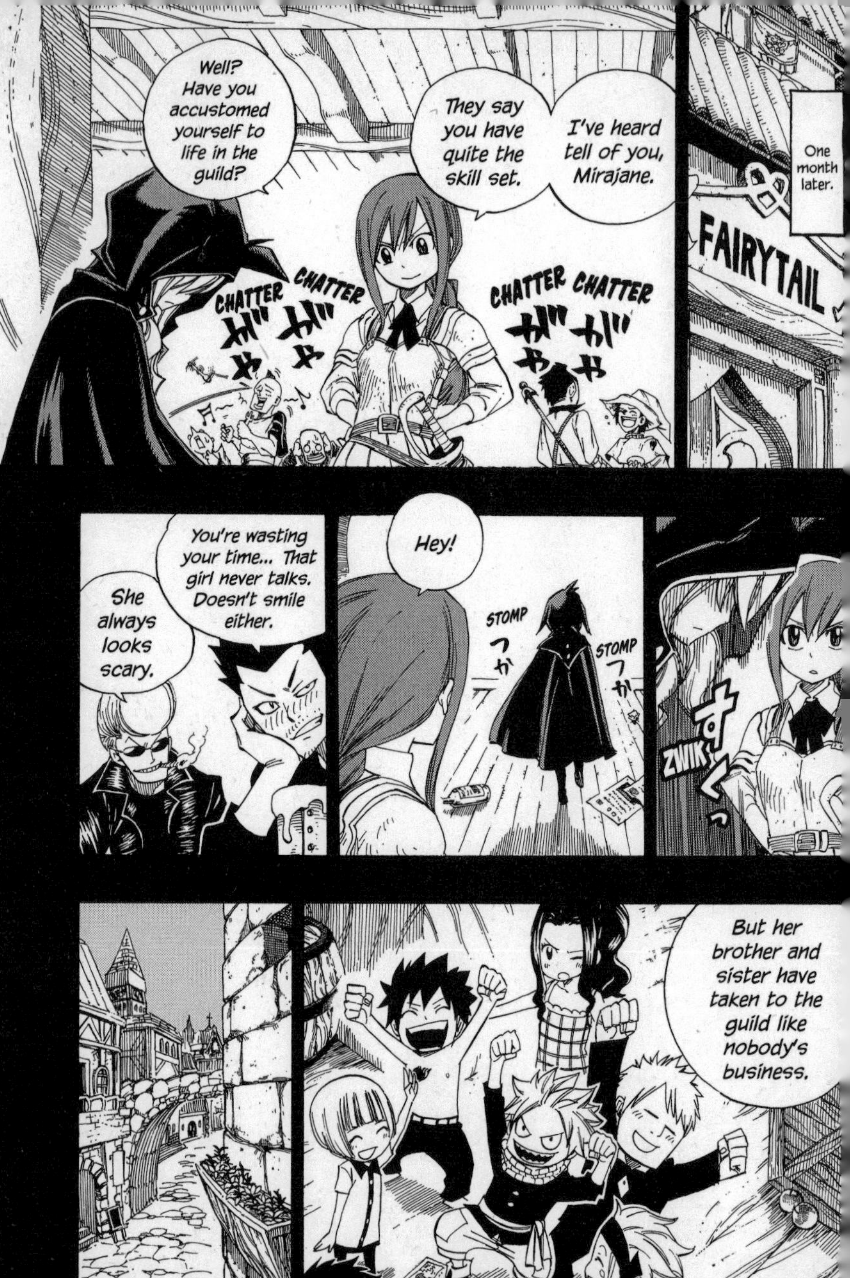

One month later.
FAIRYTAIL
I've heard tell of you, Mirajane.
They say you have quite the skill set.
Well? Have you accustomed yourself to life in the guild?
CHATTER CHATTER
ガヤガヤ
CHATTER CHATTER
ガヤガヤ
ZWIK
すくっ
Hey!
STOMP
つか
STOMP
つか
You're wasting your time... That girl never talks. Doesn't smile either.
She always looks scary.
But her brother and sister have taken to the guild like nobody's business.

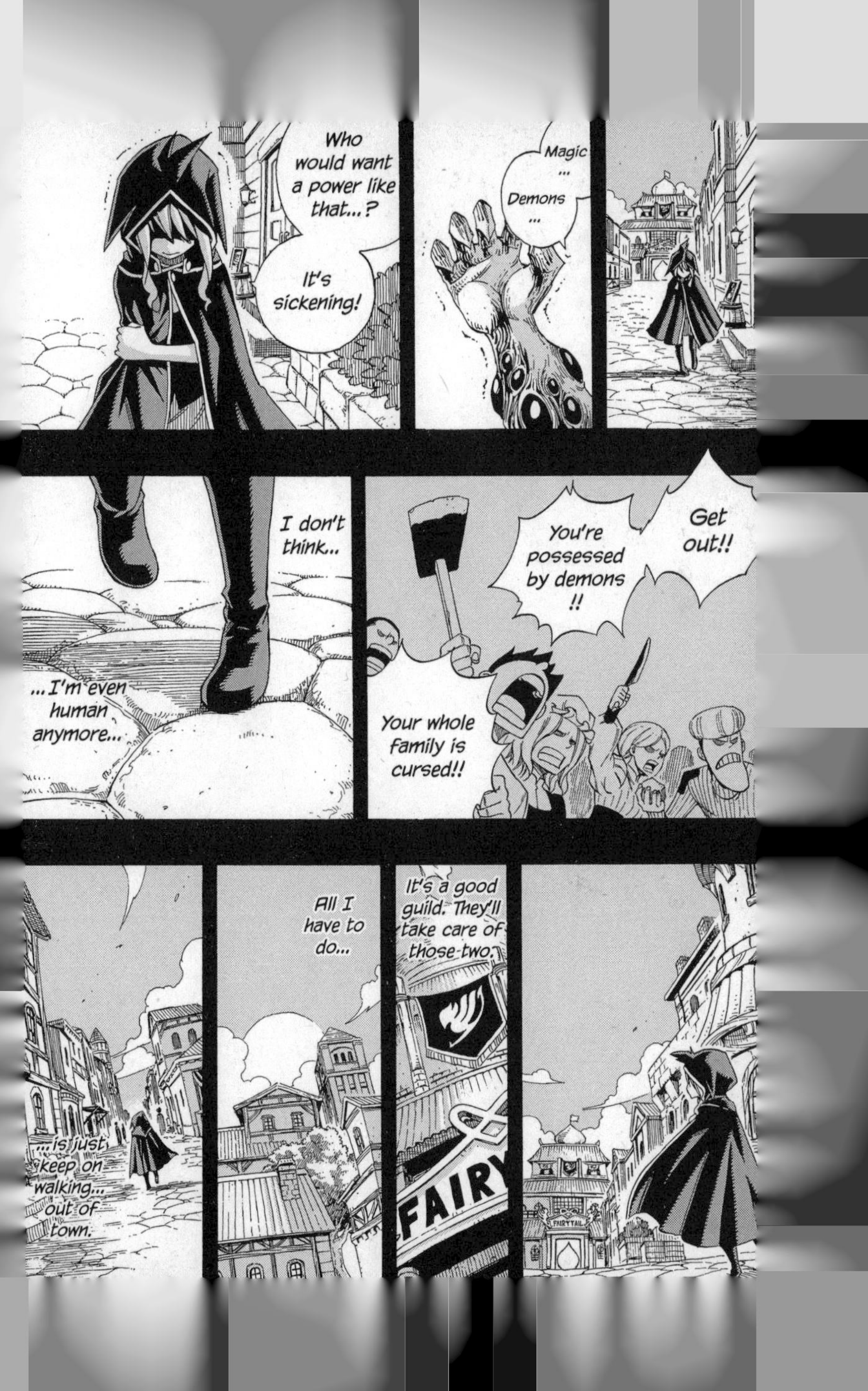
Magic ... Demons ...
Who would want a power like that...?
It's sickening!
Get out!!
You're possessed by demons !!
Your whole family is cursed!!
I don't think...
...I'm even human anymore...
It's a good guild. They'll take care of those two.
FAIRY
All I have to do...
...is just keep on walking... out of town.

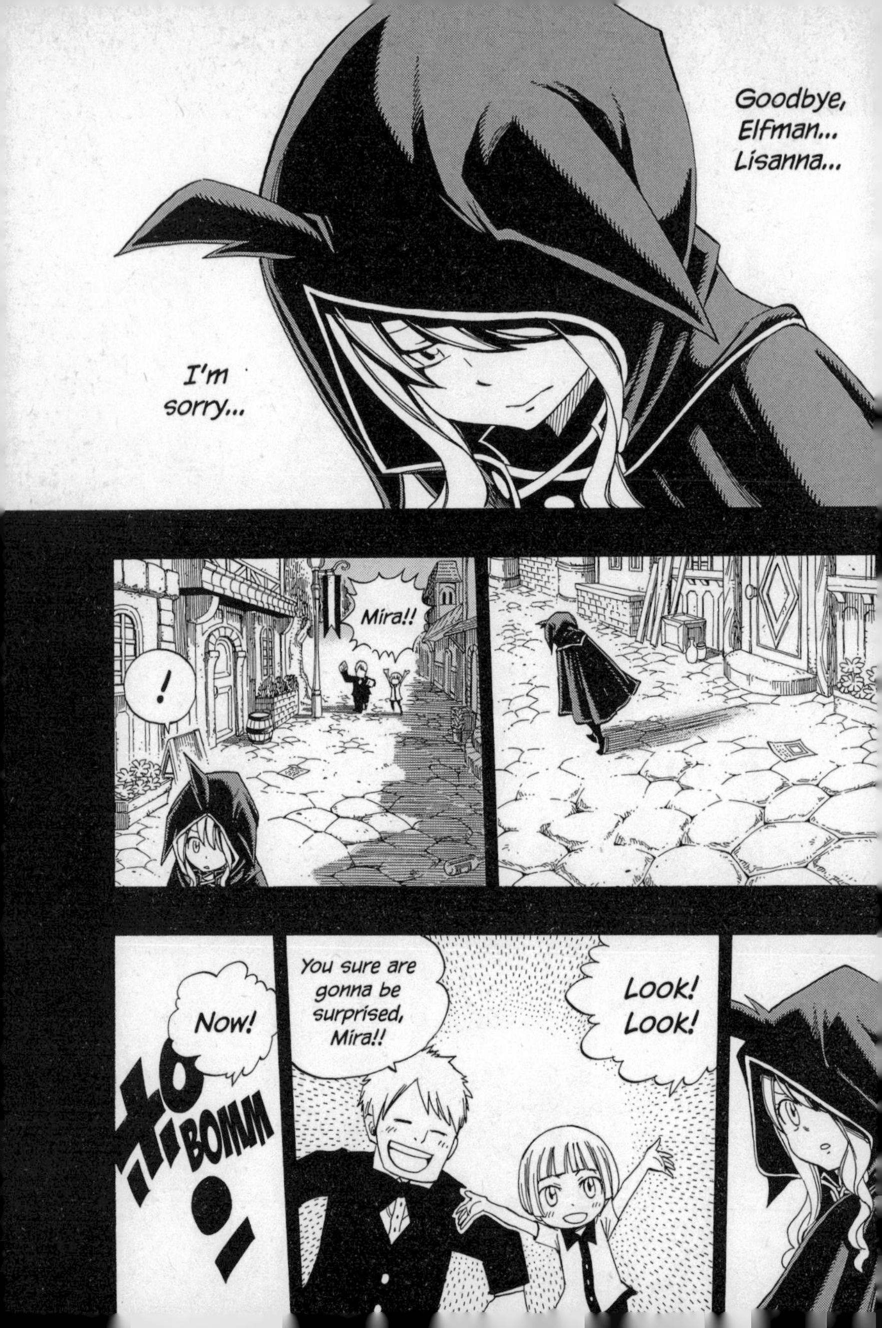
Goodbye, Elfman... Lisanna...
I'm sorry...
Mira!!
!
Look! Look!
You sure are gonna be surprised, Mira!!
Now!
BOMM

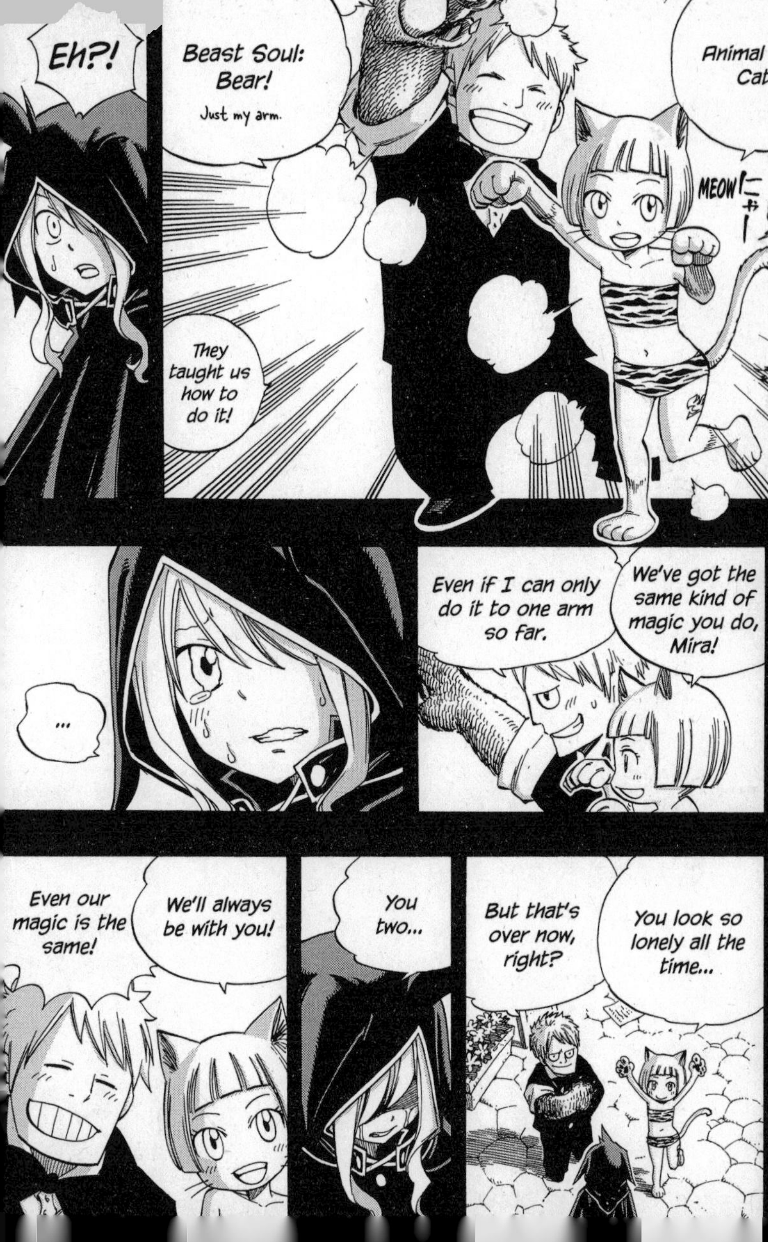

Animal Soul: Cat!!
MEOW!
Beast Soul: Bear!
Just my arm.
They taught us how to do it!
Eh?!
We've got the same kind of magic you do, Mira!
Even if I can only do it to one arm so far.
...
You look so lonely all the time...
But that's over now, right?
You two...
We'll always be with you!
Even our magic is the same!

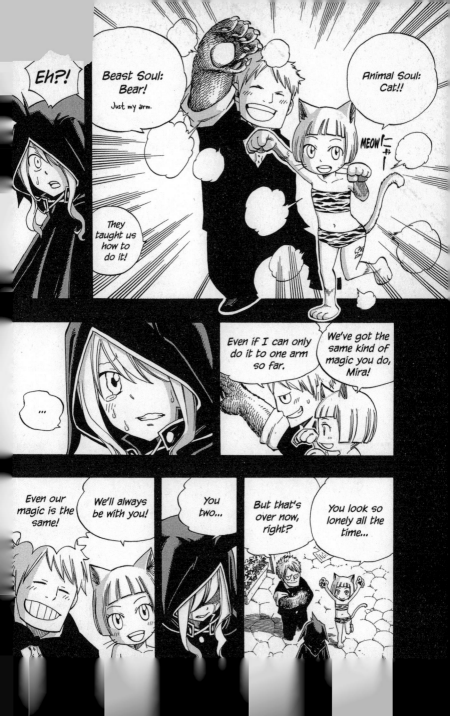

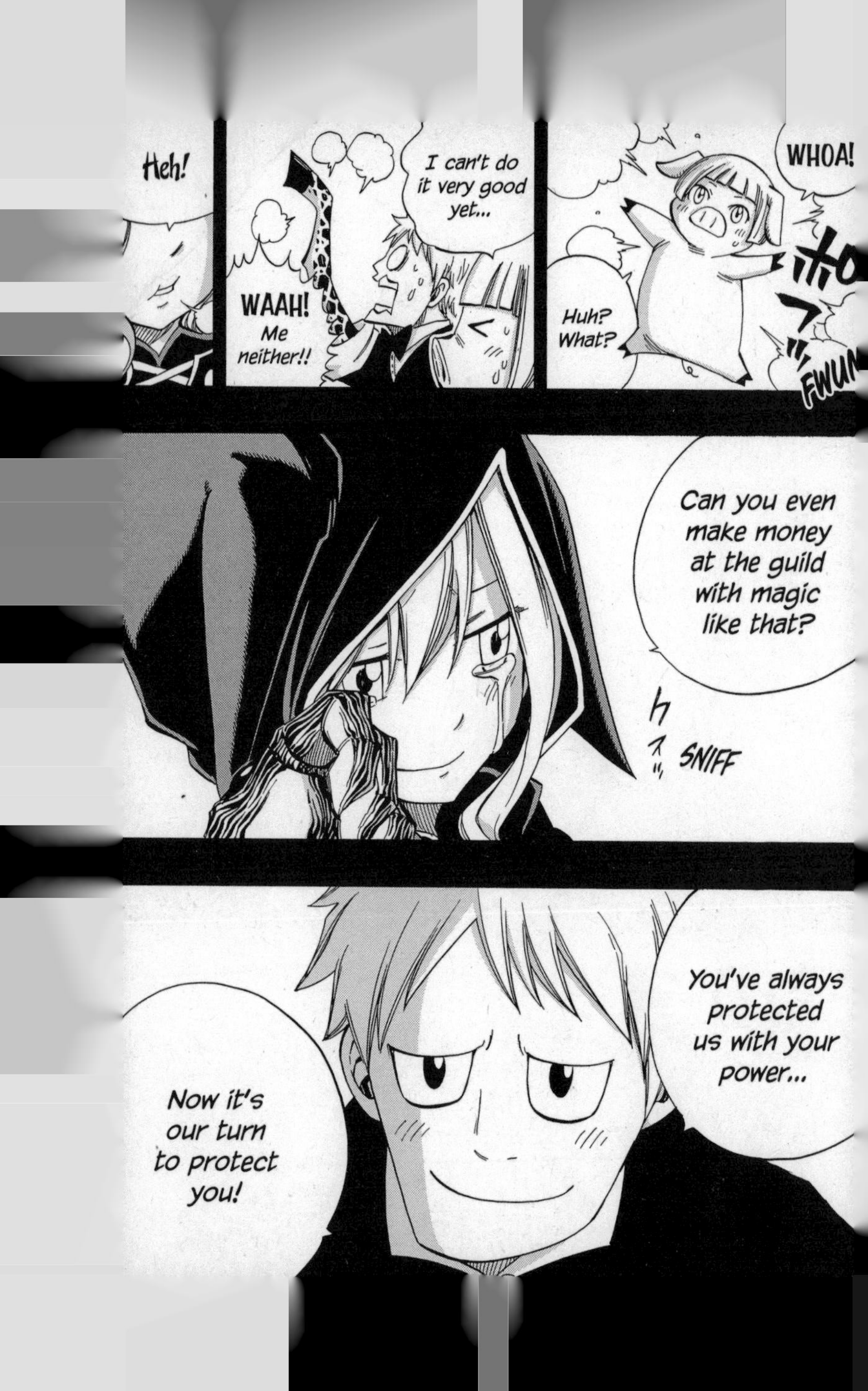
WHOA!
FWUN
Huh? What?
I can't do it very good yet...
WAAH! Me neither!!
Heh!
Can you even make money at the guild with magic like that?
SNIFF
You've always protected us with your power...
Now it's our turn to protect you!

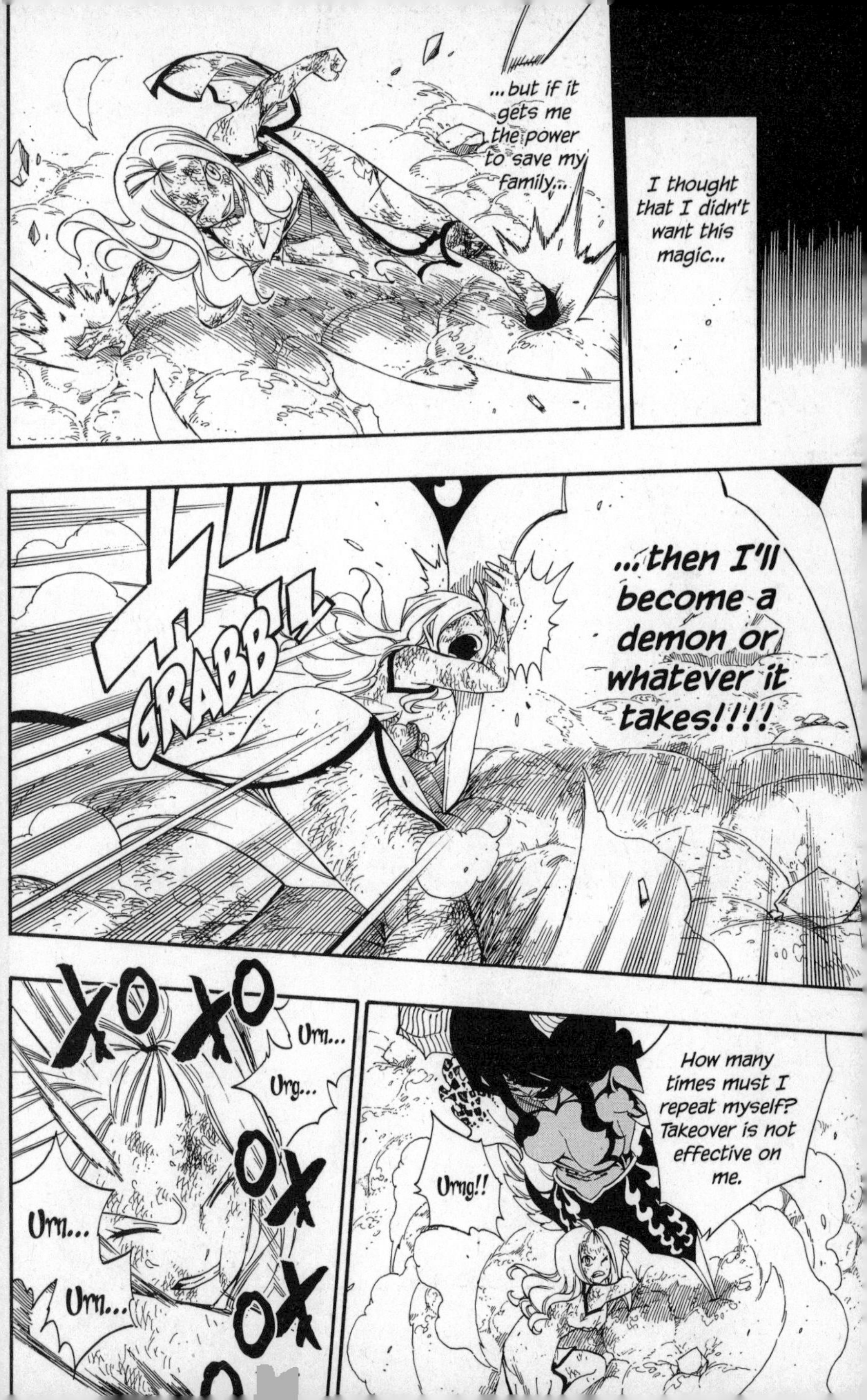
I thought that I didn't want this magic...
...but if it gets me the power to save my family...
GRABB
...then I'll become a demon or whatever it takes!!!!
How many times must I repeat myself? Takeover is not effective on me.
Urng!!
Urn...
Urg...
Urn...
Urn...

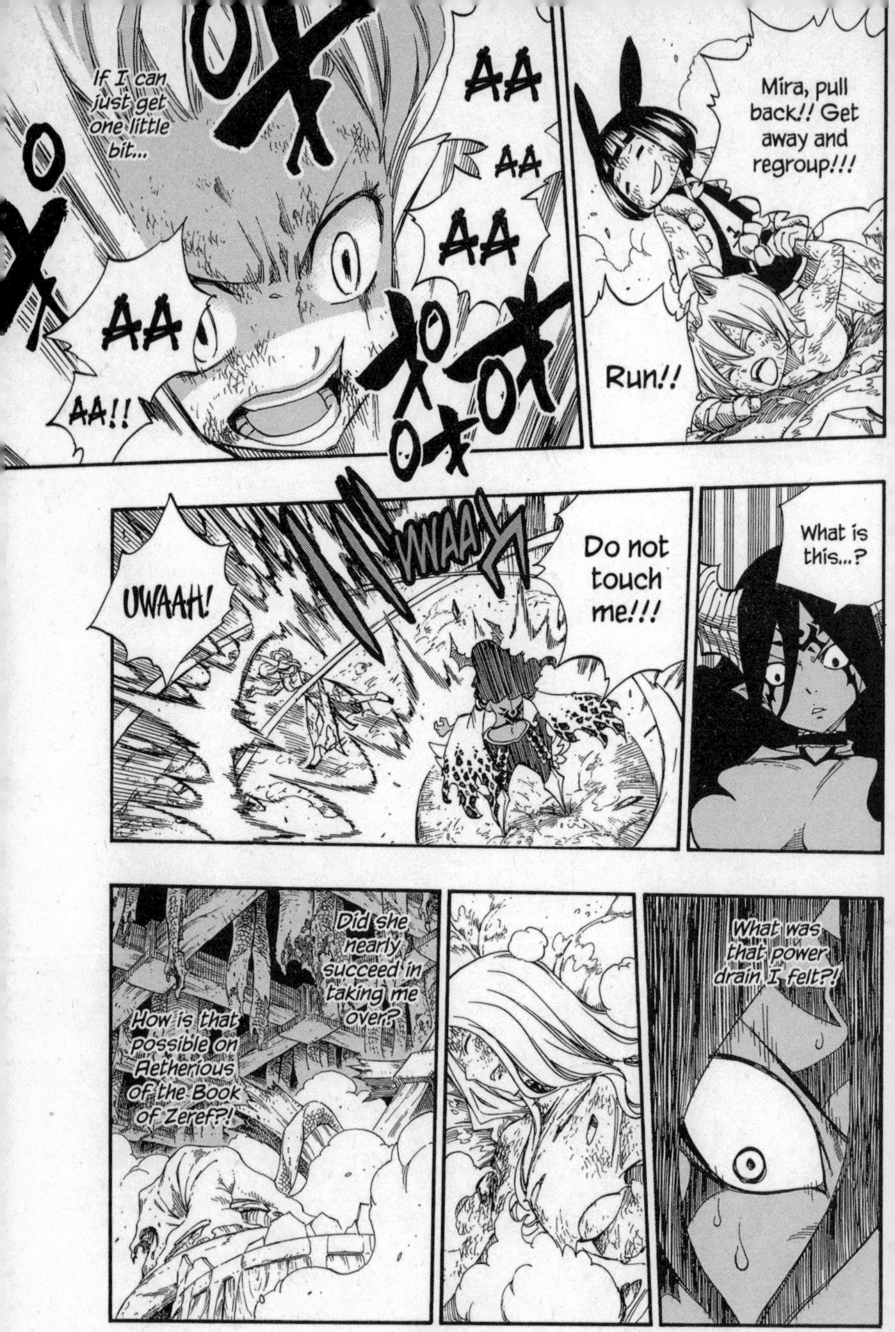
Mira, pull back!! Get away and regroup!!!
Run!!
AA
AA
AA
If I can just get one little bit...
AA
AA!!
What is this...?
Do not touch me!!!
UWAAH!
What was that power drain I felt?!
Did she nearly succeed in taking me over?
How is that possible on Aetherious of the Book of Zeref?!

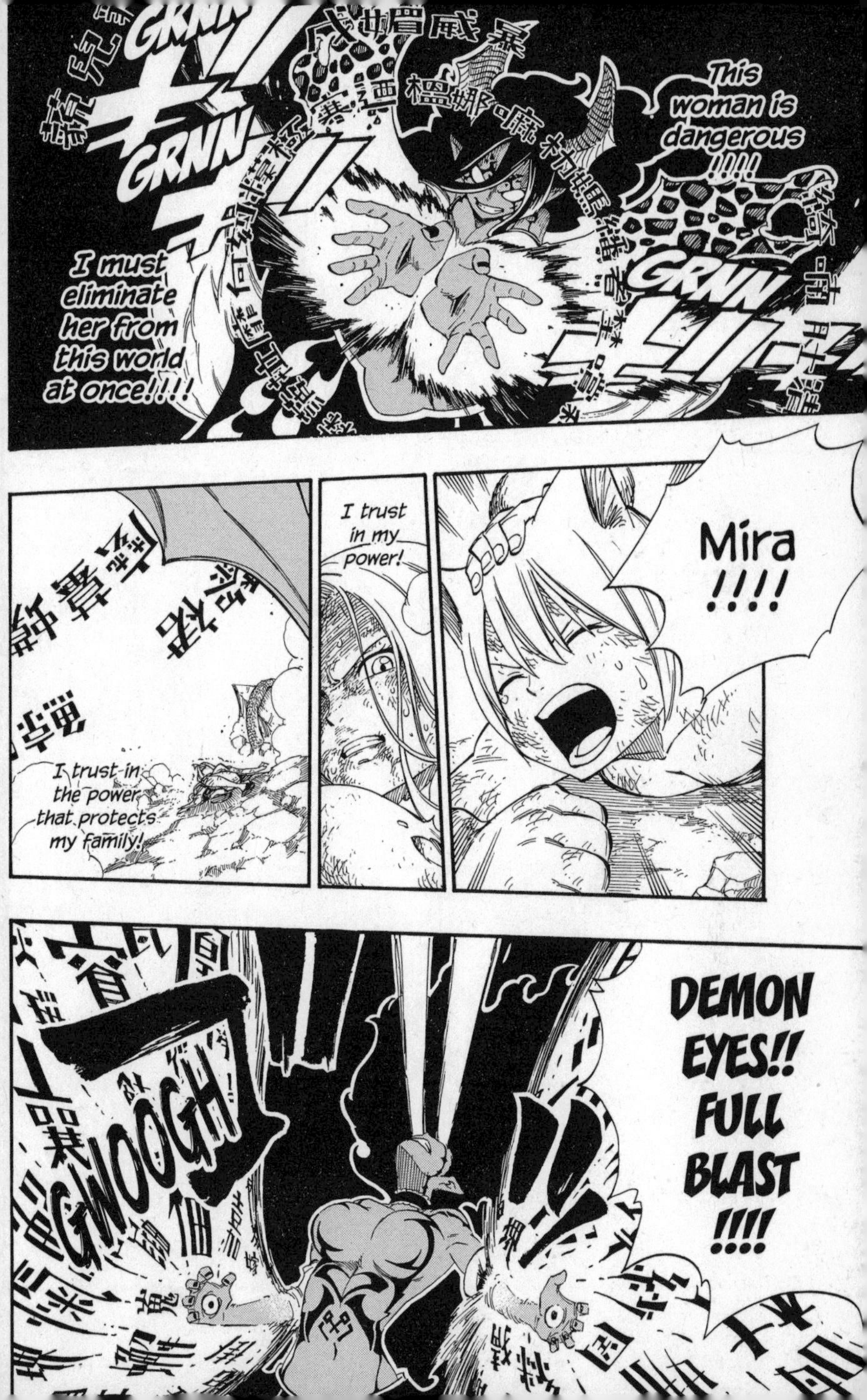
This woman is dangerous!!!!
GRNN
GRNN
GRNN
I must eliminate her from this world at once!!!!
Mira!!!!
I trust in my power!
I trust in the power that protects my family!
DEMON EYES!! FULL BLAST!!!!
GWOOGH

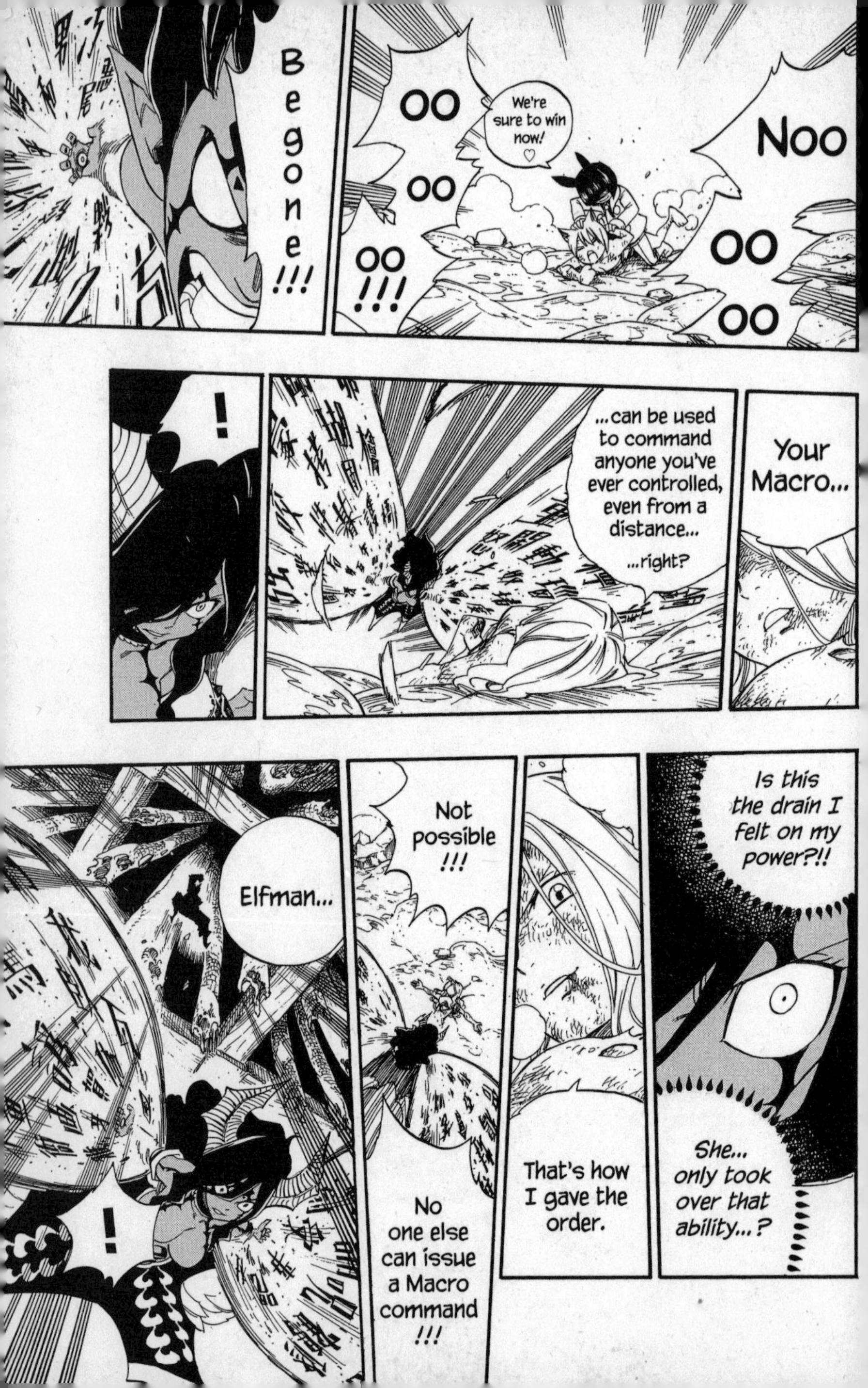
Noo
OO
OO
We're sure to win now! ♡
OO
OO
OO!!!
Begone!!!
Your Macro...
...can be used to command anyone you've ever controlled, even from a distance...
...right?
!
Is this the drain I felt on my power?!!
She... only took over that ability...?
That's how I gave the order.
Not possible!!!
No one else can issue a Macro command!!!
Elfman...
!

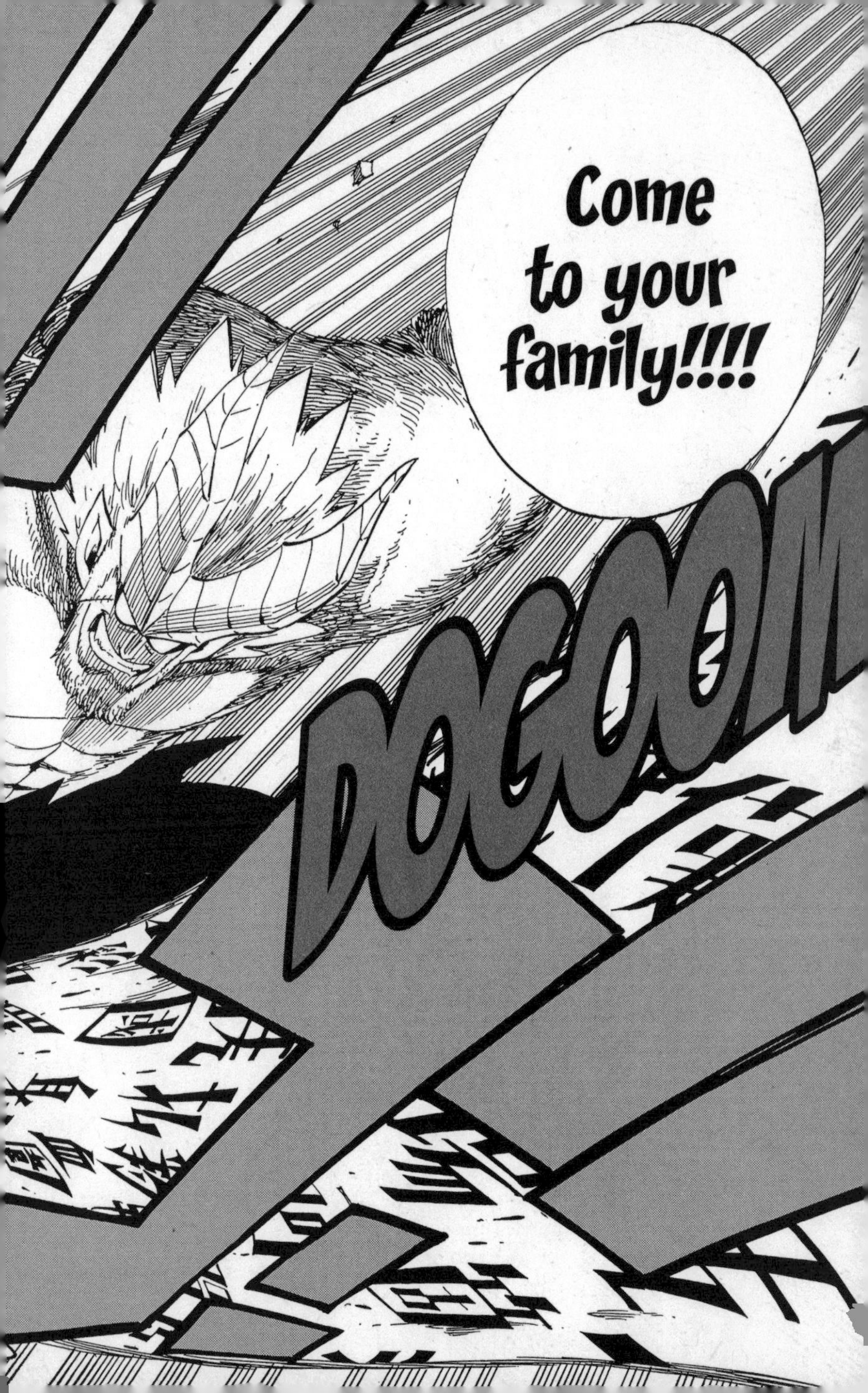
Come to your family!!!!
DOGOOM

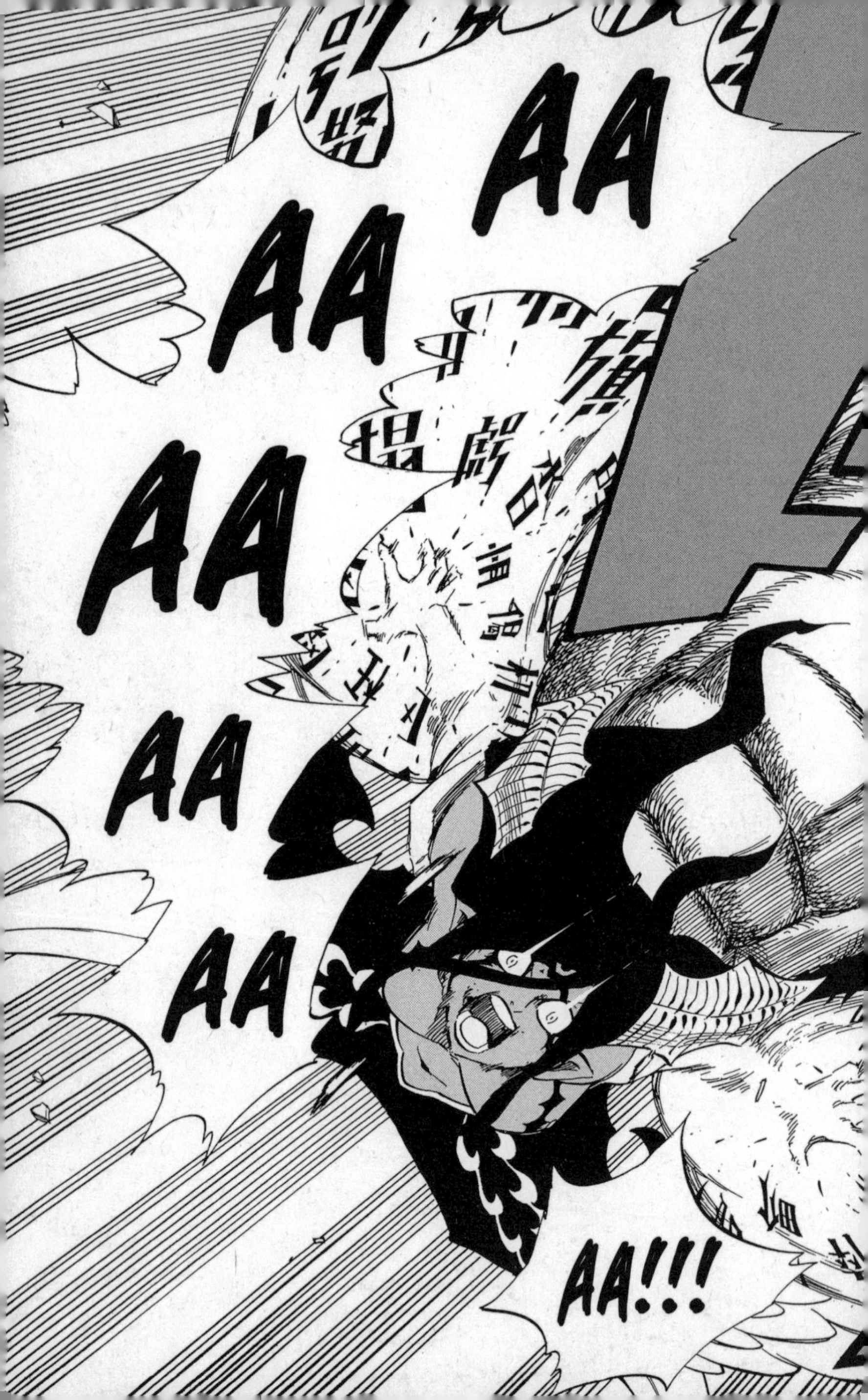

AA
AA
AA
AA
AA
AA!!!

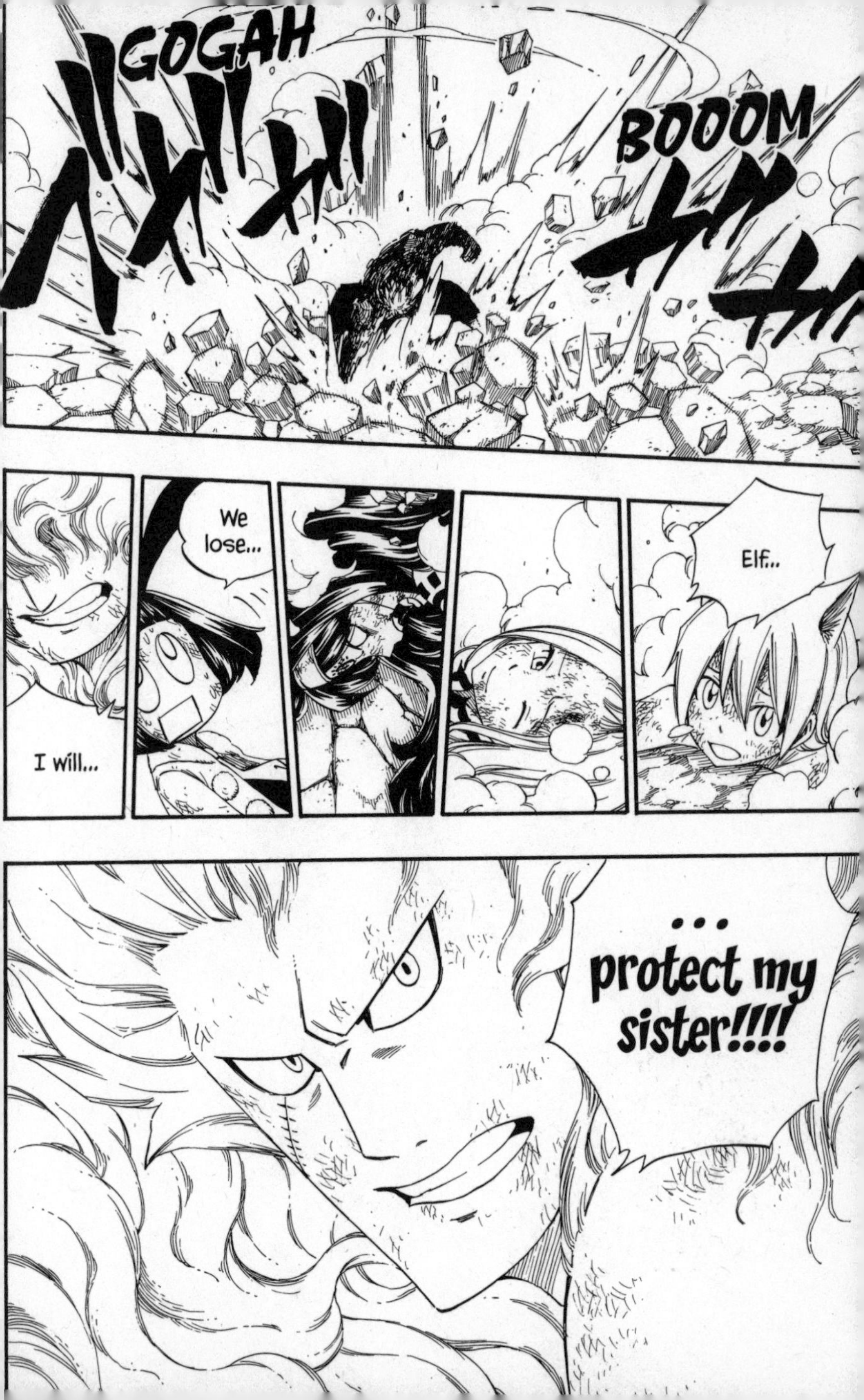
BOOOM
GOGAH
Elf...
We lose...
I will...
... protect my sister!!!!

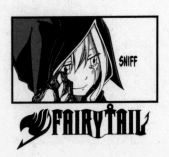
SNIFF

FAIRYTAIL

FAIRY TAIL

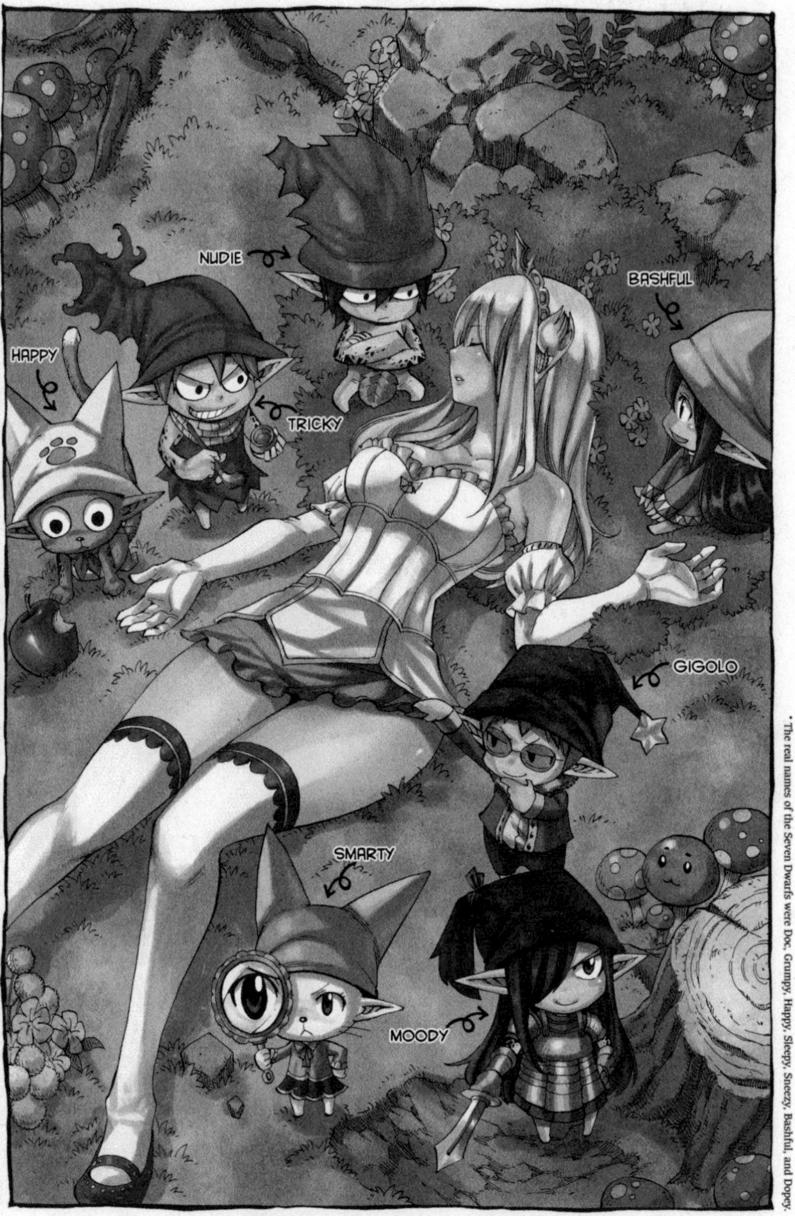
BASHFUL
NUDIE
TRICKY
HAPPY
GIGOLO
SMARTY
MOODY

* The real names of the Seven Dwarfs were Doc, Grumpy, Happy, Sleepy, Sneezy, Bashful, and Dopey.

Chapter 382: Alegria

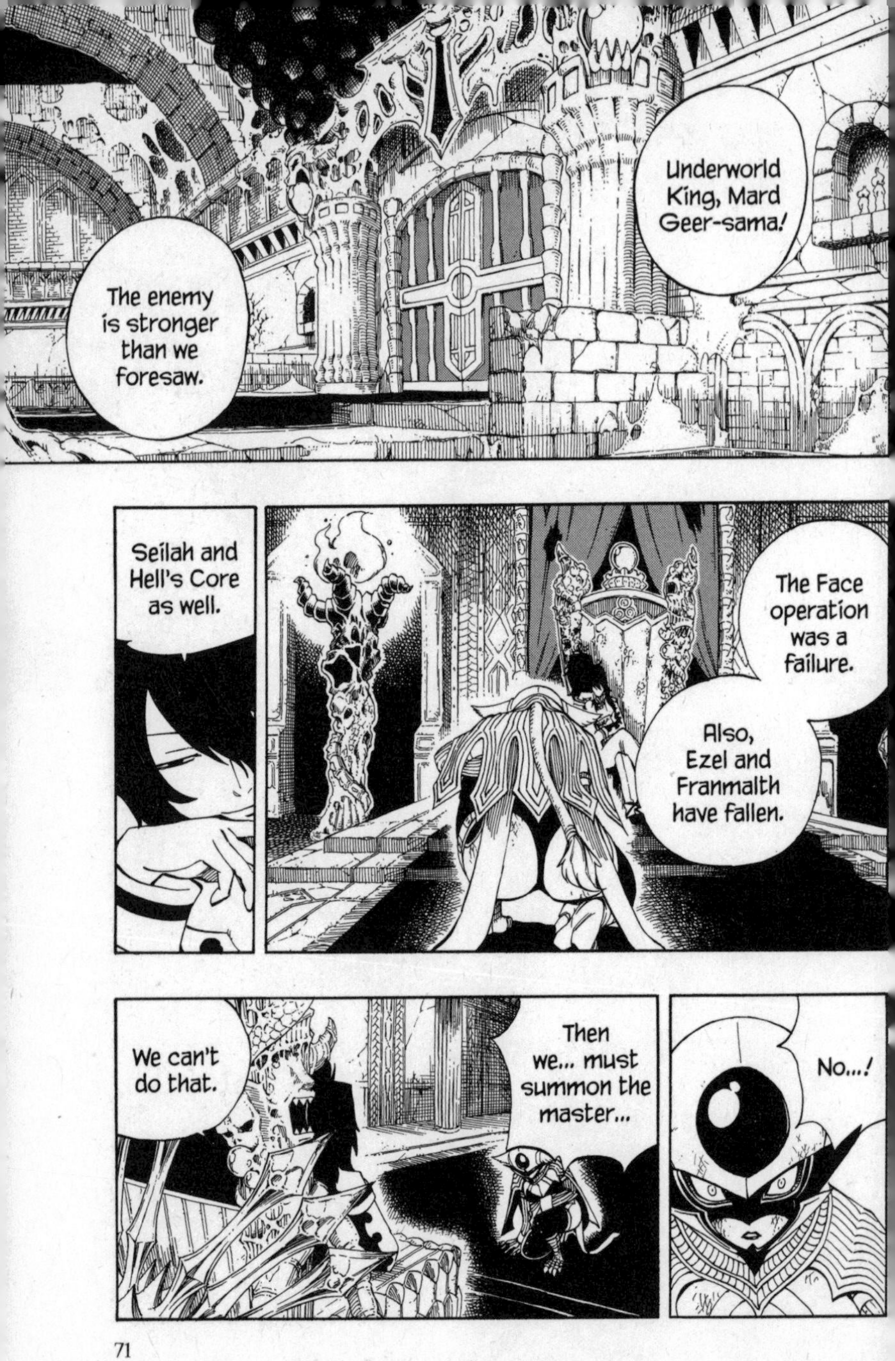
Underworld King, Mard Geer-sama!
The enemy is stronger than we foresaw.
The Face operation was a failure.
Also, Ezel and Franmalth have fallen.
Seilah and Hell's Core as well.
No...!
Then we... must summon the master...
We can't do that.

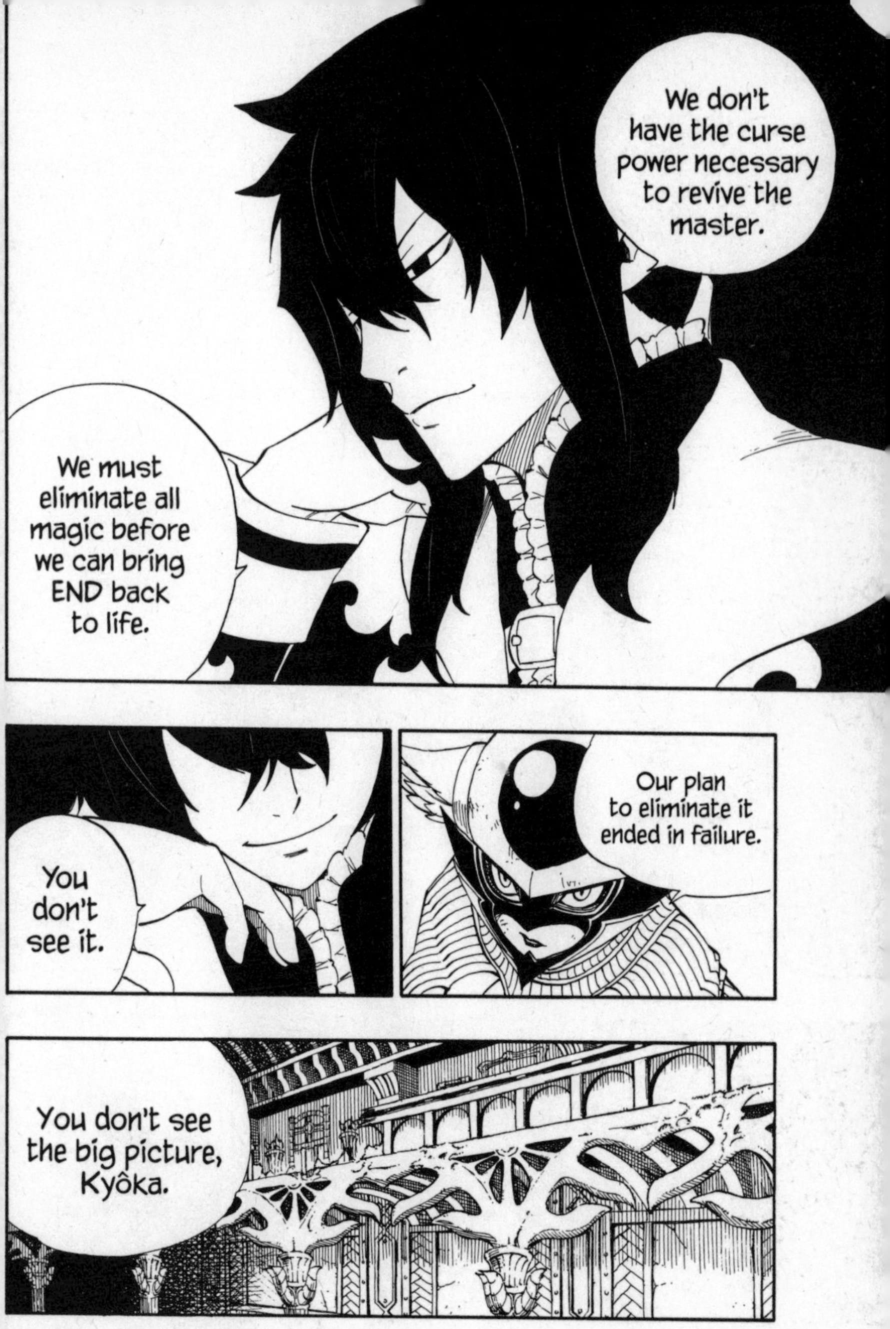
We don't have the curse power necessary to revive the master.
We must eliminate all magic before we can bring END back to life.
Our plan to eliminate it ended in failure.
You don't see it.
You don't see the big picture, Kyôka.

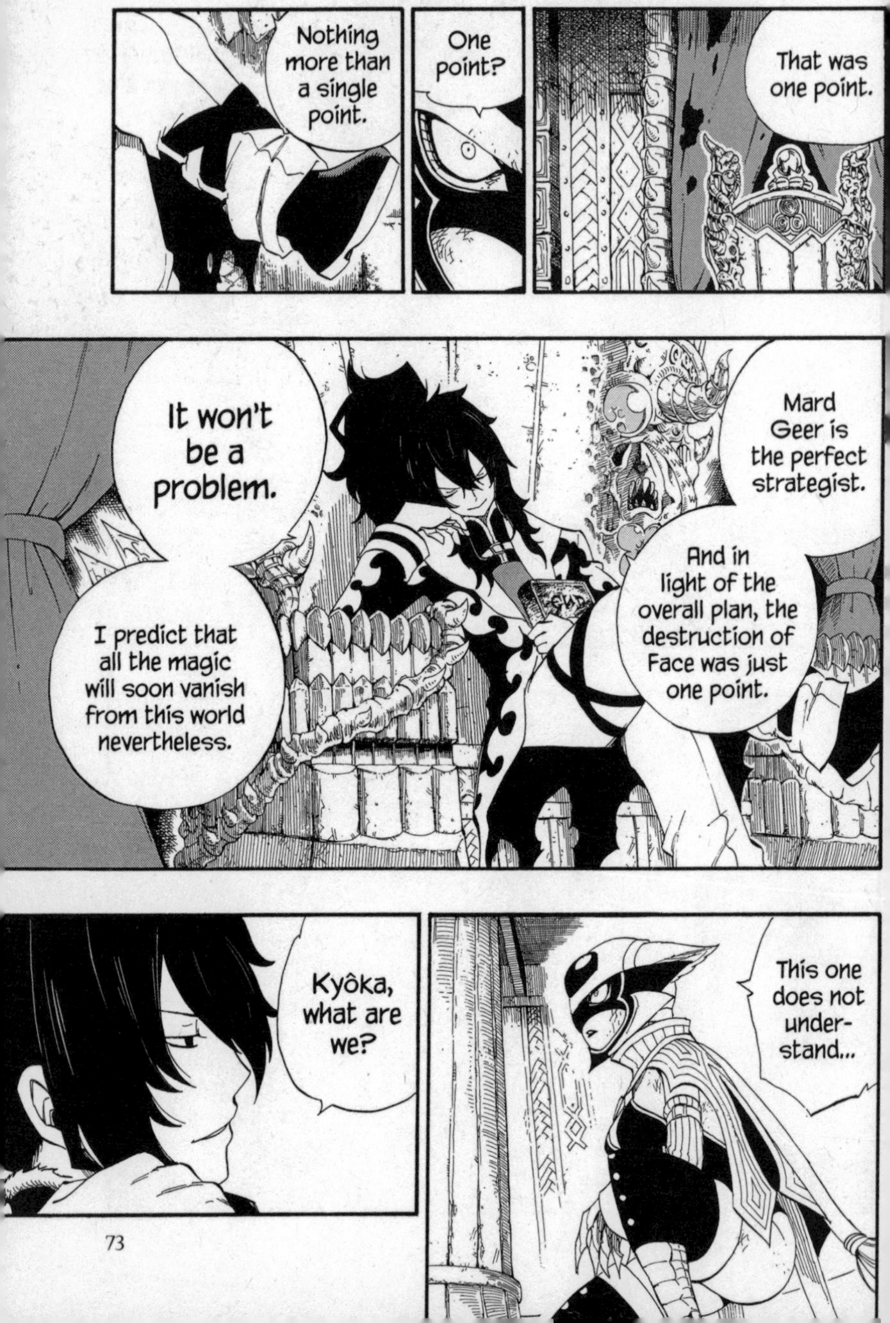

That was one point.
One point?
Nothing more than a single point.
Mard Geer is the perfect strategist.
And in light of the overall plan, the destruction of Face was just one point.
It won't be a problem.
I predict that all the magic will soon vanish from this world nevertheless.
This one does not under-stand...
Kyôka, what are we?

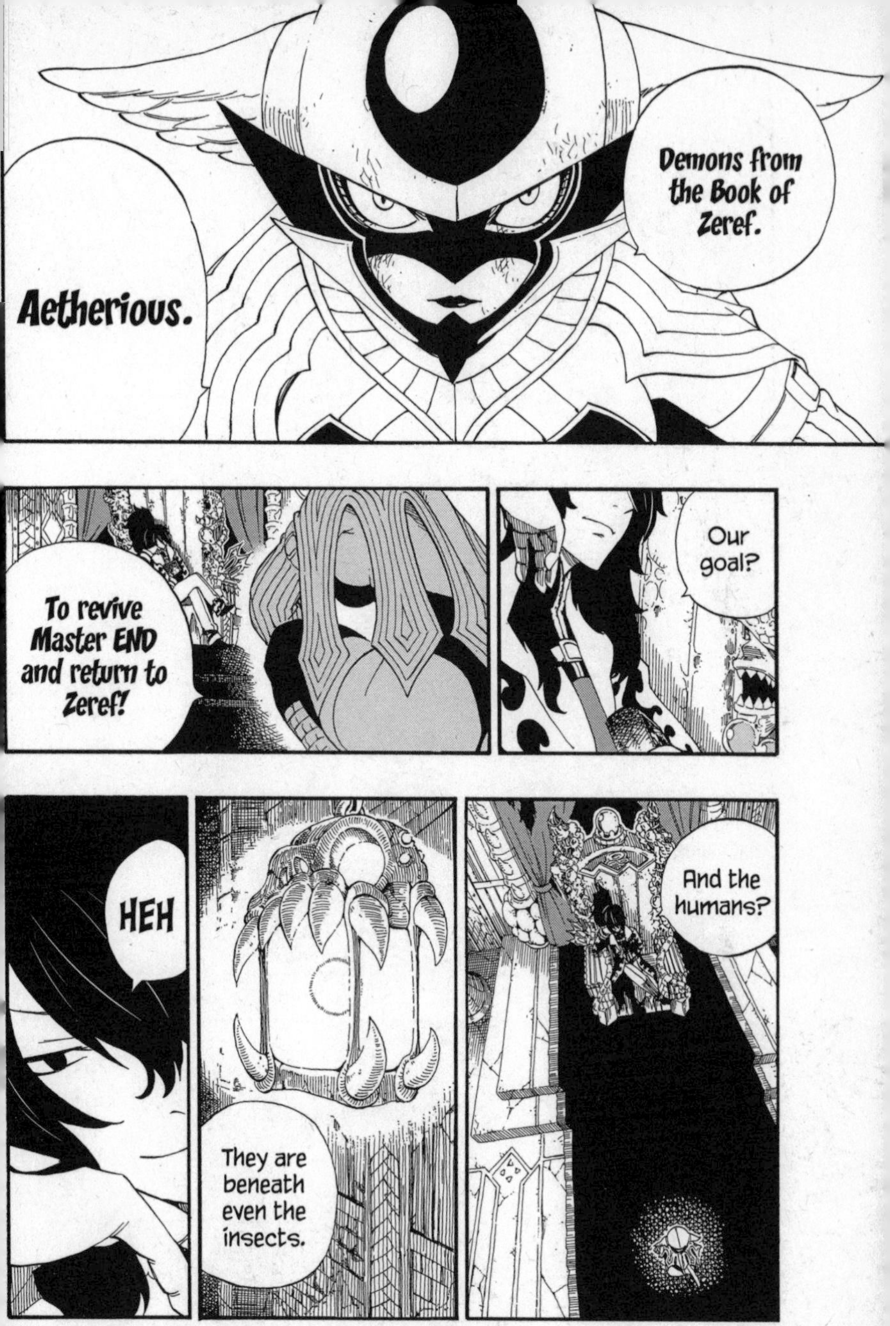
Demons from the Book of Zeref.
Aetherious.
Our goal?
To revive Master END and return to Zeref!
And the humans?
They are beneath even the insects.
HEH

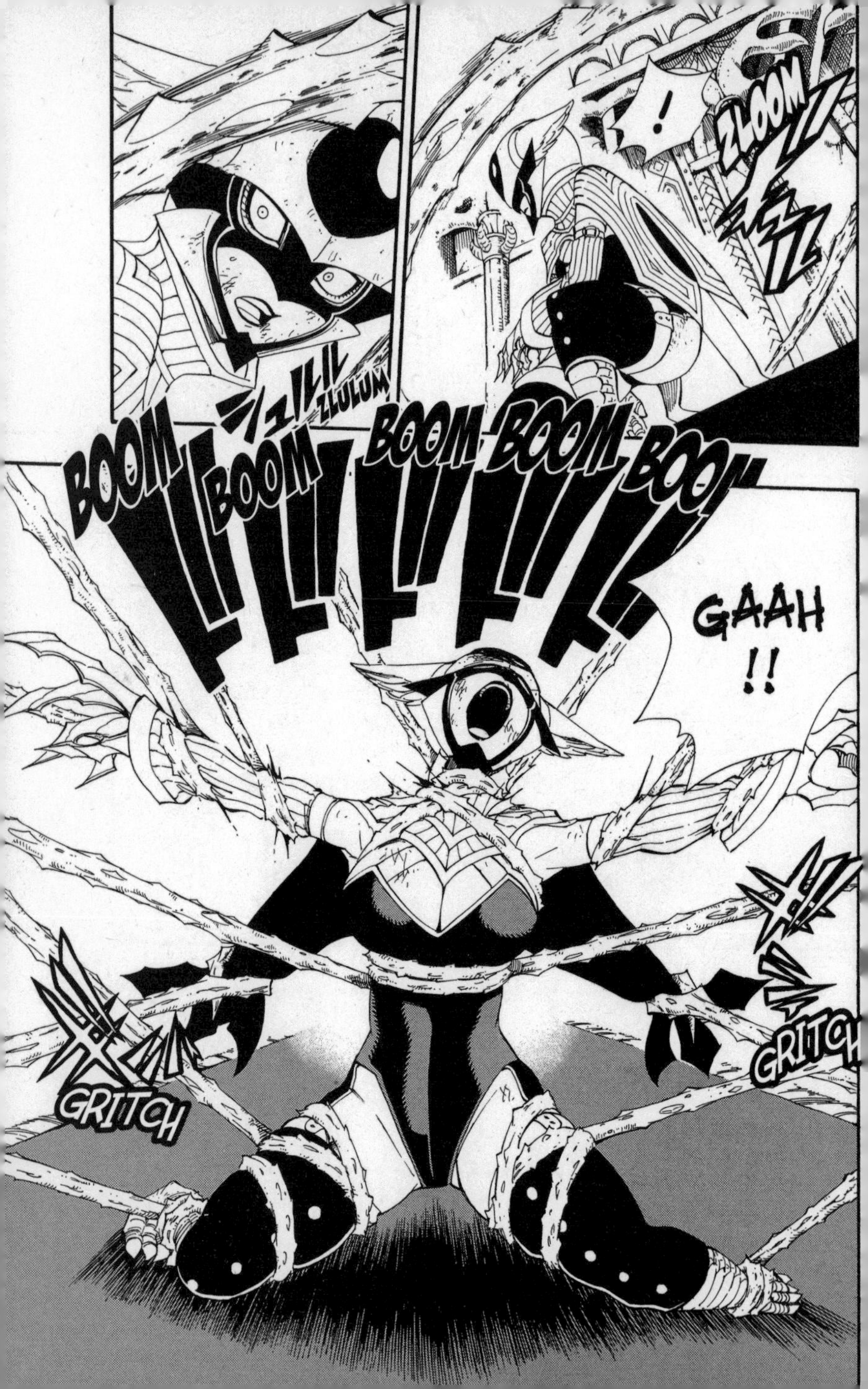
!
ZLOOM!!
シュルル
ZLULUM
BOOM BOOM BOOM BOOM BOOM
GAAH!!
GRITCH
GRITCH

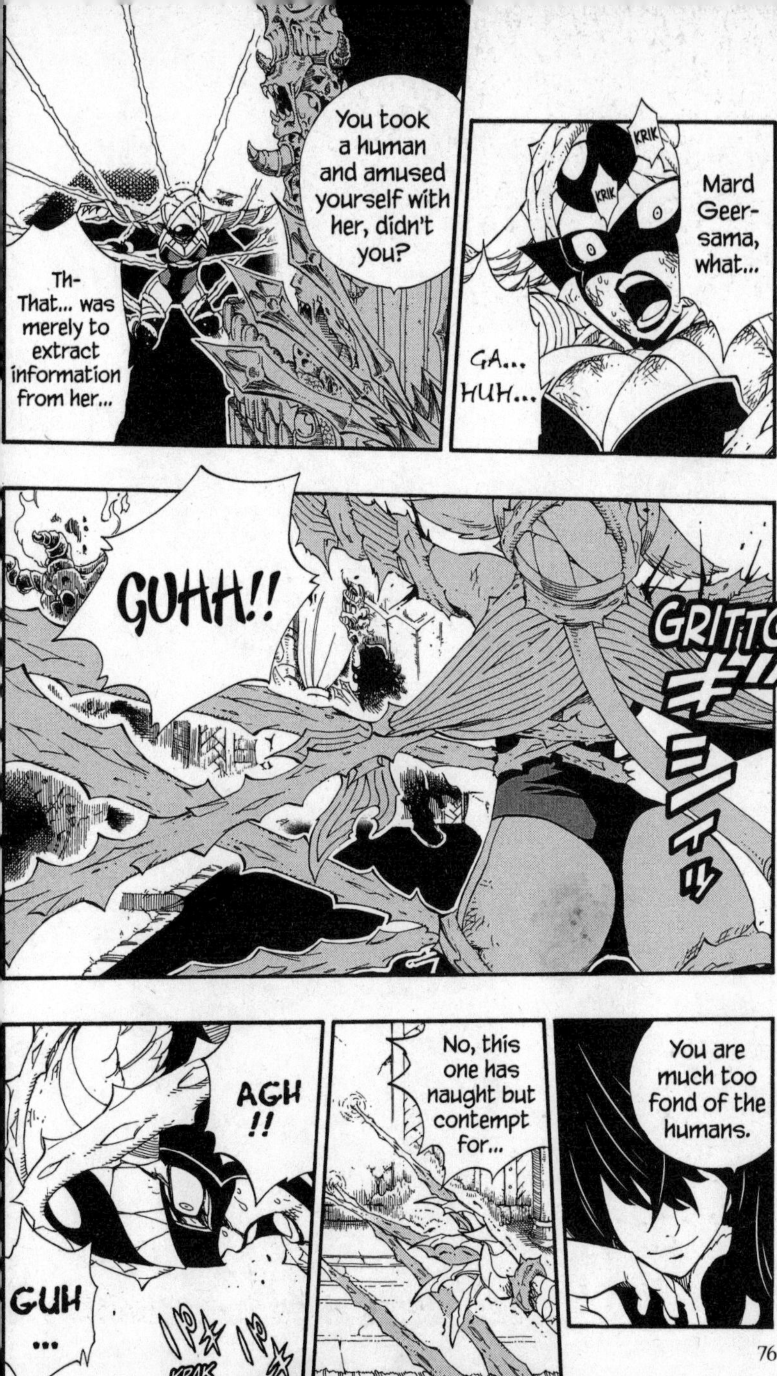

KRIK
KRIK
Mard Geer-sama, what...
GA... HUH...
You took a human and amused yourself with her, didn't you?
Th- That... was merely to extract information from her...
GRITTCH
GUHH!!
You are much too fond of the humans.
No, this one has naught but contempt for...
AGH!!
GUH...
KRAK
KRAK

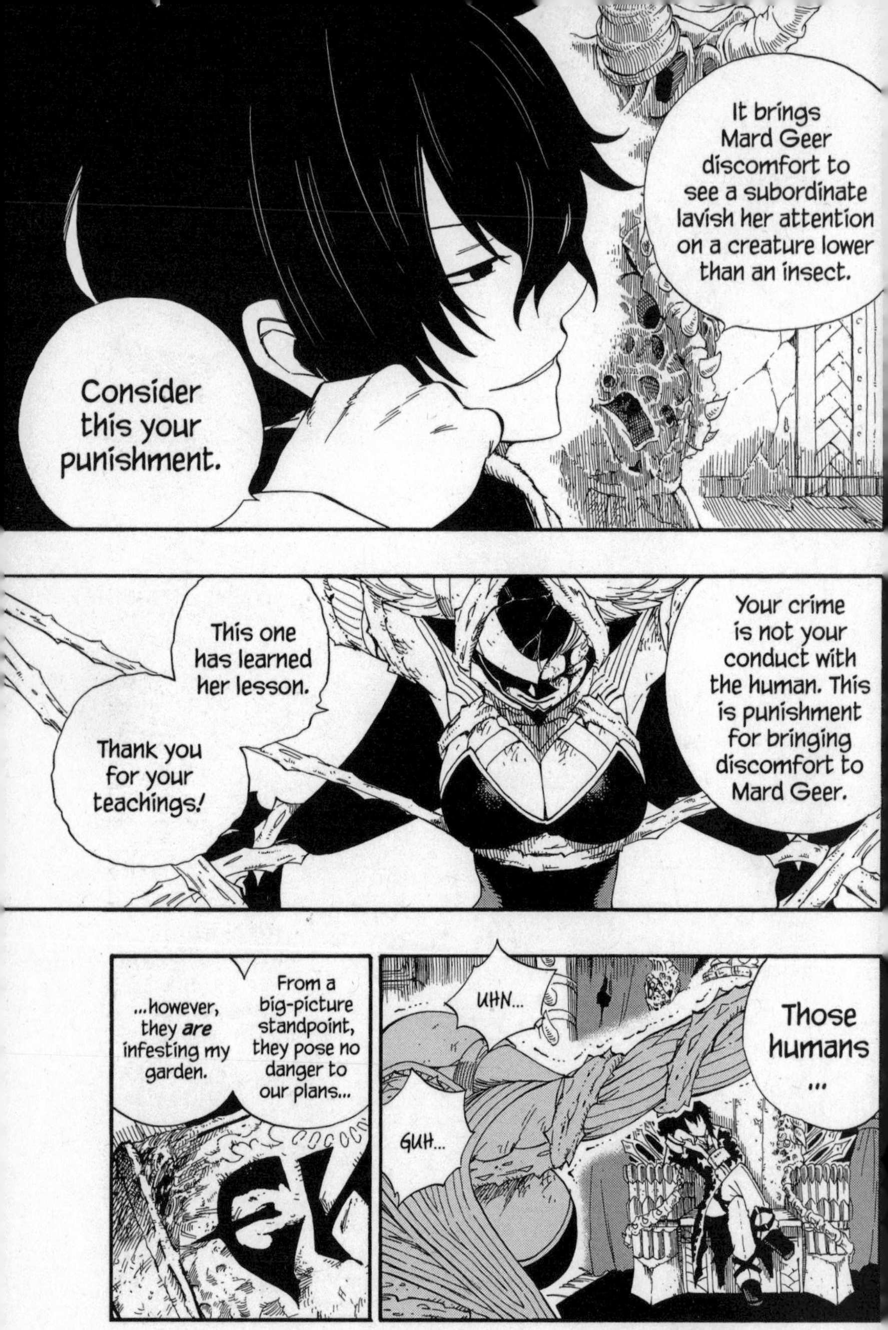

It brings Mard Geer discomfort to see a subordinate lavish her attention on a creature lower than an insect.
Consider this your punishment.
Your crime is not your conduct with the human. This is punishment for bringing discomfort to Mard Geer.
This one has learned her lesson.
Thank you for your teachings!
Those humans ...
UHN...
GUH...
From a big-picture standpoint, they pose no danger to our plans...
...however, they *are* infesting my garden.

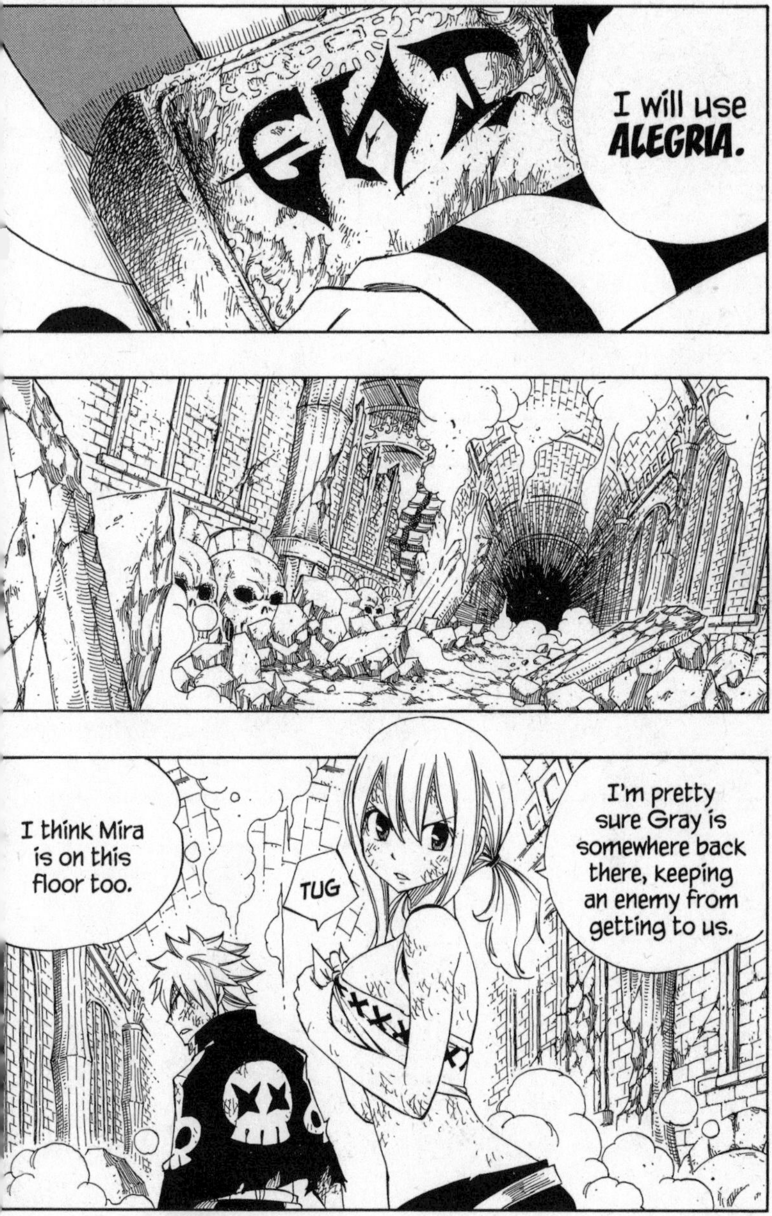
I will use **ALEGRIA.**
I'm pretty sure Gray is somewhere back there, keeping an enemy from getting to us.
TUG
I think Mira is on this floor too.

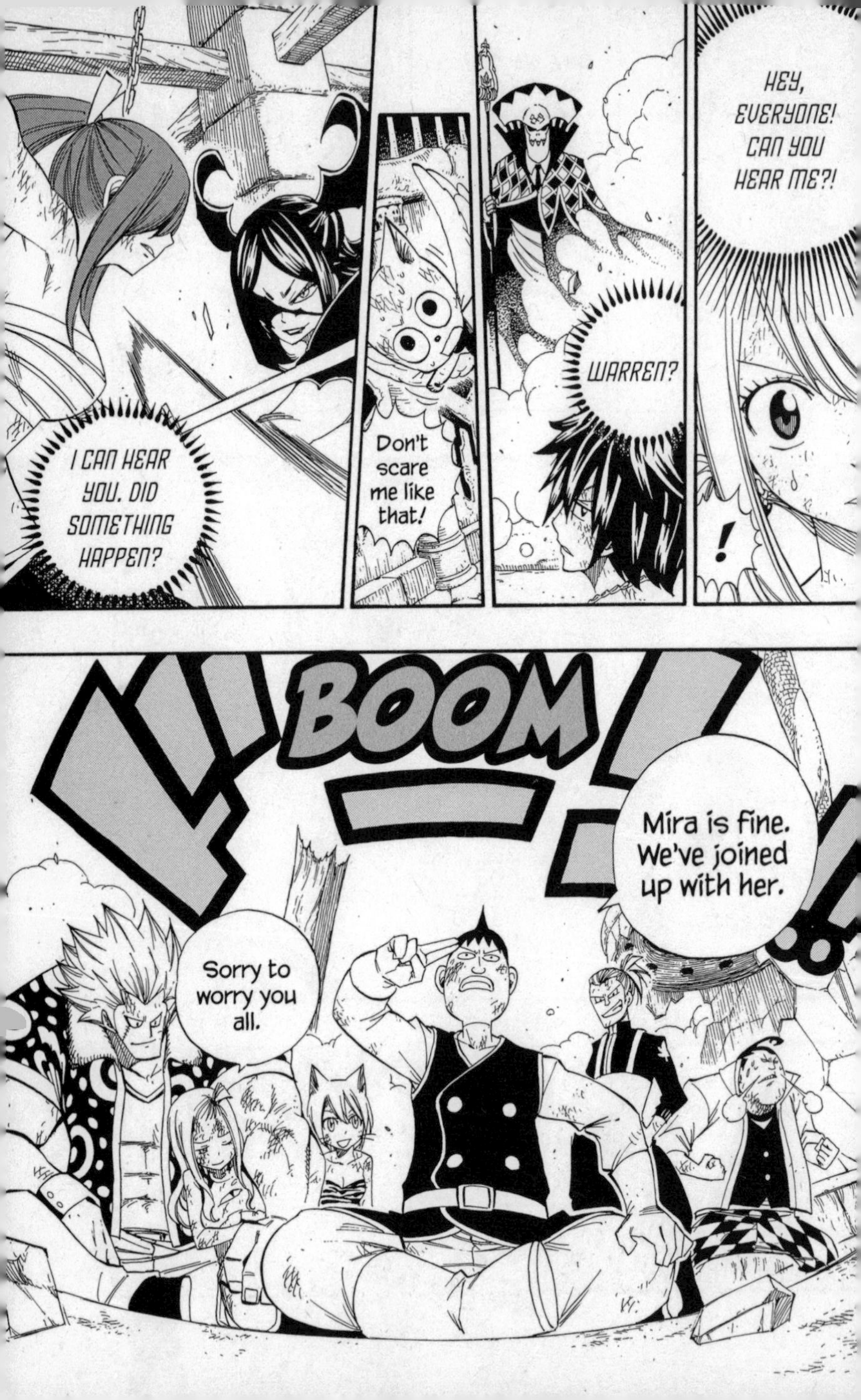
HEY, EVERYONE! CAN YOU HEAR ME?!
!
WARREN?
Don't scare me like that!
I CAN HEAR YOU. DID SOMETHING HAPPEN?
BOOM
Mira is fine. We've joined up with her.
Sorry to worry you all.

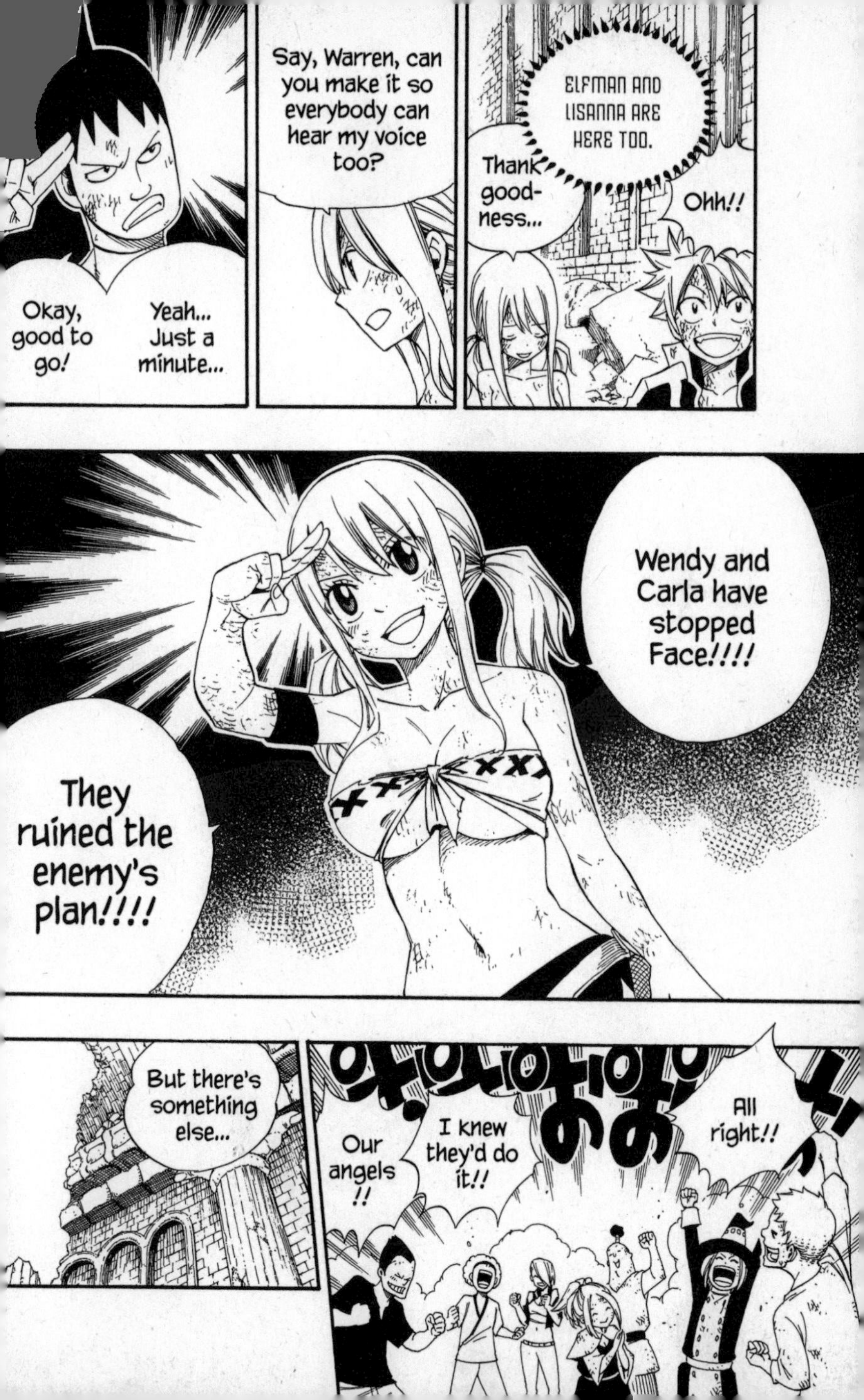
ELFMAN AND LISANNA ARE HERE TOO.
Ohh!!
Thank goodness...
Say, Warren, can you make it so everybody can hear my voice too?
Yeah... Just a minute...
Okay, good to go!
Wendy and Carla have stopped Face!!!!
They ruined the enemy's plan!!!!
All right!!
I knew they'd do it!!
Our angels!!
But there's something else...

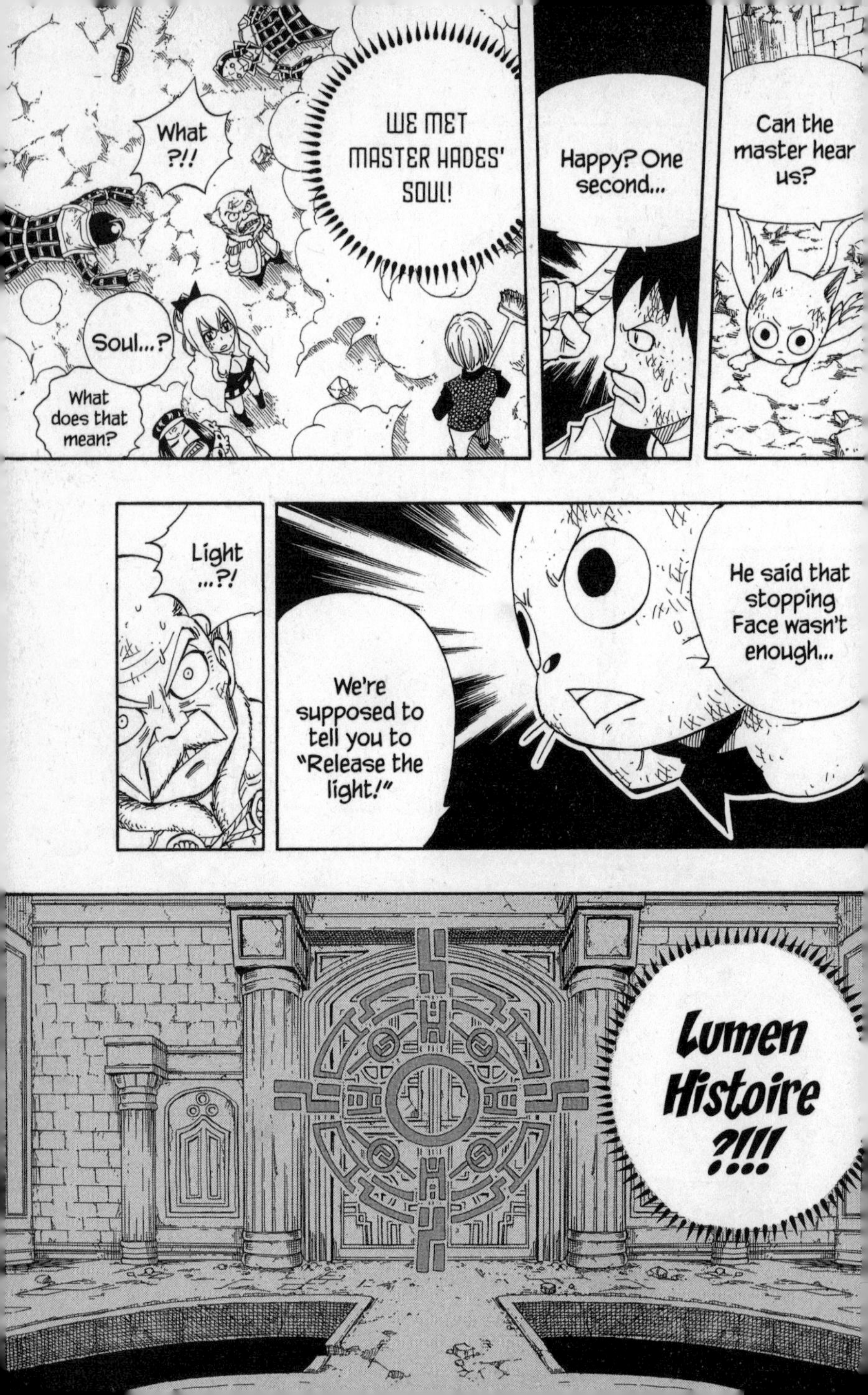
Can the master hear us?
Happy? One second...
WE MET MASTER HADES' SOUL!
What ?!!
Soul...?
What does that mean?
He said that stopping Face wasn't enough...
We're supposed to tell you to "Release the light!"
Light ...?!
Lumen Histoire ?!!!

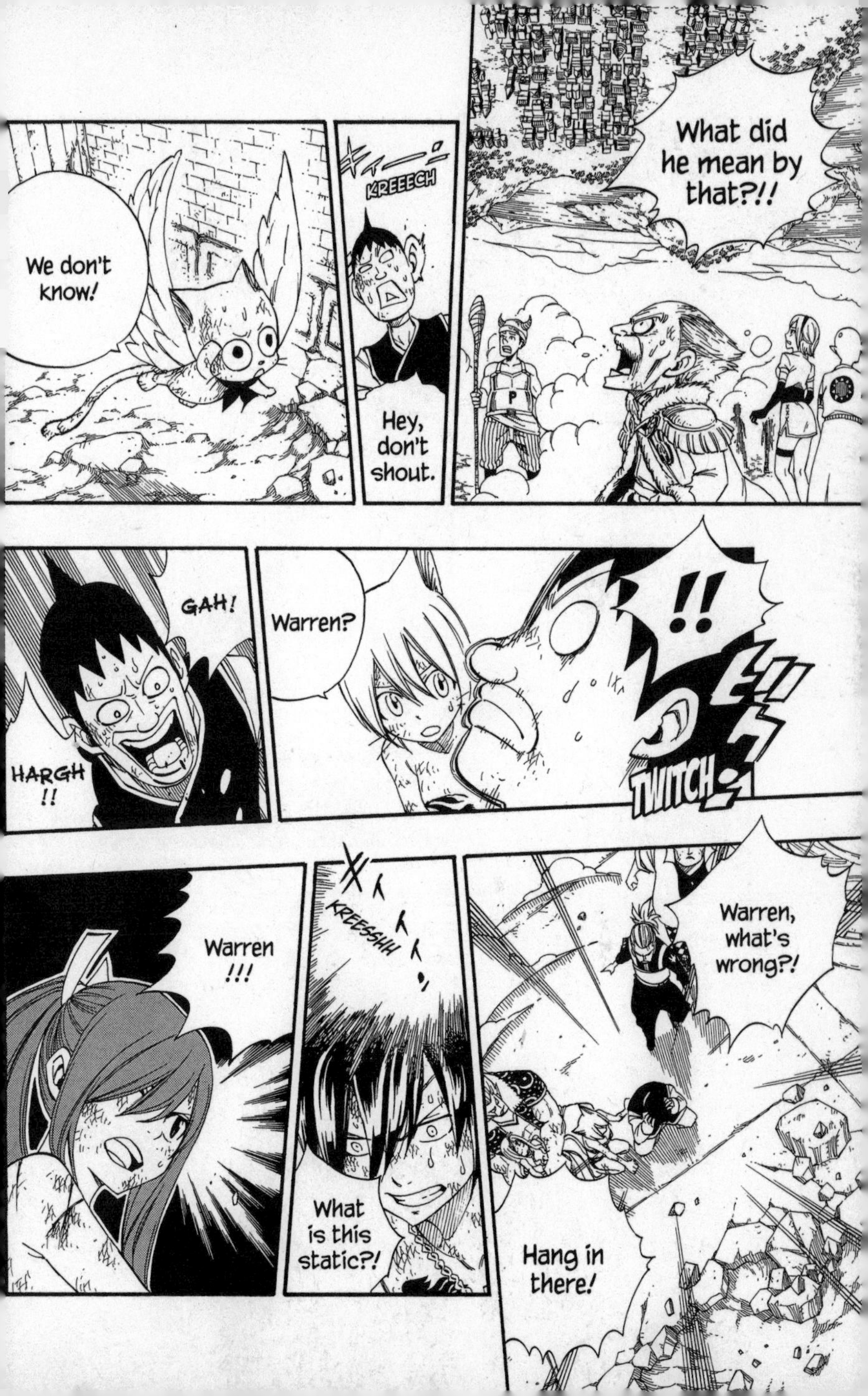
What did he mean by that?!!
KREEECH
Hey, don't shout.
We don't know!
!!
TWITCH
Warren?
GAH!
HARGH !!
Warren, what's wrong?!
Hang in there!
KREESSHH
What is this static?!
Warren !!!

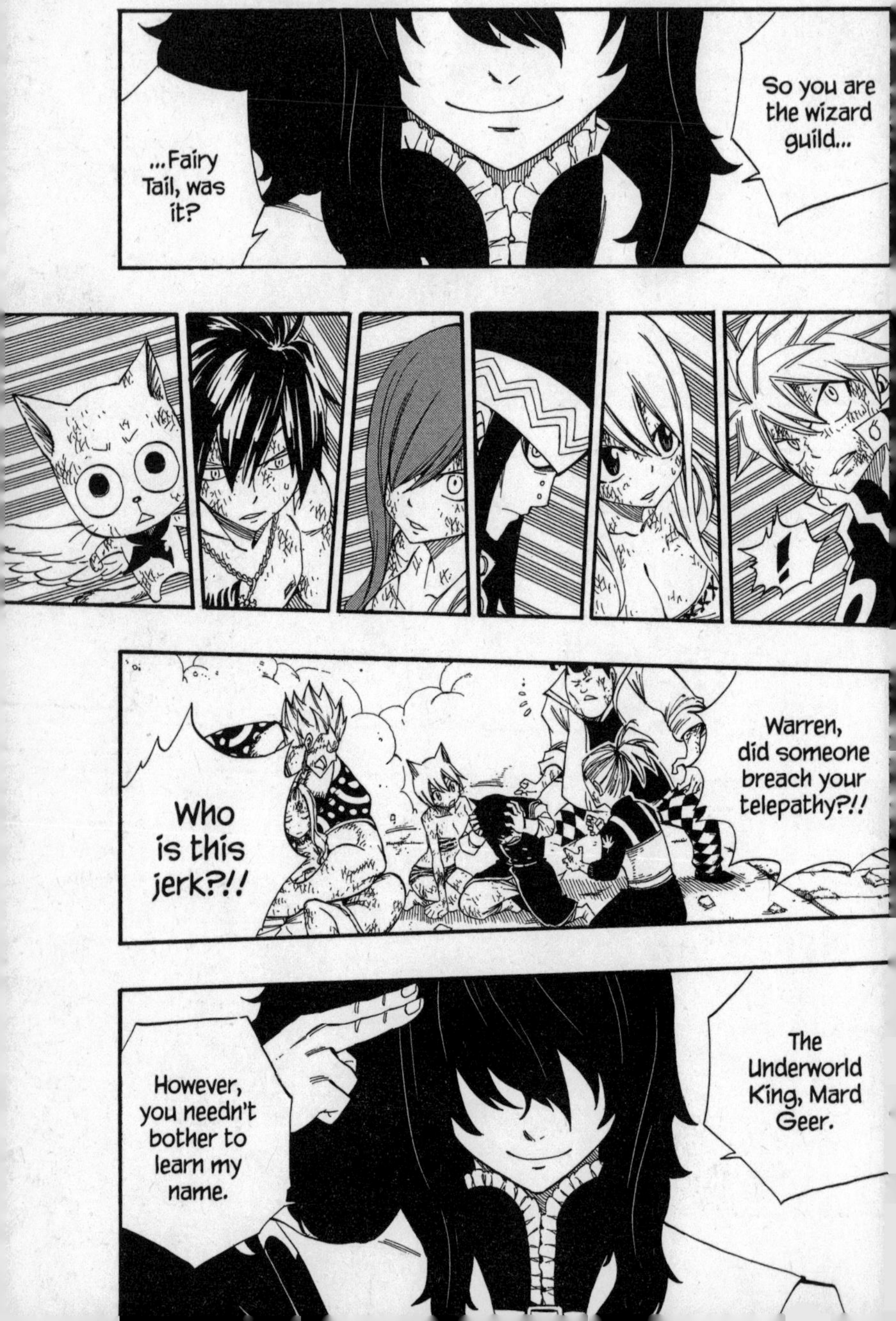
So you are the wizard guild...
...Fairy Tail, was it?
Warren, did someone breach your telepathy?!!
Who is this jerk?!!
The Underworld King, Mard Geer.
However, you needn't bother to learn my name.

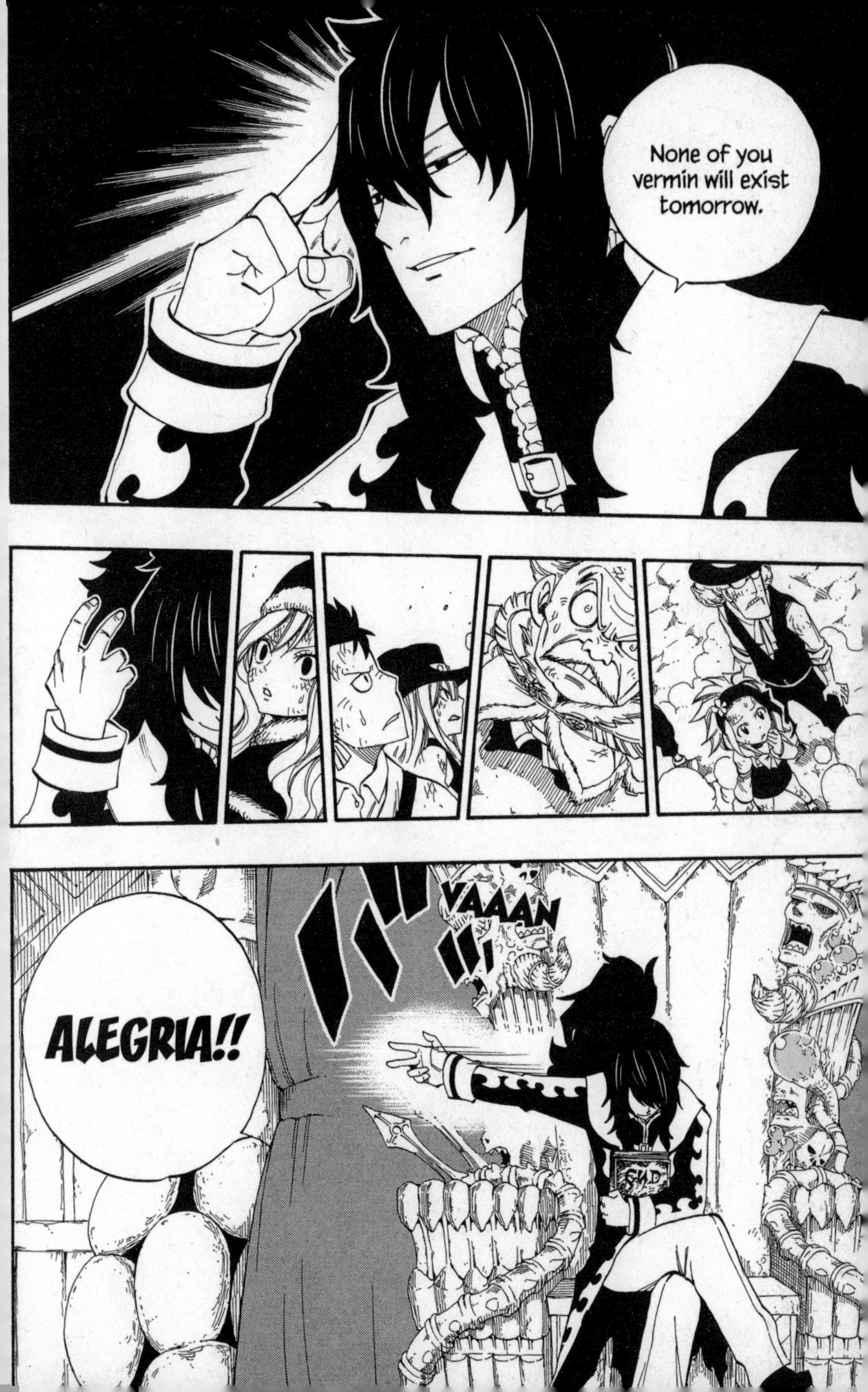
None of you vermin will exist tomorrow.
VAAAN
ALEGRIA!!

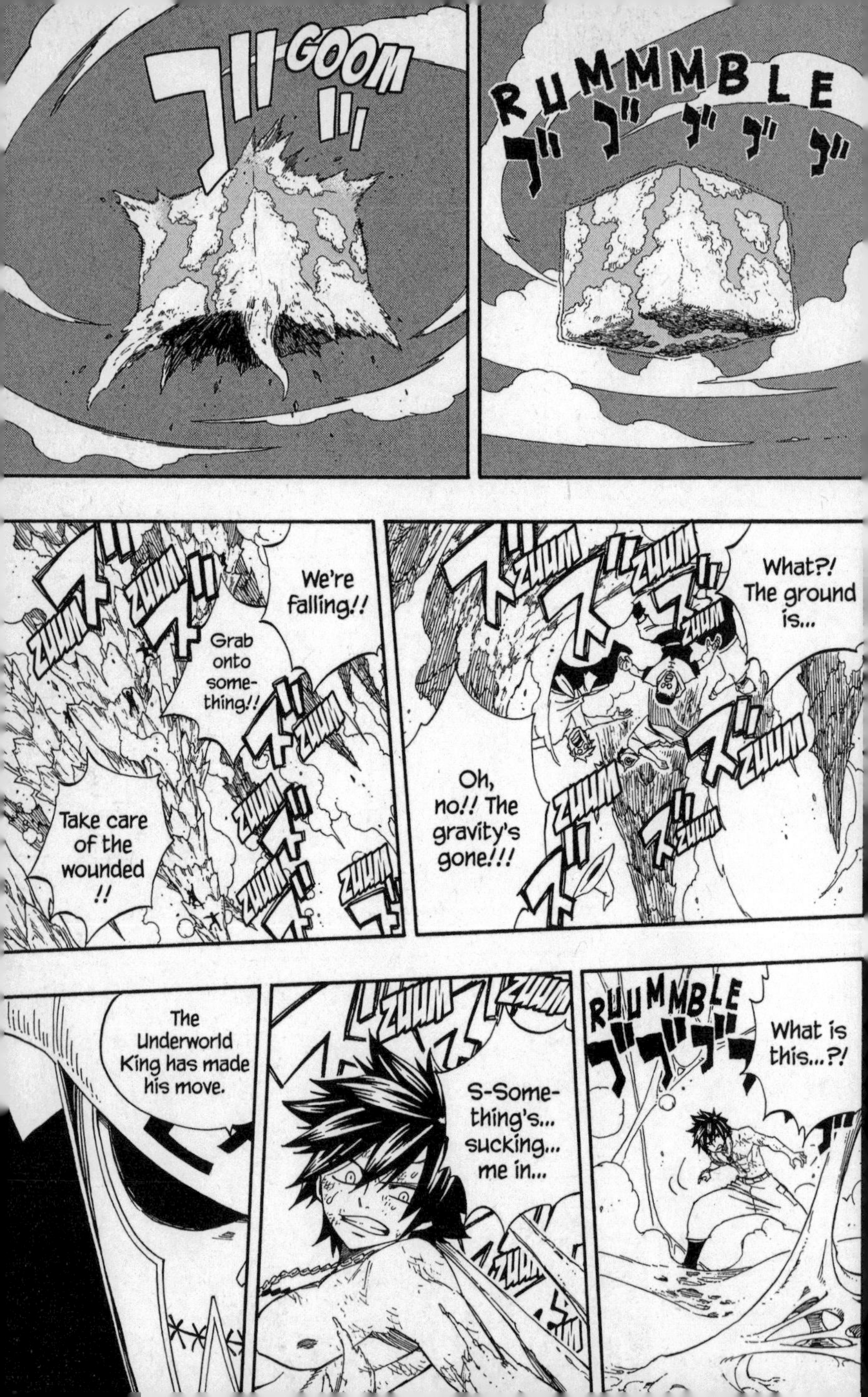
RUMMMBLE
GOOM
What?! The ground is...
ZUUM
ZUUM
ZUUM
Oh, no!! The gravity's gone!!!
We're falling!!
Grab onto some-thing!!
ZUUM
ZUUM
Take care of the wounded!!
RUMMBLE
What is this...?!
ZUUM
ZUUM
S-Some-thing's... sucking... me in...
The Underworld King has made his move.

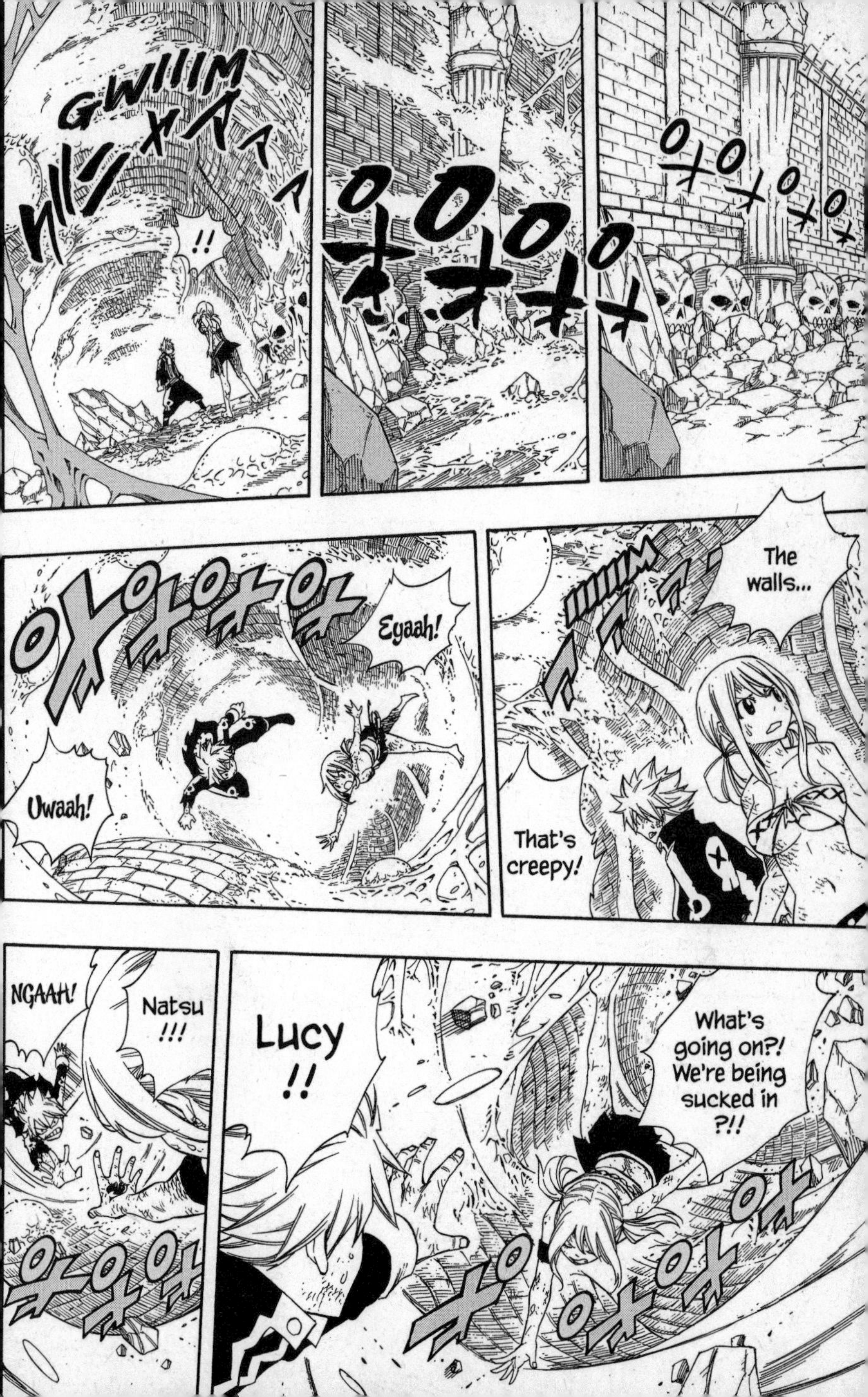
GWIIIM
!!
The walls...
That's creepy!
Eyaah!
Uwaah!
What's going on?! We're being sucked in ?!!
Lucy !!
Natsu !!!
NGAAH!

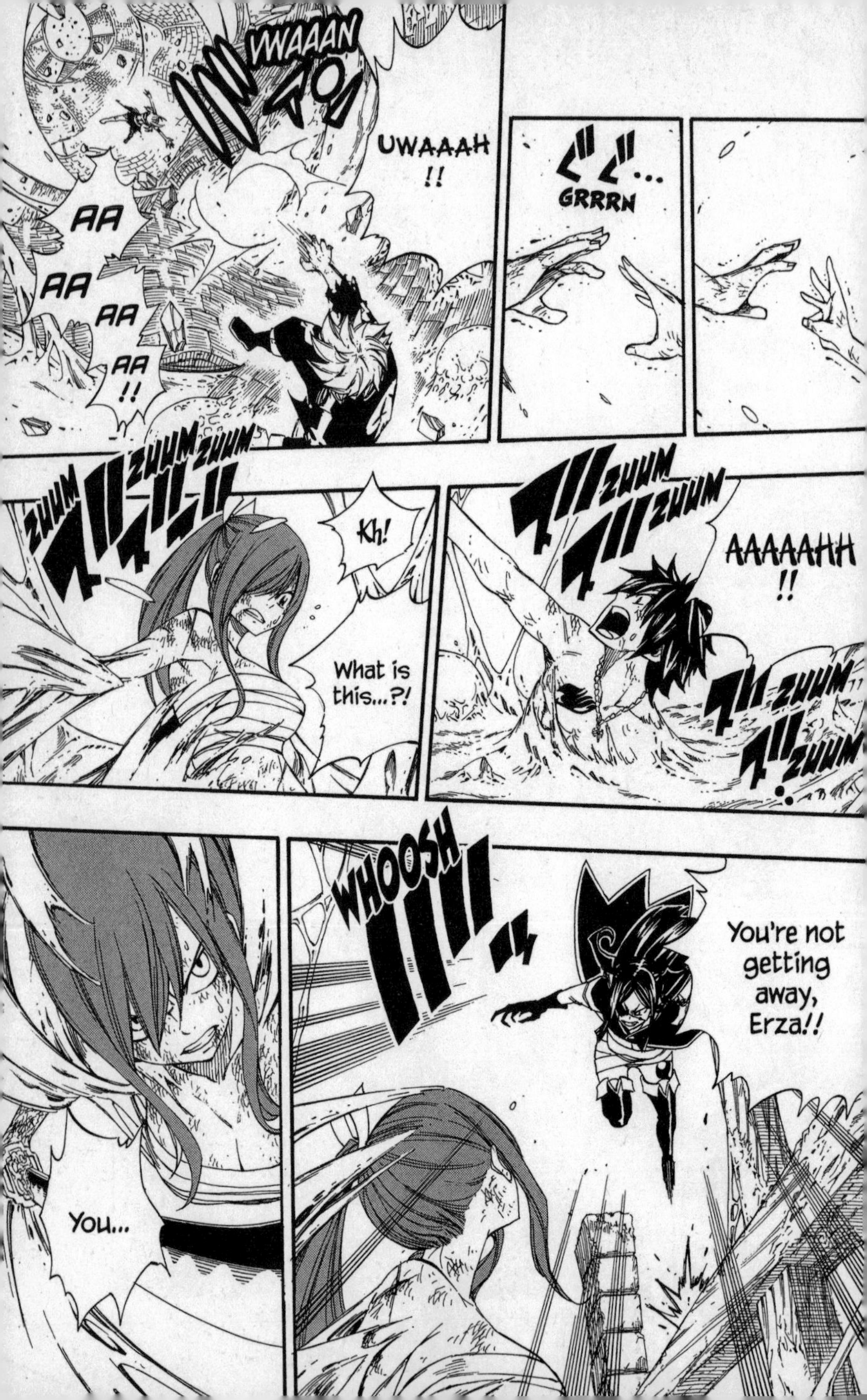
GRRRN
VWAAAN
UWAAAH!!
AA AA AA AA!!
ZUUM ZUUM
AAAAAH!!
ZUUM ZUUM
ZUUM ZUUM ZUUM
Kh!
What is this...?!
You're not getting away, Erza!!
WHOOSH
You...

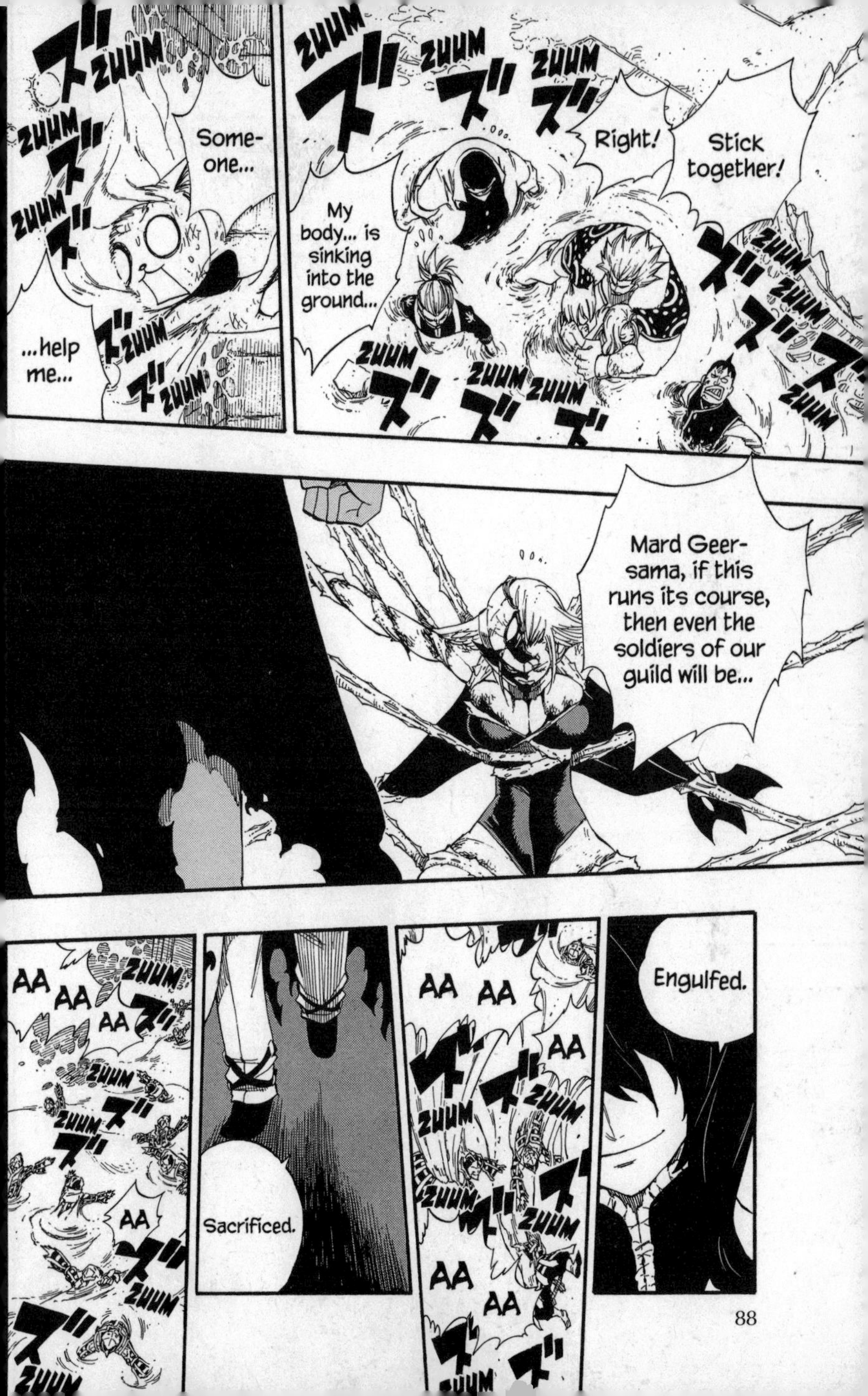
ZUUM
ZUUM
ZUUM
Stick together!
Right!
My body... is sinking into the ground...
ZUUM
ZUUM
ZUUM
Some-one...
...help me...
ZUUM
ZUUM
ZUUM
Mard Geer-sama, if this runs its course, then even the soldiers of our guild will be...
Engulfed.
AA
AA
AA
AA
AA
ZUUM
ZUUM
ZUUM
Sacrificed.
AA
AA
AA
AA
ZUUM
ZUUM
ZUUM
ZUUM

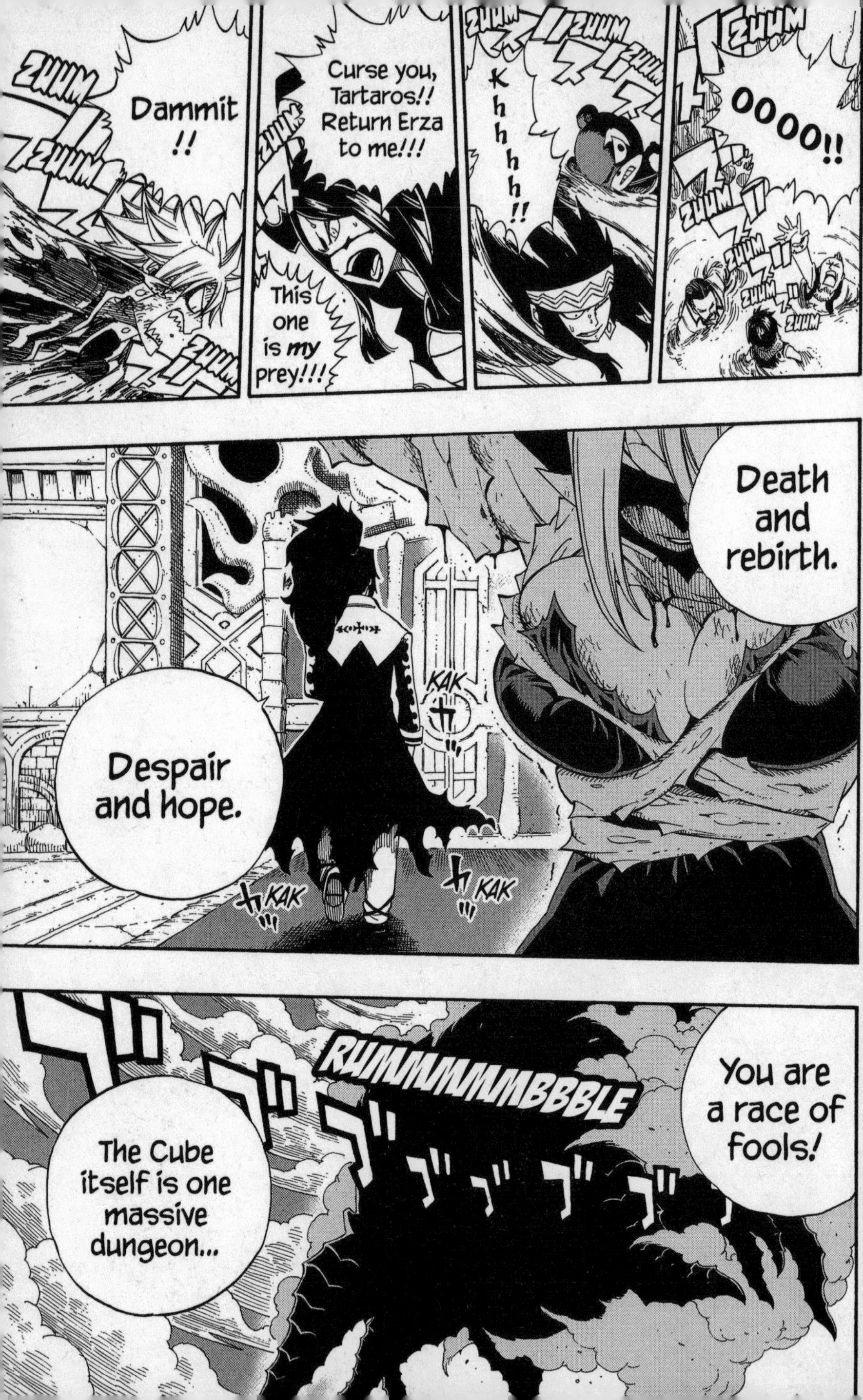
ZUUM
OOOO!!
ZUUM
ZUUM
ZUUM
ZUUM
ZUUM
Khhhh!!
Curse you, Tartaros!! Return Erza to me!!!
This one is my prey!!!
ZUUM
Dammit!!
ZUUM
ZUUM
ZUUM
Death and rebirth.
KAK
Despair and hope.
KAK
KAK
You are a race of fools!
RUMMMMMMBBBLE
The Cube itself is one massive dungeon...

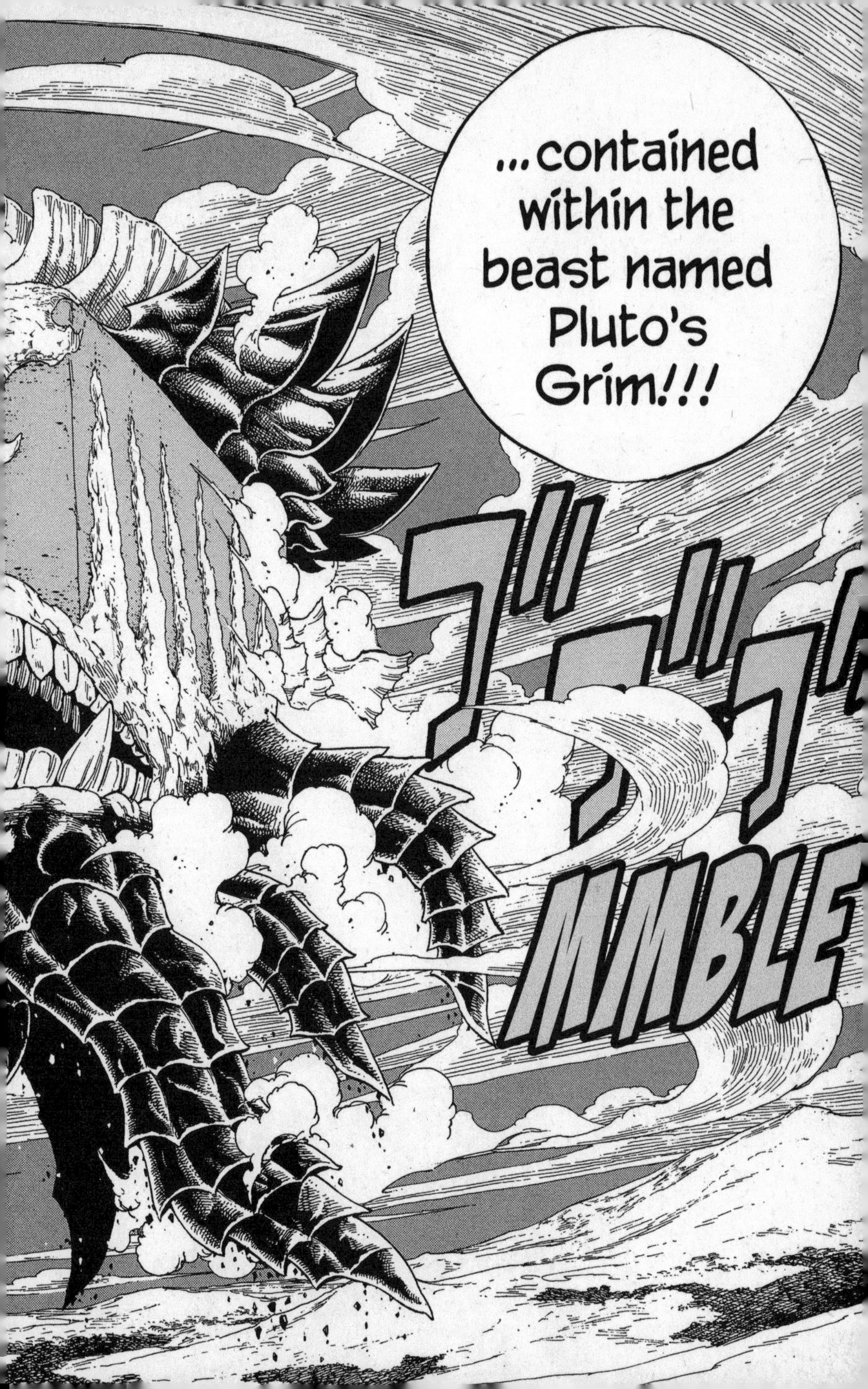
...contained within the beast named Pluto's Grim!!!
MMBLE

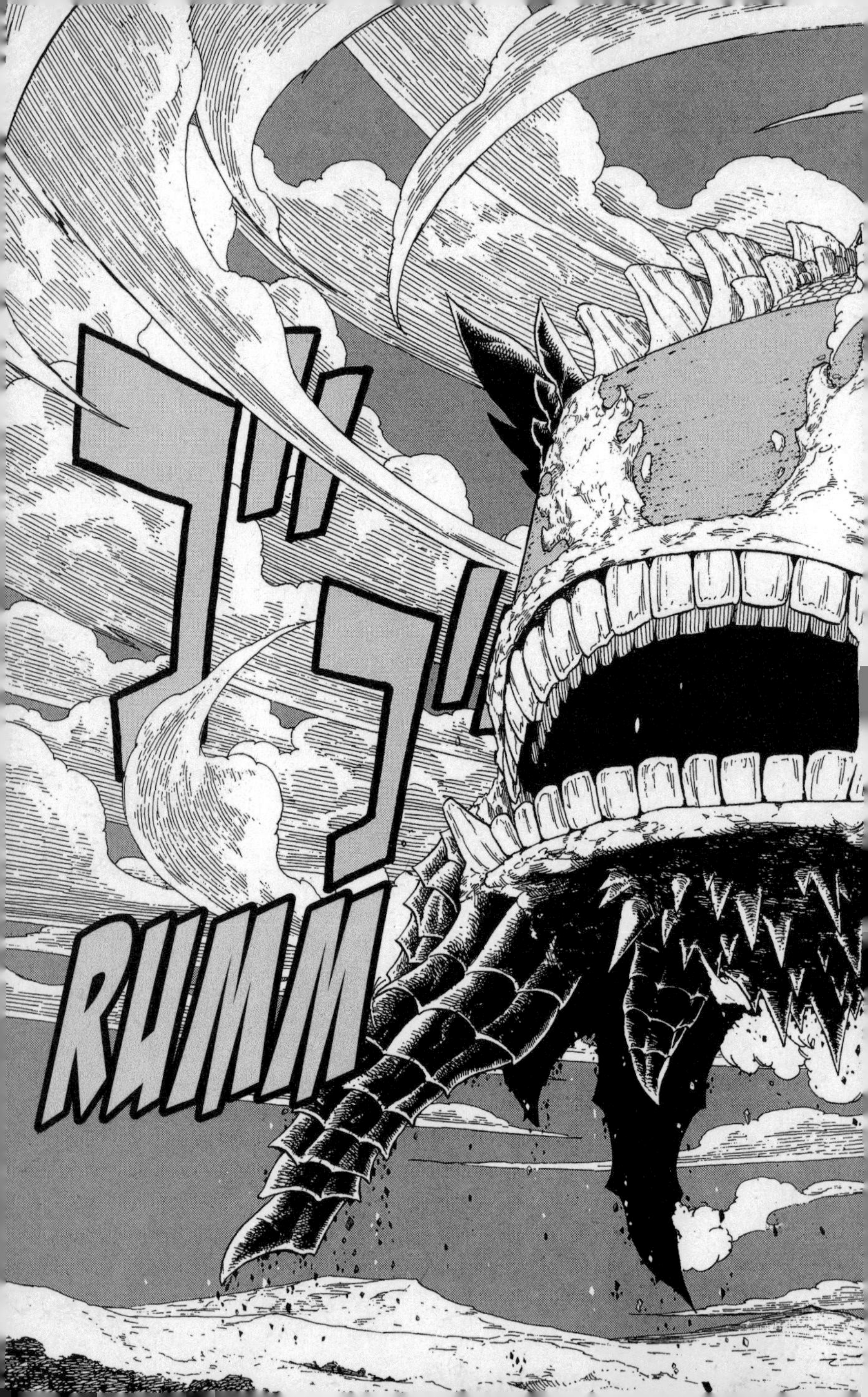
RHMM

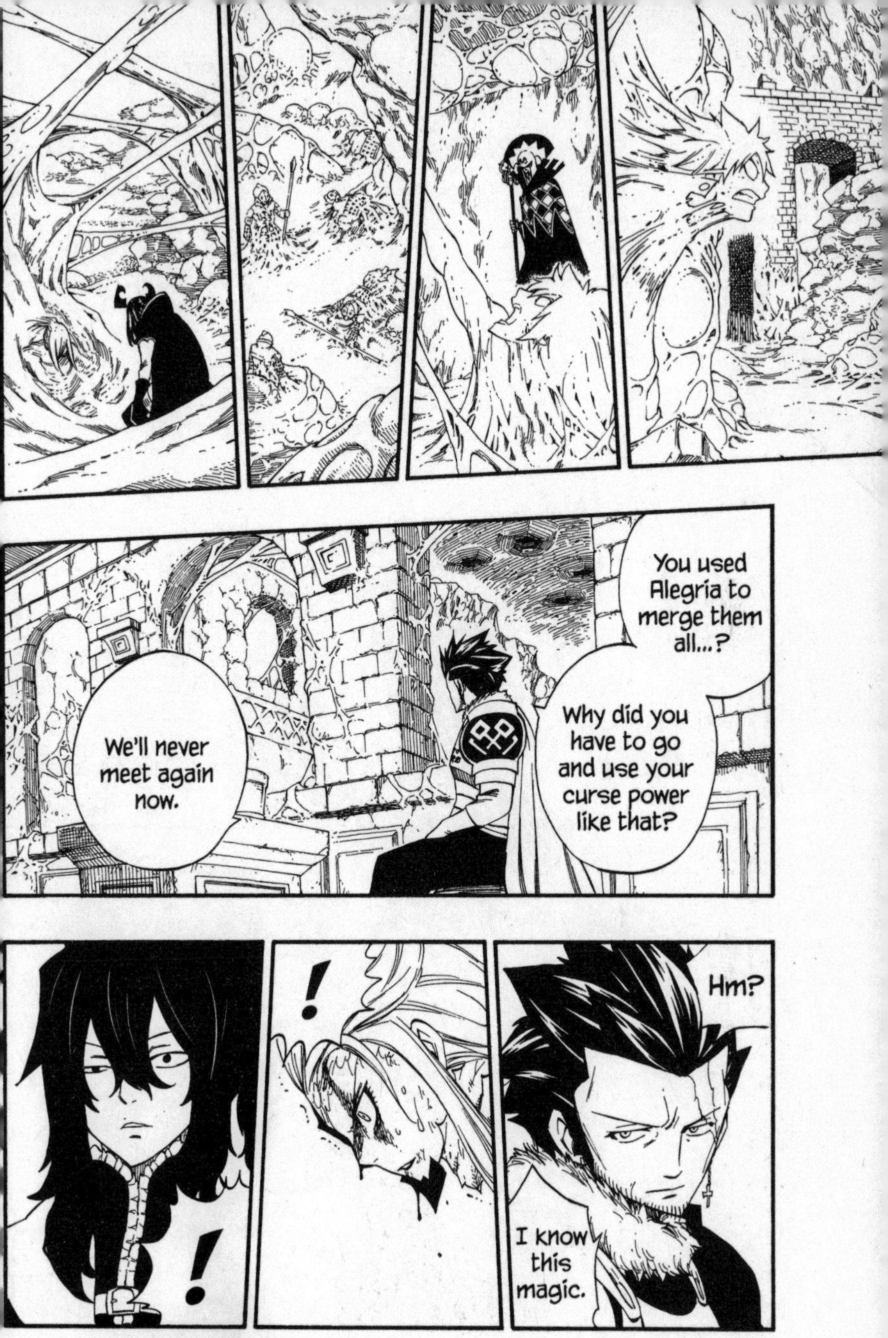
You used Alegria to merge them all...?
Why did you have to go and use your curse power like that?
We'll never meet again now.
Hm?
I know this magic.
!
!

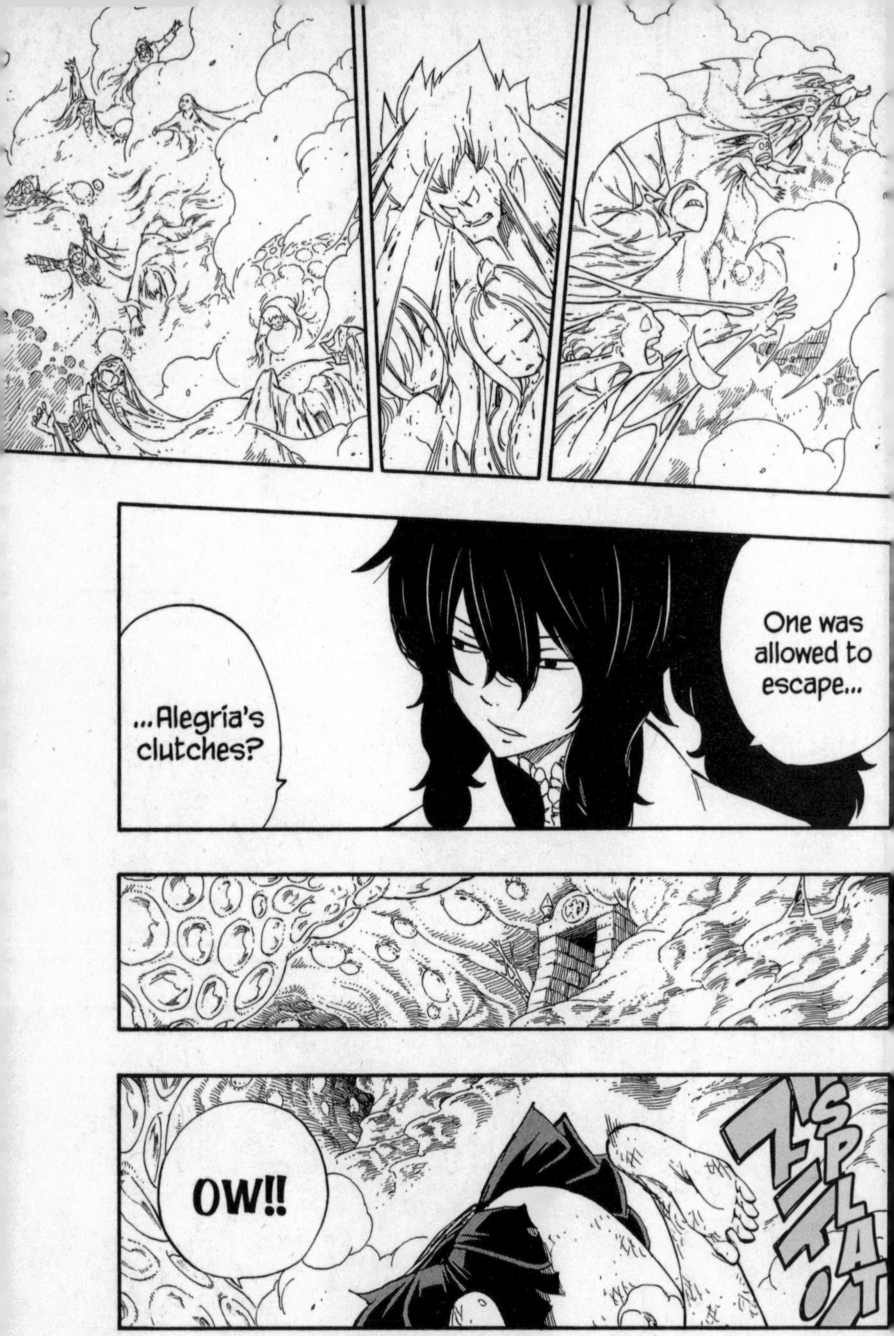
One was allowed to escape...
...Alegria's clutches?
SPLAT
OW!!

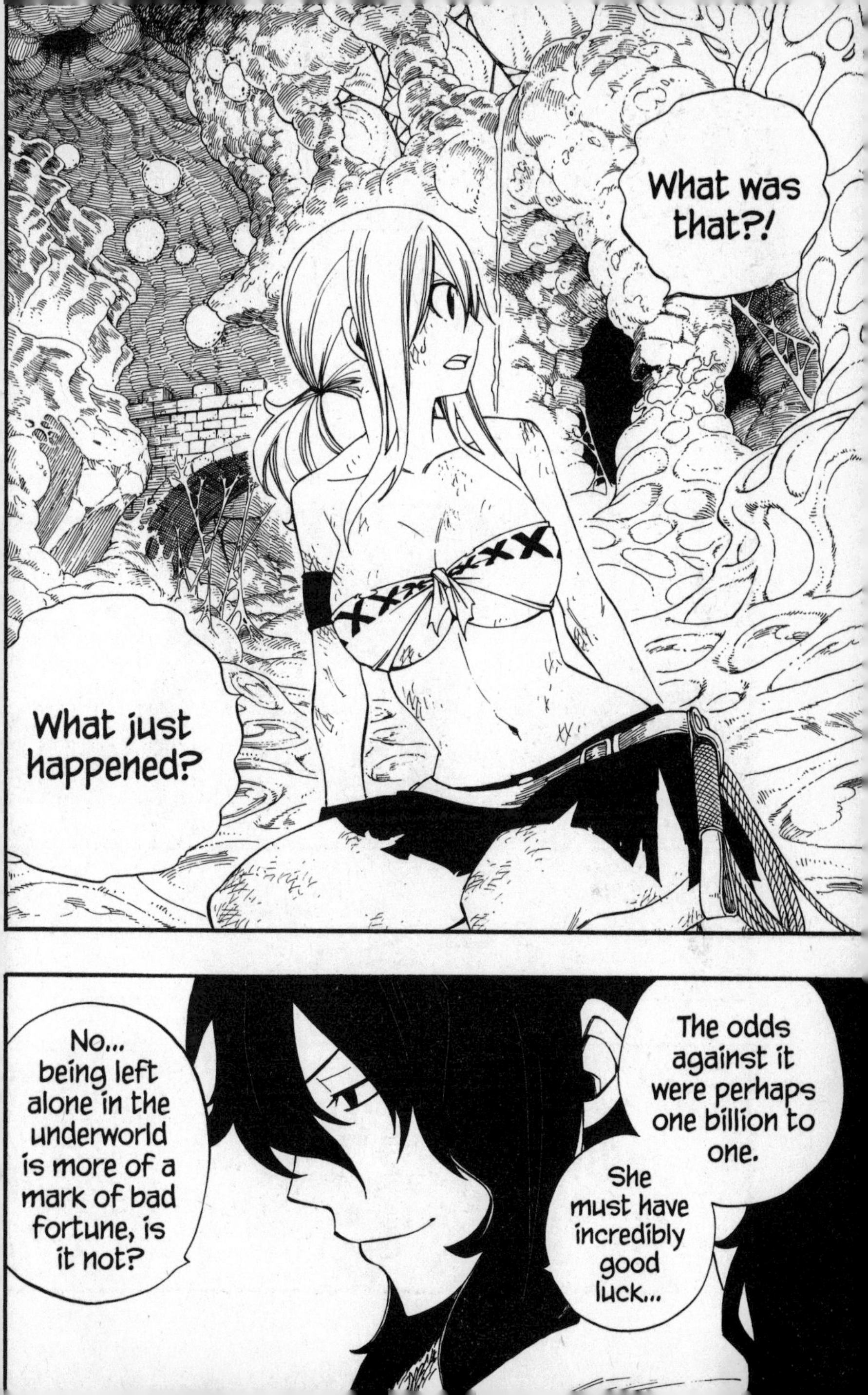
What was that?!
What just happened?
The odds against it were perhaps one billion to one.
She must have incredibly good luck...
No... being left alone in the underworld is more of a mark of bad fortune, is it not?

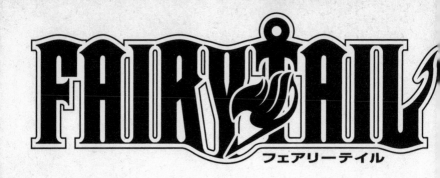

Chapter 383: Wave Rider Lucy

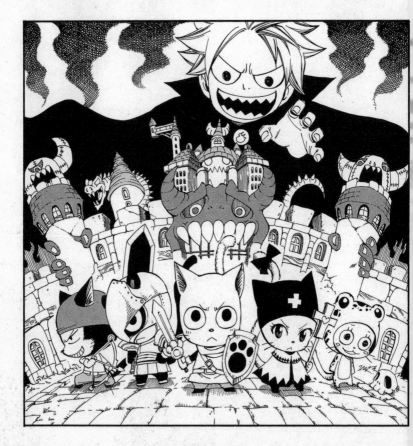

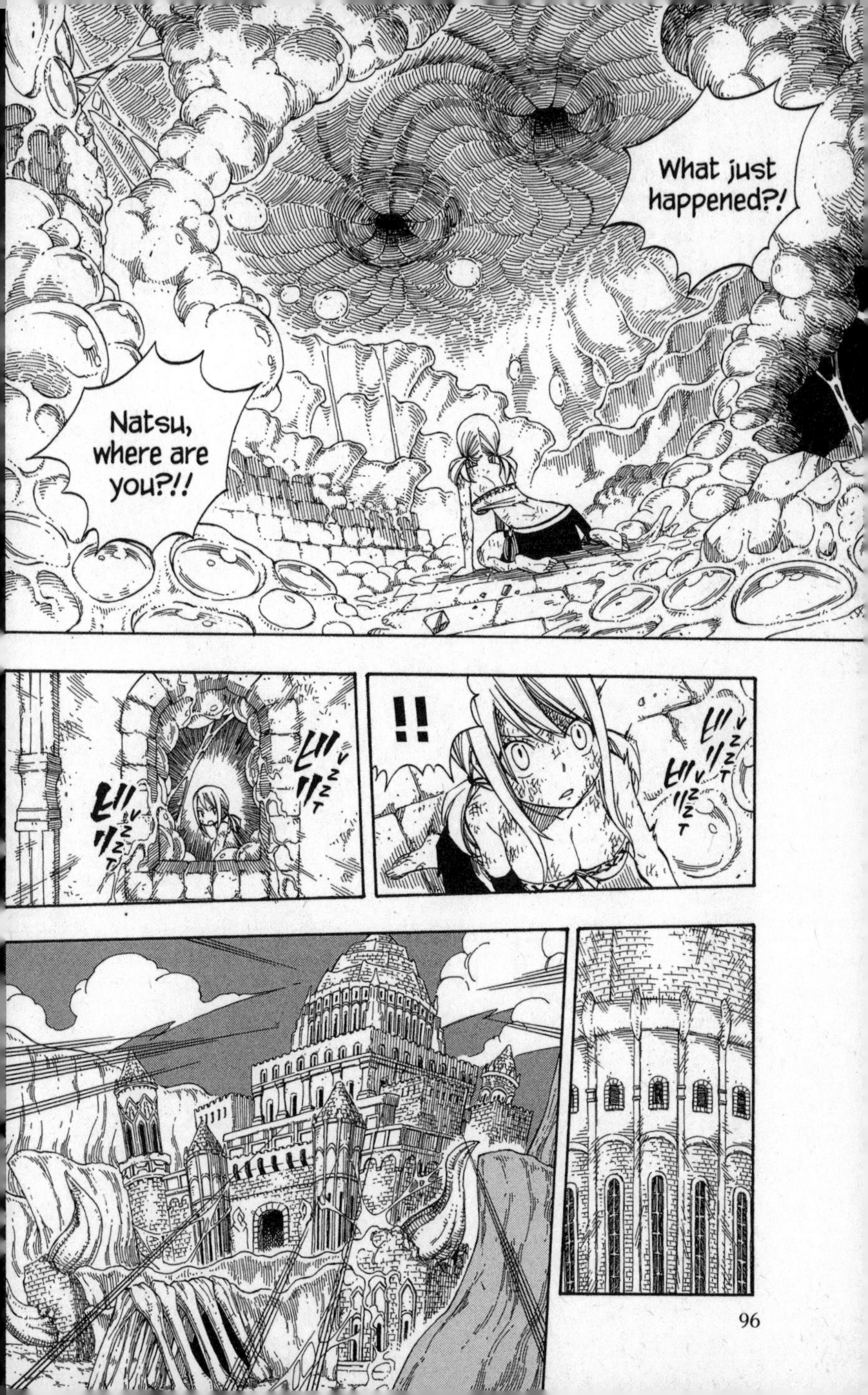
What just happened?!
Natsu, where are you?!!
!!
ビリ VZZT
ビリ VZZT
ビリ VZZT
ビリ VZZT

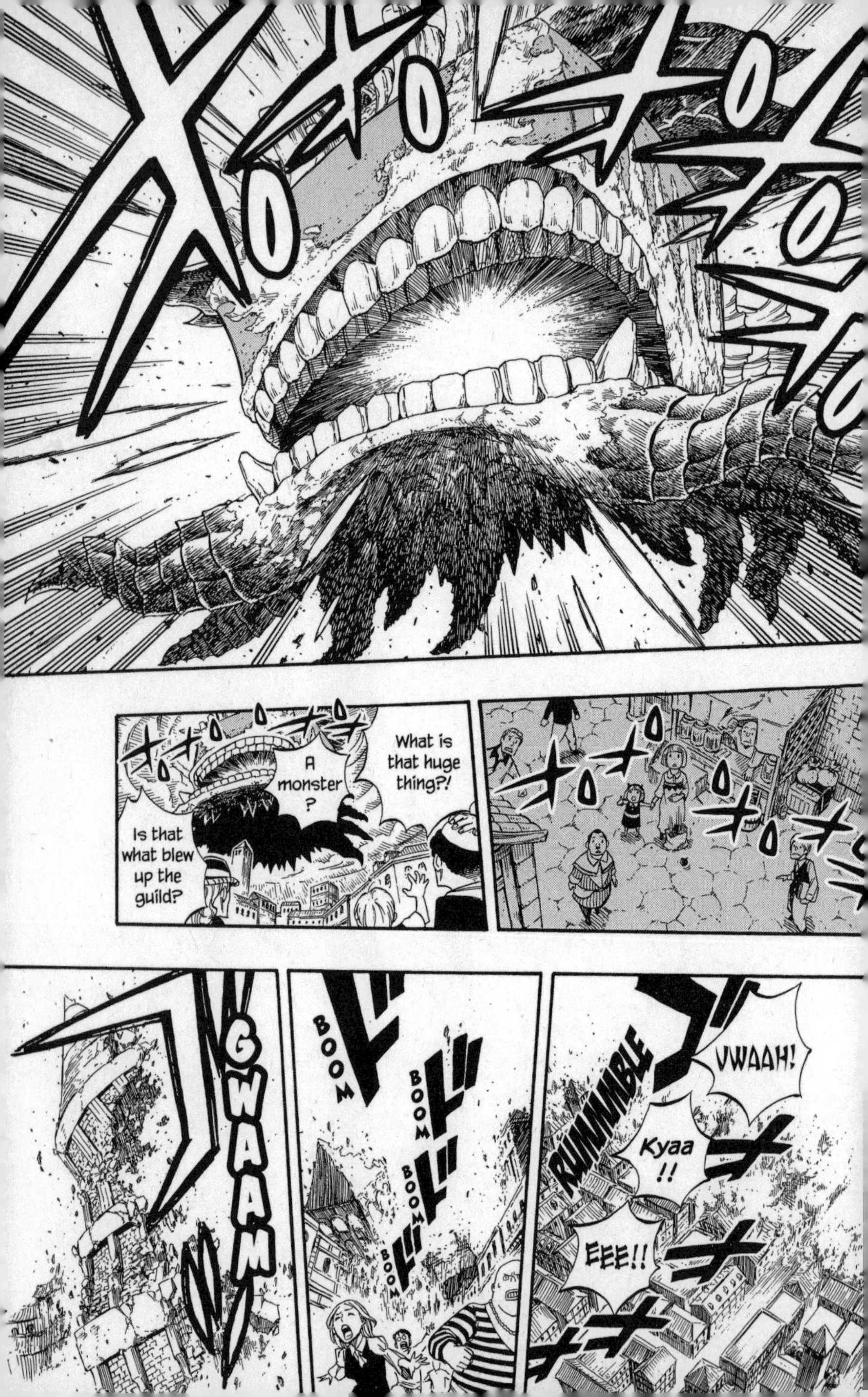
What is that huge thing?!
A monster?
Is that what blew up the guild?
VWAAH!
RUMMMBLE
Kyaa !!
EEE!!
BOOM
BOOM
BOOM
BOOM
BOOM
GWAAM

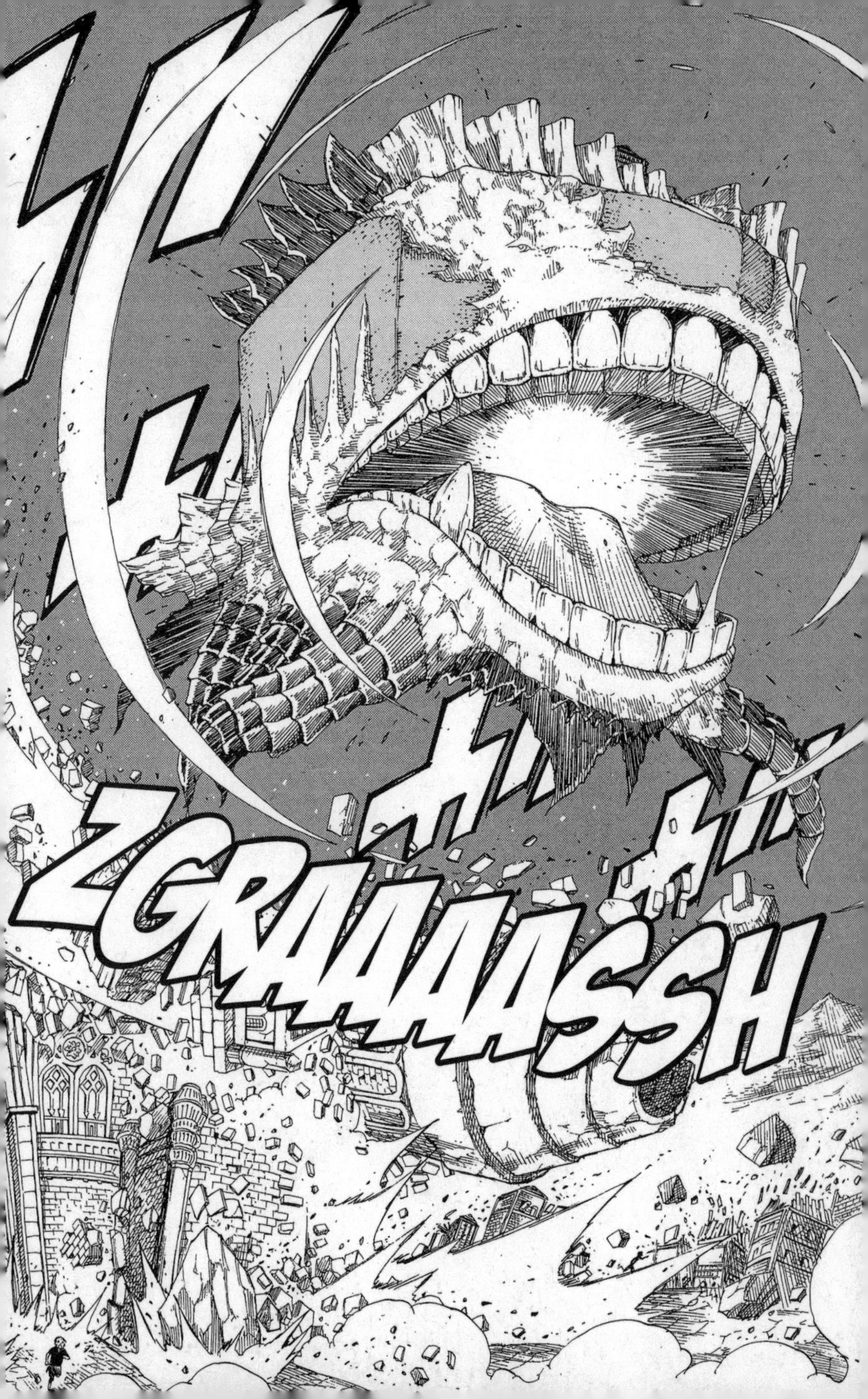
ZGRAAAASSH

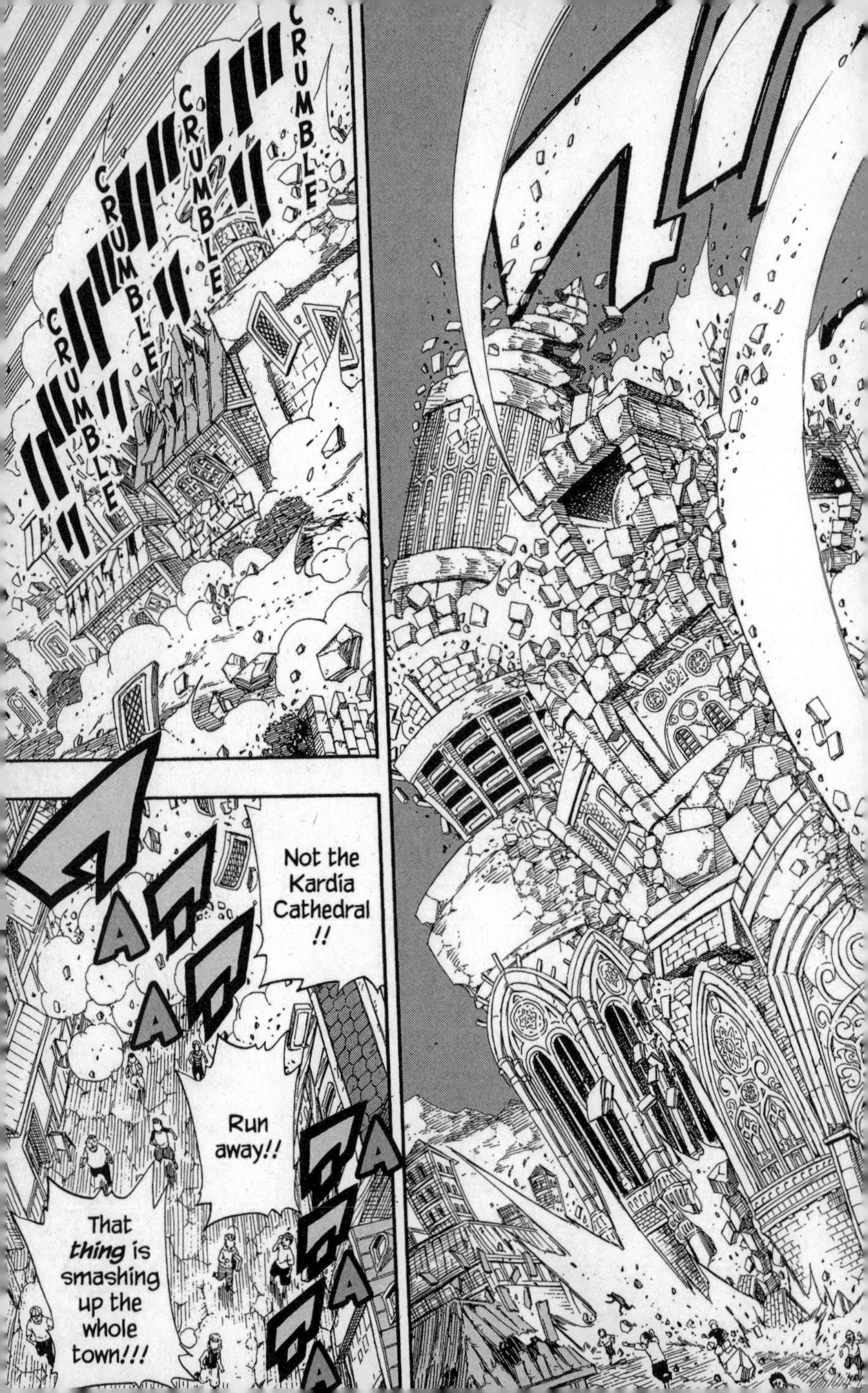
CRUMBLE
CRUMBLE
CRUMBLE
CRUMBLE
Not the Kardia Cathedral!!
AAA
Run away!!
That *thing* is smashing up the whole town!!!
AAAA

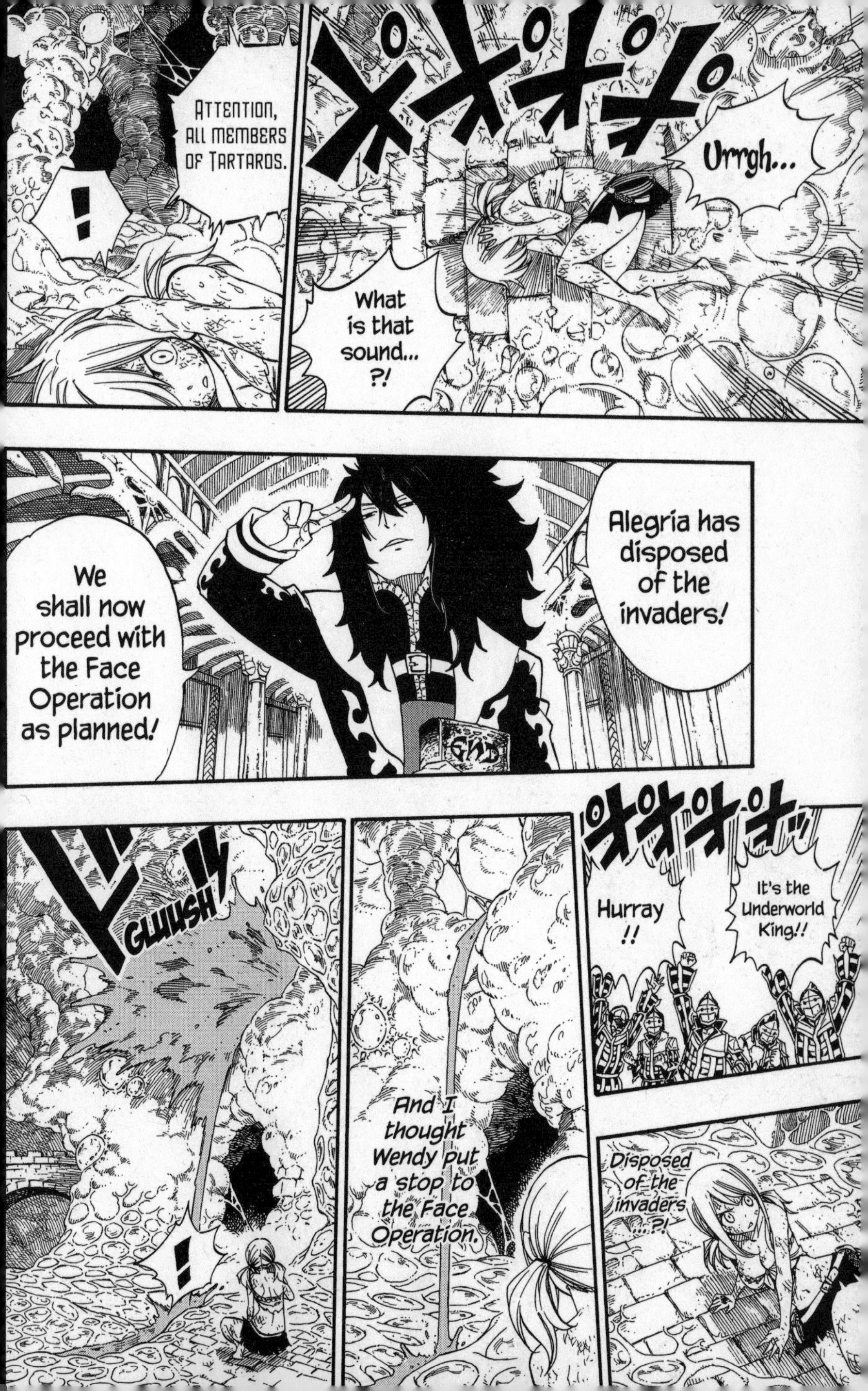
Urrgh...
What is that sound...?!
Attention, all members of Tartaros.
!
Alegria has disposed of the invaders!
We shall now proceed with the Face Operation as planned!
It's the Underworld King!!
Hurray!!
Disposed of the invaders...?!
And I thought Wendy put a stop to the Face Operation.
GLUUSH!!
!

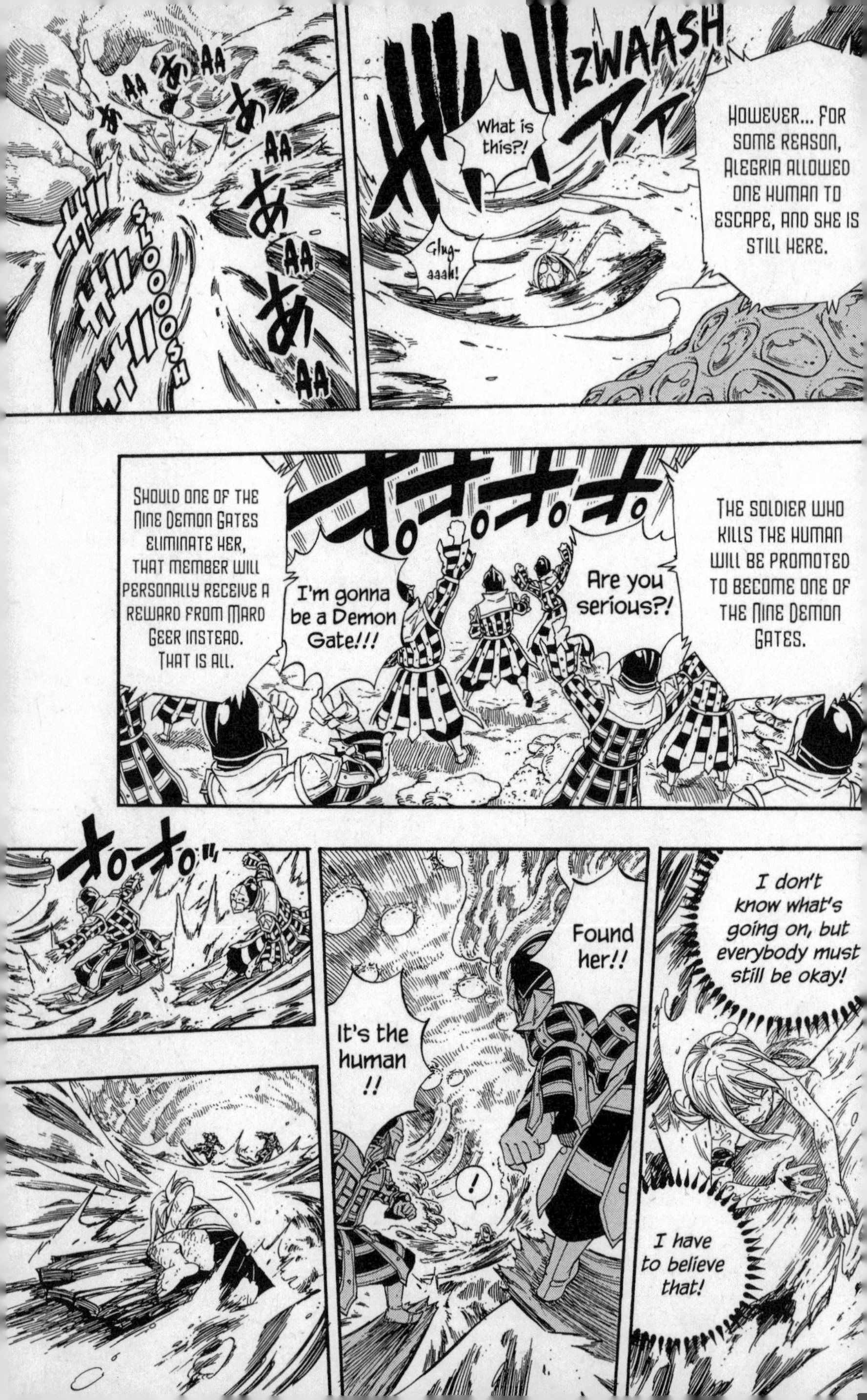
ZWAASH
What is this?!
Glug-aaah!
However... for some reason, Alegria allowed one human to escape, and she is still here.
AA
AA
AA
AA
AA
SHOOOOOSH
The soldier who kills the human will be promoted to become one of the Nine Demon Gates.
Are you serious?!
I'm gonna be a Demon Gate!!!
Should one of the Nine Demon Gates eliminate her, that member will personally receive a reward from Mard Geer instead. That is all.
I don't know what's going on, but everybody must still be okay!
I have to believe that!
Found her!!
It's the human!!
!

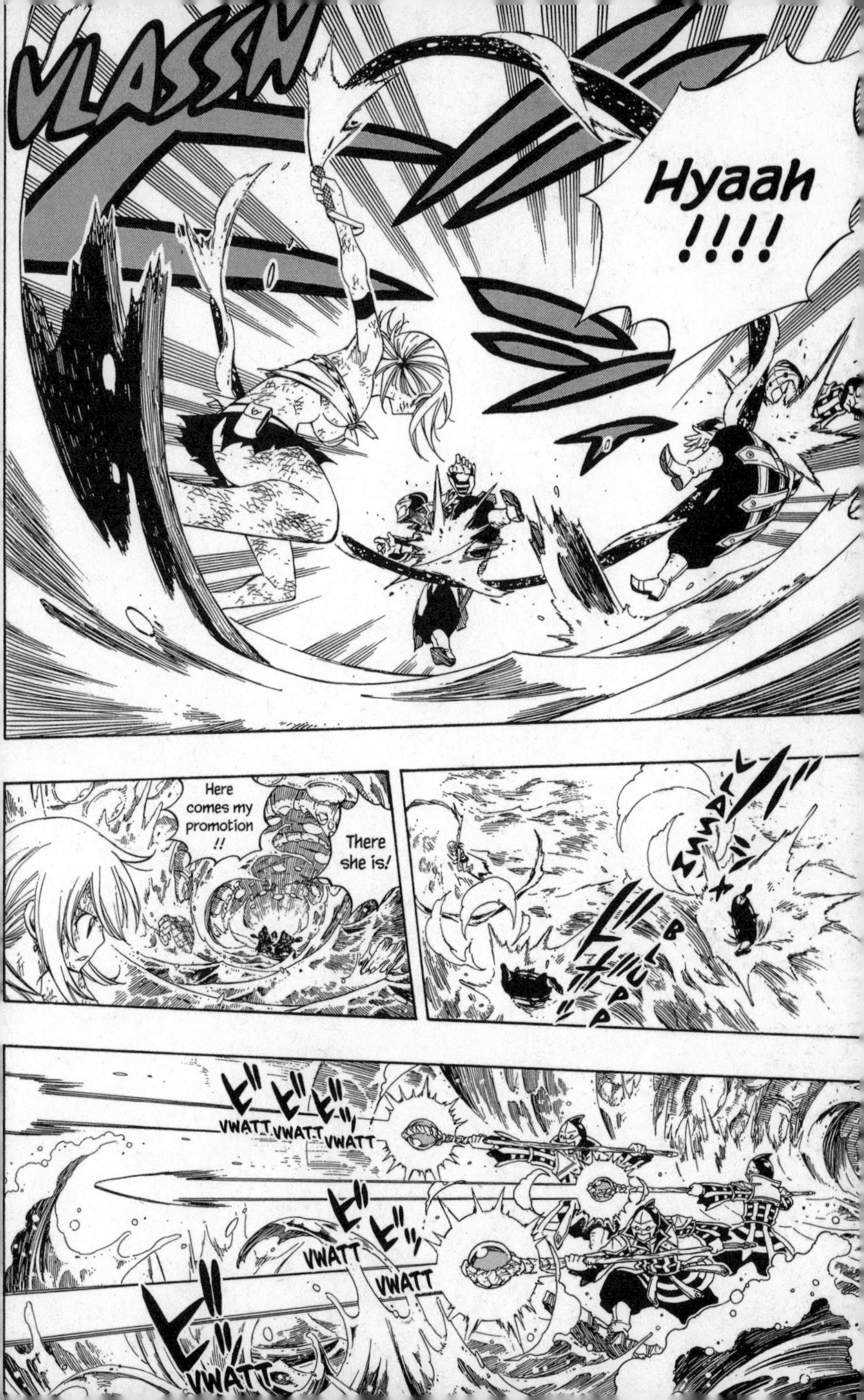
VLASSH
Hyaah !!!!
BLUPP
There she is!
Here comes my promotion !!
VWATT VWATT VWATT
VWATT
VWATT
VWATT

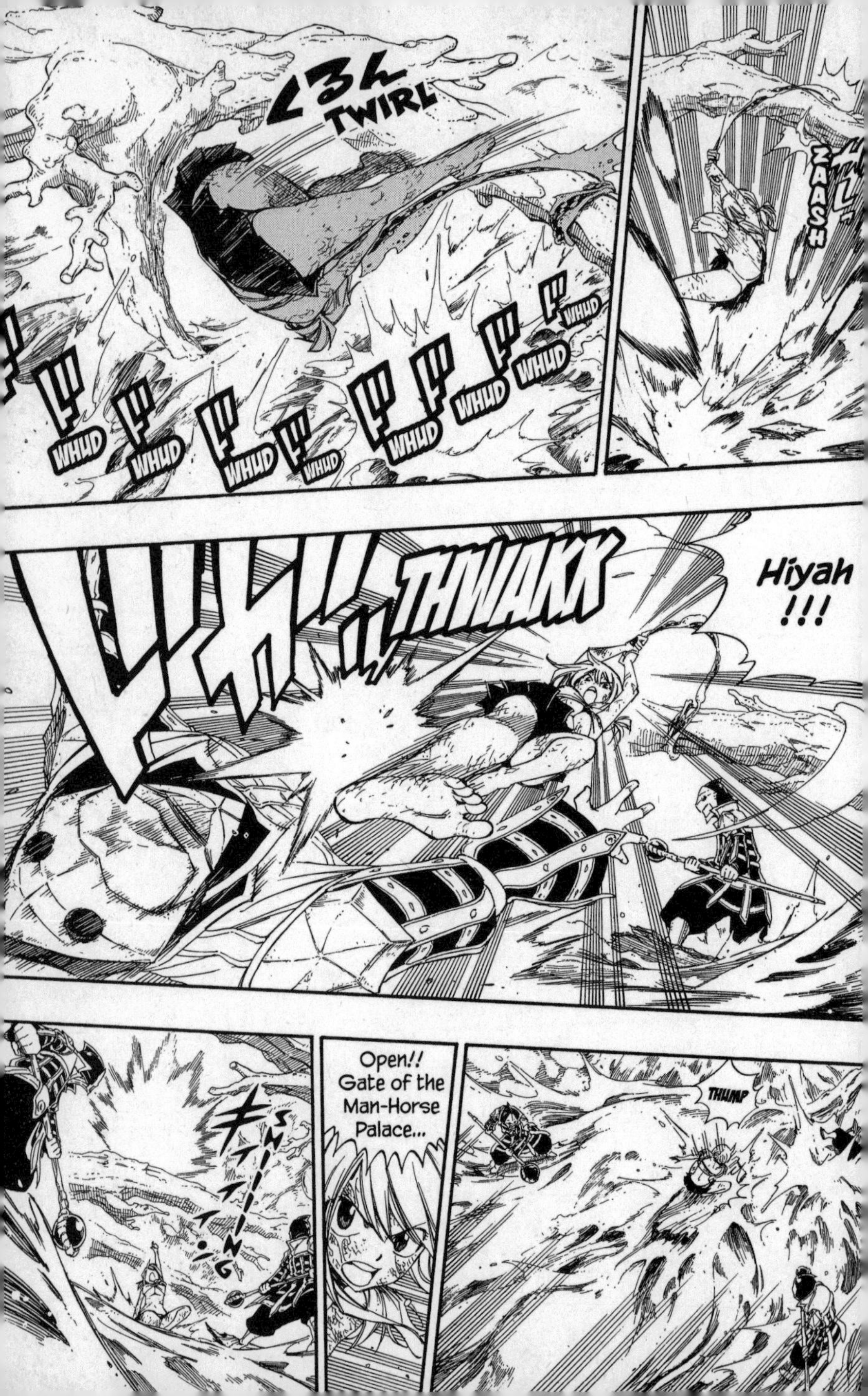

ZAASH
くるん
TWIRL
WHUD
WHUD
WHUD
WHUD
WHUD
WHUD
WHUD
WHUD
WHUD
Hiyah!!!
THWAKK
THUMP
Open!! Gate of the Man-Horse Palace...
SHIIIING

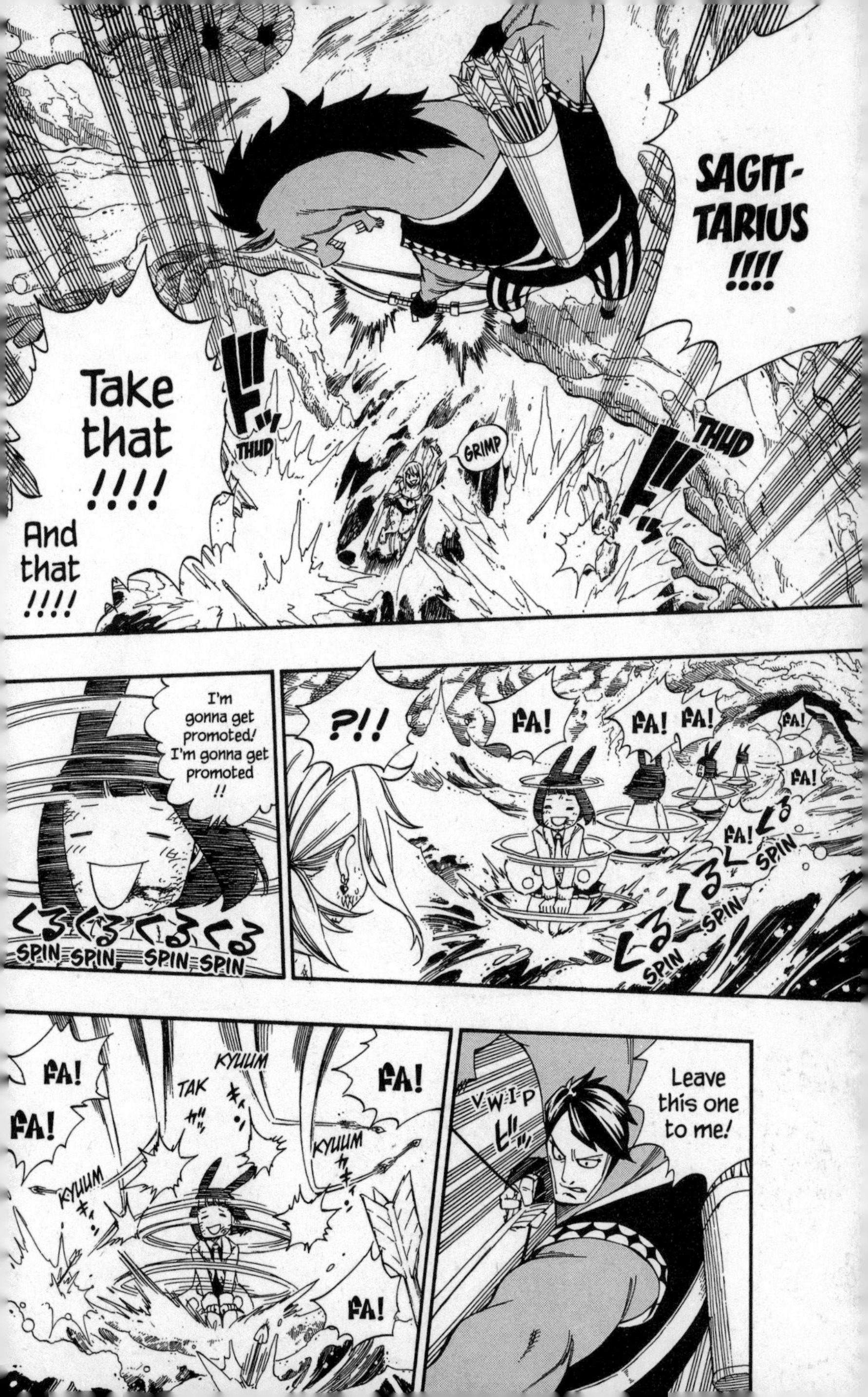
SAGIT-TARIUS!!!!
THUD
GRIMP
THUD
Take that!!!!
And that!!!!
FA!
FA!
FA!
FA!
?!!
FA!
FA! くる SPIN
くる SPIN
くる SPIN
I'm gonna get promoted! I'm gonna get promoted!!
くるくる くるくる
SPIN SPIN SPIN SPIN
Leave this one to me!
VWIP
FA!
KYUUM
TAK
FA!
FA!
KYUUM
KYUUM
FA!

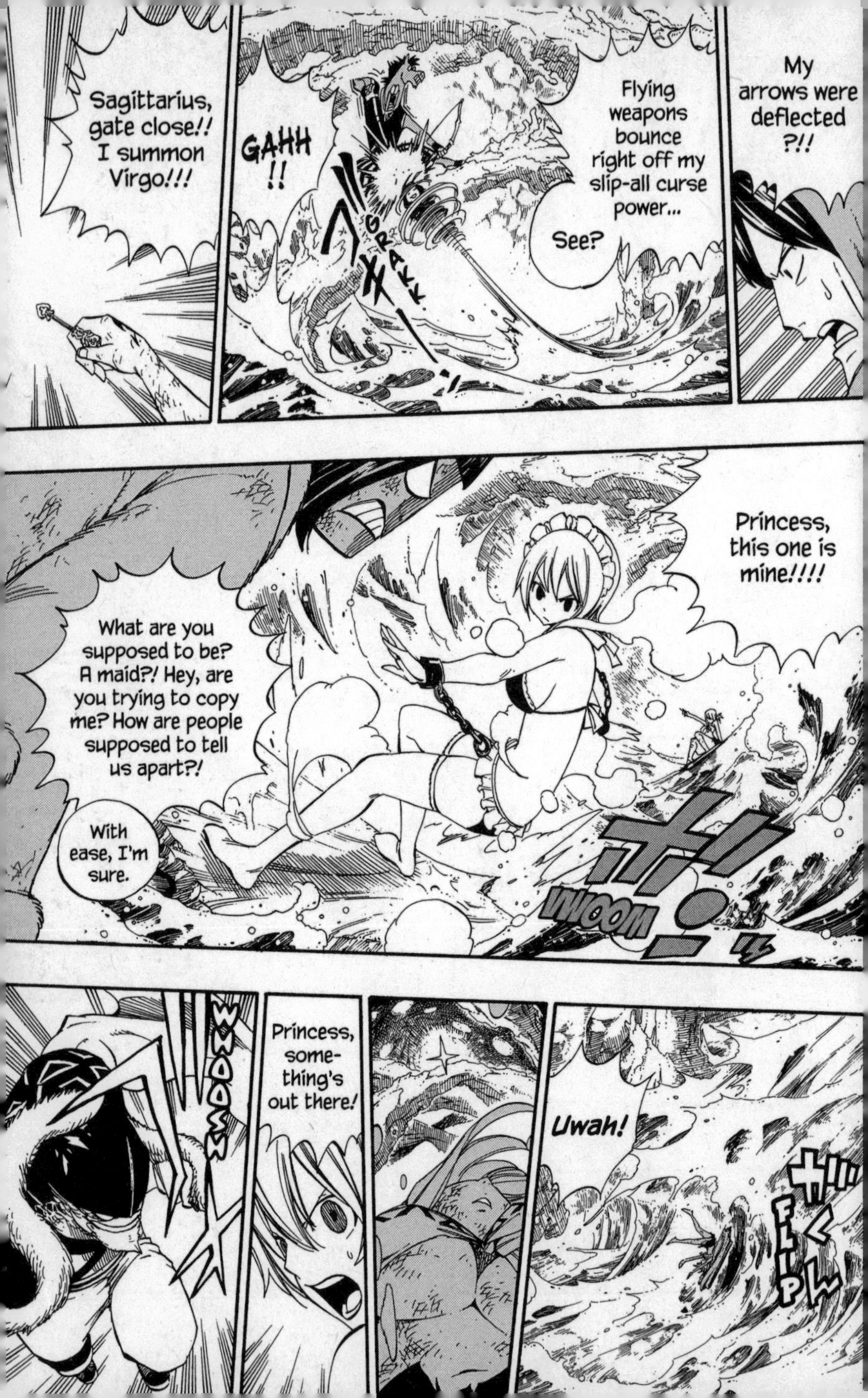
My arrows were deflected?!!
Flying weapons bounce right off my slip-all curse power...
See?
GAHH!!
GRAKK
Sagittarius, gate close!! I summon Virgo!!!
Princess, this one is mine!!!!
What are you supposed to be? A maid?! Hey, are you trying to copy me? How are people supposed to tell us apart?!
With ease, I'm sure.
Uwah!
FLIP
Princess, some-thing's out there!
WHOOSH

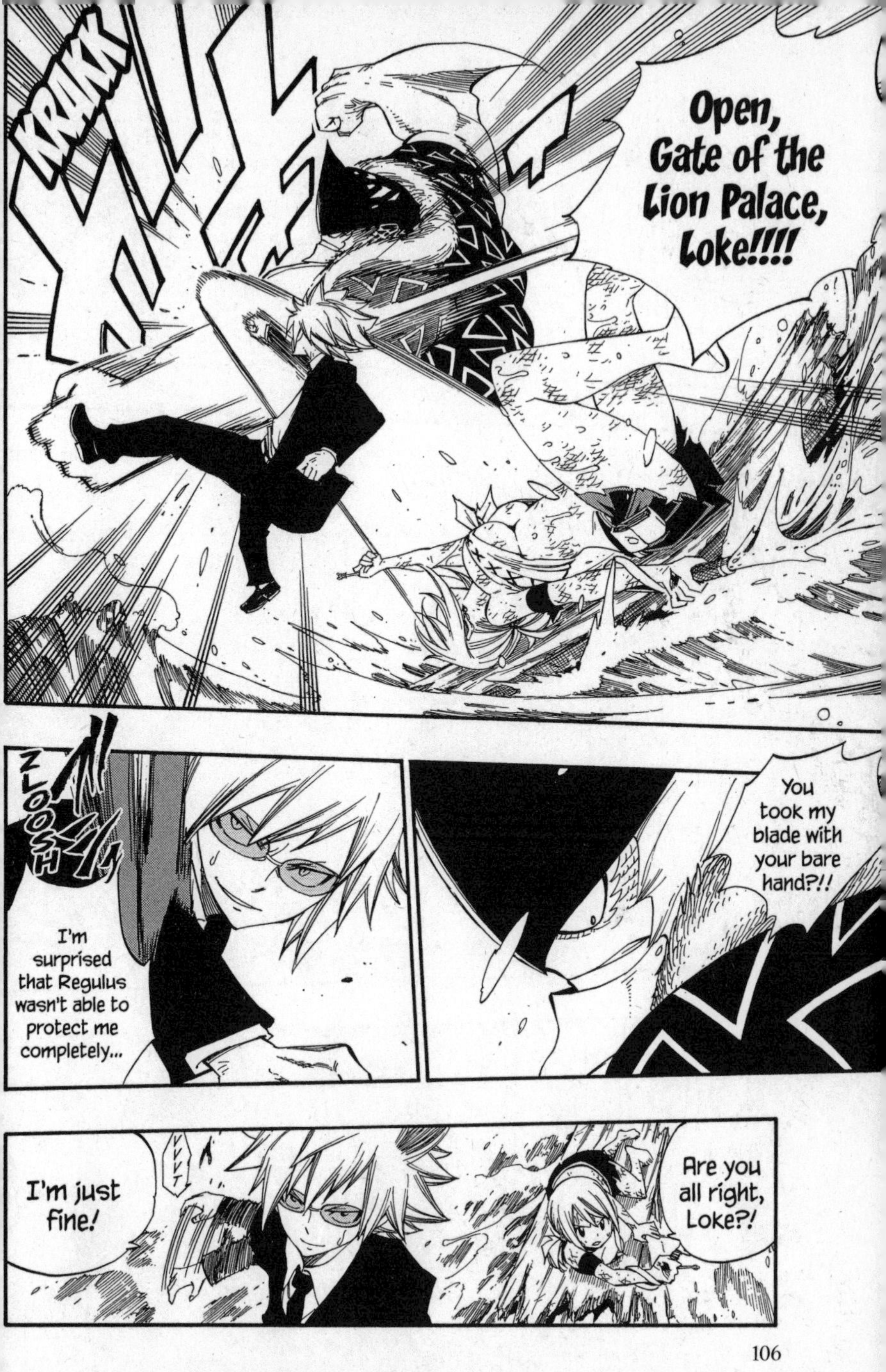
Open, Gate of the Lion Palace, Loke!!!!
KRAKK
You took my blade with your bare hand?!!
ZLOOSH
I'm surprised that Regulus wasn't able to protect me completely...
Are you all right, Loke?!
I'm just fine!

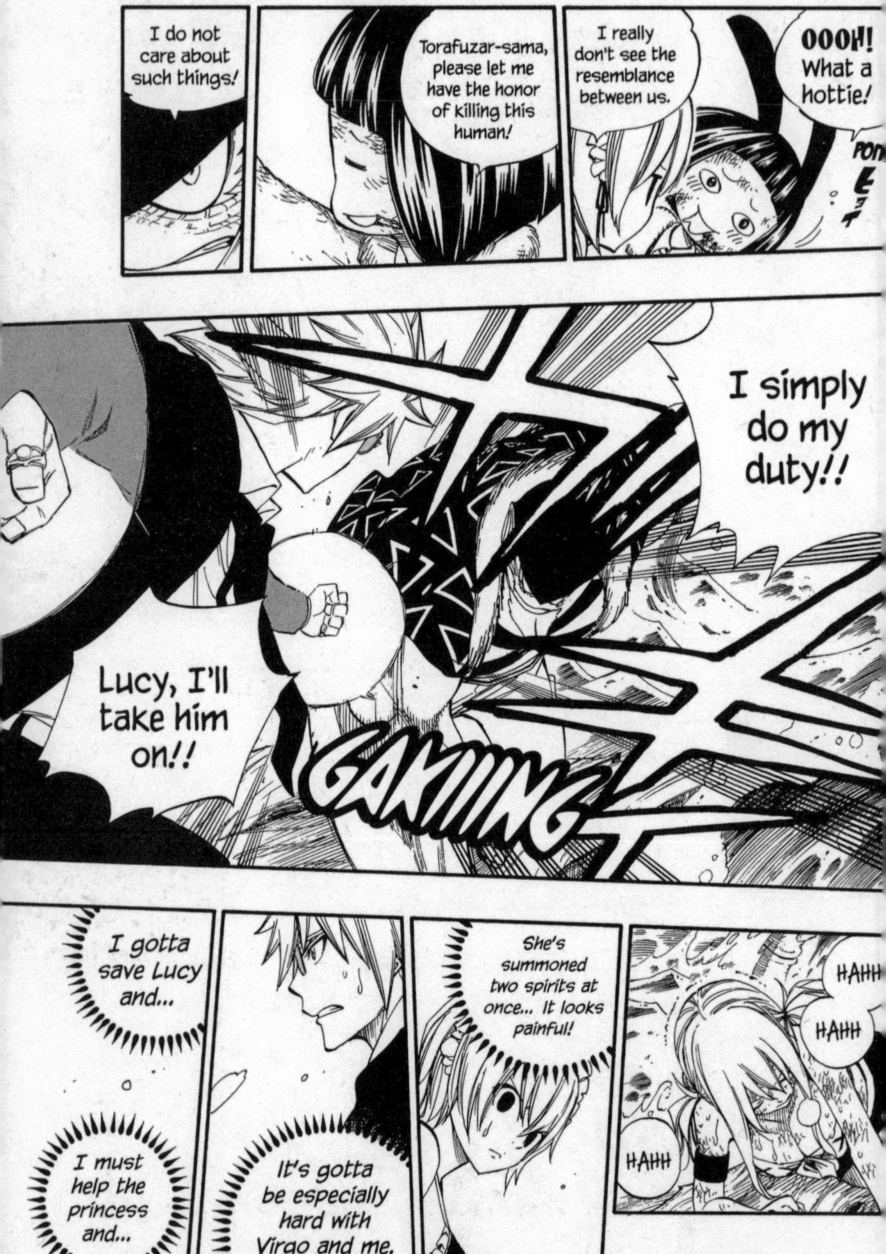
OOOH!! What a hottie!
I really don't see the resemblance between us.
Torafuzar-sama, please let me have the honor of killing this human!
I do not care about such things!
I simply do my duty!!
GAKIING
Lucy, I'll take him on!!
HAHH
HAHH
HAHH
She's summoned two spirits at once... It looks painful!
It's gotta be especially hard with Virgo and me. We take a lot of magic!
I gotta save Lucy and...
I must help the princess and...

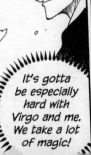

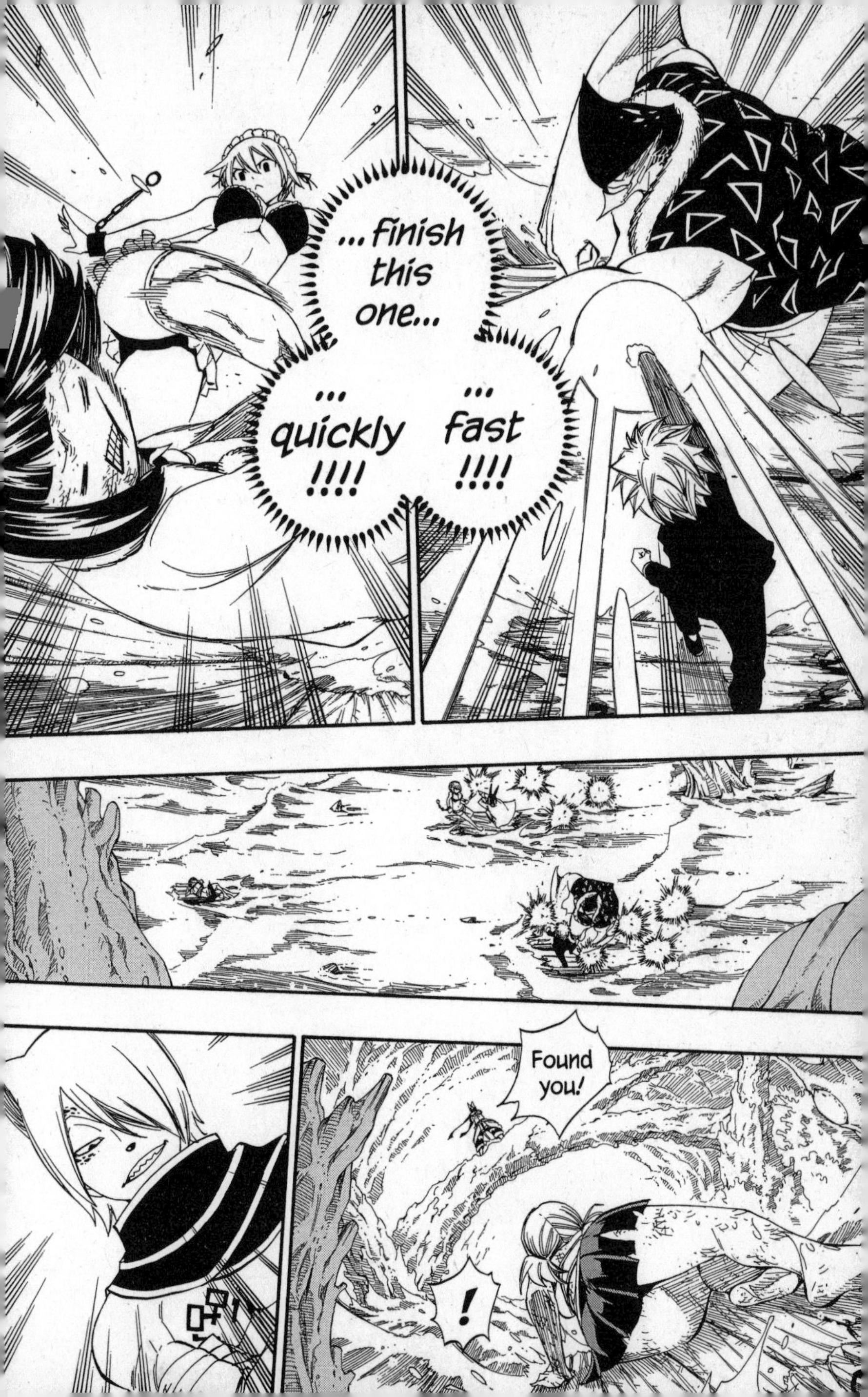
...finish this one...
...fast!!!!
...quickly!!!!
Found you!
!

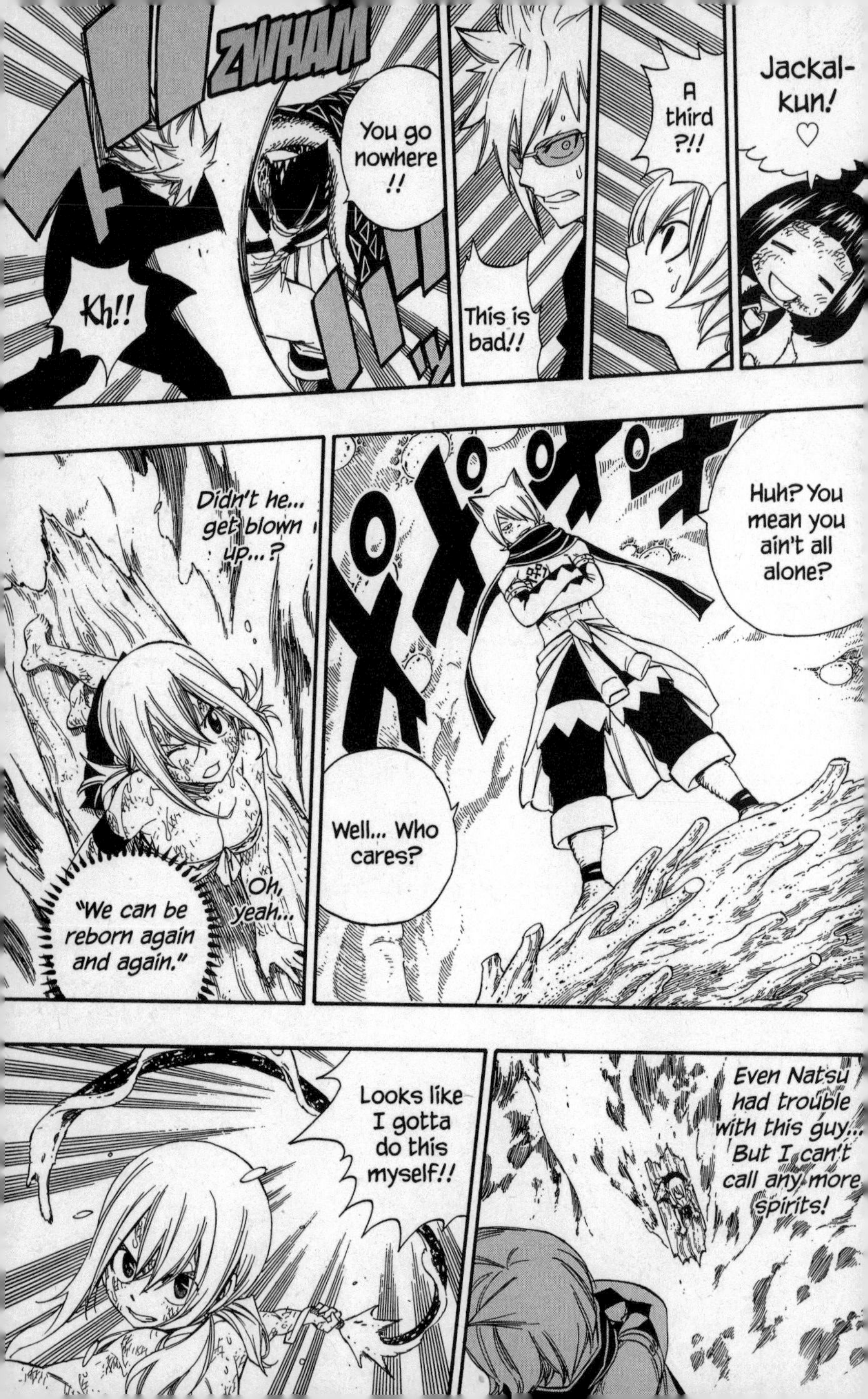
Jackal-kun! ♡
A third ?!!
This is bad!!
You go nowhere !!
ZWHAM
Kh!!
Huh? You mean you ain't all alone?
Well... Who cares?
Didn't he... get blown up...?
Oh, yeah...
"We can be reborn again and again."
Even Natsu had trouble with this guy... But I can't call any more spirits!
Looks like I gotta do this myself!!

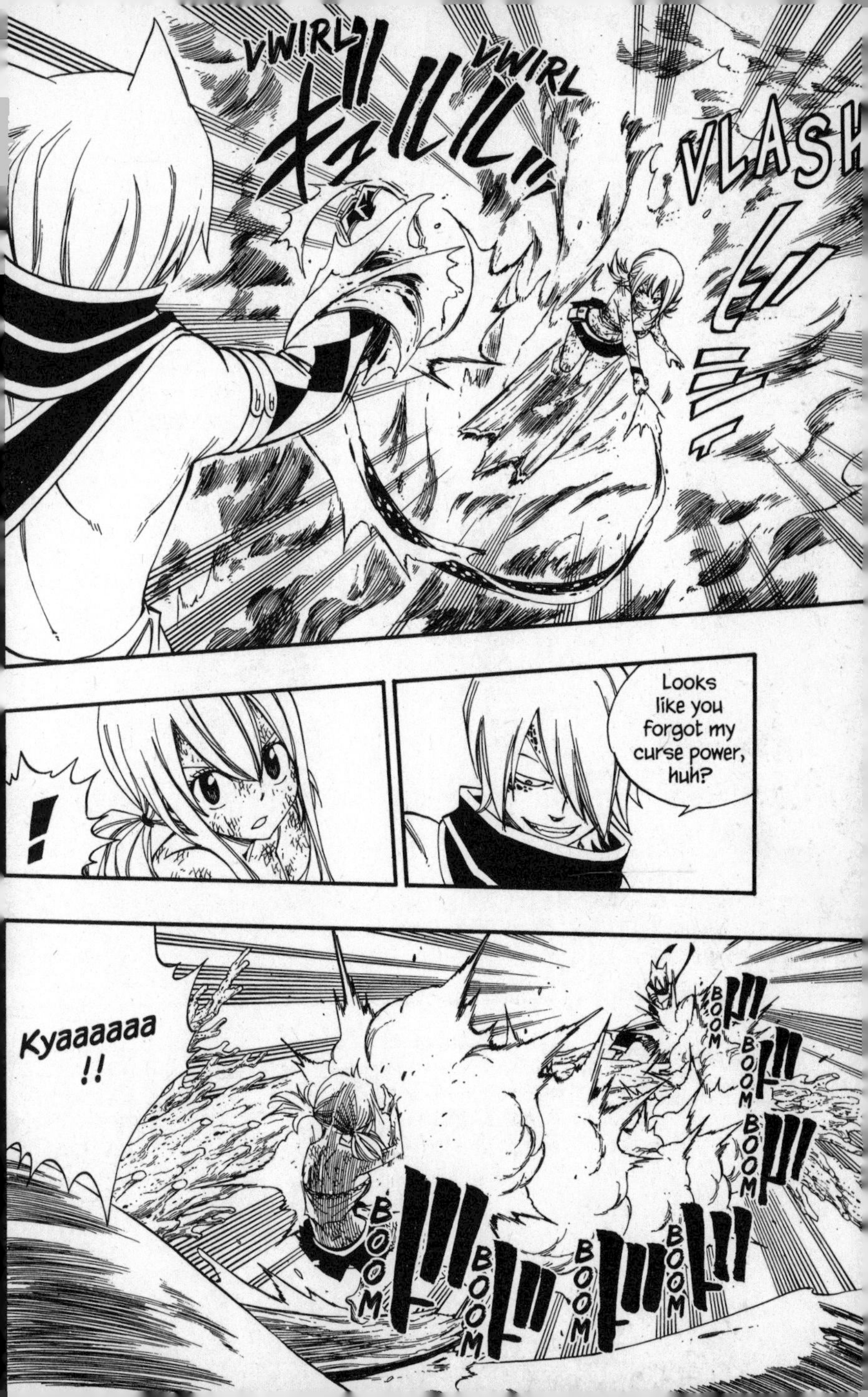
VLASH
VWIRL
VWIRL
Looks like you forgot my curse power, huh?
!
BOOM
BOOM
BOOM
BOOM
BOOM
BOOM
BOOM
BOOM
Kyaaaaaa !!

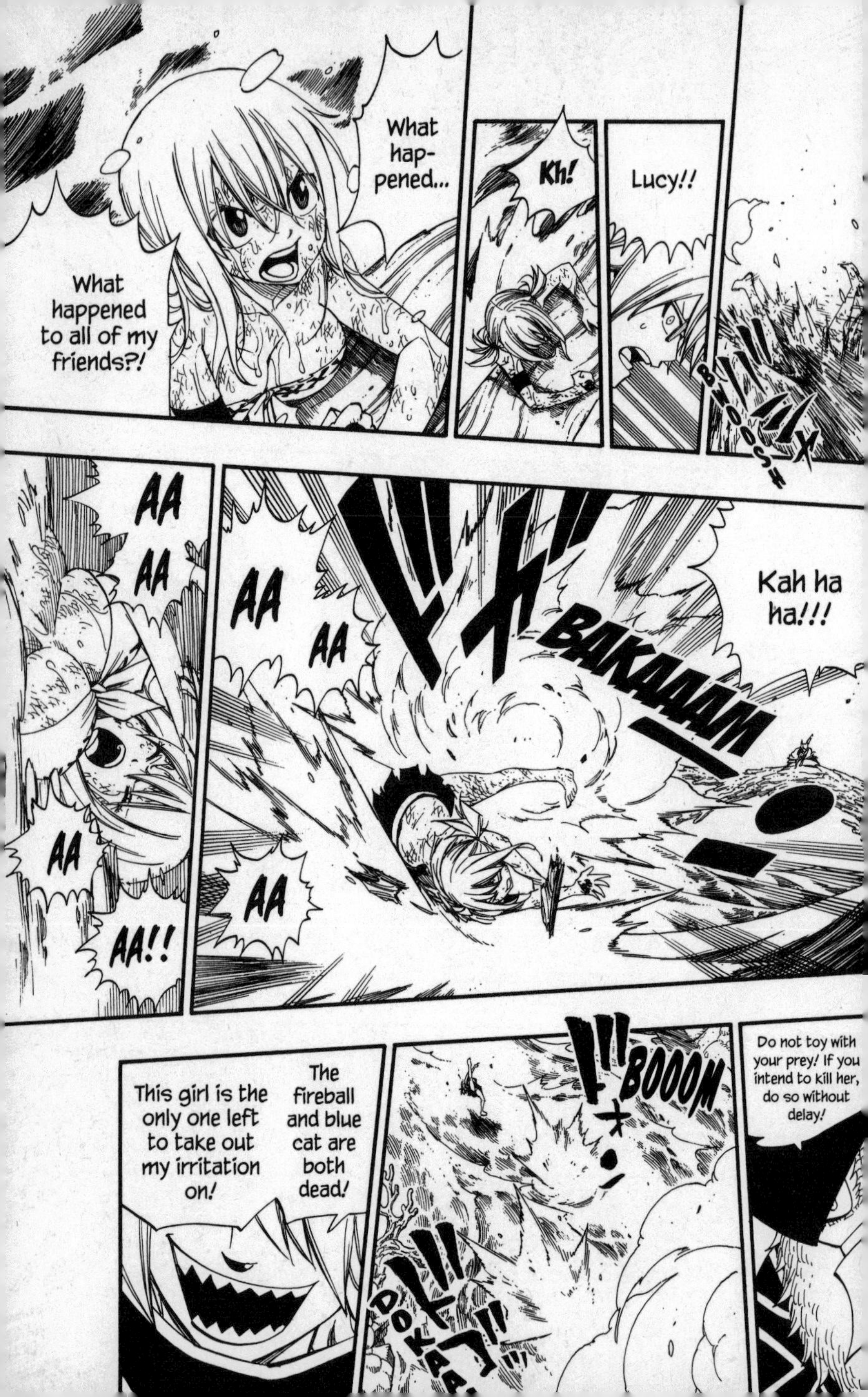
BWOOSH
Lucy!!
Kh!
What hap-pened...
What happened to all of my friends?!
Kah ha ha!!!
BAKAAAM
AA AA
AA
AA
AA AA
AA
AA!!
Do not toy with your prey! If you intend to kill her, do so without delay!
BOOOM
DOKAA
The fireball and blue cat are both dead!
This girl is the only one left to take out my irritation on!

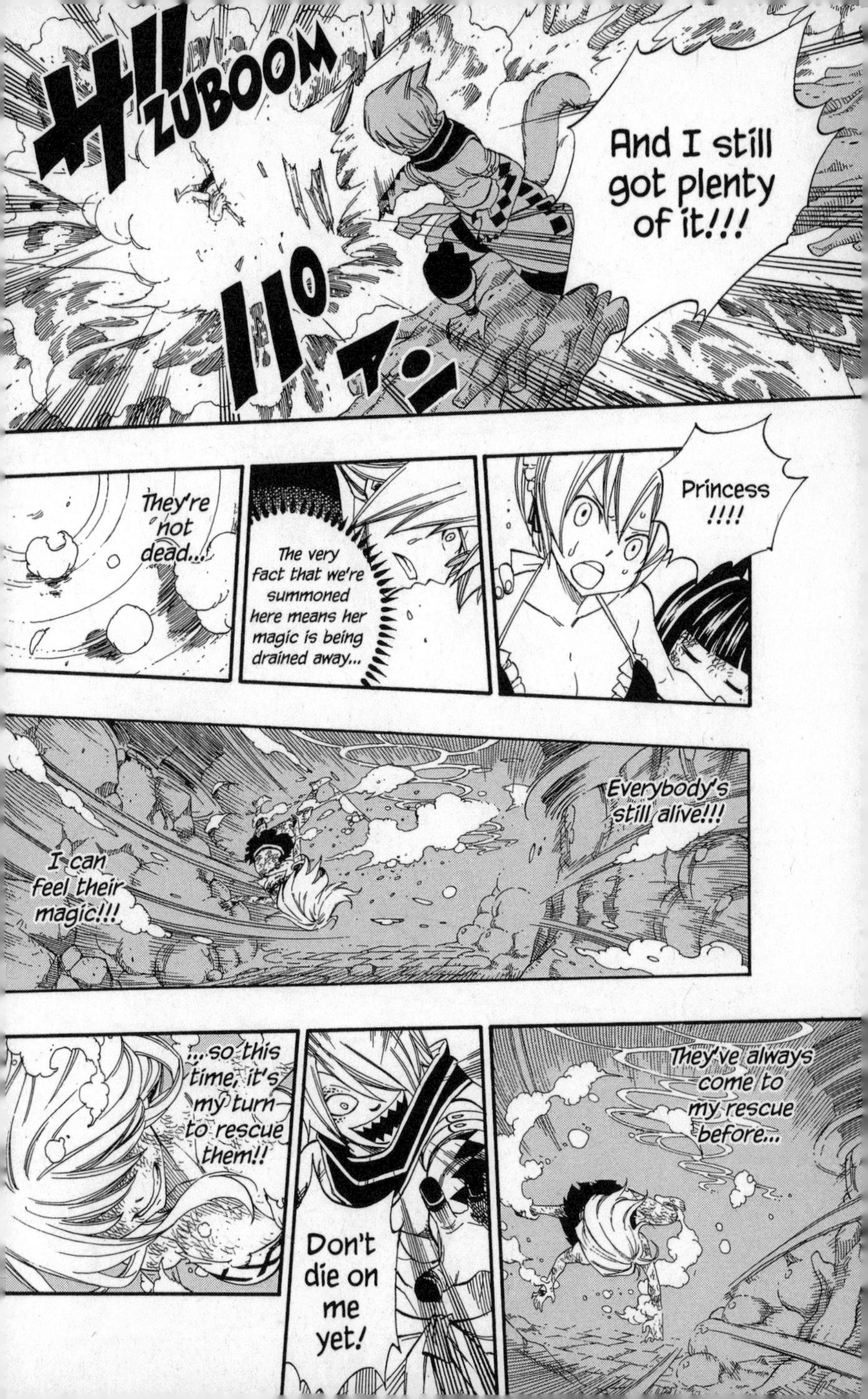
And I still got plenty of it!!!
ZUBOOM
Princess !!!!
The very fact that we're summoned here means her magic is being drained away...
They're not dead...
Everybody's still alive!!!
I can feel their magic!!!
They've always come to my rescue before...
Don't die on me yet!
...so this time, it's my turn to rescue them!!

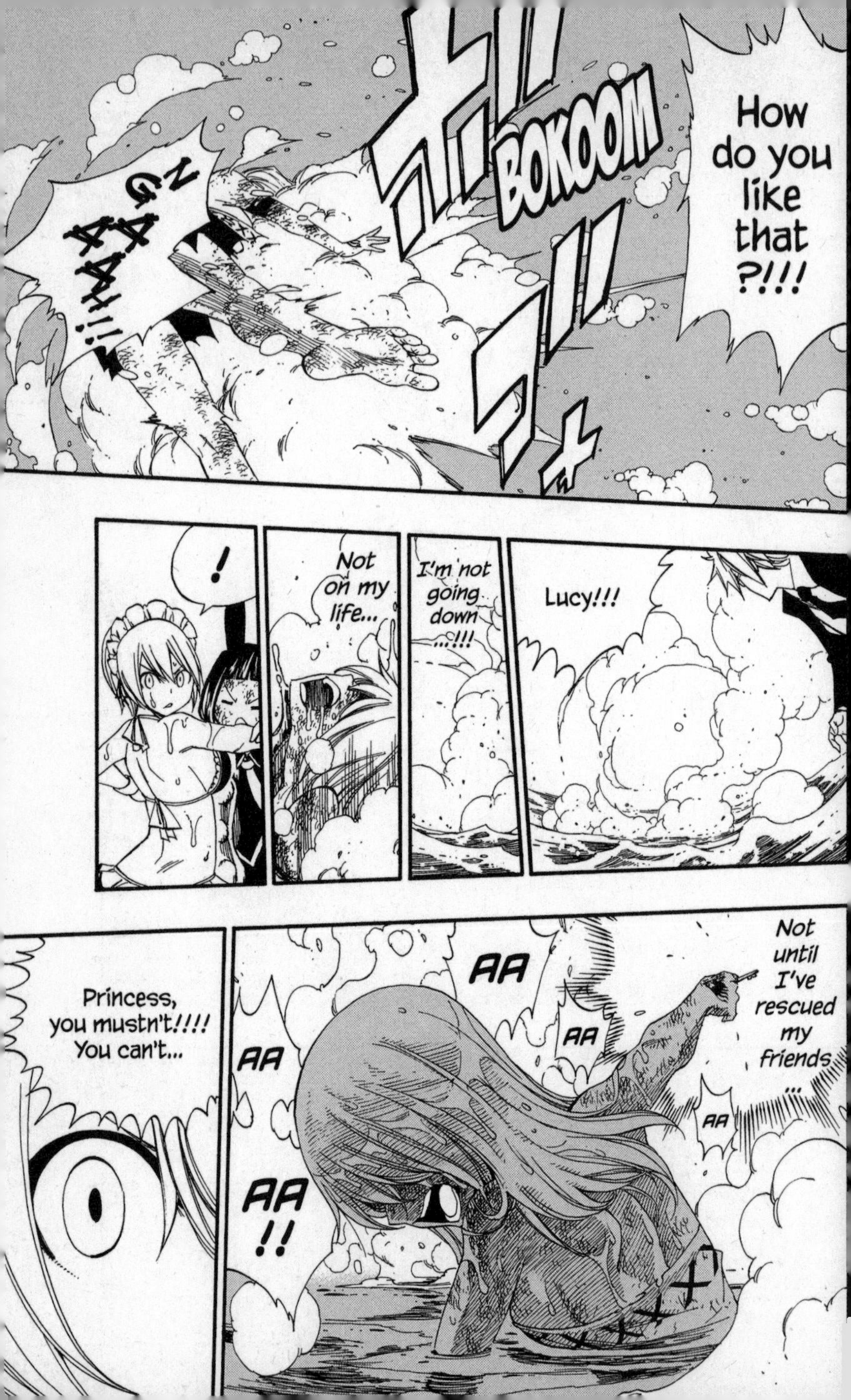
How do you like that?!!!
BOKOOM
GNAAAH!!!
Lucy!!!
I'm not going down ...!!!
Not on my life...
!
Not until I've rescued my friends ...
AA
AA
AA
AA
AA !!
Princess, you mustn't!!!! You can't...

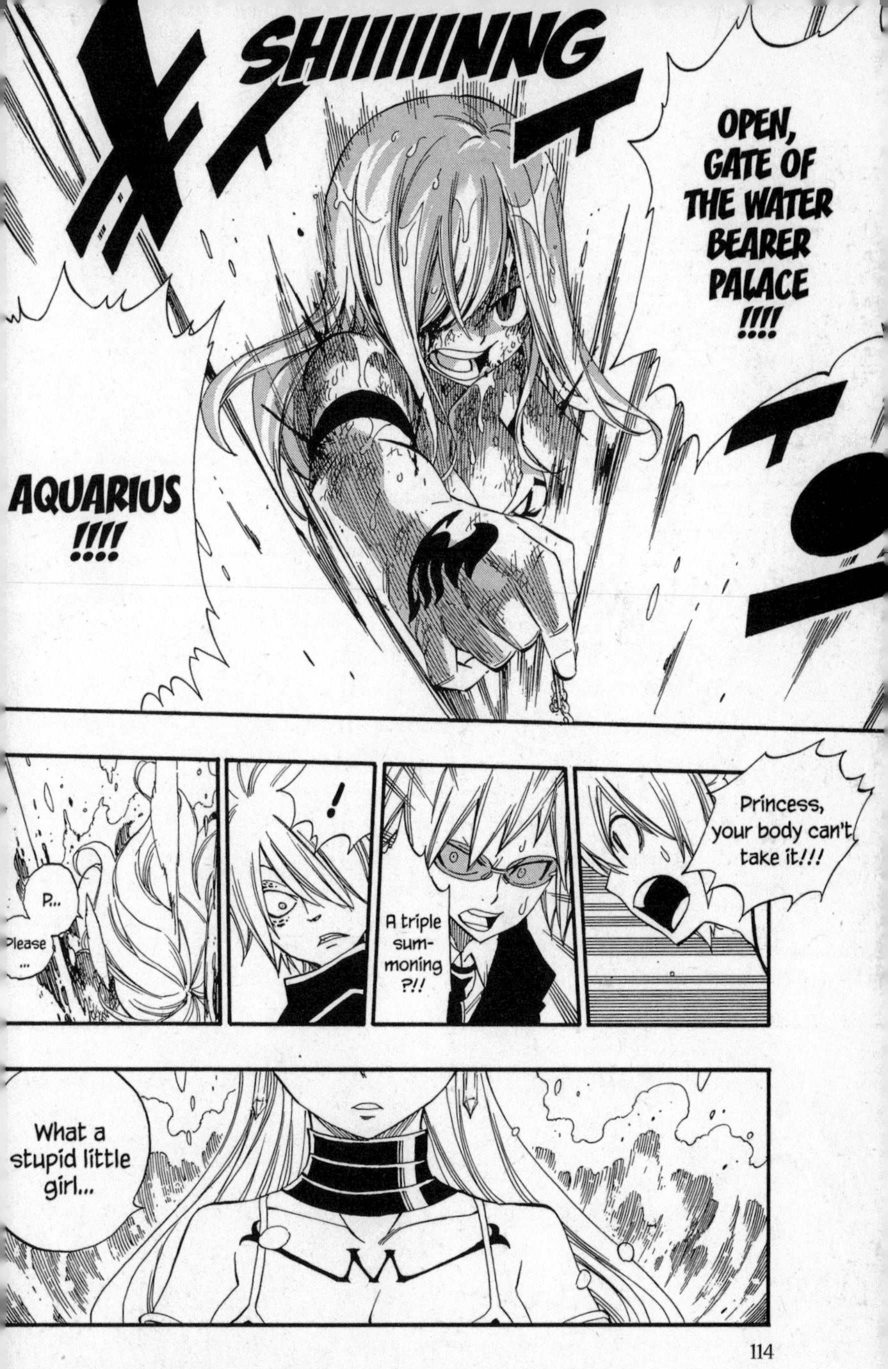
SHIIIIINNG
OPEN, GATE OF THE WATER BEARER PALACE!!!!
AQUARIUS!!!!
Princess, your body can't take it!!!
A triple sum-moning?!!
!
P... Please ...
What a stupid little girl...

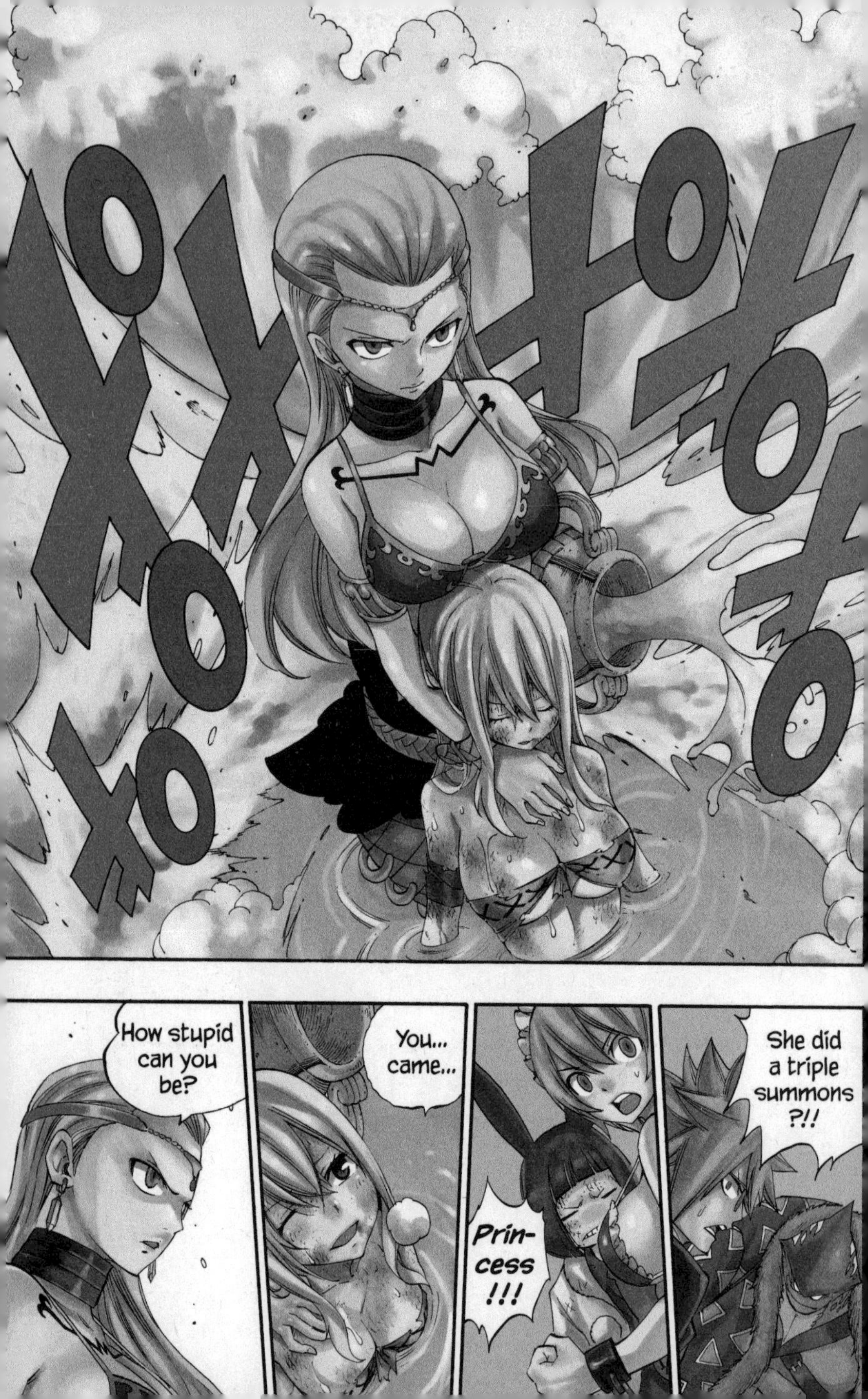
She did a triple summons ?!!
Prin-cess !!!
You... came...
How stupid can you be?

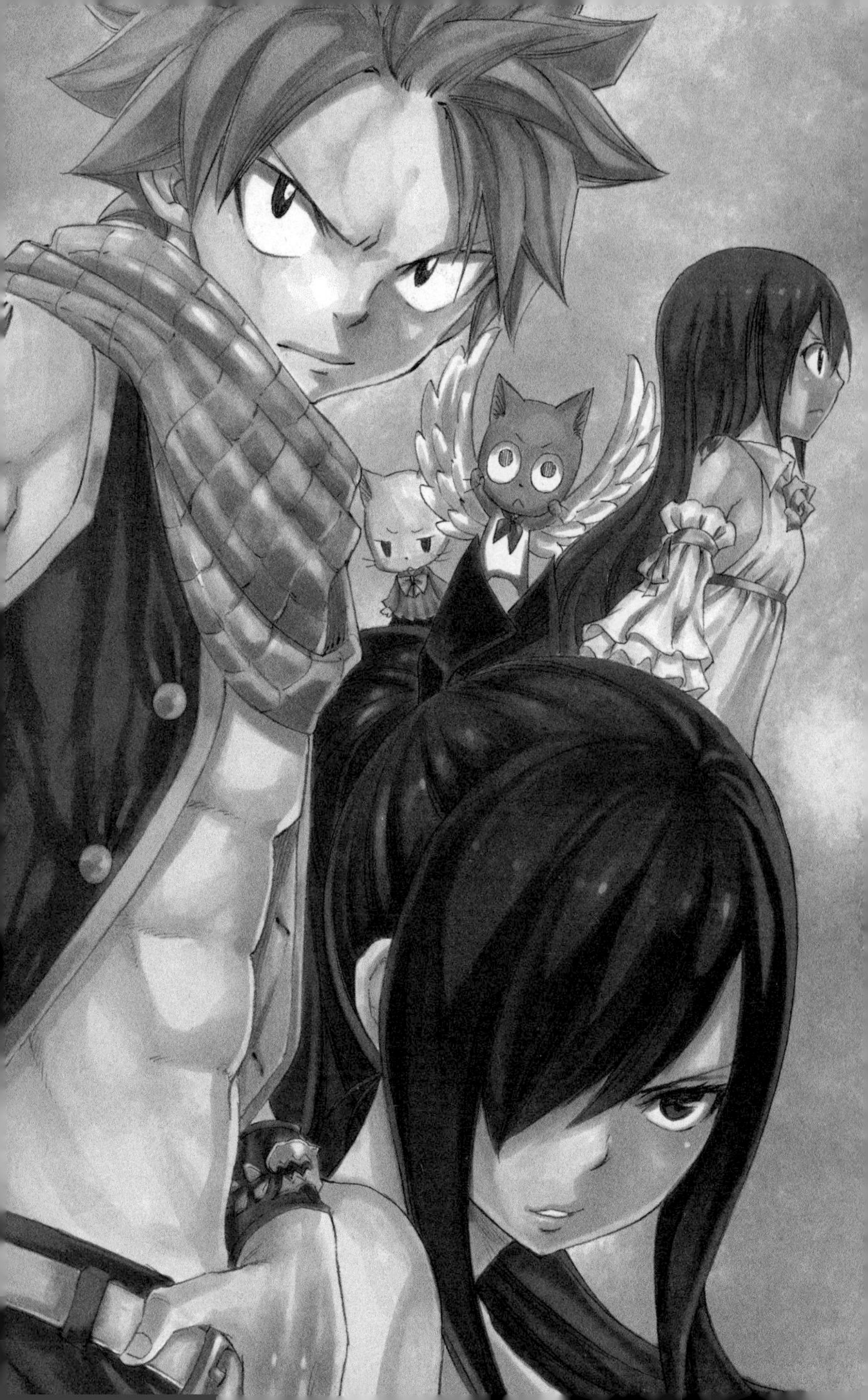

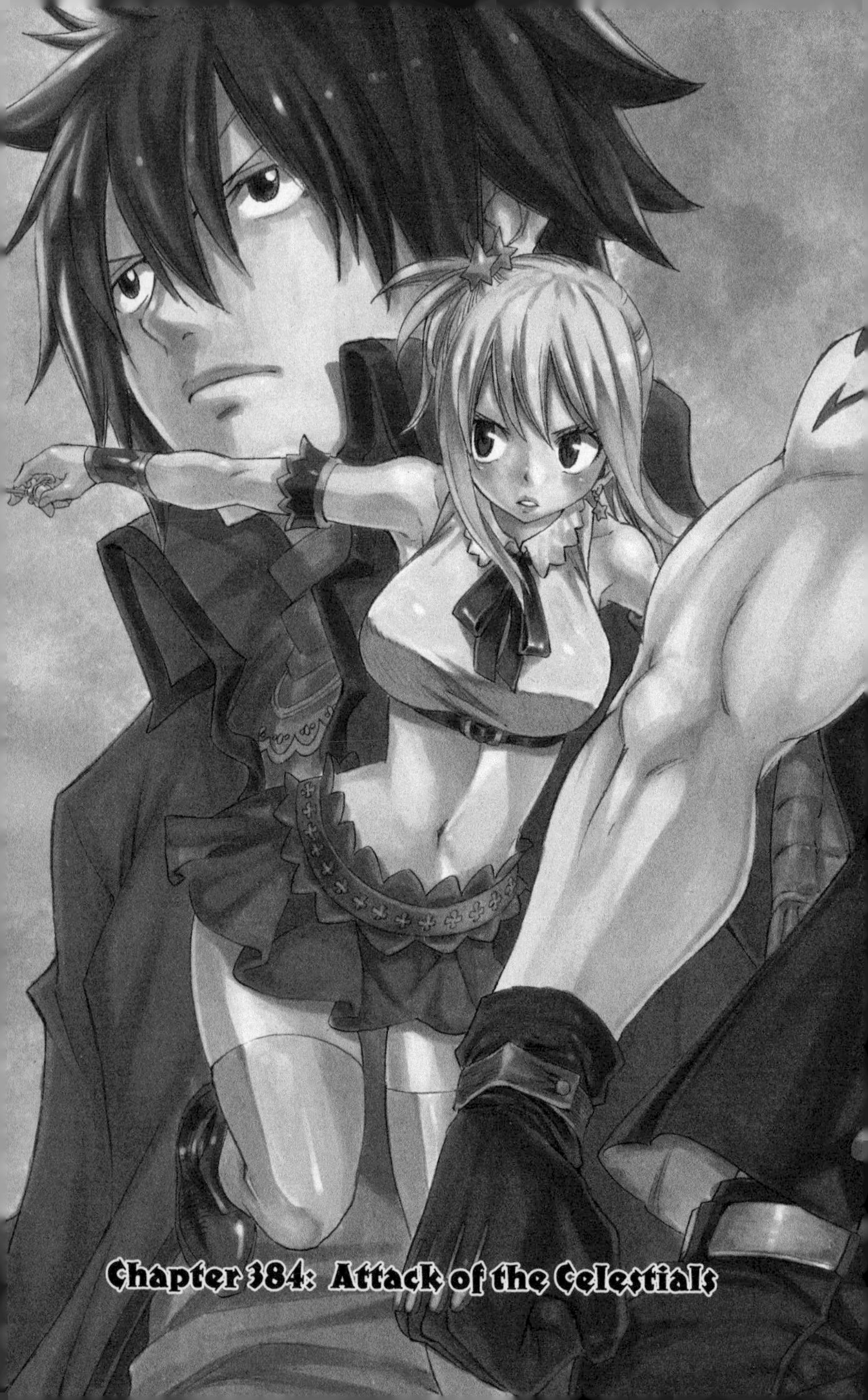

Chapter 384: Attack of the Celestials

FAIRY TAIL
フェアリーテイル

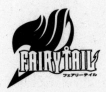

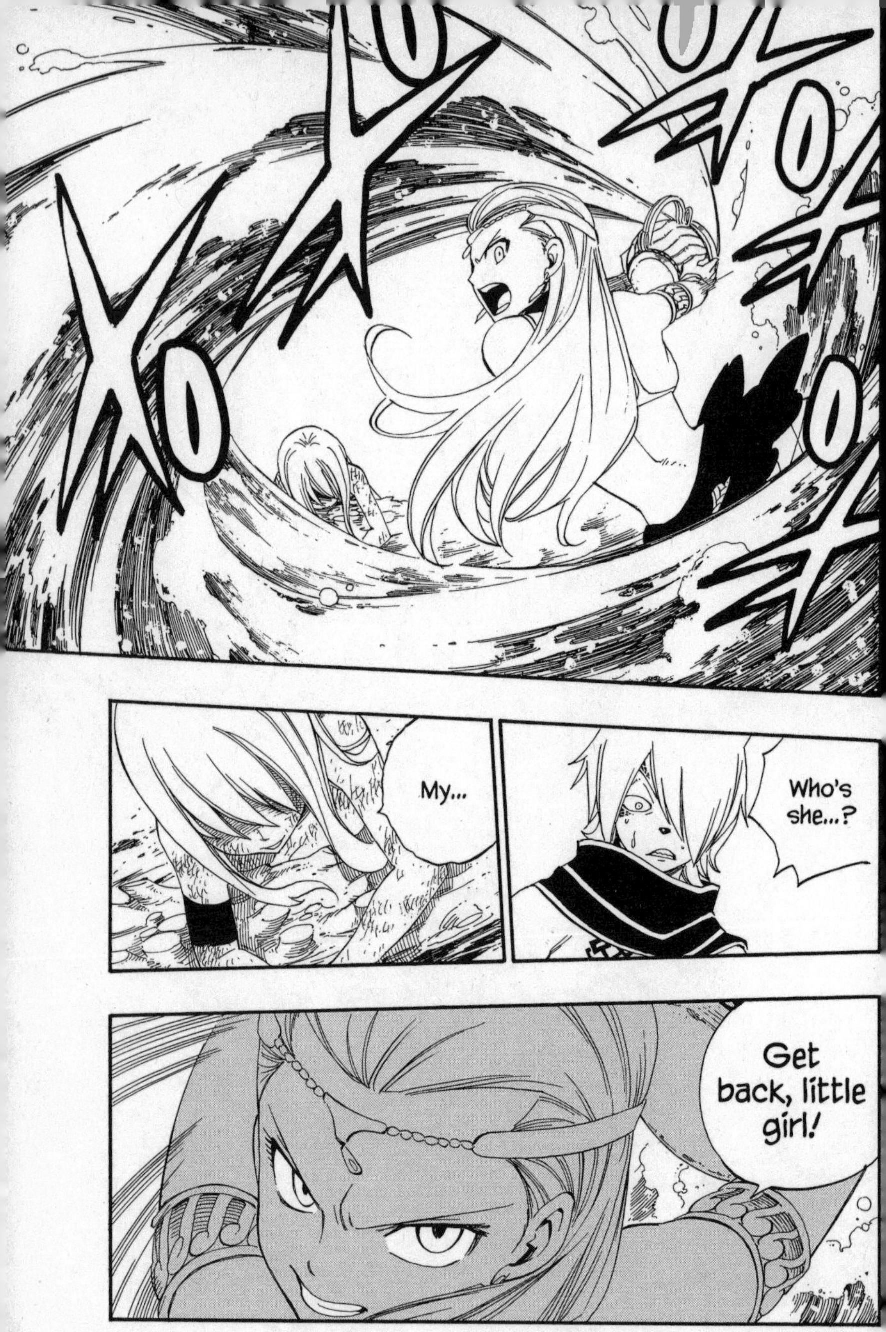
Who's she...?
My...
Get back, little girl!

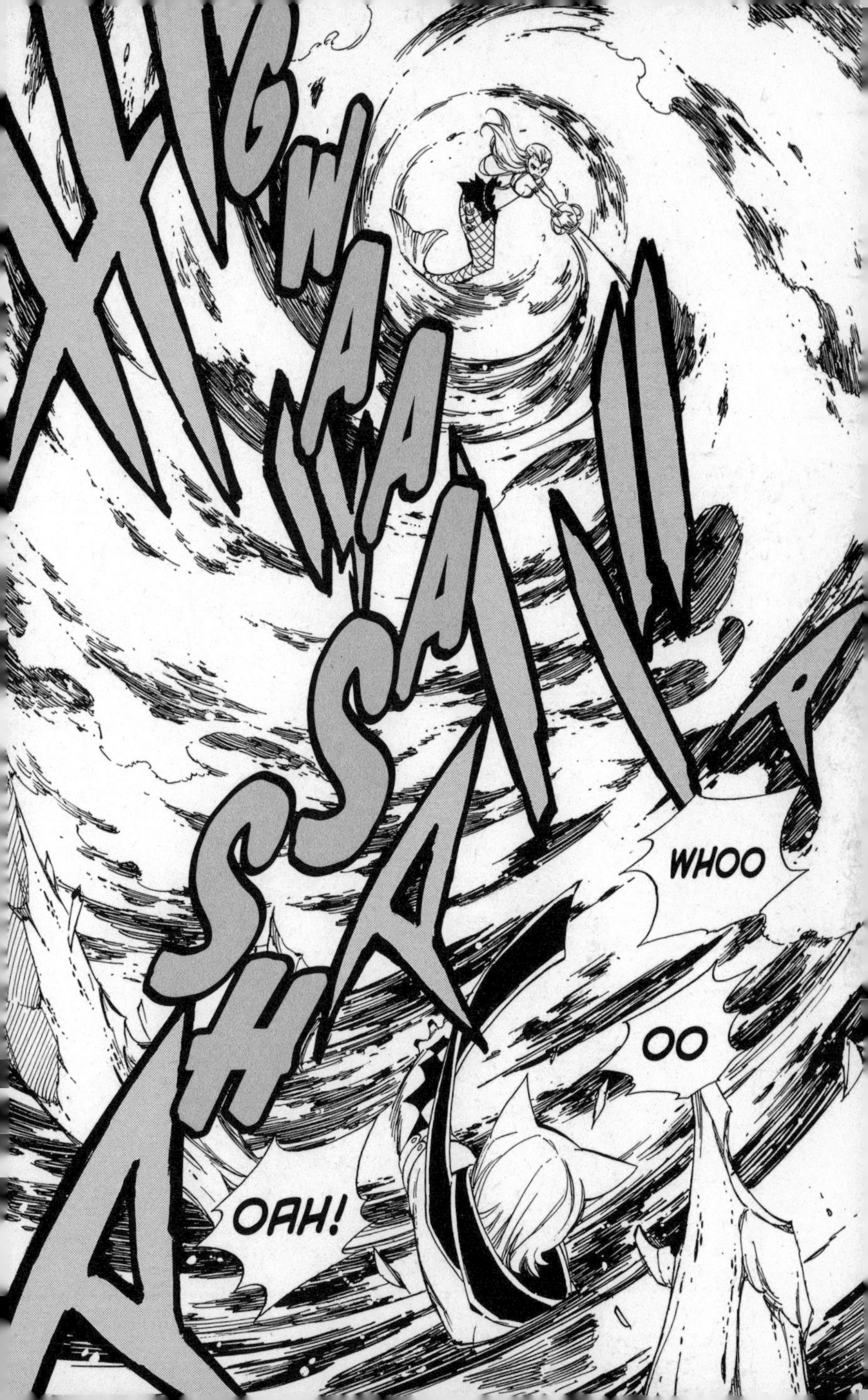
WHOO
OO
OAH!

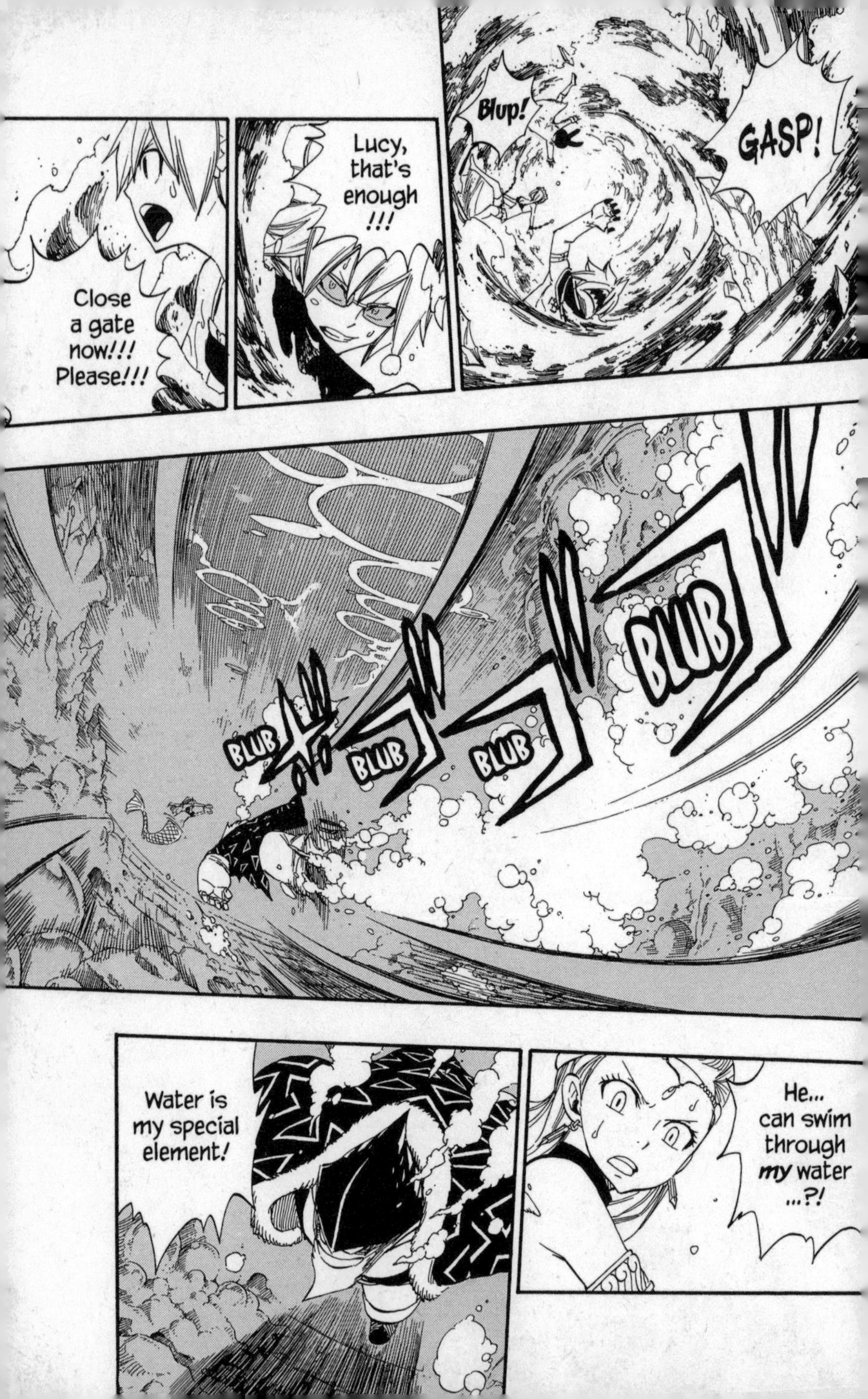
GASP!
Blup!
Lucy, that's enough!!!
Close a gate now!!! Please!!!
BLUB
BLUB
BLUB
BLUB
He... can swim through *my* water ...?!
Water is my special element!

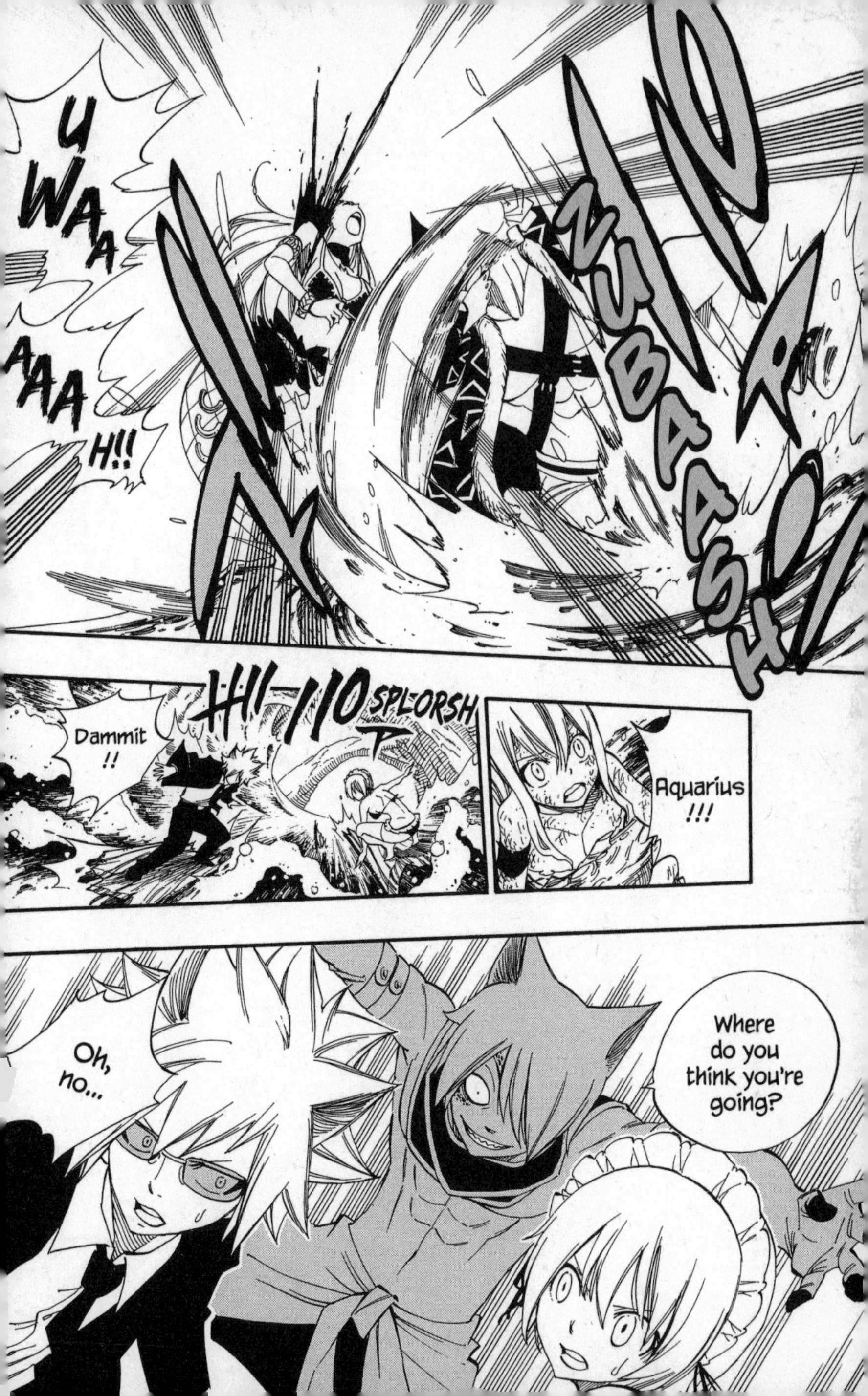
NUBAASH!!
UWAAAAAAH!!
Aquarius!!!
SPLORSH
Dammit!!
Where do you think you're going?
Oh, no...

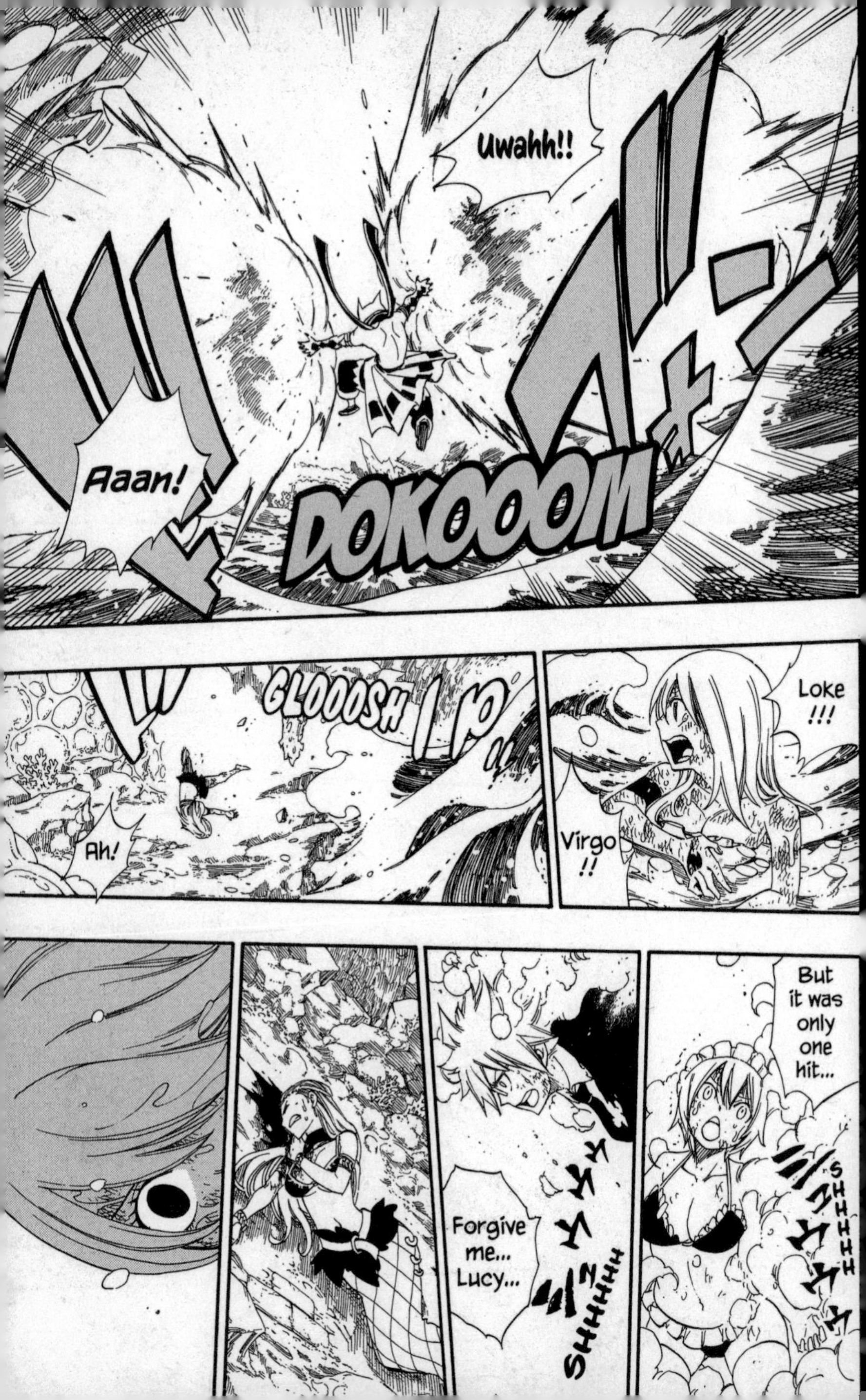
Uwahh!!
Aaan!
DOKOOOM
Loke!!!
Virgo!!
GLOOOSH
Ah!
But it was only one hit...
SHHHHH
Forgive me... Lucy...
SHHHHHH

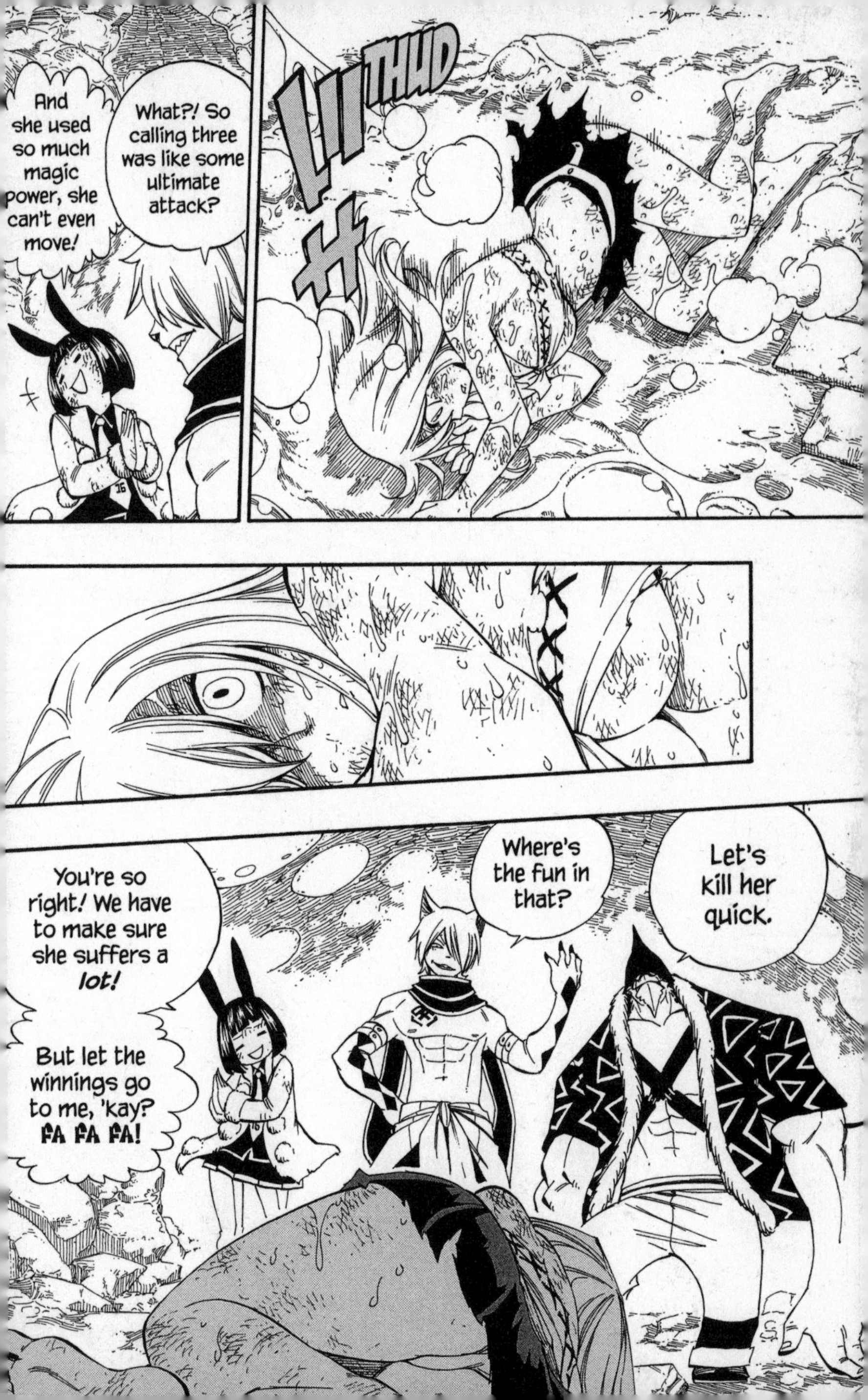
THUD
What?! So calling three was like some ultimate attack?
And she used so much magic power, she can't even move!
Let's kill her quick.
Where's the fun in that?
You're so right! We have to make sure she suffers a *lot!*
But let the winnings go to me, 'kay? **FA FA FA!**

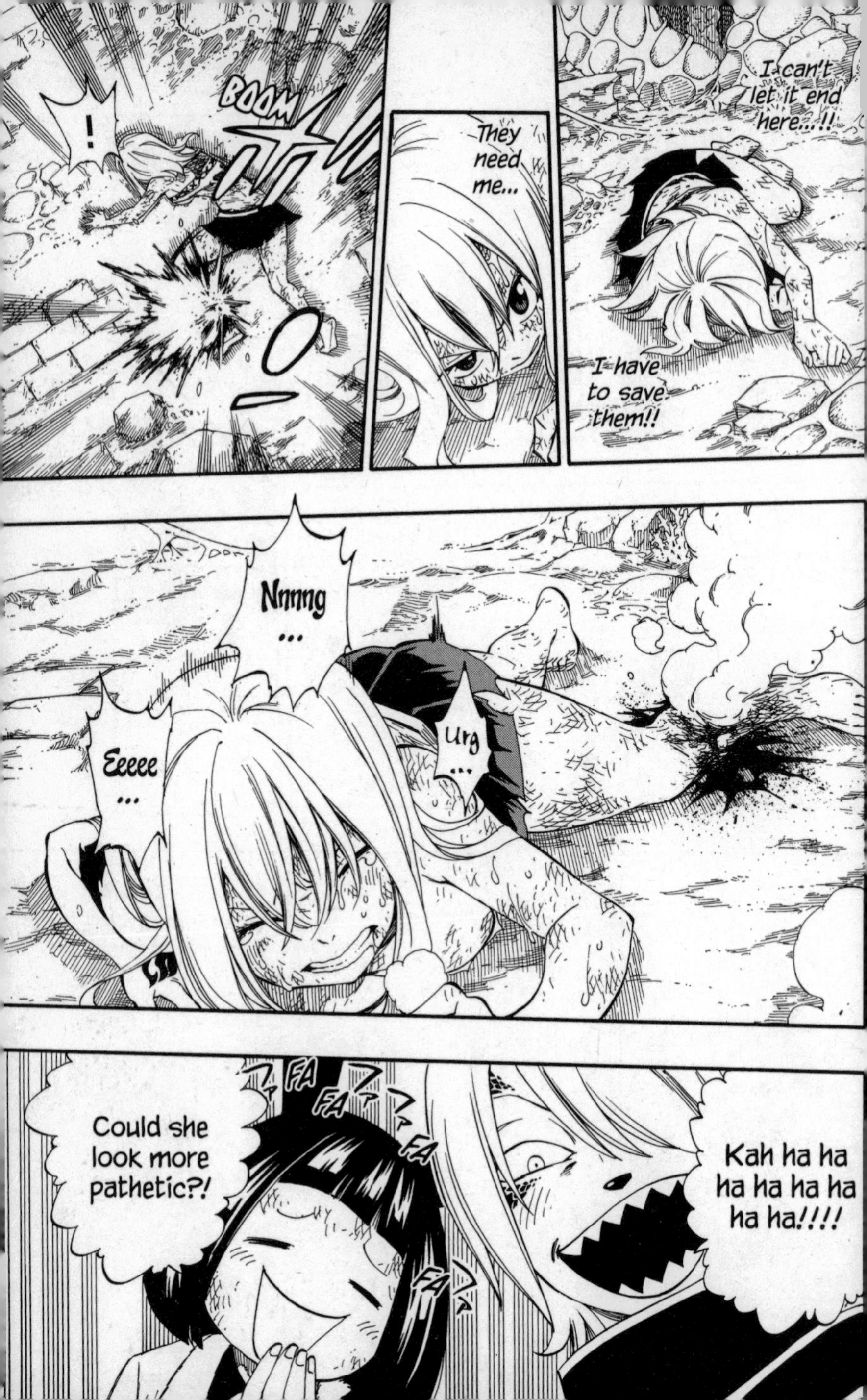
I can't let it end here...!!
I have to save them!!
They need me...
!
BOOM
Nnnng...
Urg...
Eeeee...
Kah ha ha ha ha ha ha ha ha!!!!
FA
FA
FA
FA
FA
Could she look more pathetic?!

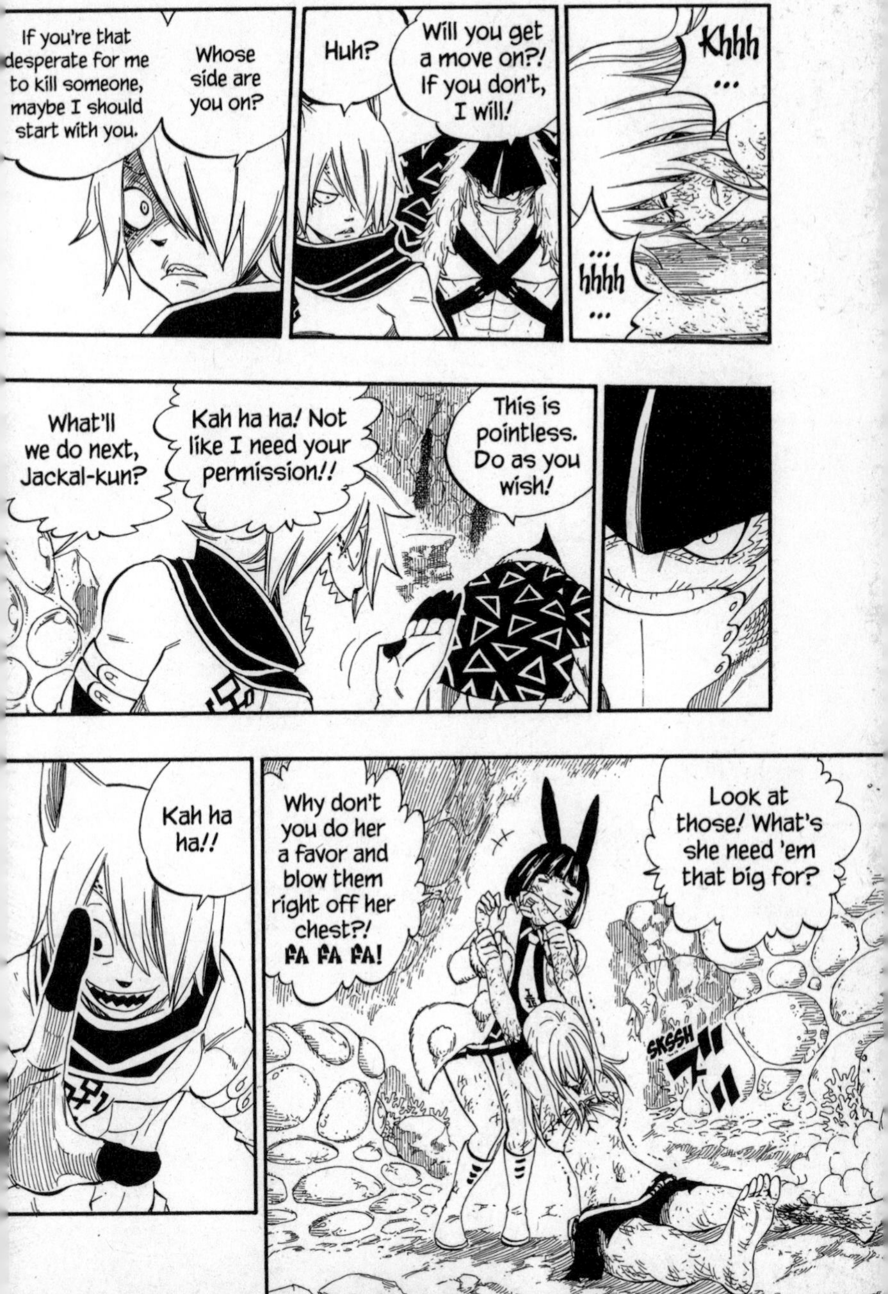
Khhh …
… hhhh …
Will you get a move on?! If you don't, I will!
Huh?
Whose side are you on?
If you're that desperate for me to kill someone, maybe I should start with you.
This is pointless. Do as you wish!
Kah ha ha! Not like I need your permission!!
What'll we do next, Jackal-kun?
Look at those! What's she need 'em that big for?
Why don't you do her a favor and blow them right off her chest?! FA FA FA!
SKSSH
Kah ha ha!!

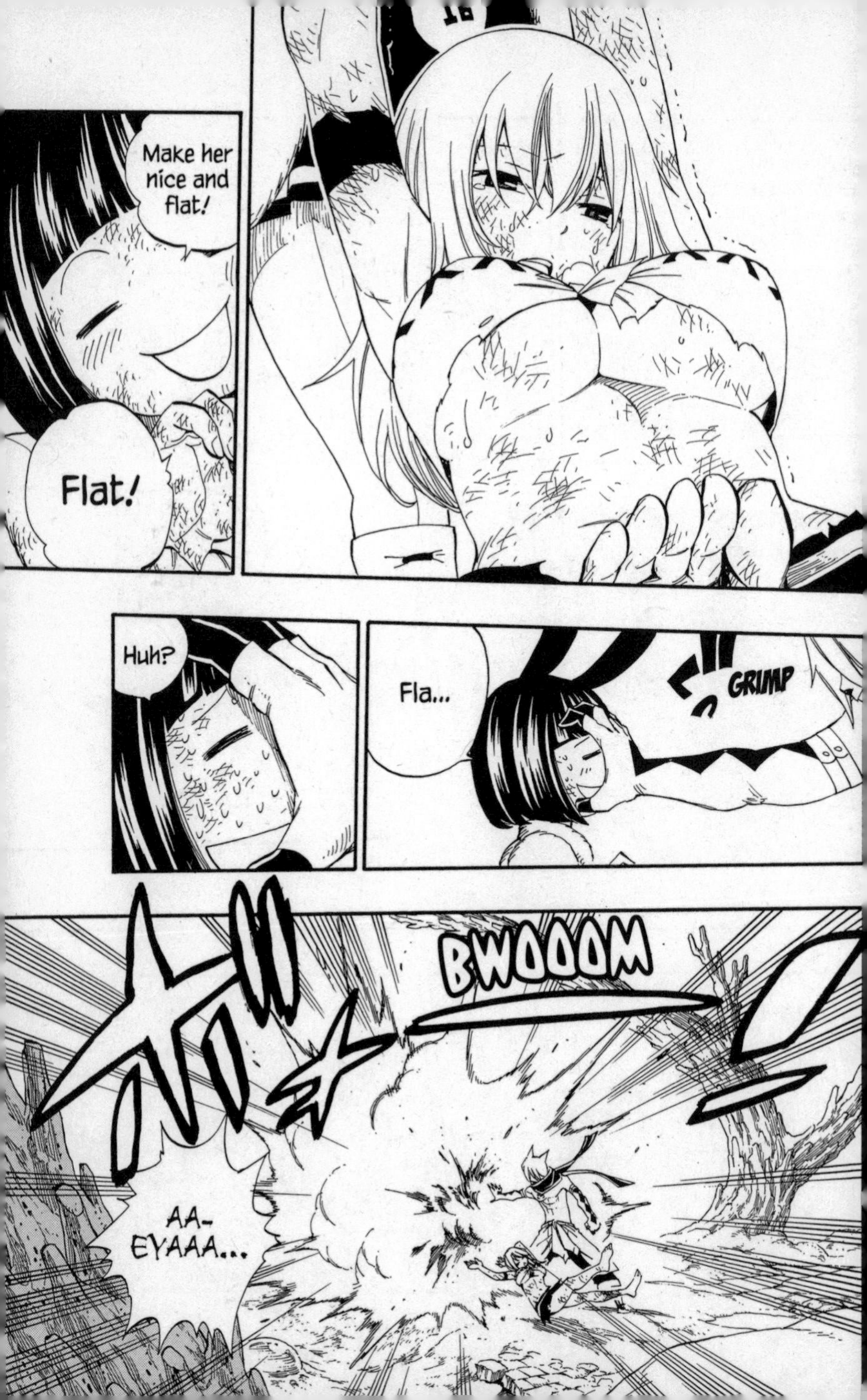

Make her nice and flat!
Flat!
GRIMP
Fla...
Huh?
BWOOOM
AA-EYAAA...

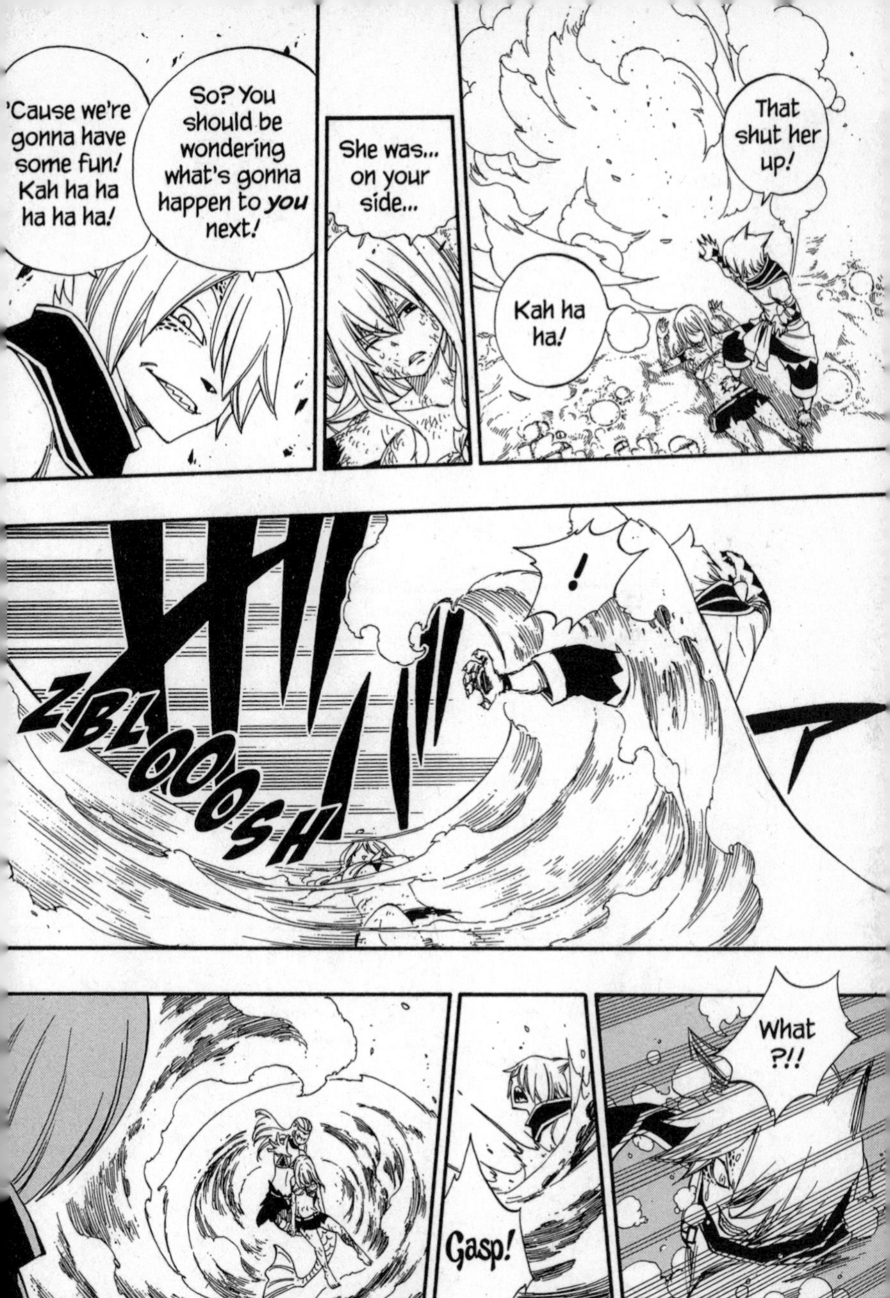
That shut her up!
Kah ha ha!
She was... on your side...
So? You should be wondering what's gonna happen to *you* next!
'Cause we're gonna have some fun! Kah ha ha ha ha ha!
!
ZBLOOOOSH
What ?!!
Gasp!

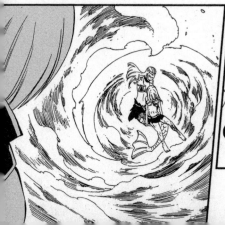

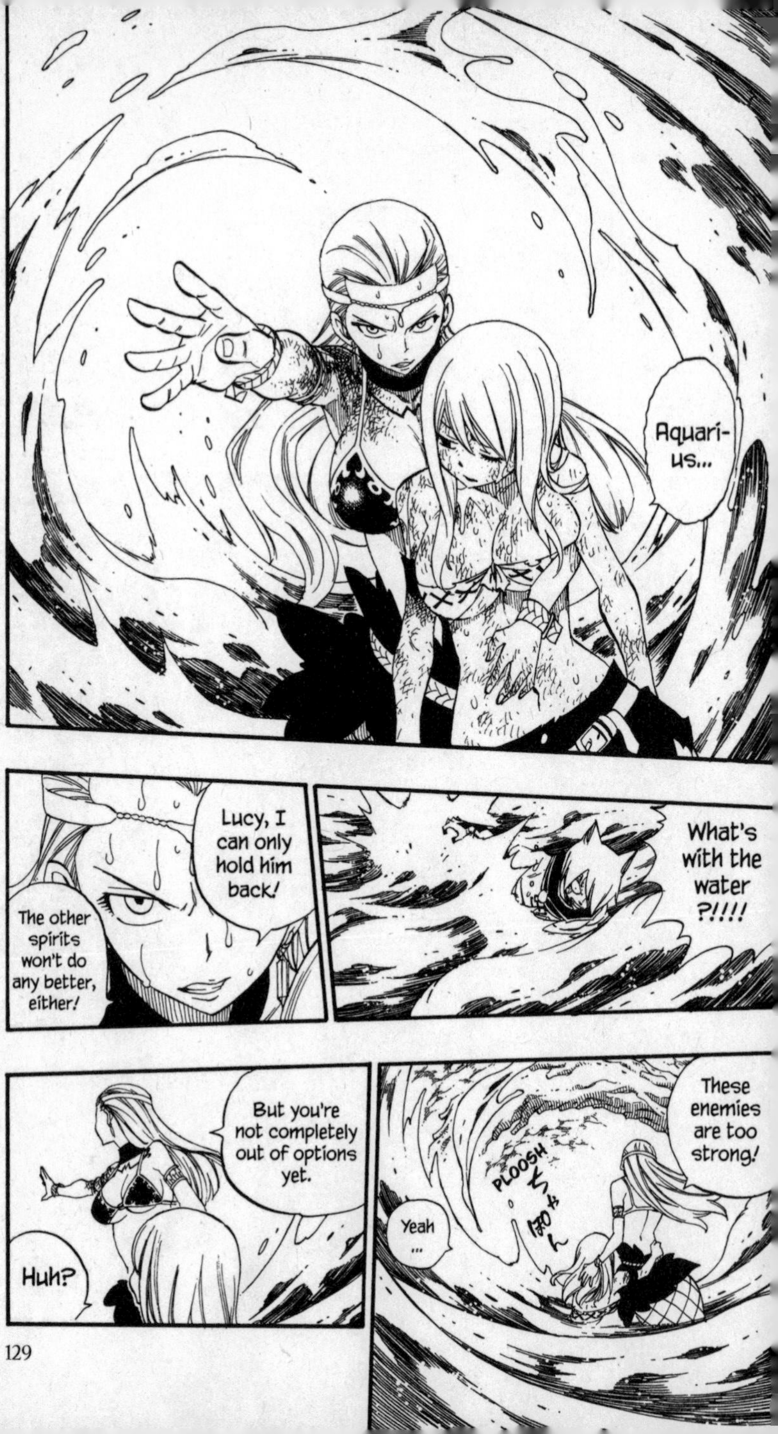
Aquari-us...
What's with the water ?!!!!
Lucy, I can only hold him back!
The other spirits won't do any better, either!
These enemies are too strong!
PLOOSH
Yeah ...
But you're not completely out of options yet.
Huh?

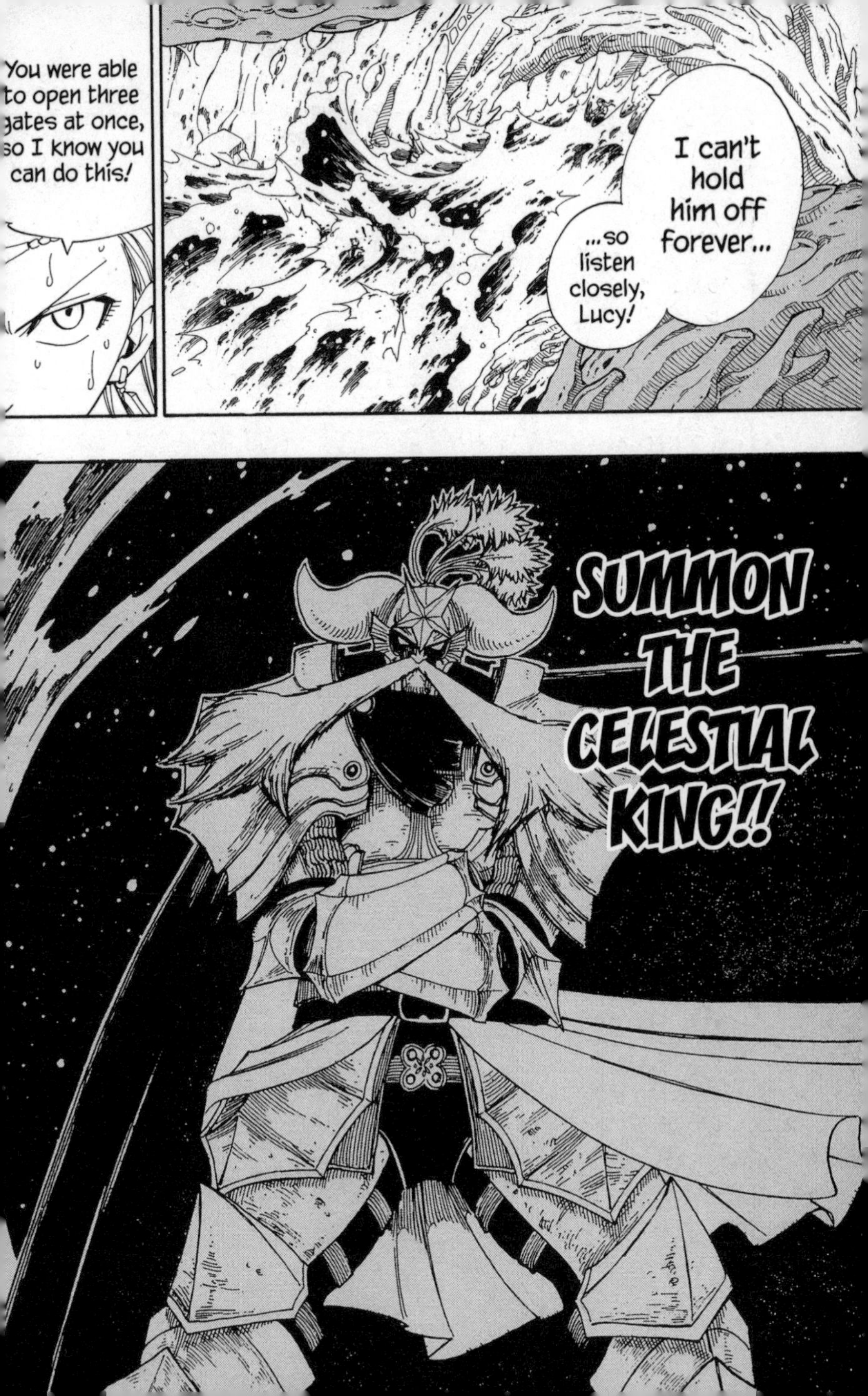
I can't hold him off forever...
...so listen closely, Lucy!
You were able to open three gates at once, so I know you can do this!
SUMMON THE CELESTIAL KING!!

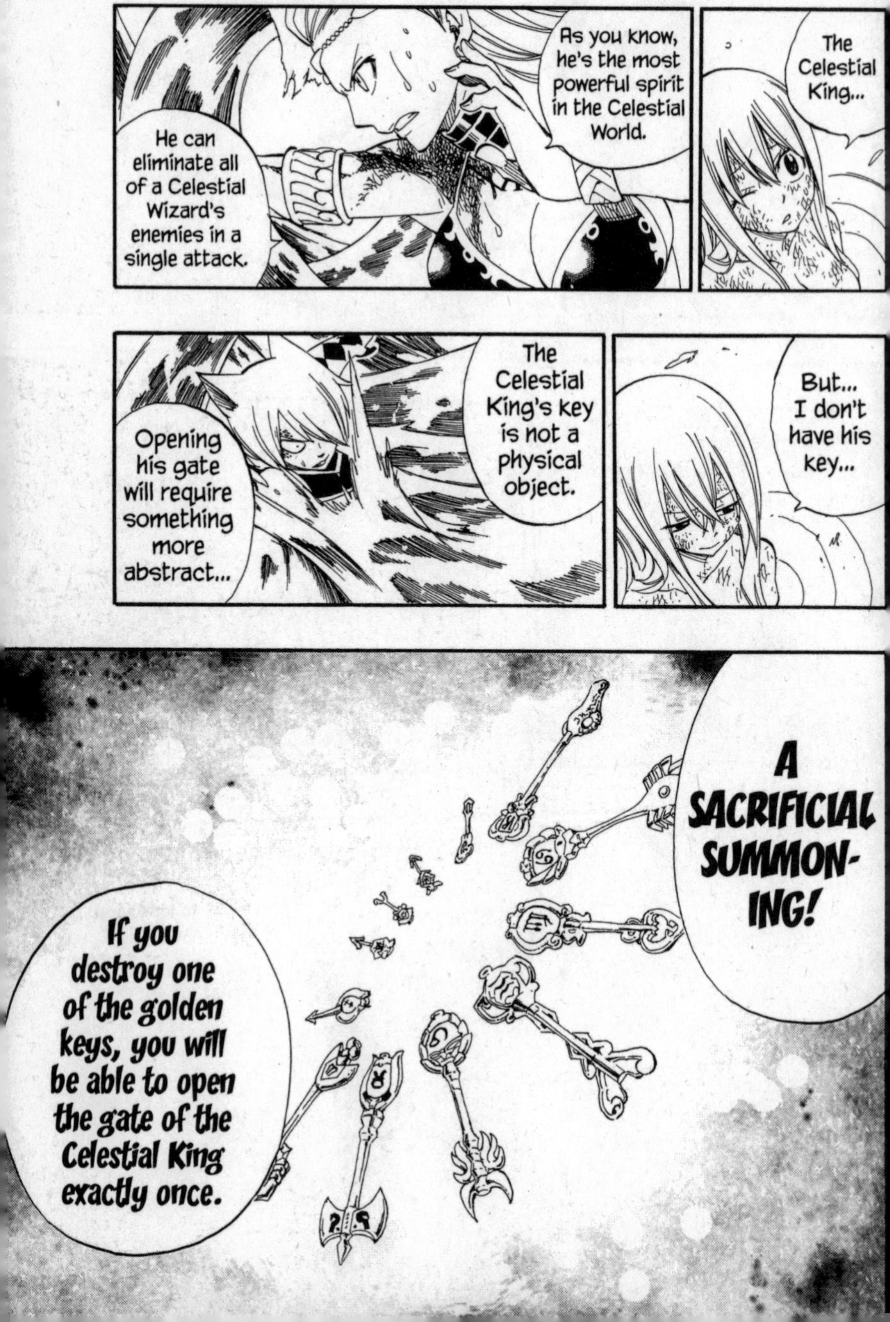
The Celestial King...
As you know, he's the most powerful spirit in the Celestial World.
He can eliminate all of a Celestial Wizard's enemies in a single attack.
But... I don't have his key...
The Celestial King's key is not a physical object.
Opening his gate will require something more abstract...
A SACRIFICIAL SUMMON-ING!
If you destroy one of the golden keys, you will be able to open the gate of the Celestial King exactly once.

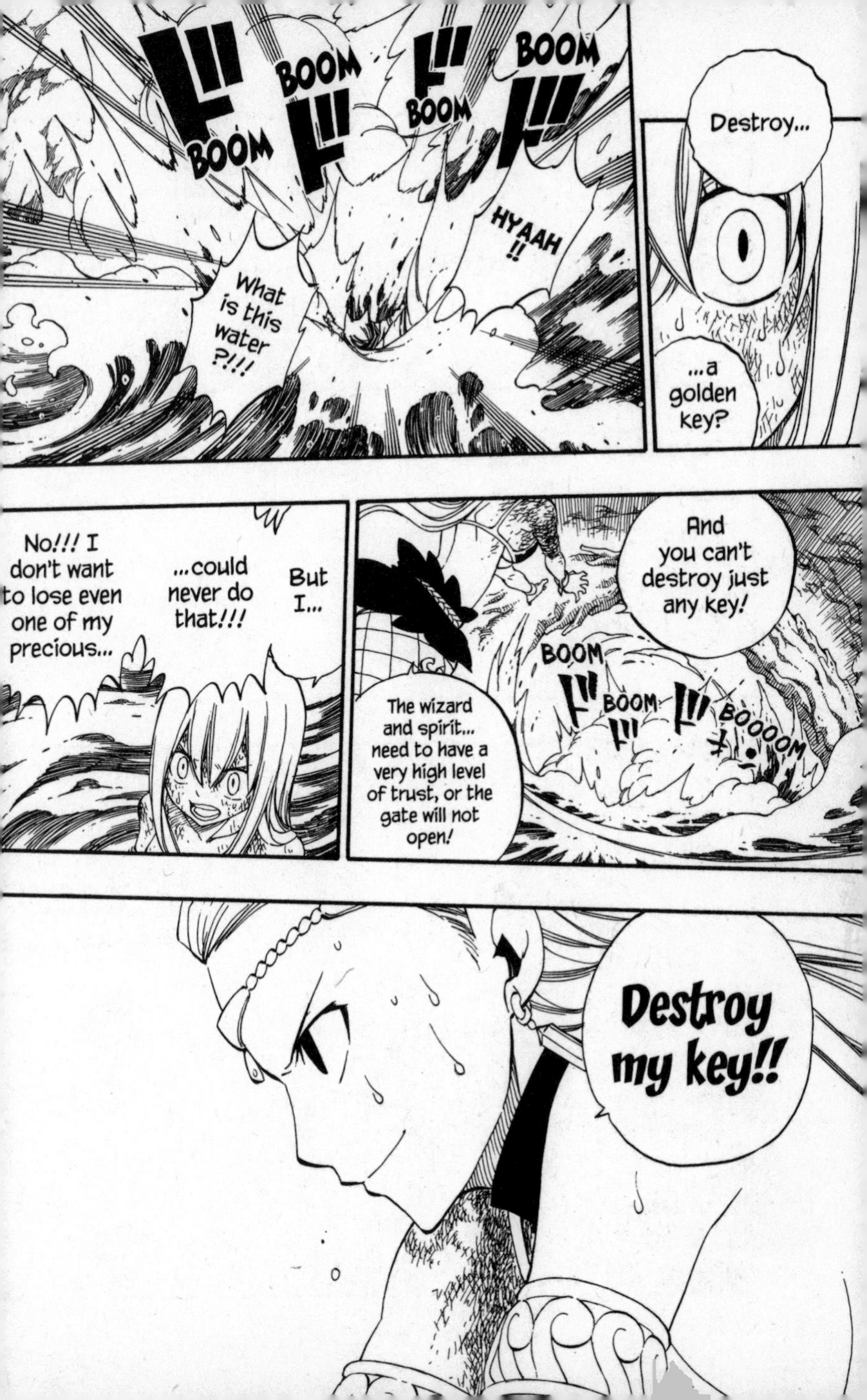
Destroy...
...a golden key?
BOOM
BOOM
BOOM
BOOM
HYAAH!!
What is this water?!!!
And you can't destroy just any key!
The wizard and spirit... need to have a very high level of trust, or the gate will not open!
BOOM
BOOM
BOOOOOM
But I...
...could never do that!!!
No!!! I don't want to lose even one of my precious...
Destroy my key!!

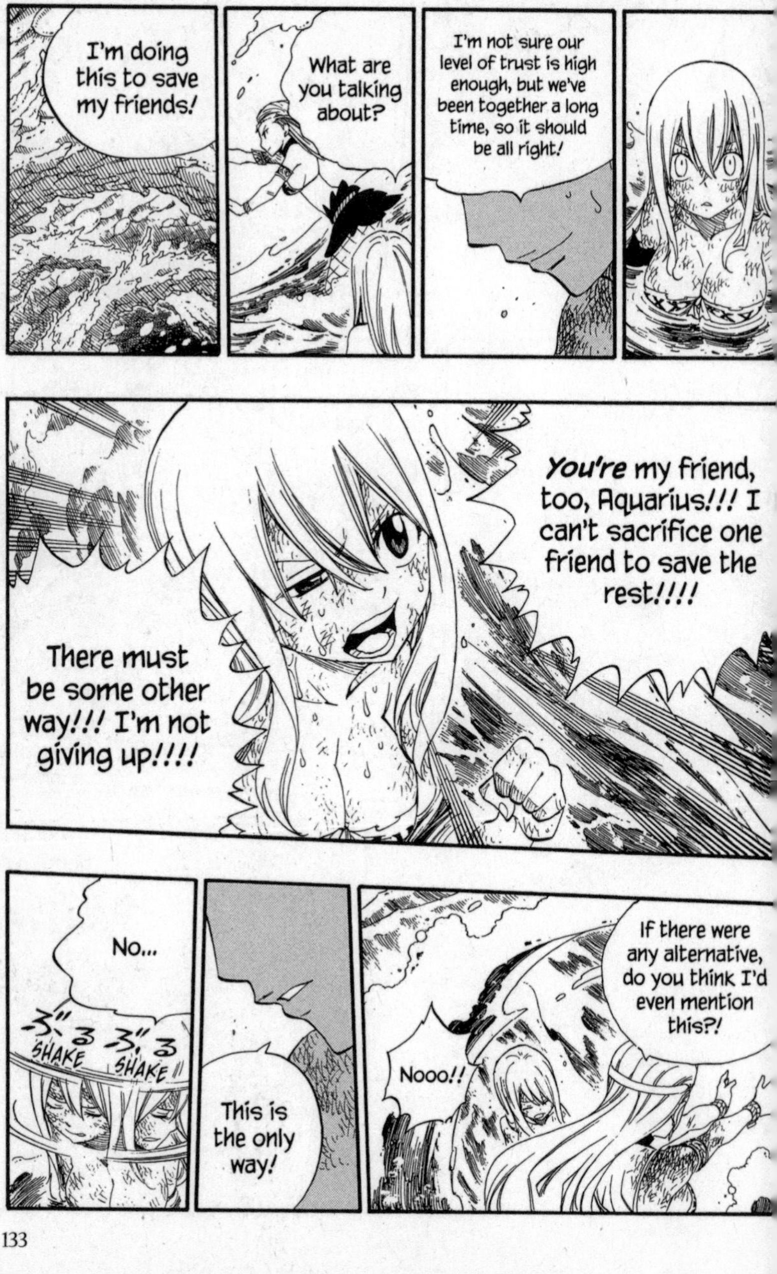
I'm not sure our level of trust is high enough, but we've been together a long time, so it should be all right!
What are you talking about?
I'm doing this to save my friends!
You're my friend, too, Aquarius!!! I can't sacrifice one friend to save the rest!!!!
There must be some other way!!! I'm not giving up!!!!
If there were any alternative, do you think I'd even mention this?!
Nooo!!
This is the only way!
No...
ぶる SHAKE ぶる SHAKE

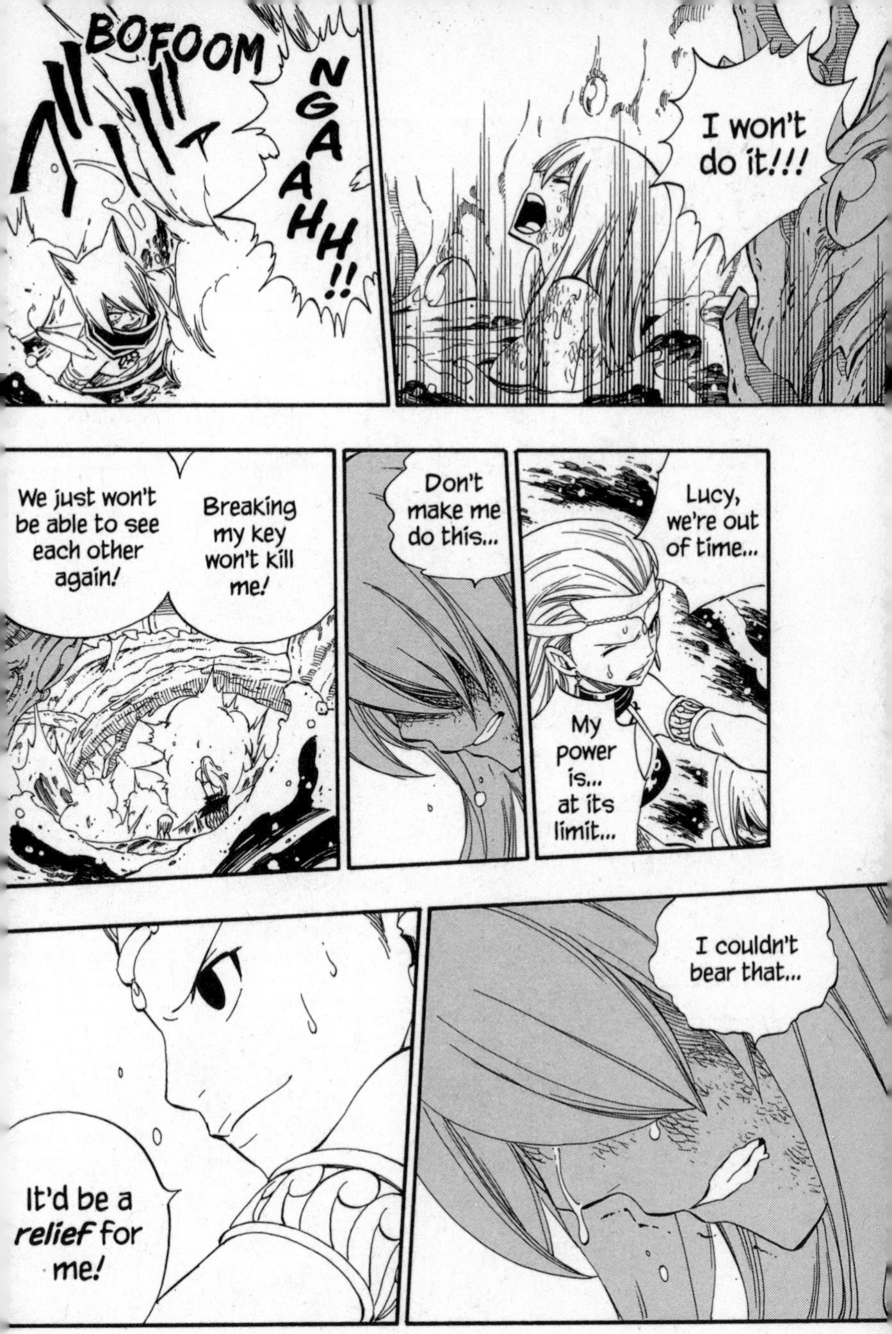
I won't do it!!!
BOFOOM
NGAAHH!!
Lucy, we're out of time...
My power is... at its limit...
Don't make me do this...
Breaking my key won't kill me!
We just won't be able to see each other again!
I couldn't bear that...
It'd be a *relief* for me!

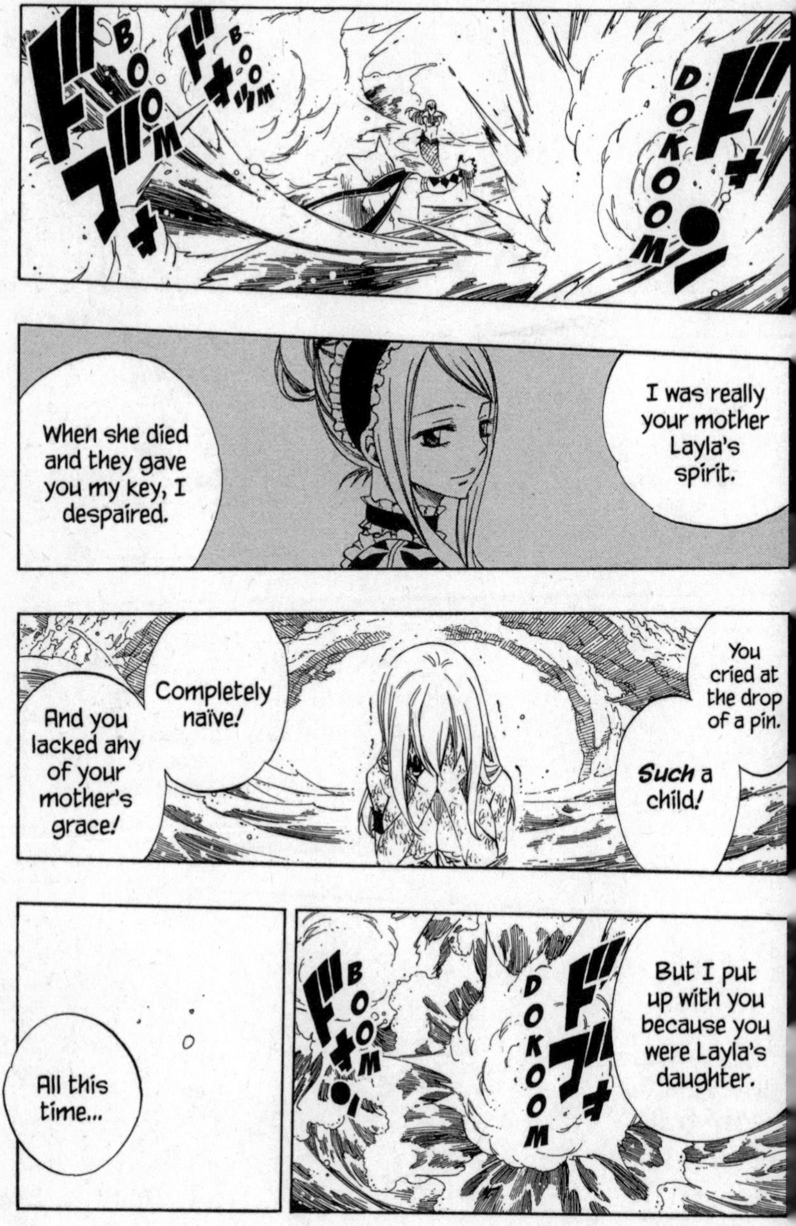
DOKOOM
BOOM
BOOM
I was really your mother Layla's spirit.
When she died and they gave you my key, I despaired.
You cried at the drop of a pin.
Such a child!
Completely naïve!
And you lacked any of your mother's grace!
But I put up with you because you were Layla's daughter.
DOKOOM
BOOM
All this time...

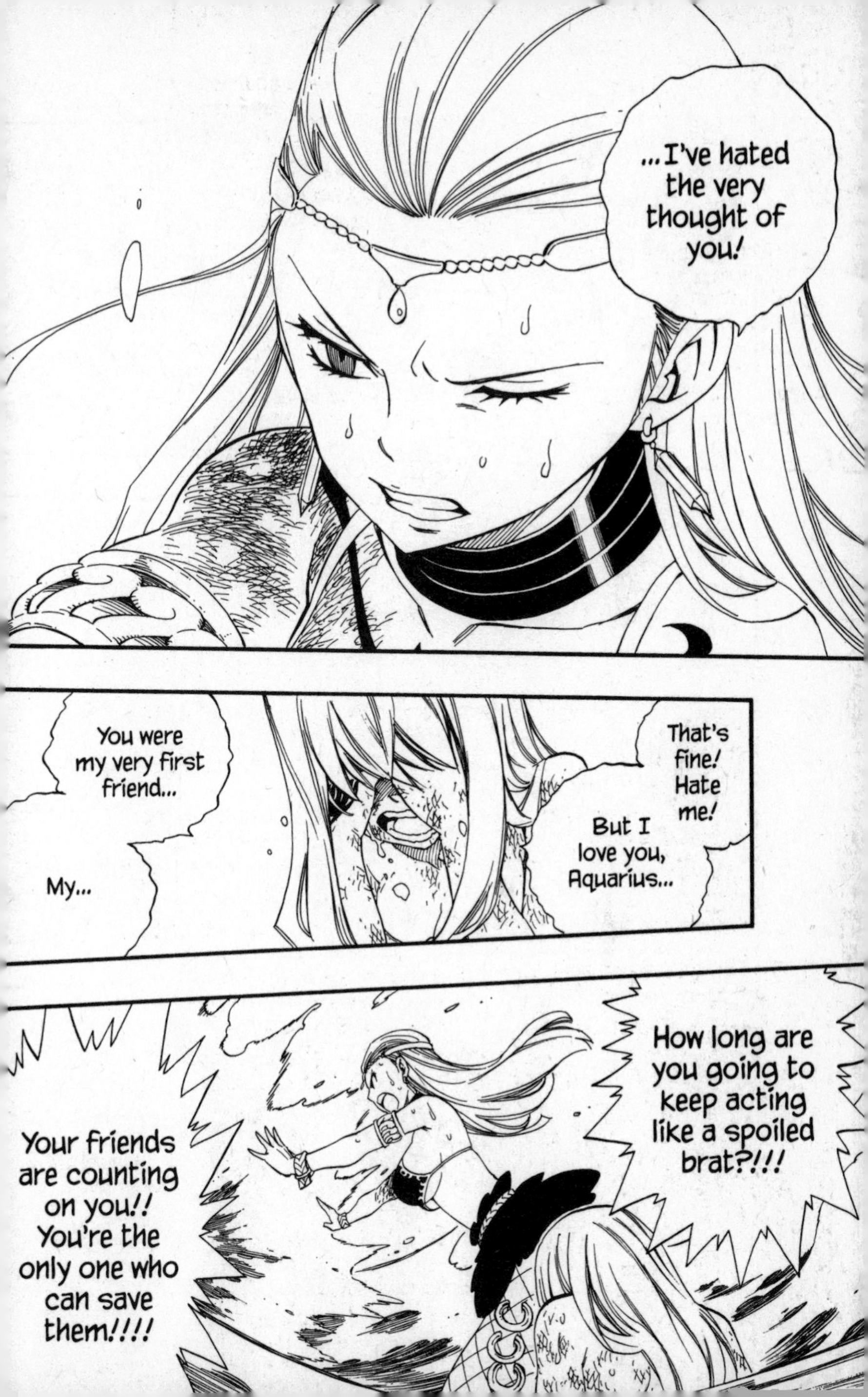
...I've hated the very thought of you!
That's fine! Hate me!
But I love you, Aquarius...
You were my very first friend...
My...
How long are you going to keep acting like a spoiled brat?!!!
Your friends are counting on you!! You're the only one who can save them!!!!

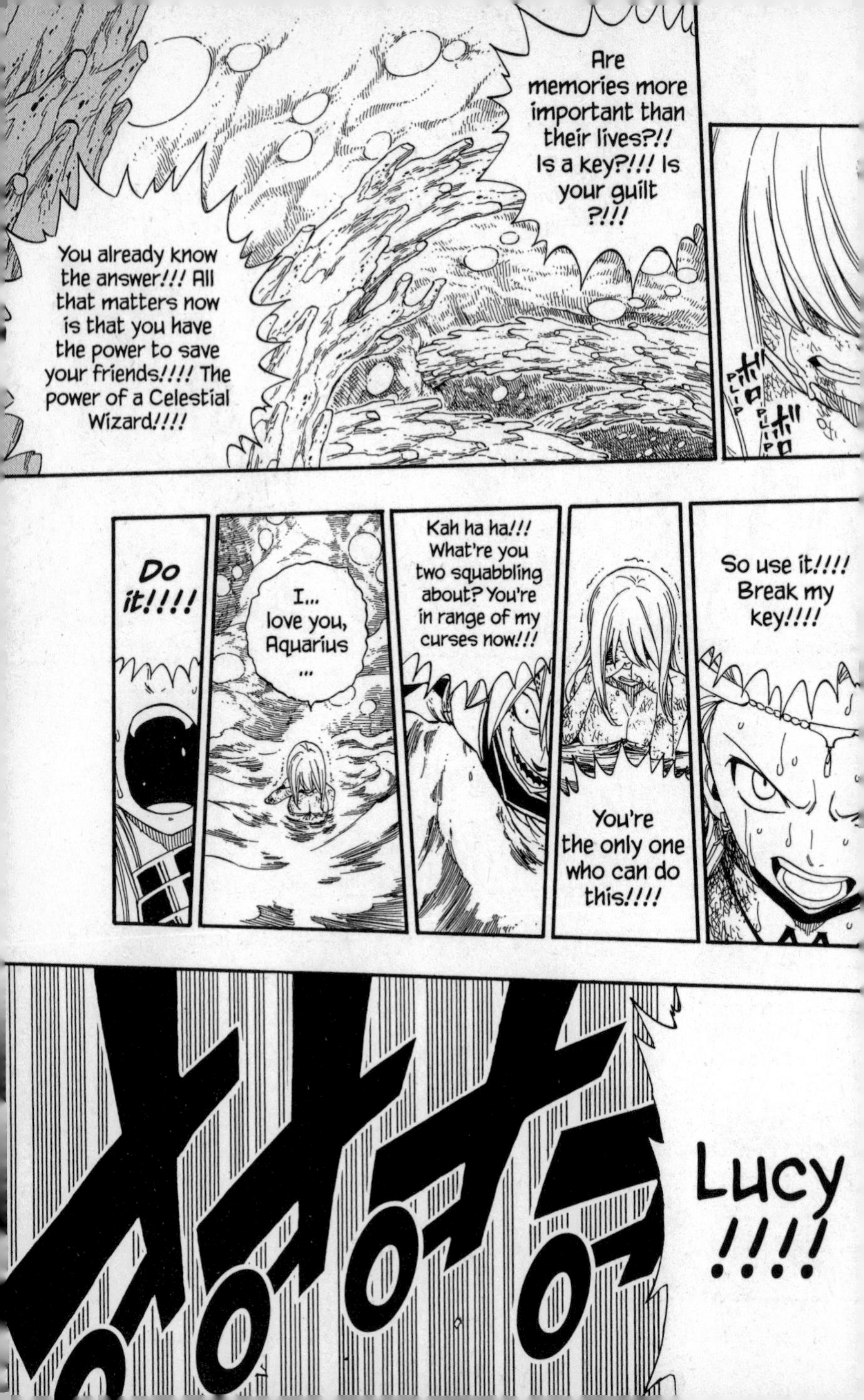
PLIP PLIP
Are memories more important than their lives?!! Is a key?!!! Is your guilt ?!!!
You already know the answer!!! All that matters now is that you have the power to save your friends!!!! The power of a Celestial Wizard!!!!
So use it!!!! Break my key!!!!
You're the only one who can do this!!!!
Kah ha ha!!! What're you two squabbling about? You're in range of my curses now!!!
I... love you, Aquarius ...
Do it!!!!
Lucy !!!!

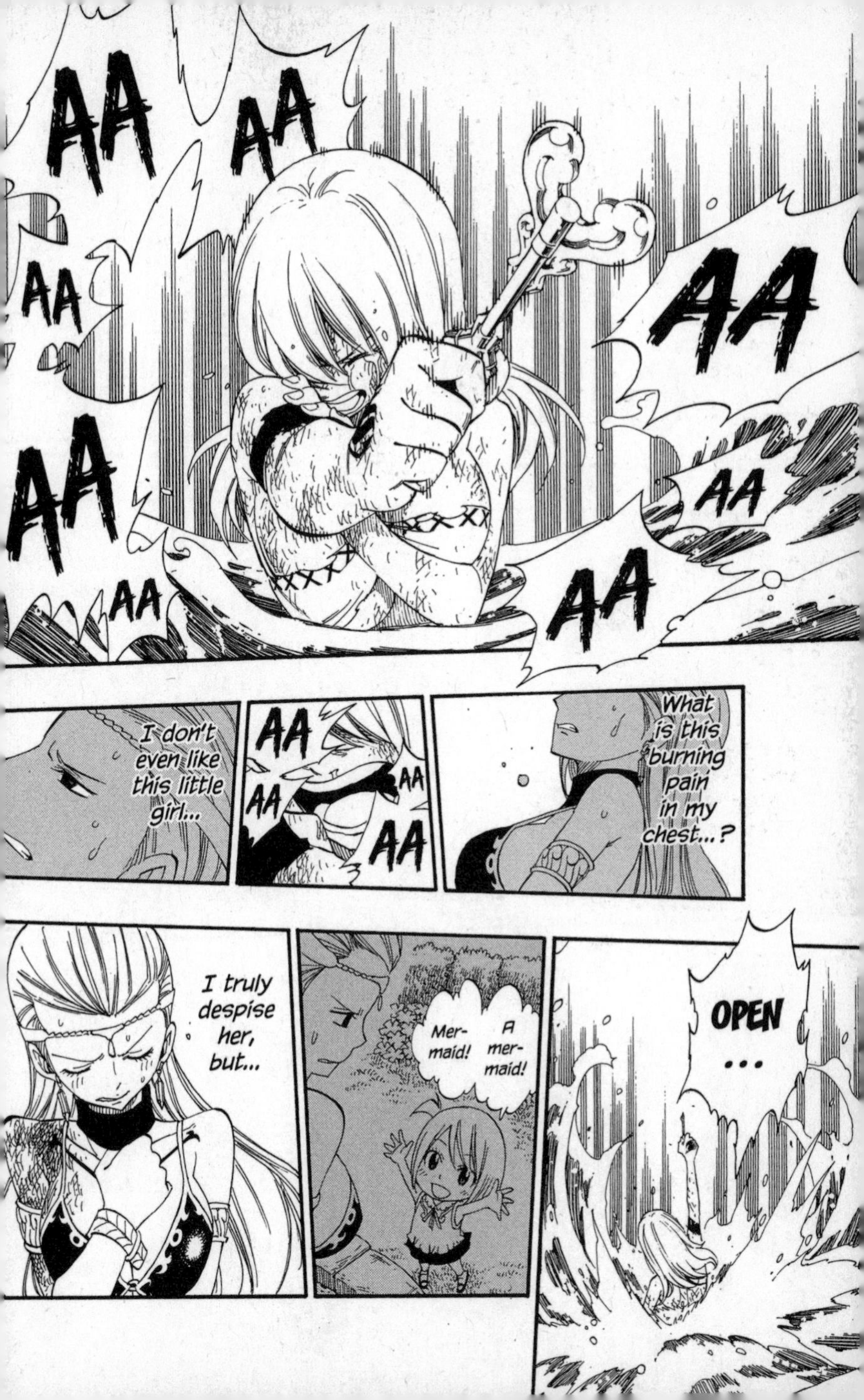
AA
AA
AA
AA
AA
AA
AA
AA
What is this burning pain in my chest...?
AA
AA
AA
AA
I don't even like this little girl...
OPEN ...
A mer-maid!
Mer-maid!
I truly despise her, but...

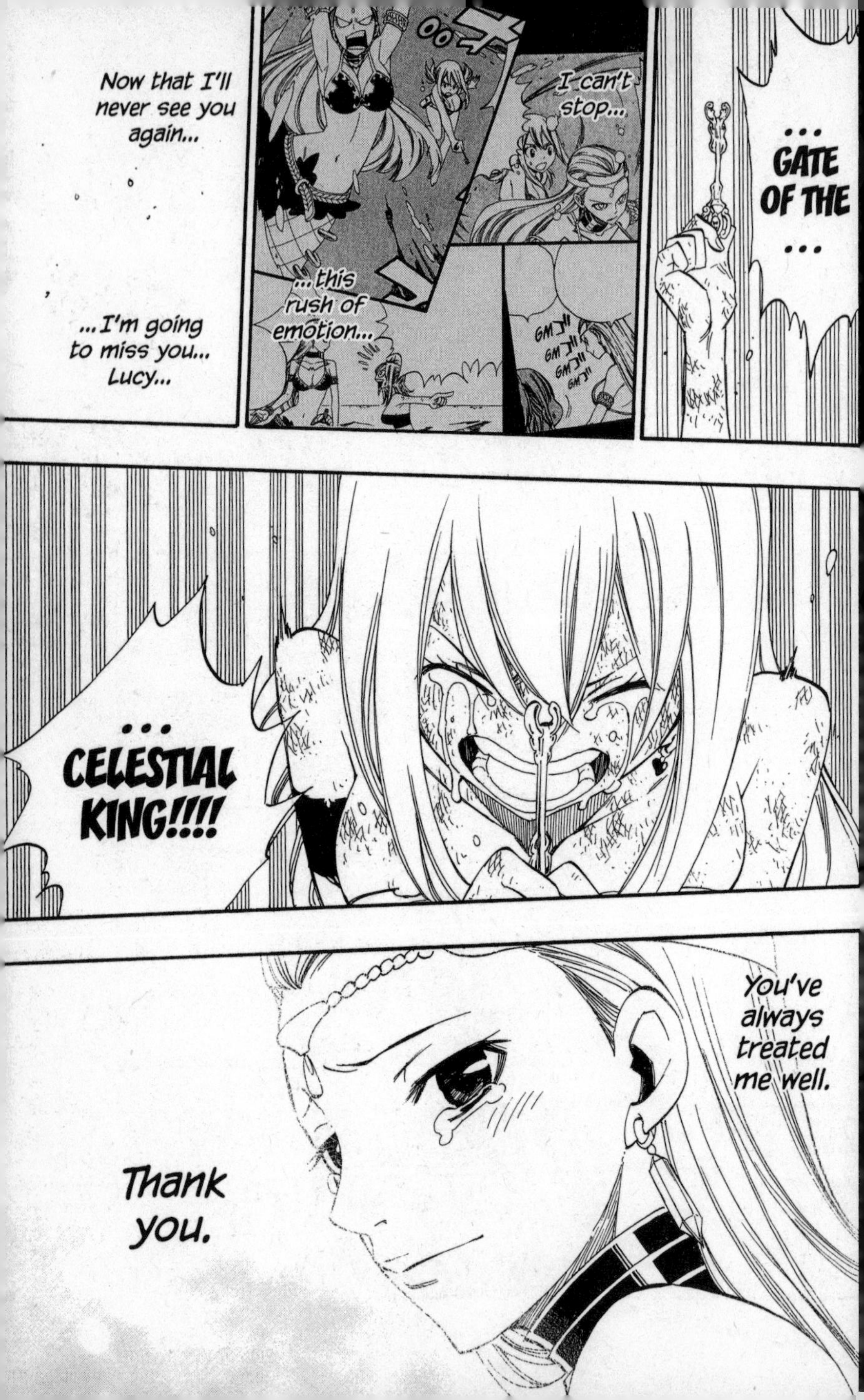
...
GATE OF THE
...
I can't stop...
...this rush of emotion...
Now that I'll never see you again...
...I'm going to miss you... Lucy...
...
CELESTIAL KING!!!!
You've always treated me well.
Thank you.

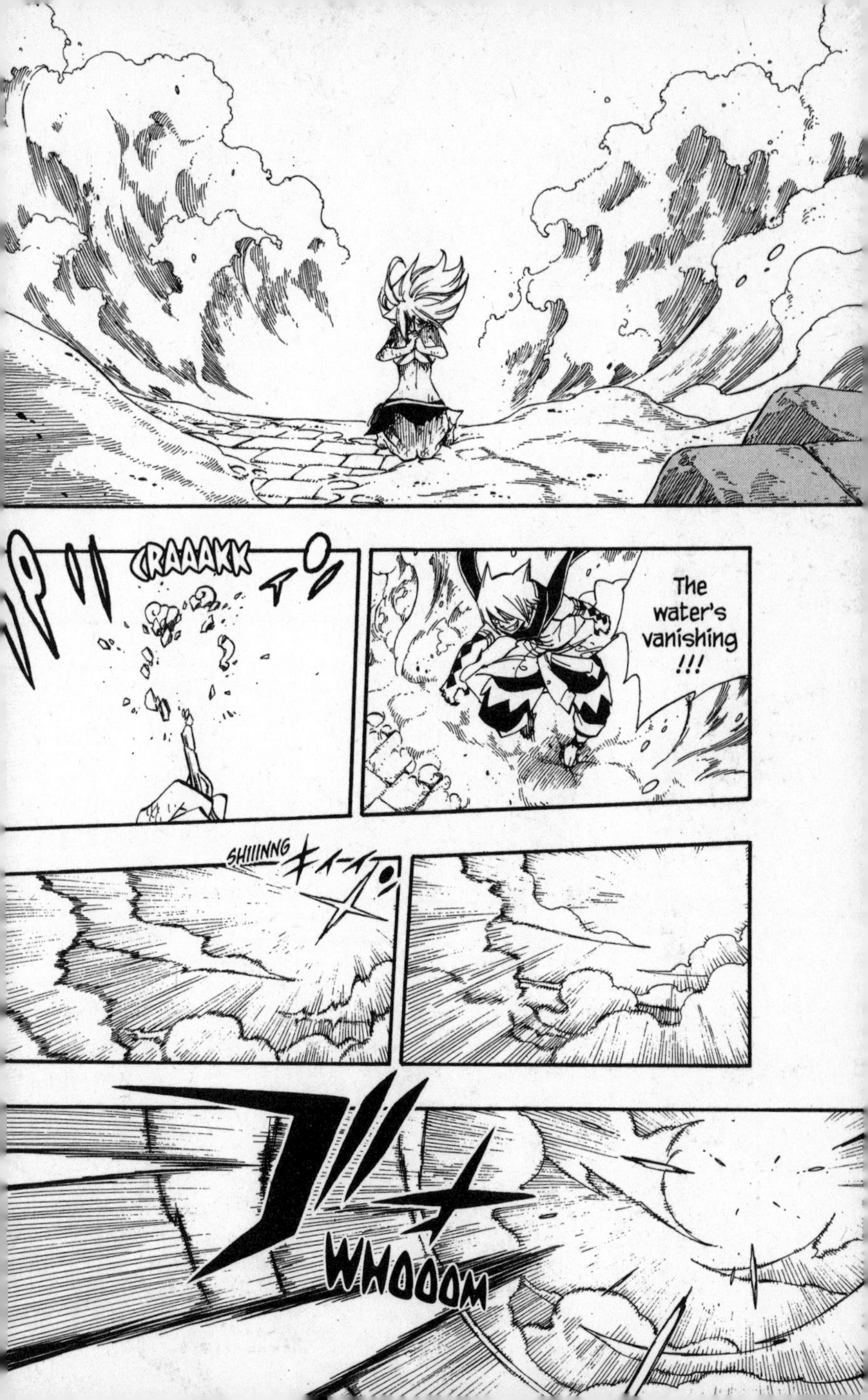
The water's vanishing !!!
CRAAAKK
SHIIINNG
WHOOOM

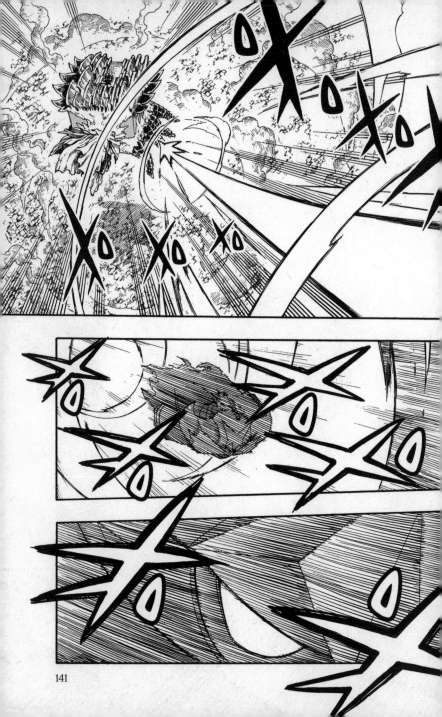

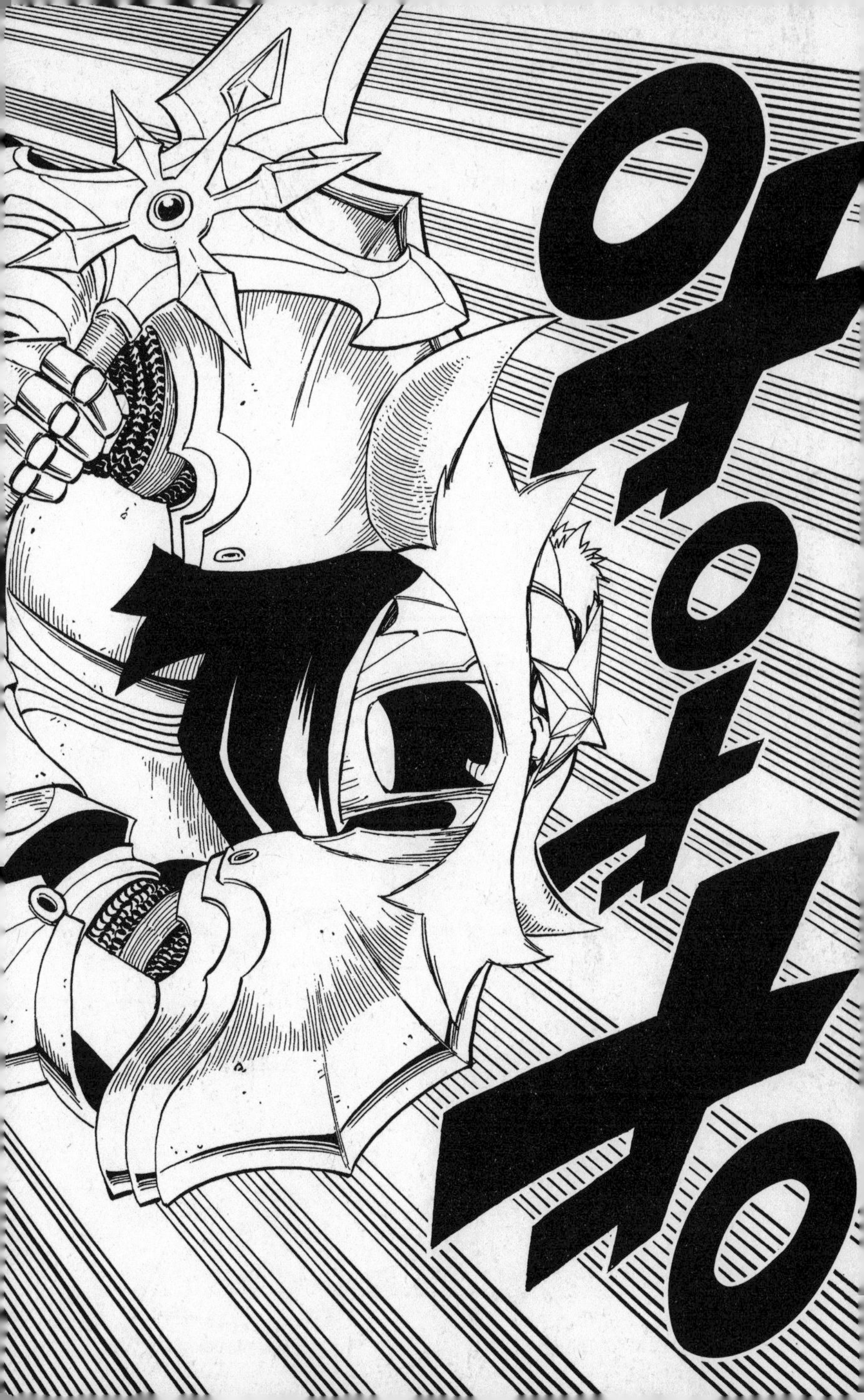

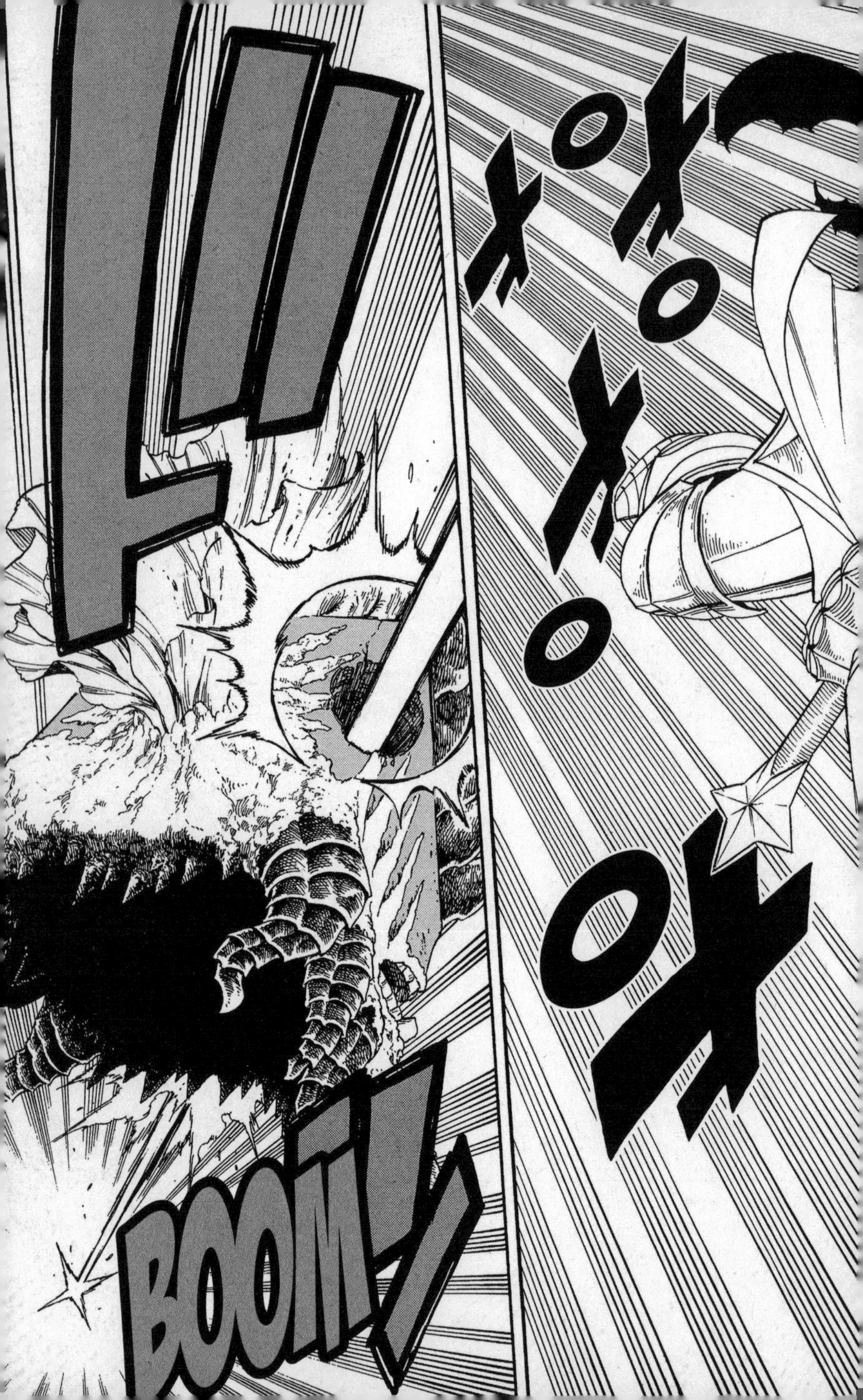
BOOM!!

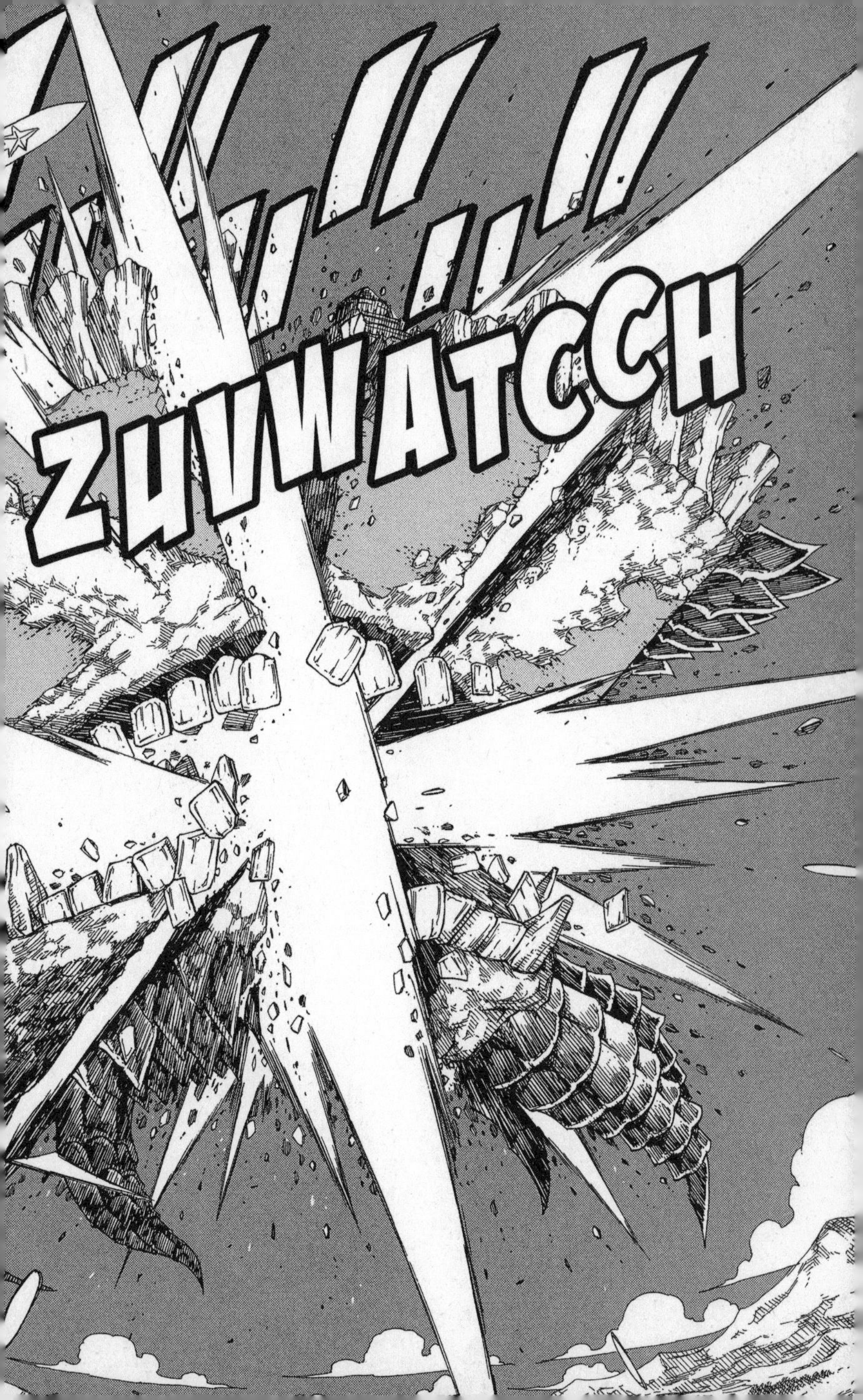
ZUVWATCCH

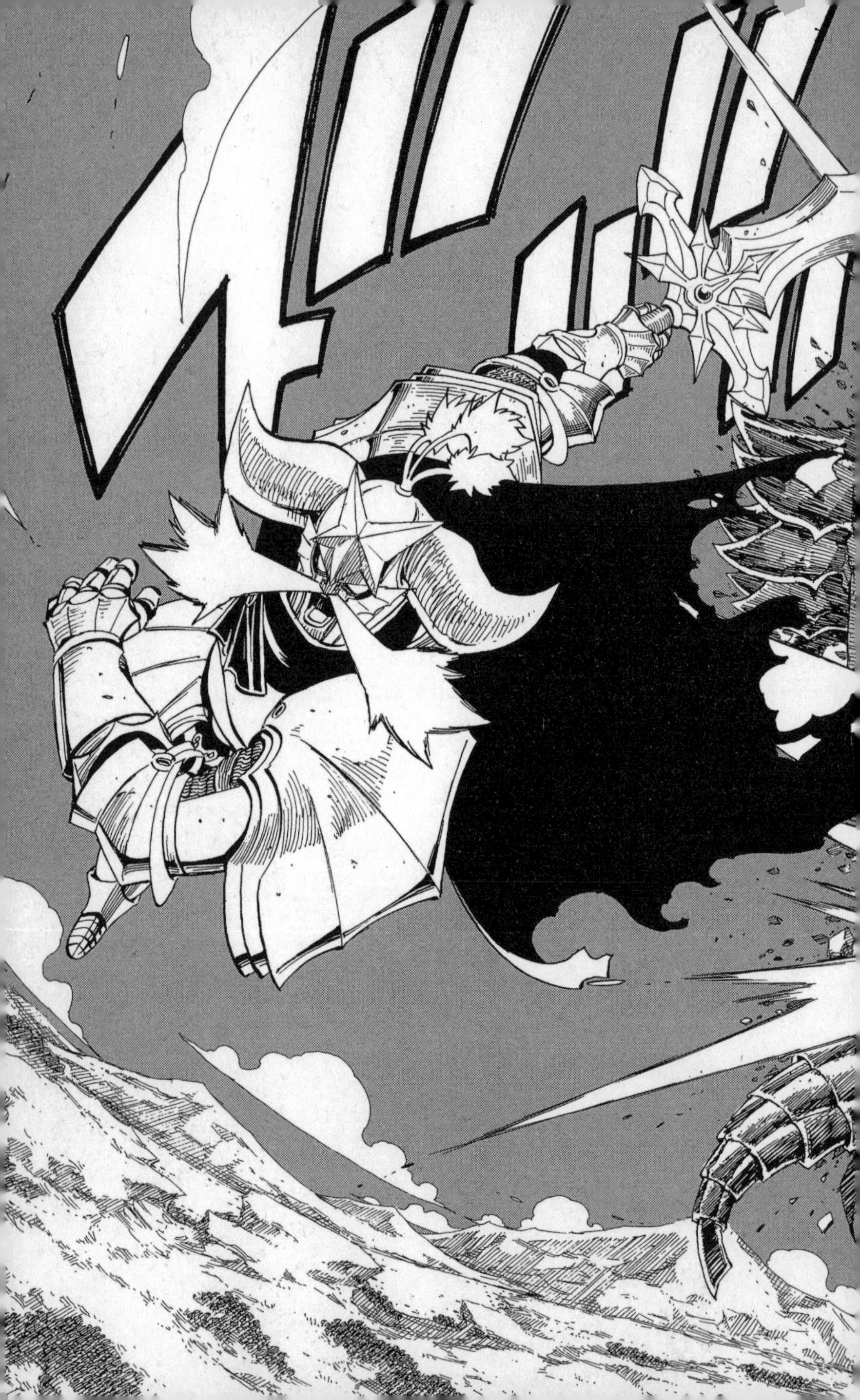

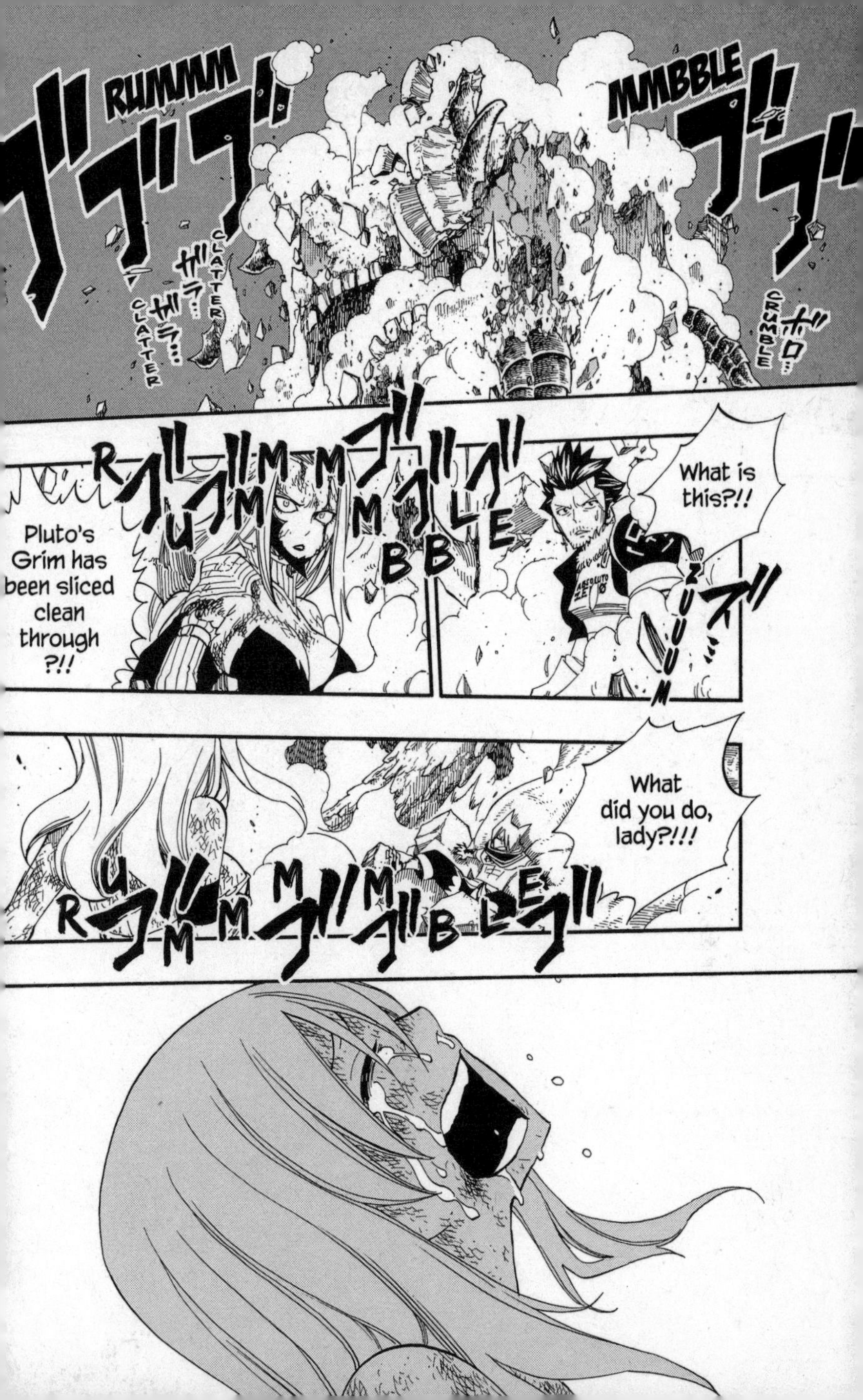
RUMMM
MMBBLE
CRUMBLE
CLATTER
CLATTER
What is this?!!
ZUUUUM
Pluto's Grim has been sliced clean through?!!
RUMMMMBBLE
What did you do, lady?!!!
RUMMMMBLE

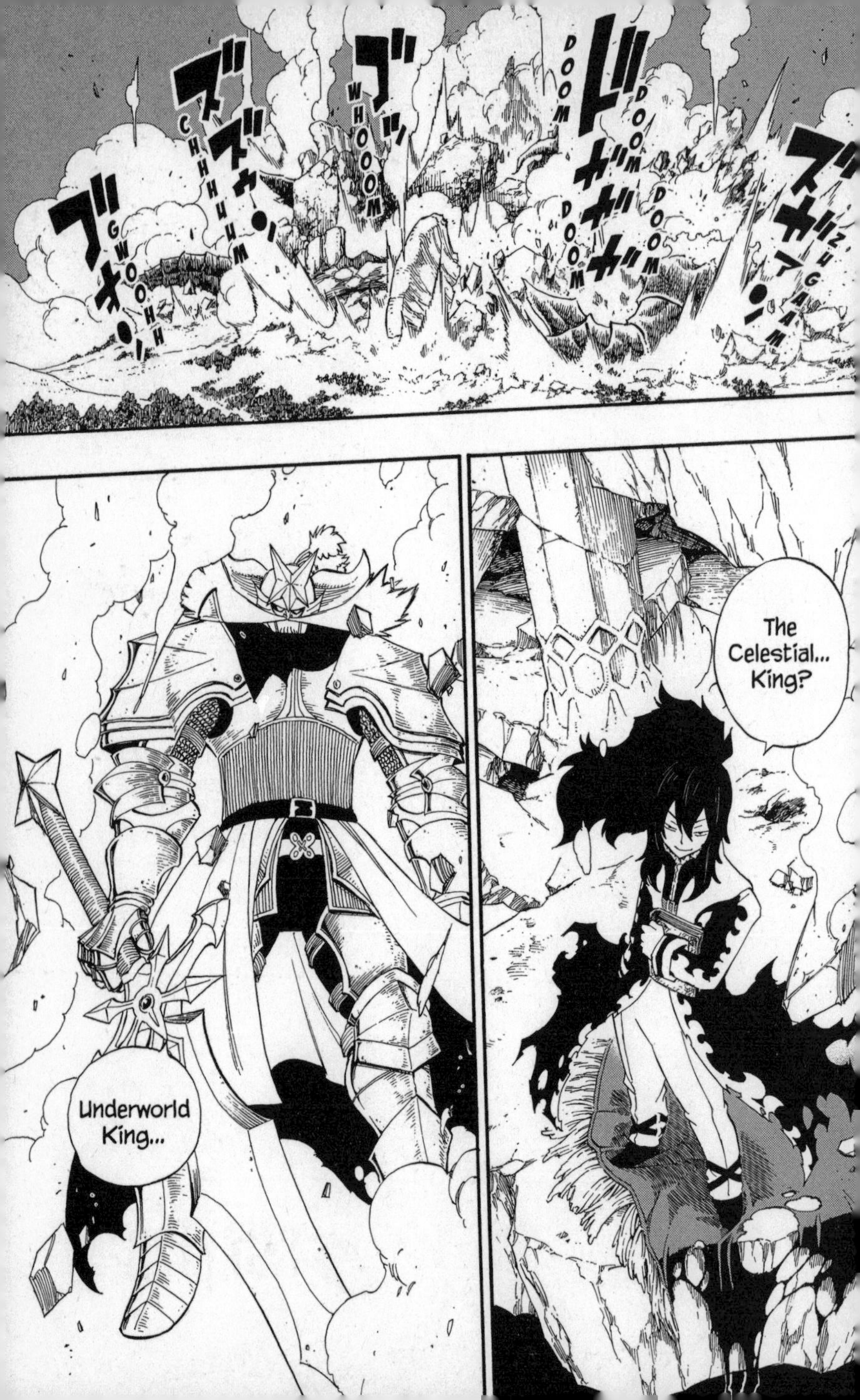

ZZGAAM
DOOM
DOOM DOOM
DOOM
WHOOOM
CHHHUUUM
GWOOOHH
The Celestial... King?
Underworld King...

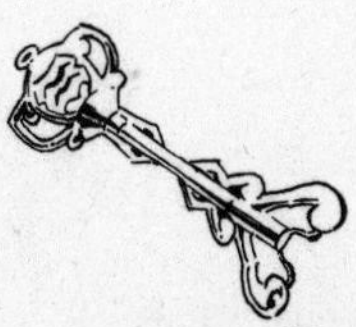

FAIRY TAIL

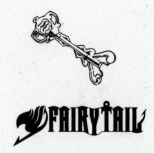

FAIRY TAIL
フェアリーテイル

Chapter 385: The Celestial King vs. the Underworld King

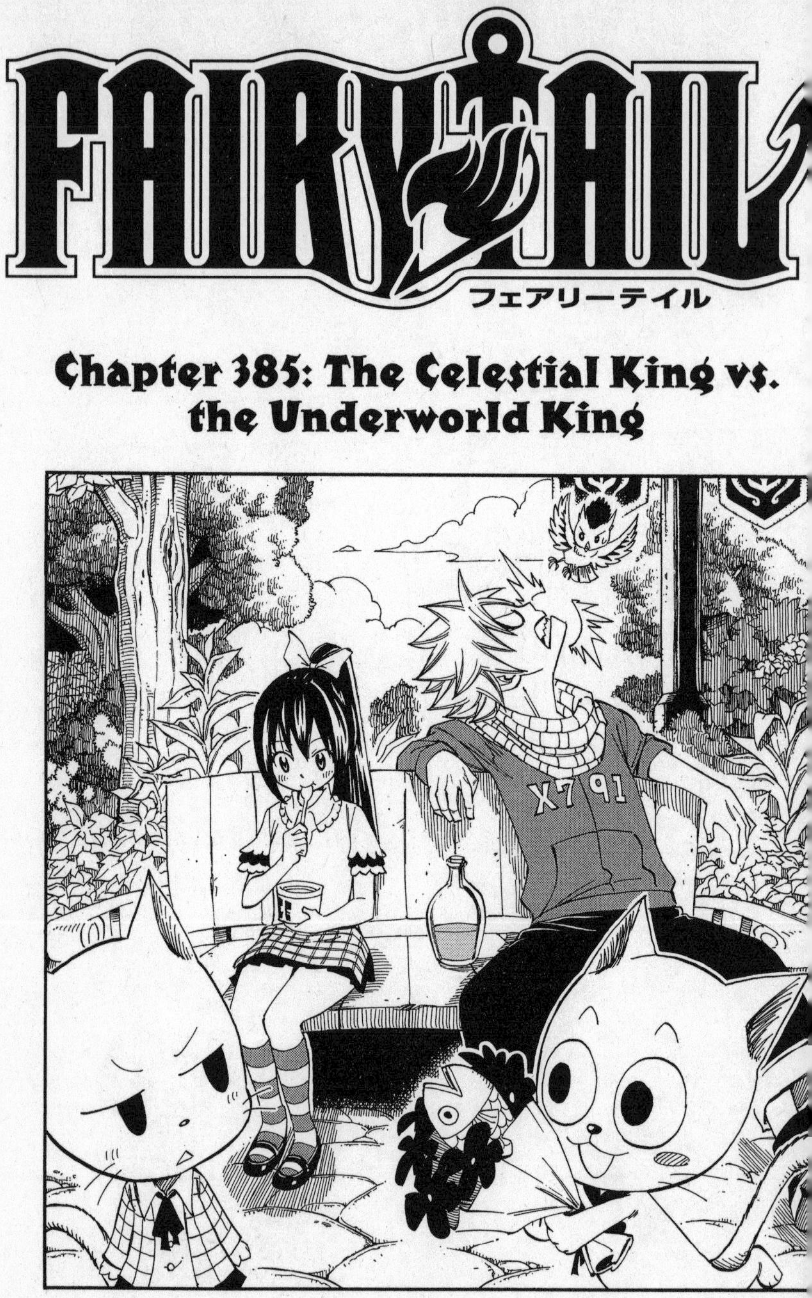
X7 91

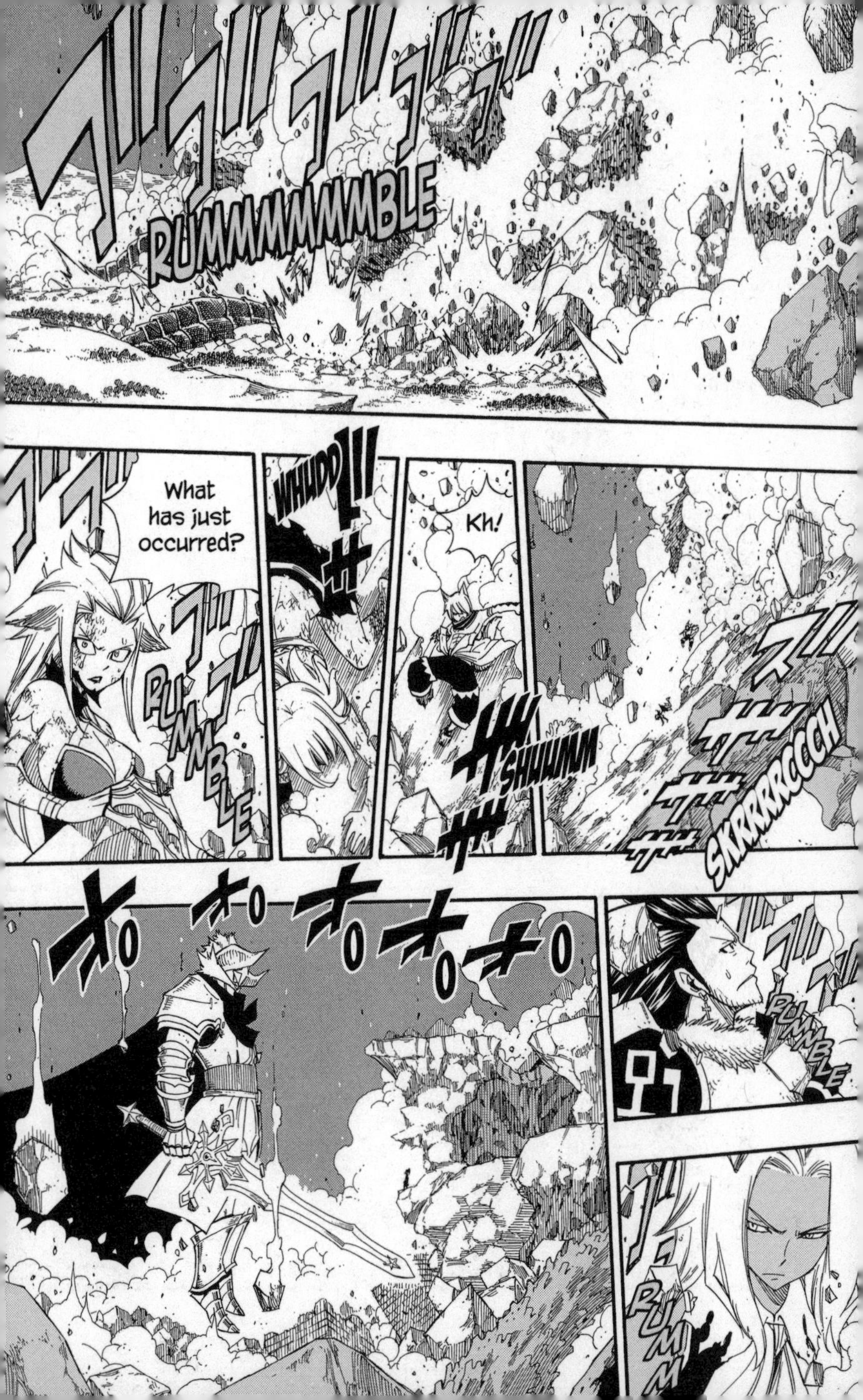
RUMMMMMMMBLE
SKRRRRCCCH
Kh!
SHHUMMM
WHUDD!!
What has just occurred?
RUMMBLE
RUMMBLE
RUMM

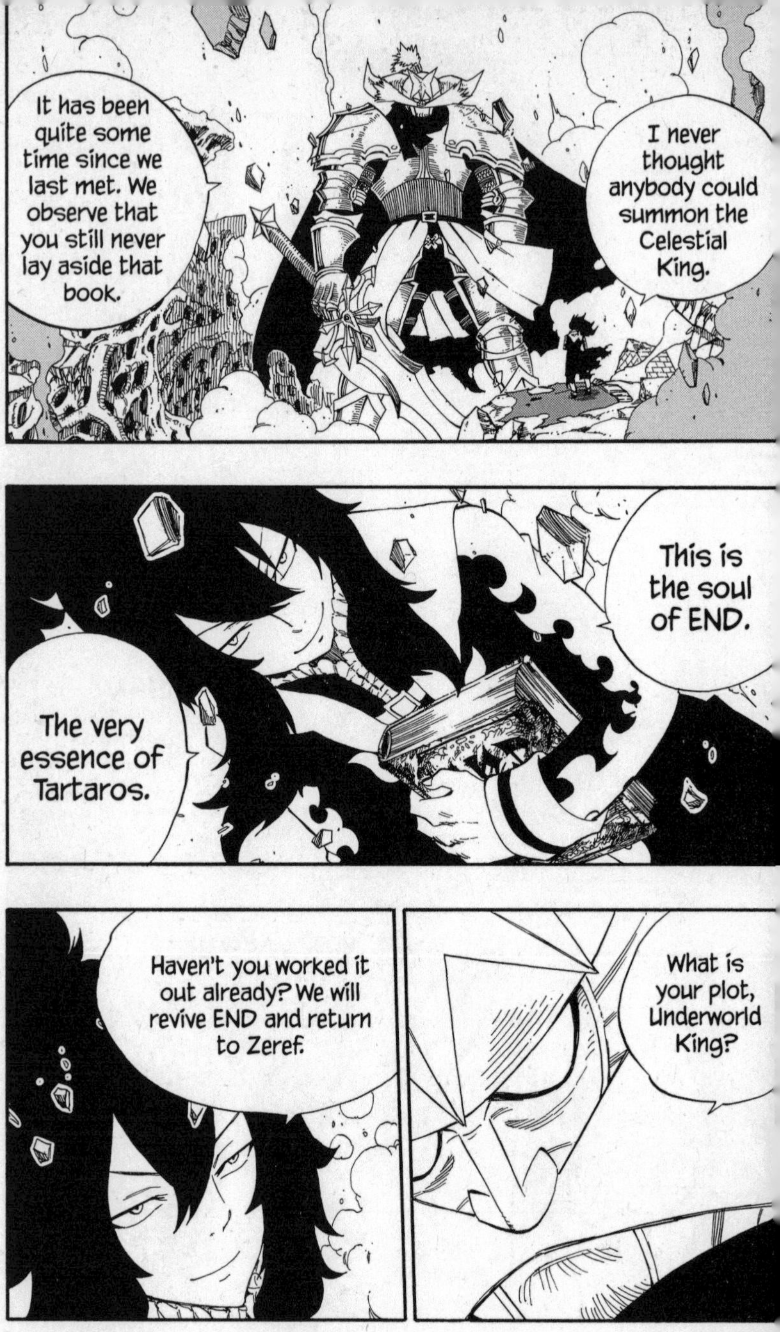
I never thought anybody could summon the Celestial King.
It has been quite some time since we last met. We observe that you still never lay aside that book.
This is the soul of END.
The very essence of Tartaros.
What is your plot, Underworld King?
Haven't you worked it out already? We will revive END and return to Zeref.

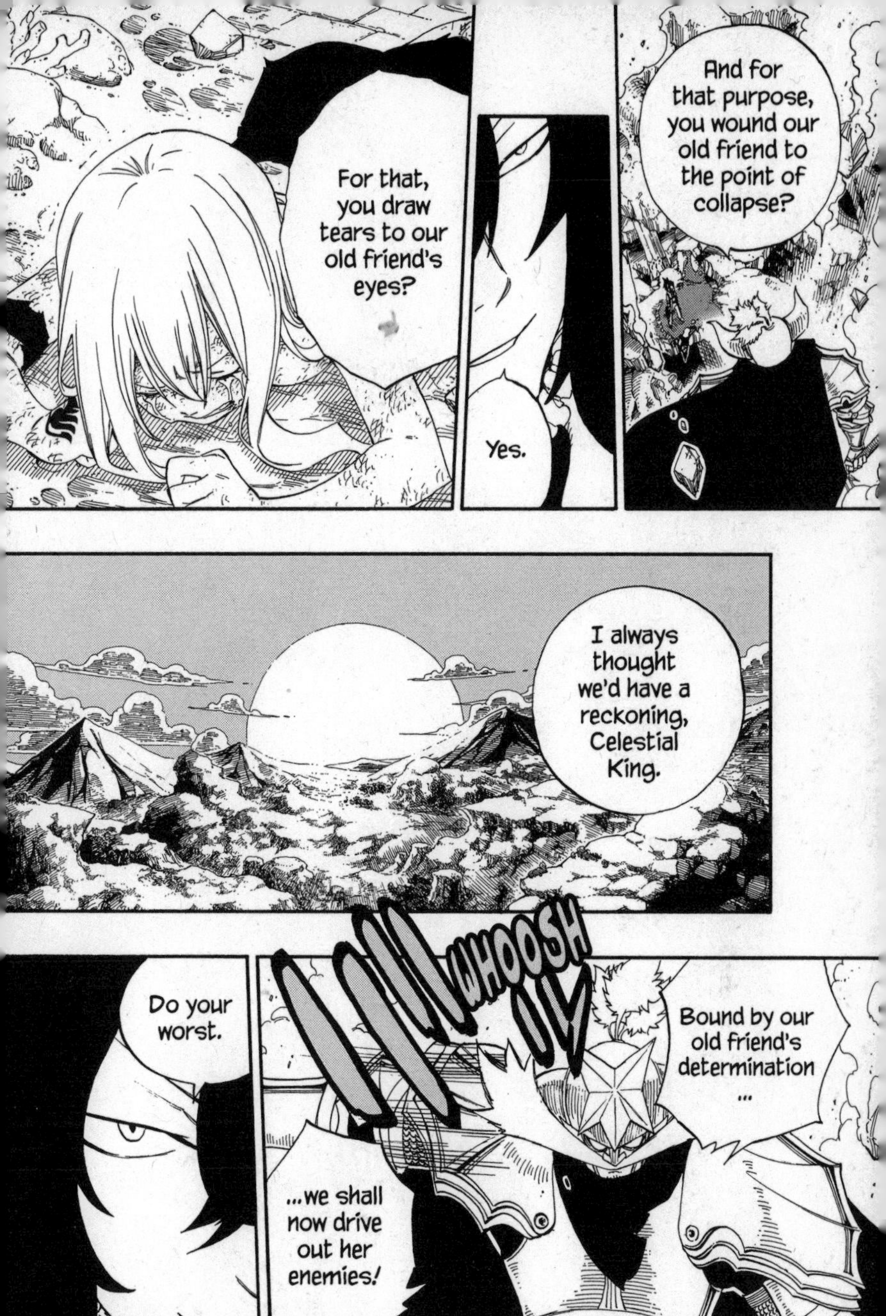
And for that purpose, you wound our old friend to the point of collapse?
Yes.
For that, you draw tears to our old friend's eyes?
I always thought we'd have a reckoning, Celestial King.
Bound by our old friend's determination ...
WHOOSH
...we shall now drive out her enemies!
Do your worst.

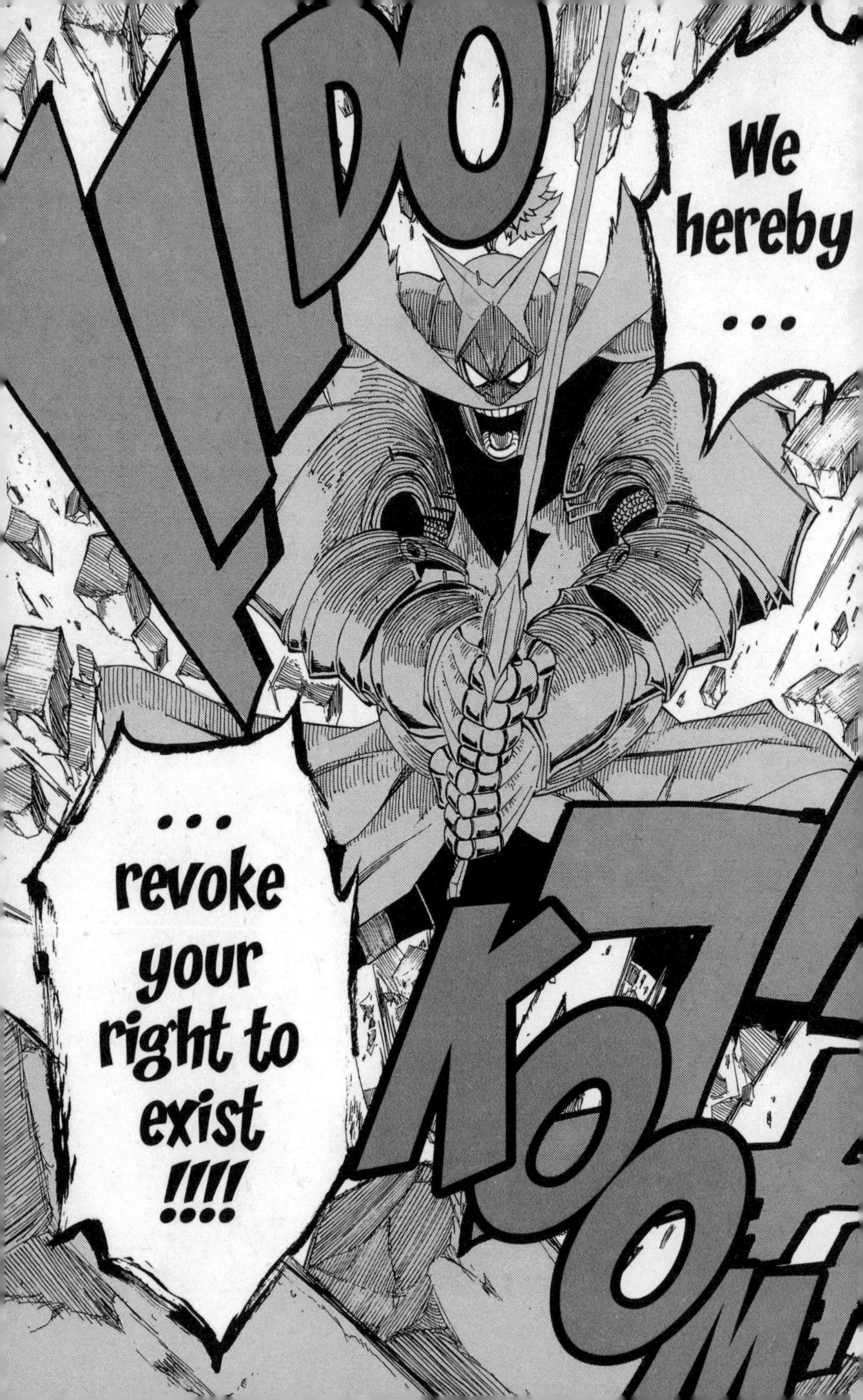
We hereby ...
... revoke your right to exist !!!!
DO
KOOM

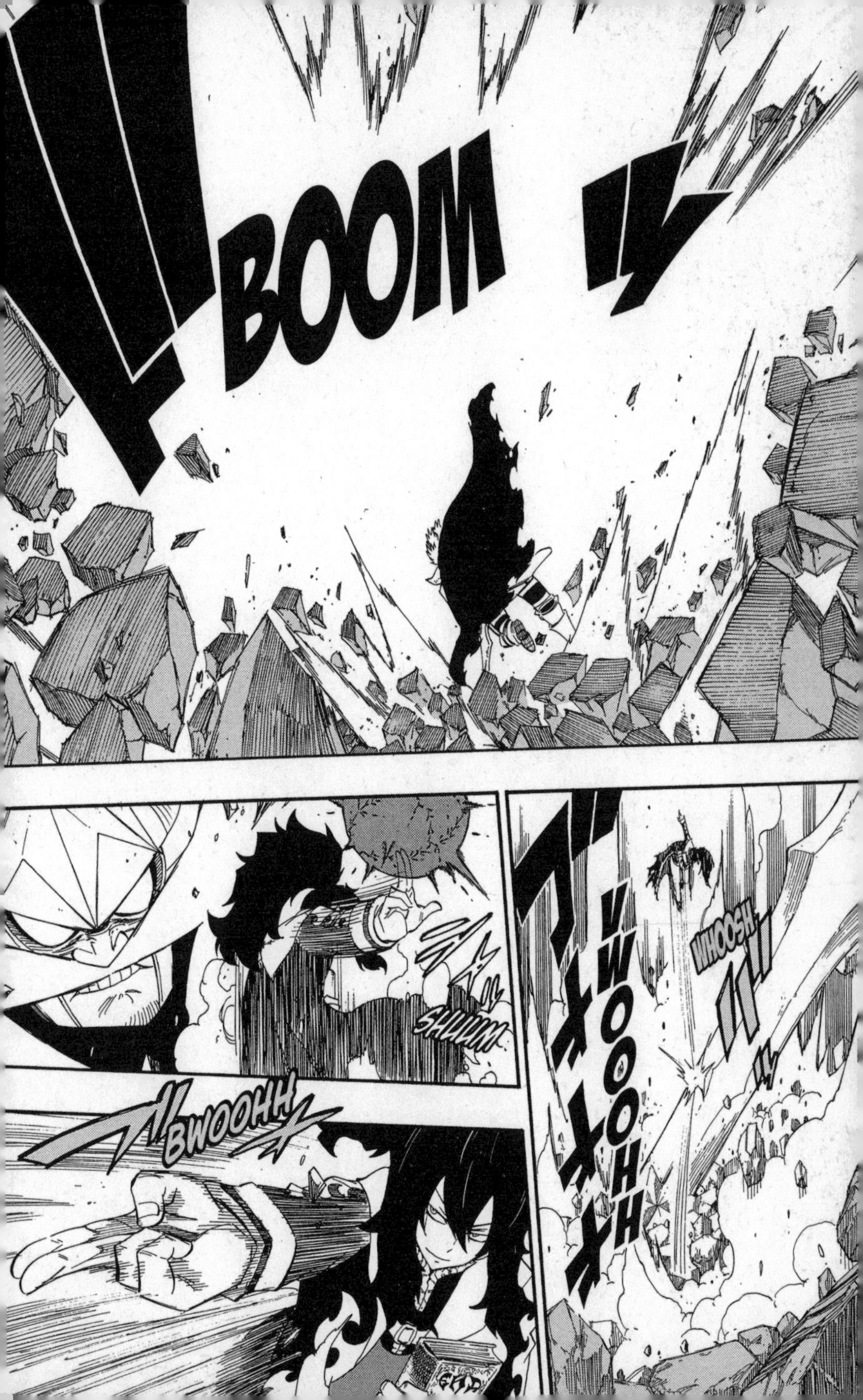
BOOM
WHOOSH
WOOOOHH
SHUUM
BWOOHH

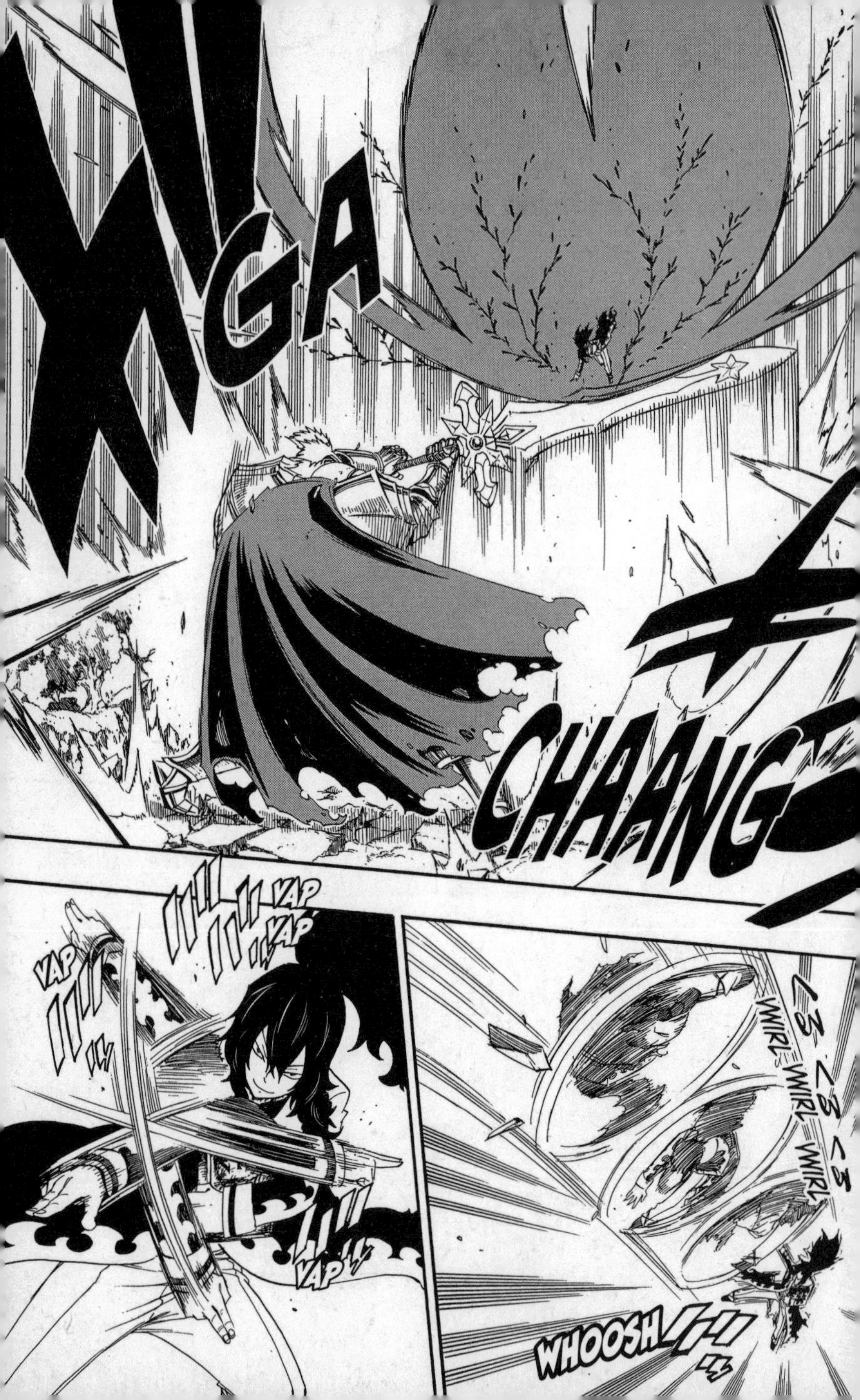
GA
CHANG
WHIRL WHIRL WHIRL
WHOOSH
VAP
VAP
VAP
VAP

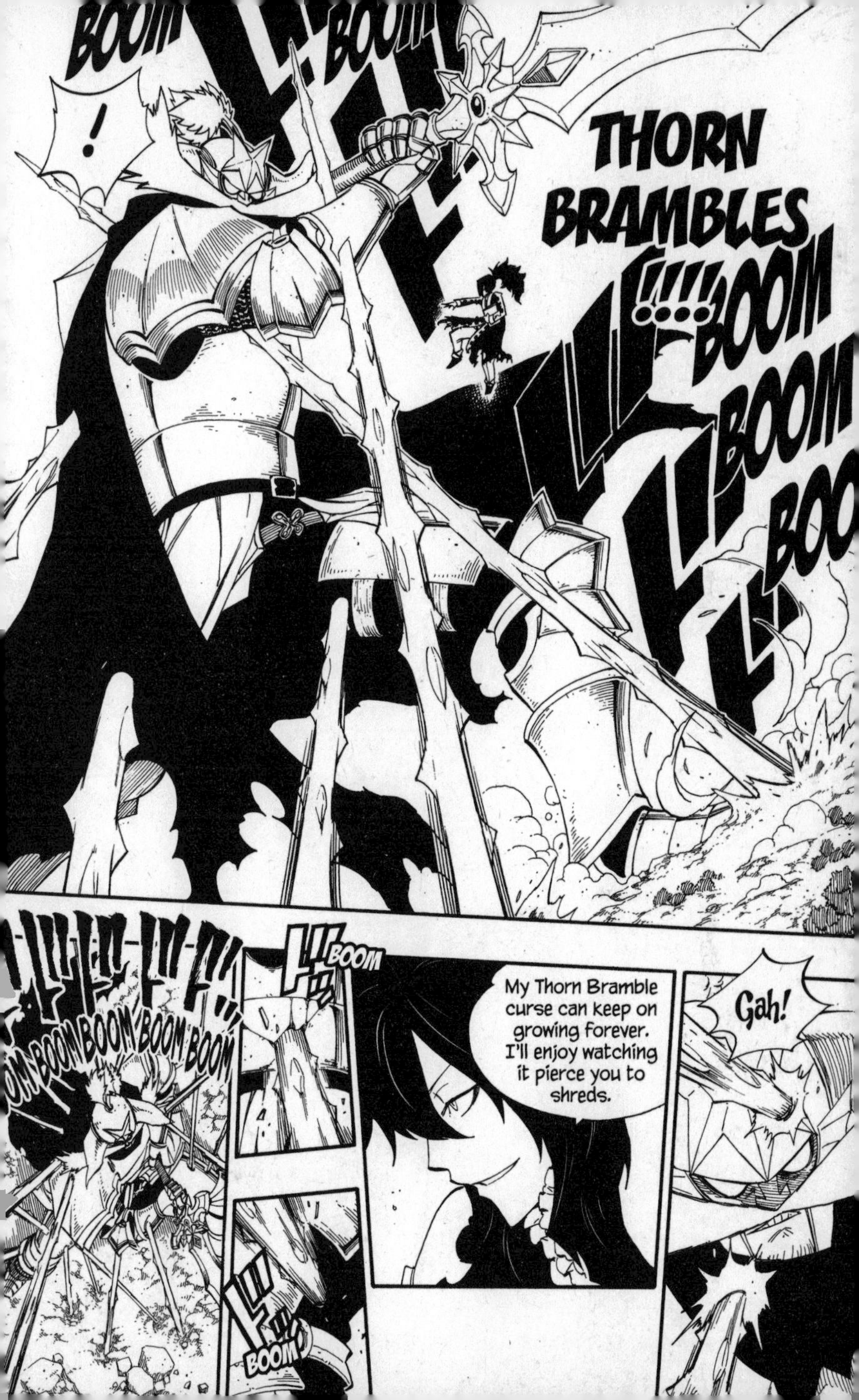

THORN BRAMBLES
BOOM
BOOM
BOOM
BOO
BOO
BOOM
BOOM
!
Gah!
My Thorn Bramble curse can keep on growing forever. I'll enjoy watching it pierce you to shreds.
BOOM
BOOM
OM BOOM BOOM BOOM BOOM

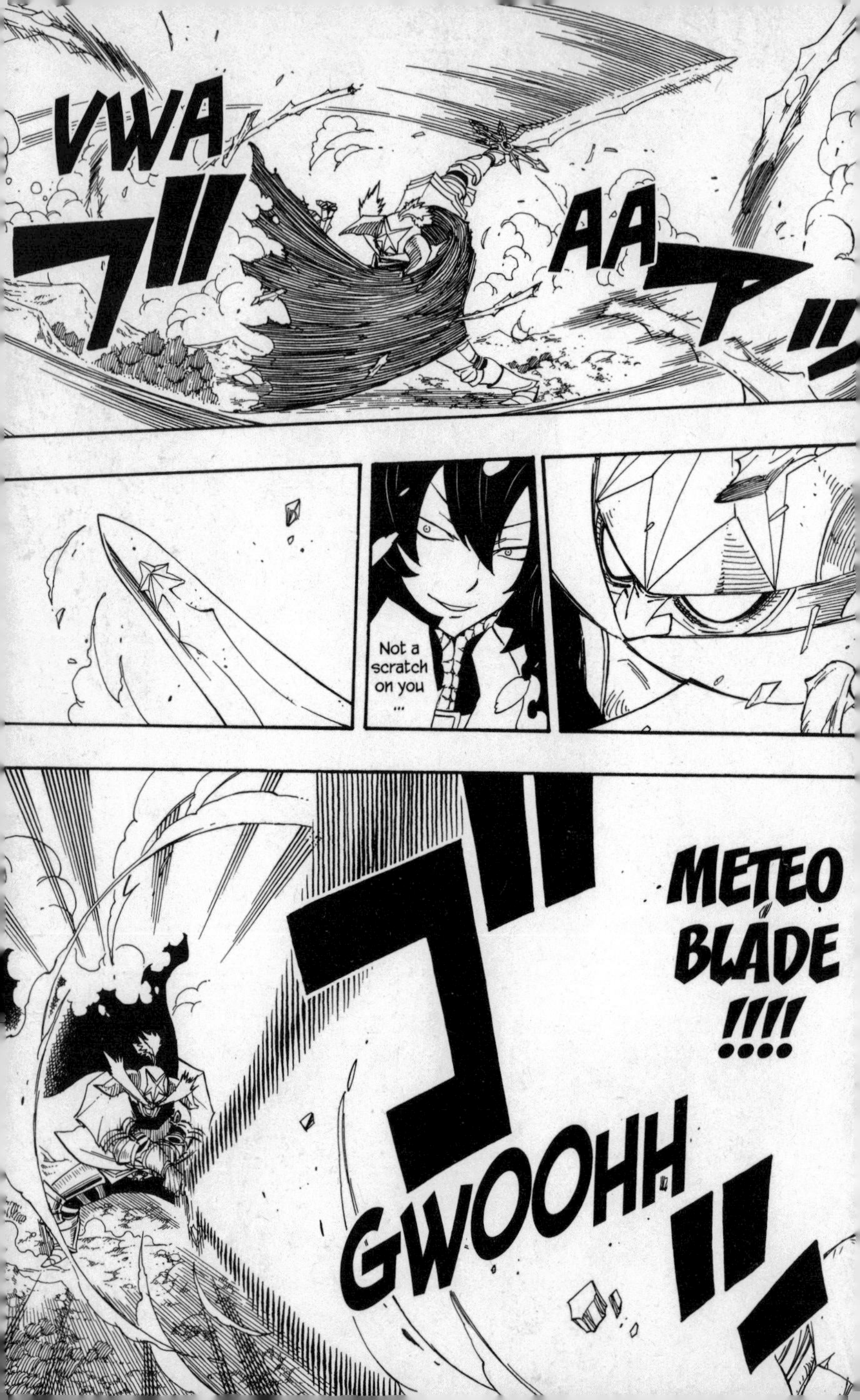
VWAAAP!!
Not a scratch on you ...
METEO BLADE!!!!
GWOOHH!!

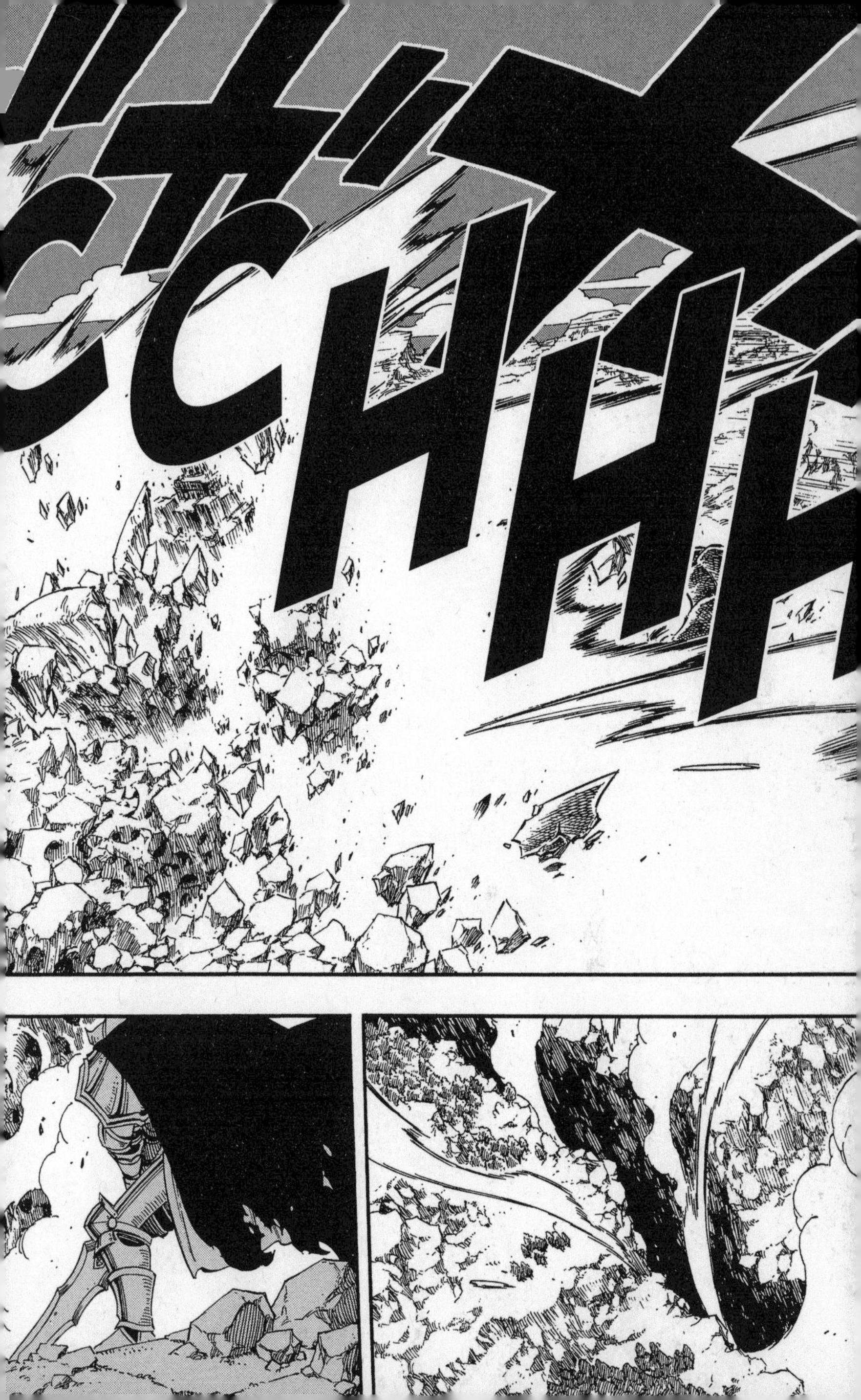
CHH

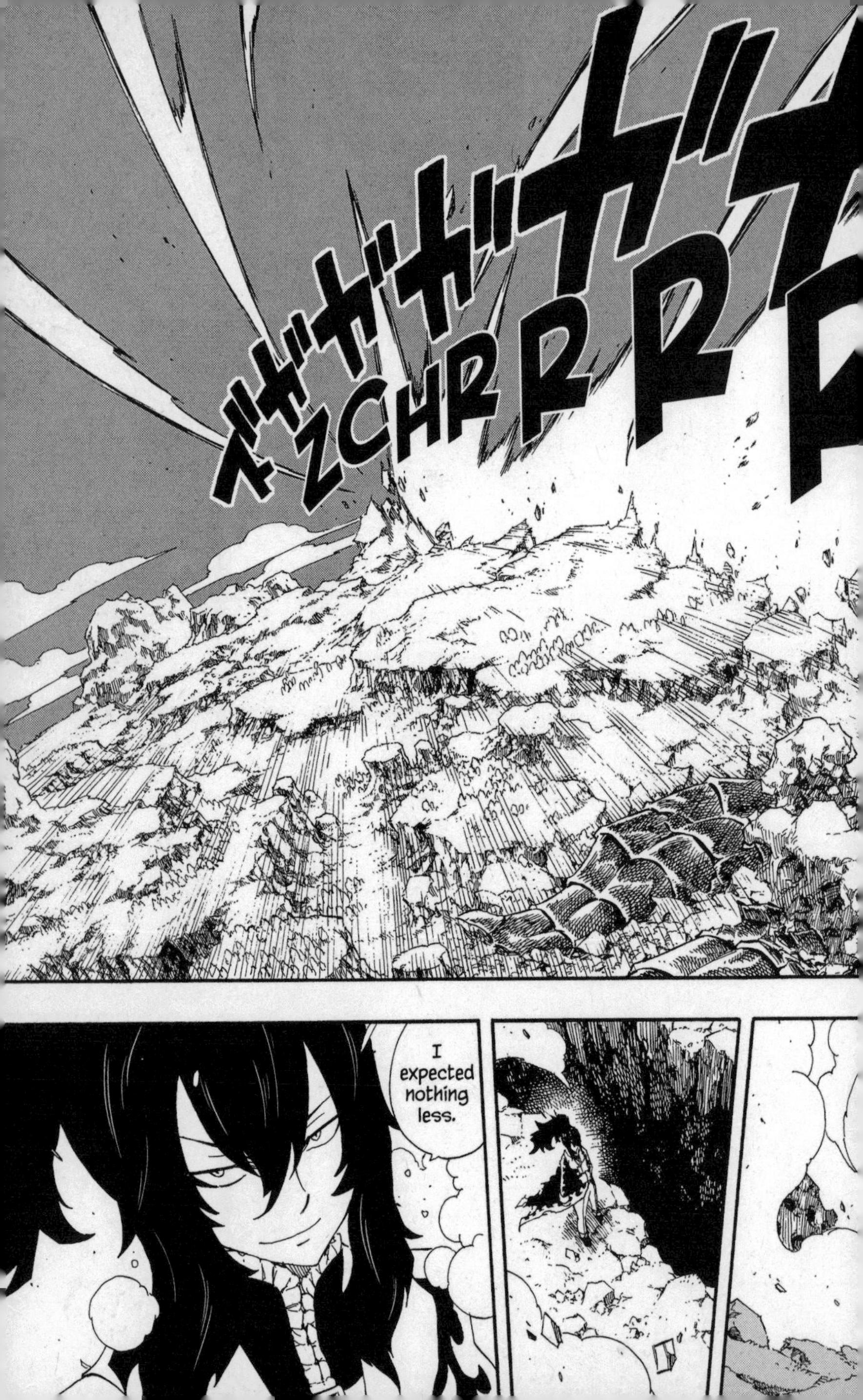

ZCHRRRR
I expected nothing less.

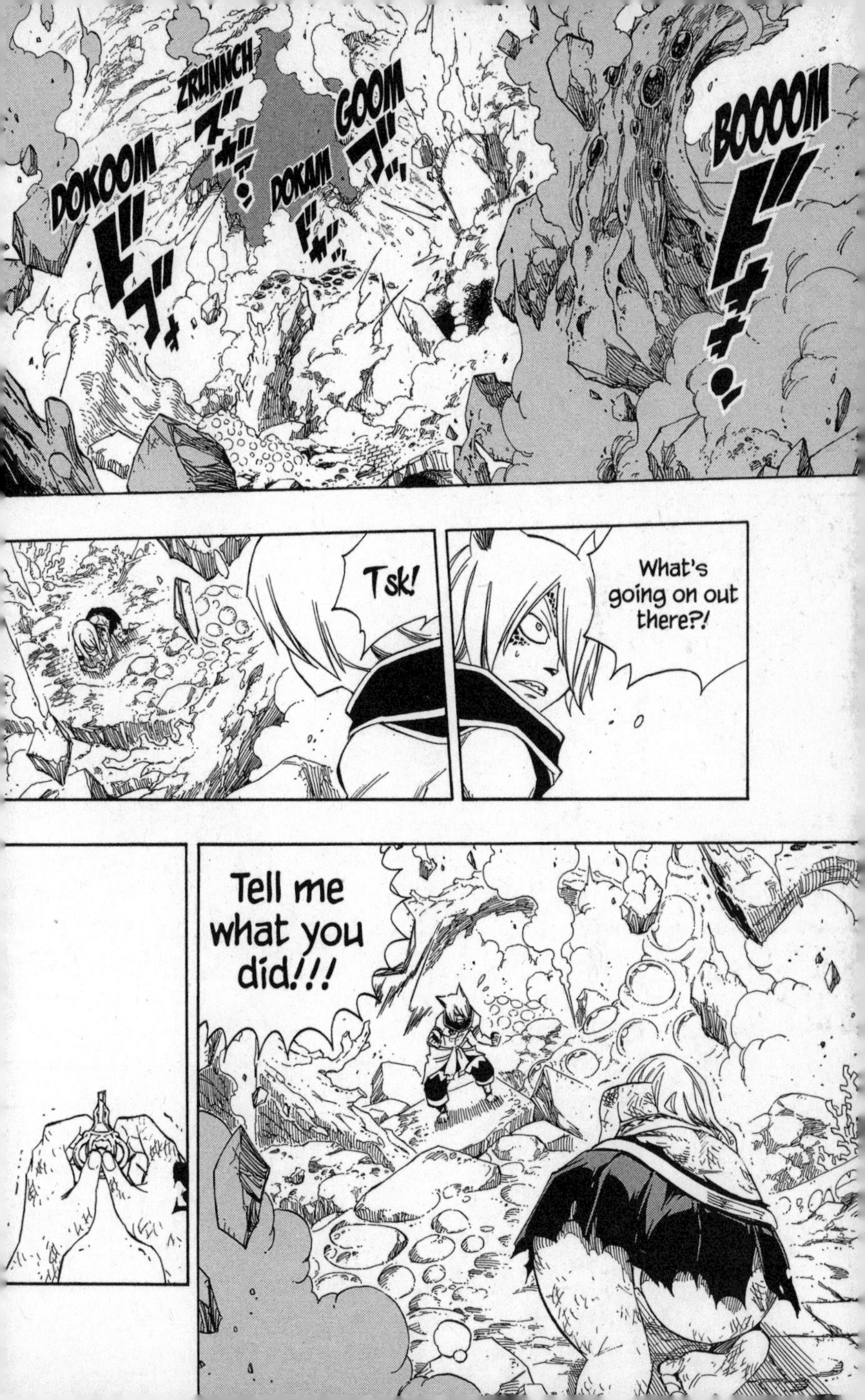
BOOOM
GOOM
DOKAM
ZRUNNCH
DOKOOM
What's going on out there?!
Tsk!
Tell me what you did!!!

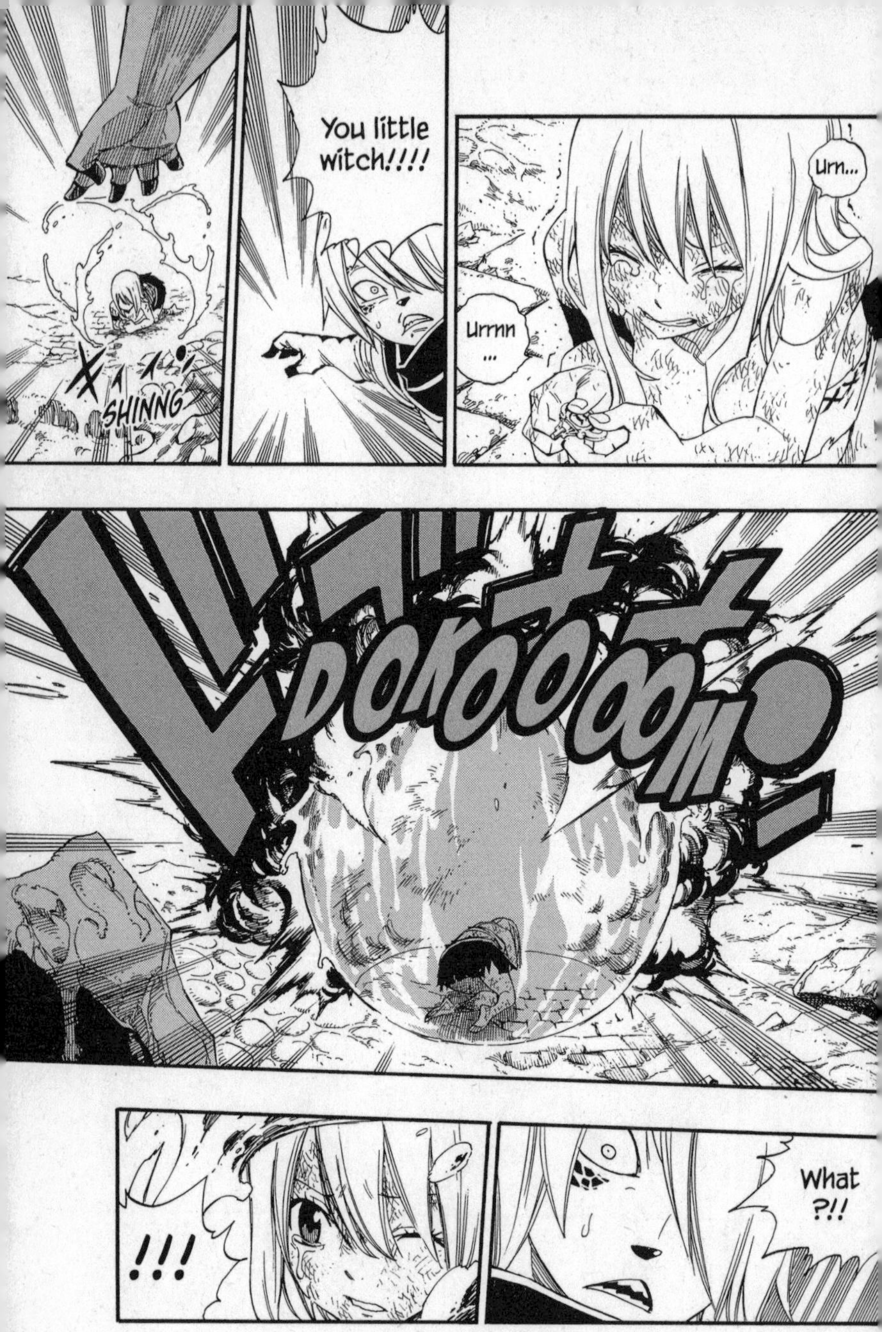
Urn...
Urrnn ...
You little witch!!!!
SHINNG
DOKOOOOM
What ?!!
!!!

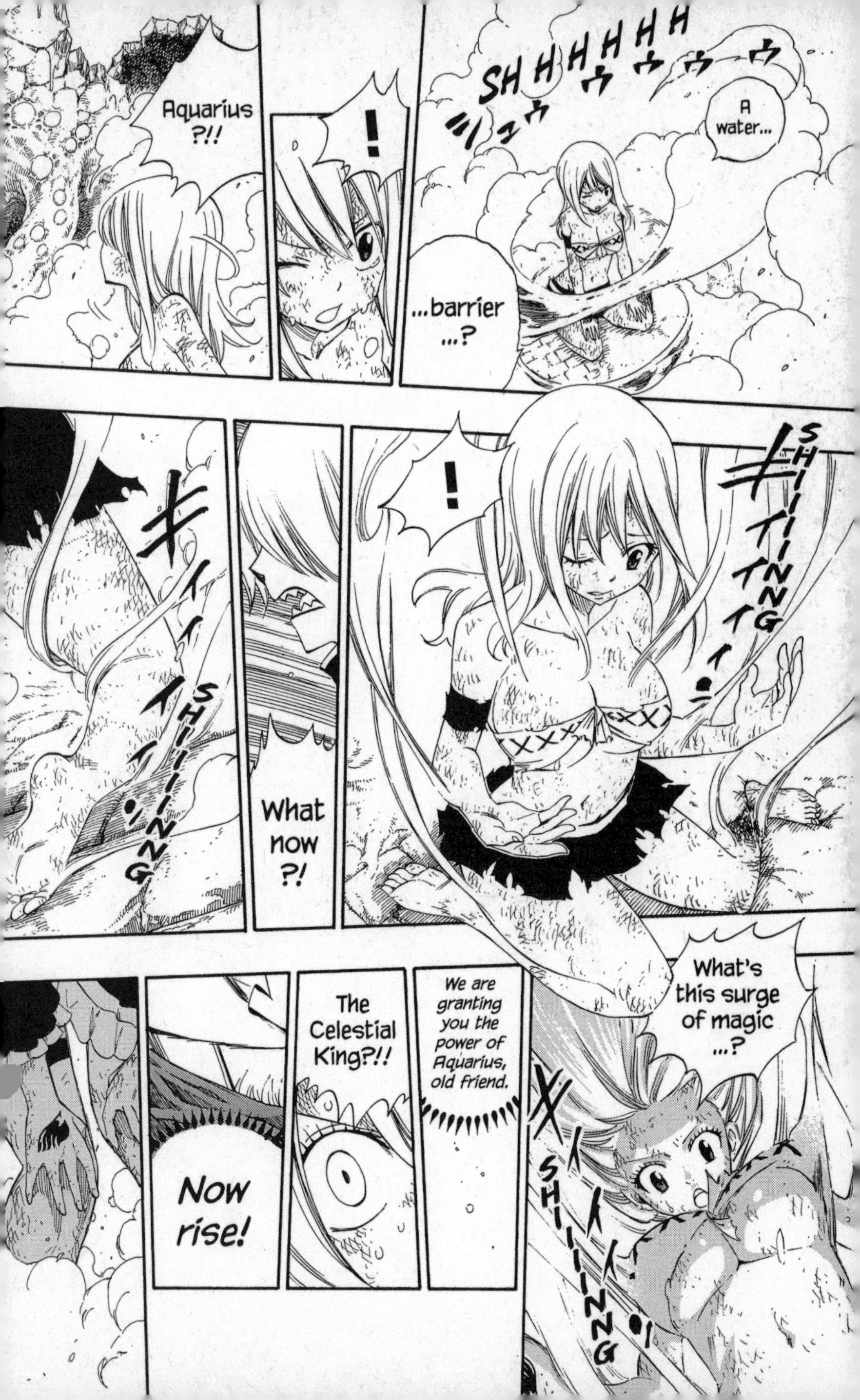
SHHHHHHH
A water...
...barrier ...?
!
Aquarius ?!!
SHIIIIINNG
!
What now ?!
SHIIIIINNG
What's this surge of magic ...?
SHIIIIINNG
We are granting you the power of Aquarius, old friend.
The Celestial King?!!
Now rise!

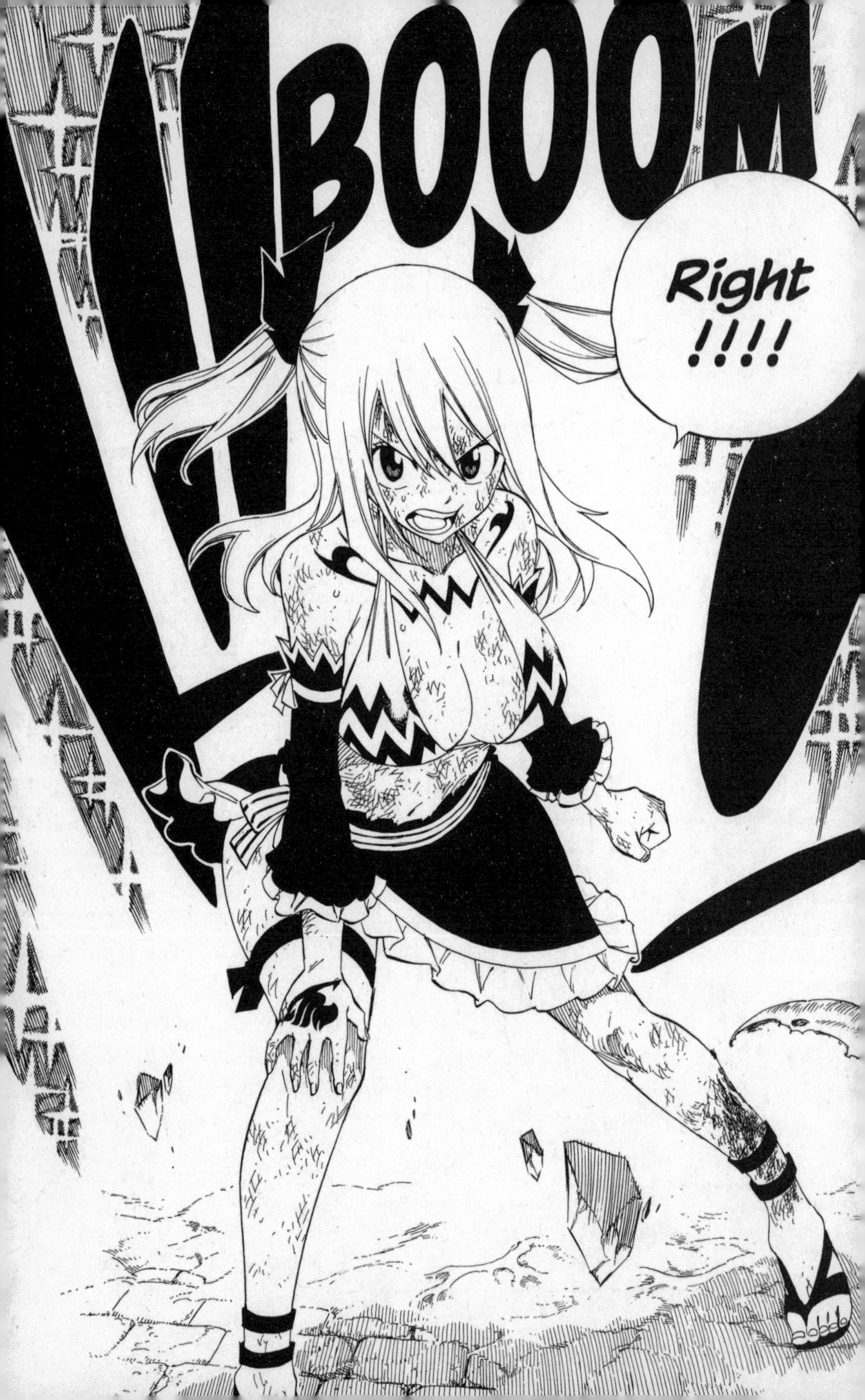
BOOOM
Right !!!!

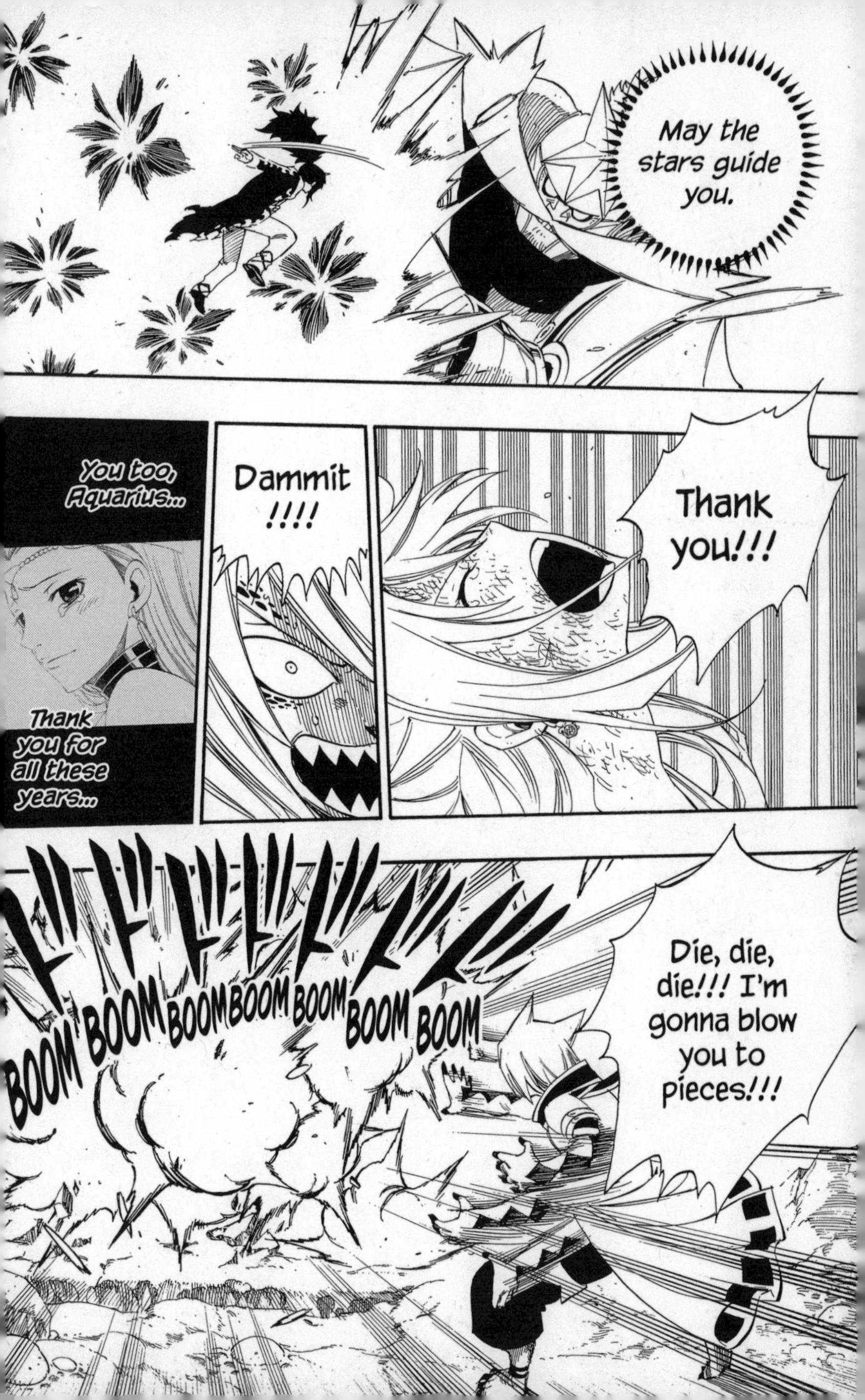
May the stars guide you.
Thank you!!!
Dammit !!!!
You too, Aquarius...
Thank you for all these years...
Die, die, die!!! I'm gonna blow you to pieces!!!
BOOM BOOM BOOM BOOM BOOM BOOM BOOM

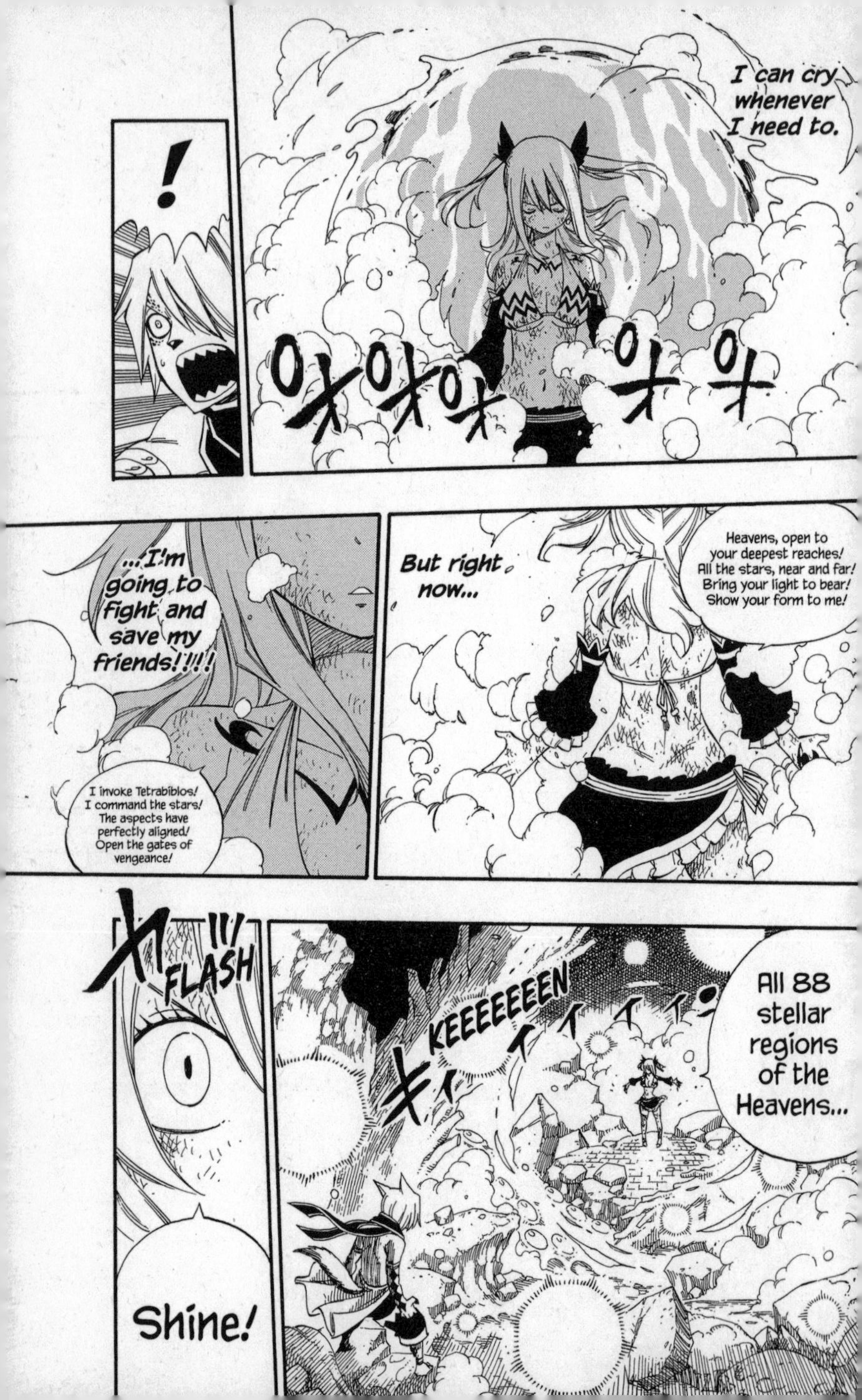
I can cry whenever I need to.
!
Heavens, open to your deepest reaches! All the stars, near and far! Bring your light to bear! Show your form to me!
But right now...
...I'm going to fight and save my friends!!!!
I invoke Tetrabiblos! I command the stars! The aspects have perfectly aligned! Open the gates of vengeance!
All 88 stellar regions of the Heavens...
KEEEEEEEN
FLASH
Shine!

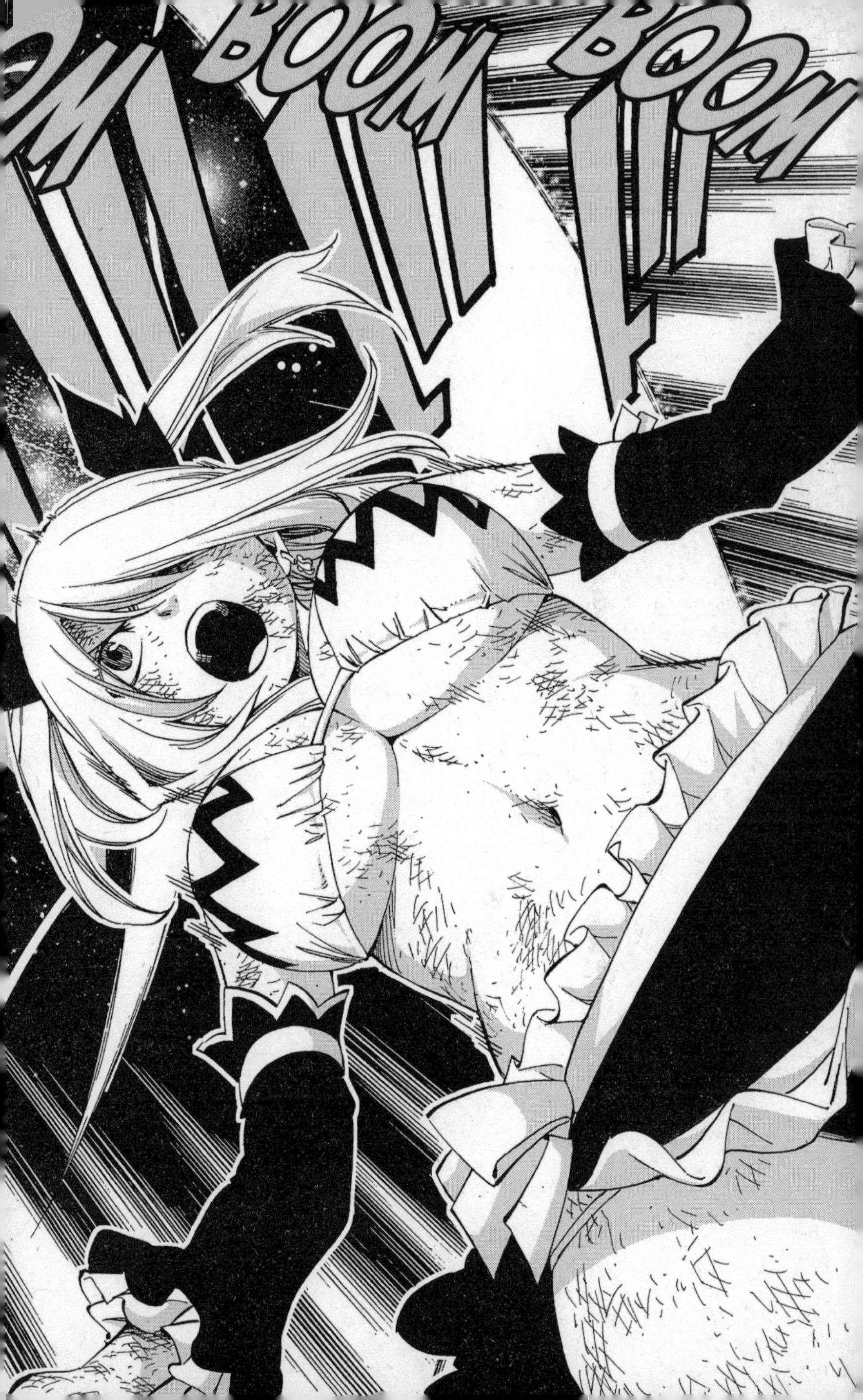
BOOM
BOOM

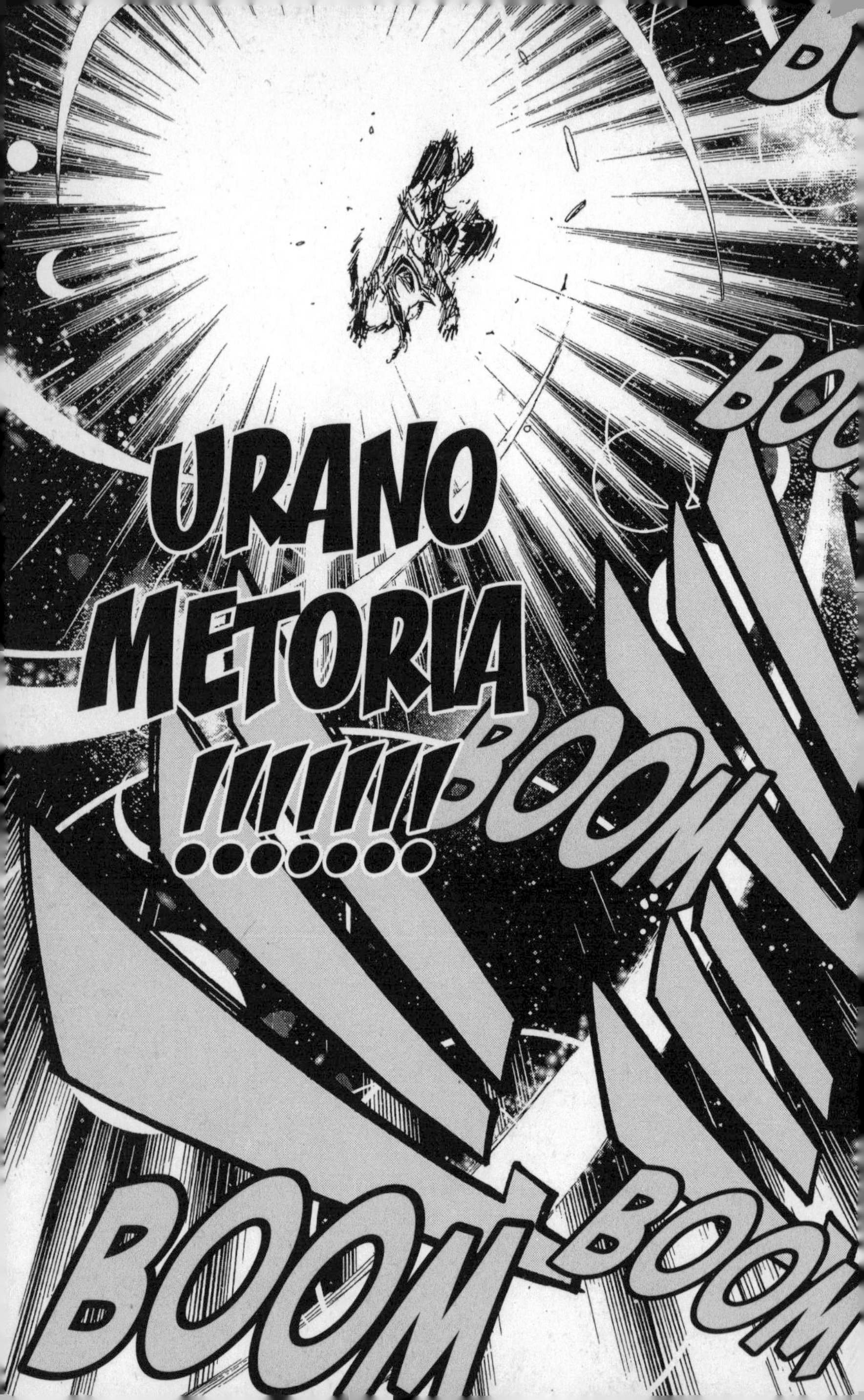
URANO METORIA!!!!!!!
....
BOOM
BOOM
BOOM
BOOM

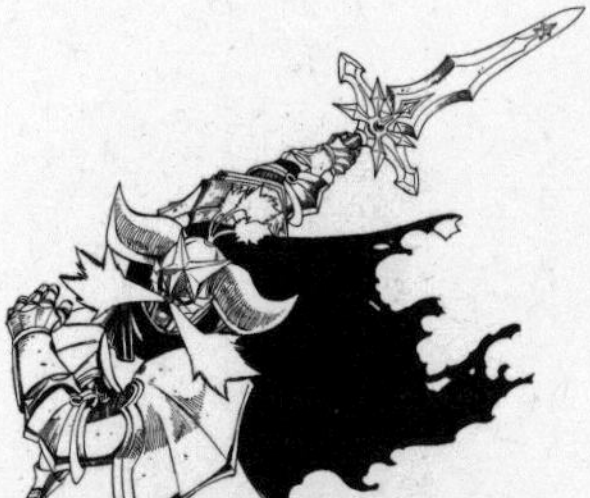

FAIRY TAIL

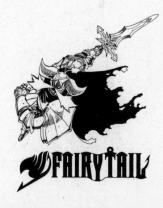

FAIRY TAIL
フェアリーテイル

Chapter 386: Galaxia Blade

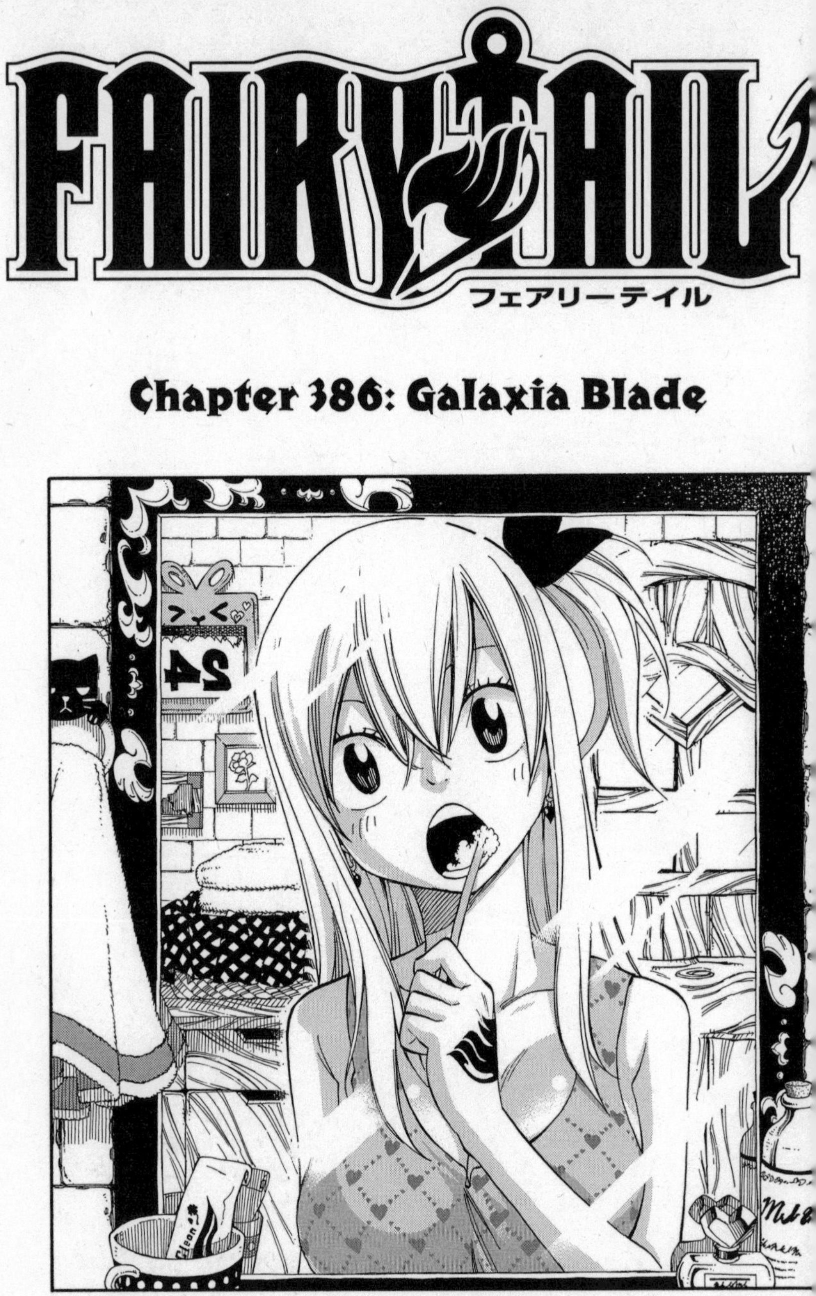
24

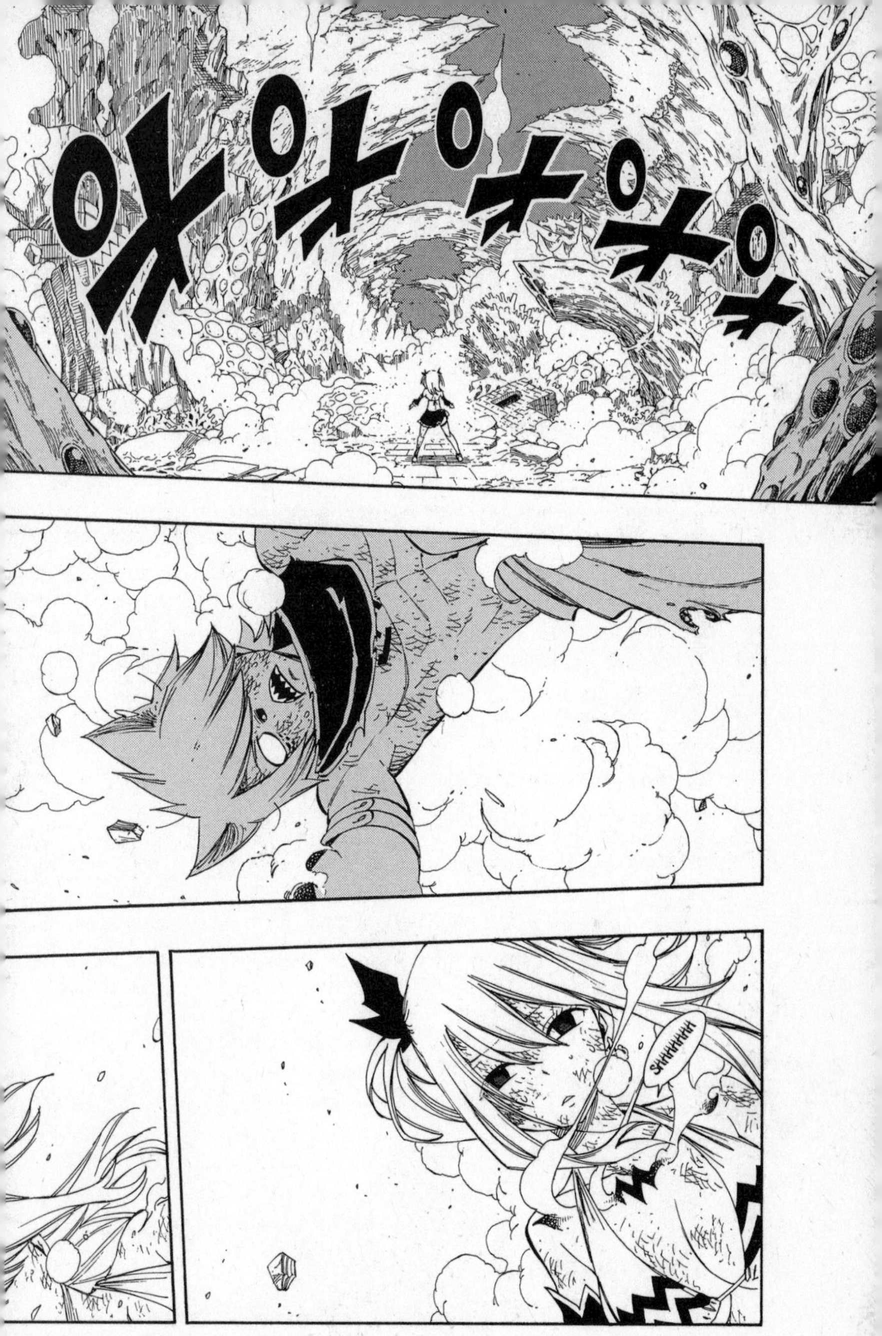
SHHHHHHH

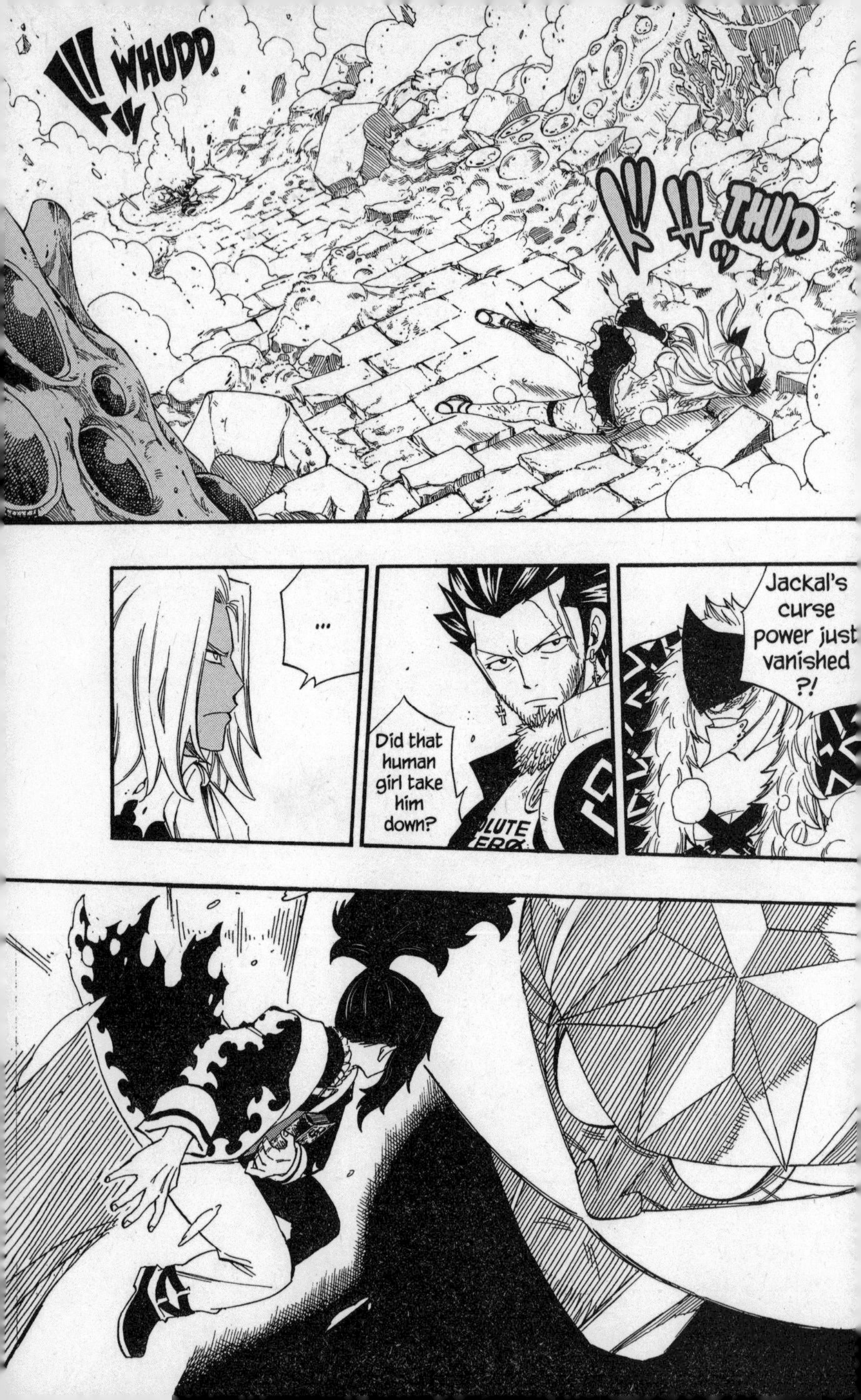
WHUDD
THUD
Jackal's curse power just vanished ?!
Did that human girl take him down?
...

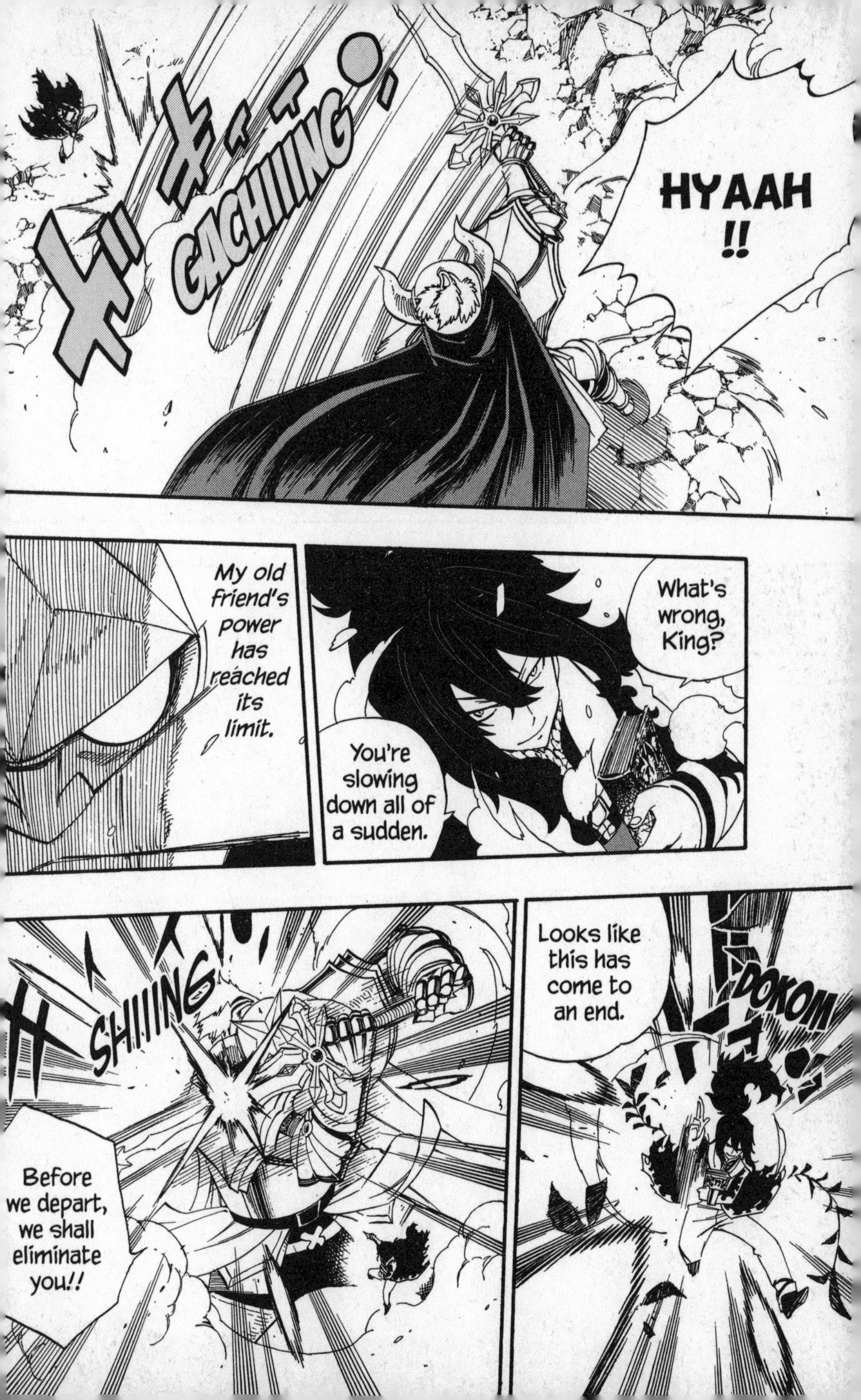
HYAAH!!
GACHIIING
What's wrong, King?
You're slowing down all of a sudden.
My old friend's power has reached its limit.
Looks like this has come to an end.
DOKOM
SHIIING
Before we depart, we shall eliminate you!!

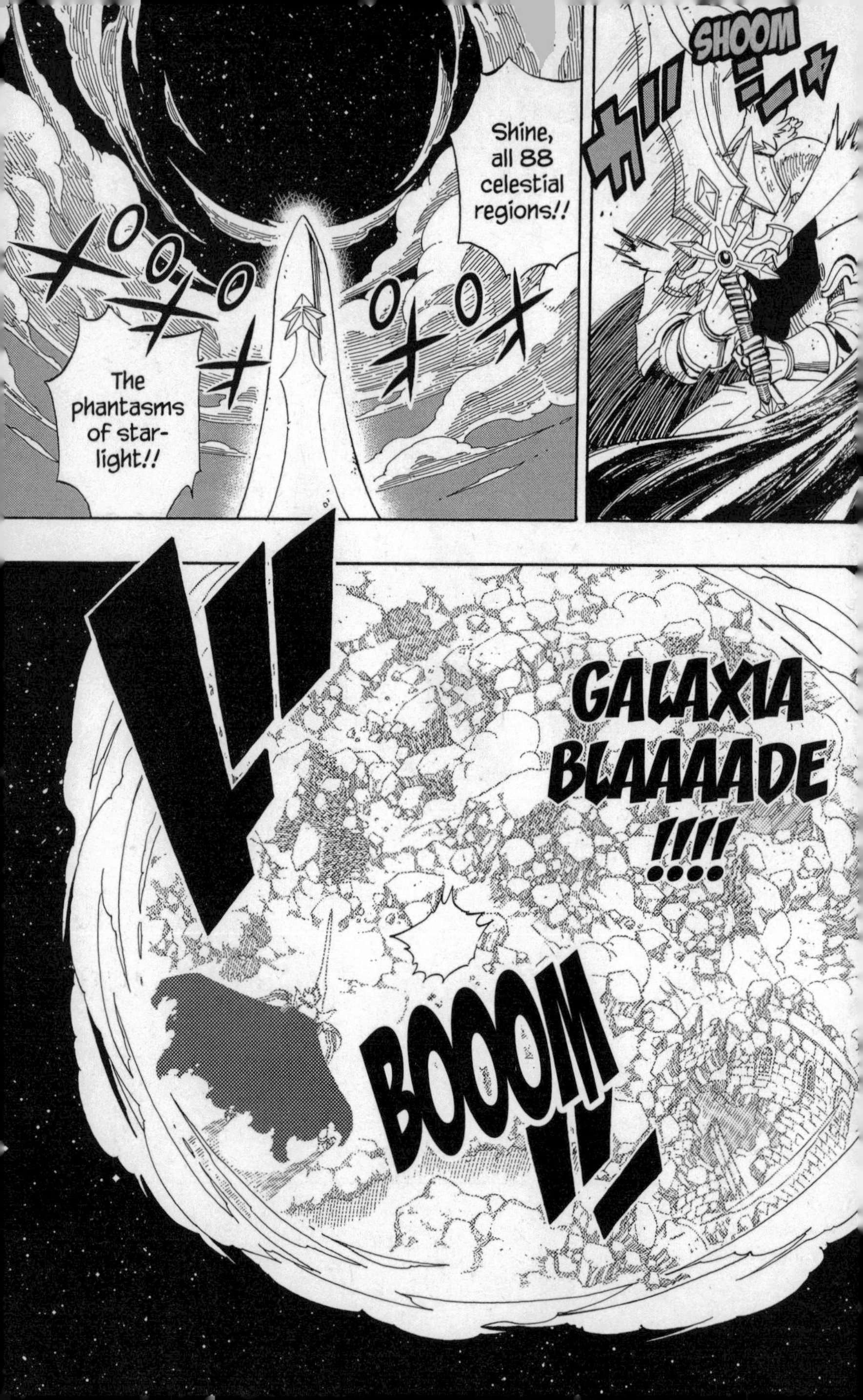

SHOOM
Shine, all 88 celestial regions!!
The phantasms of star-light!!
GALAXIA BLAAAADE!!!!
BOOOM

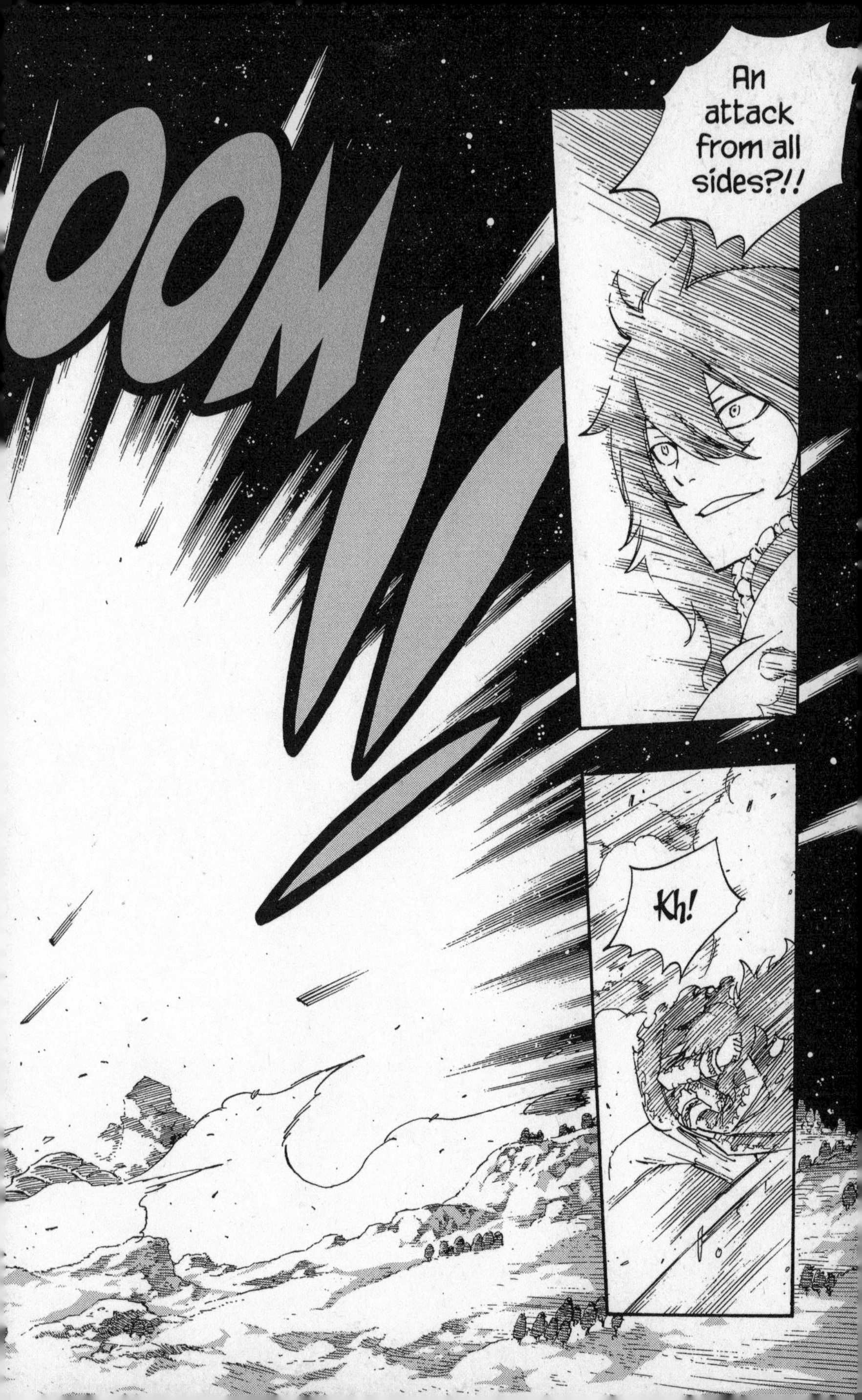
An attack from all sides?!!
Kh!
OOM

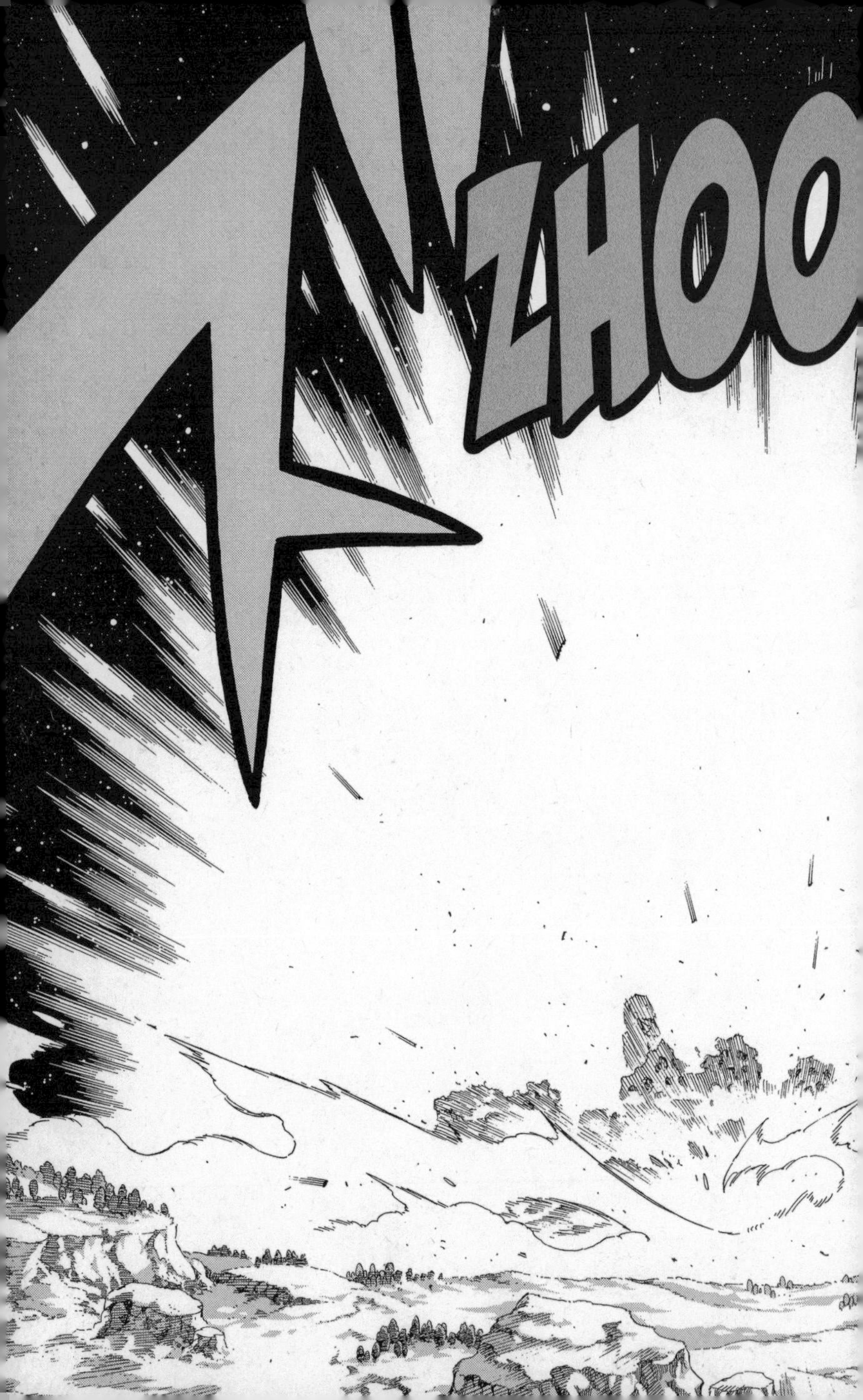
ZHOO

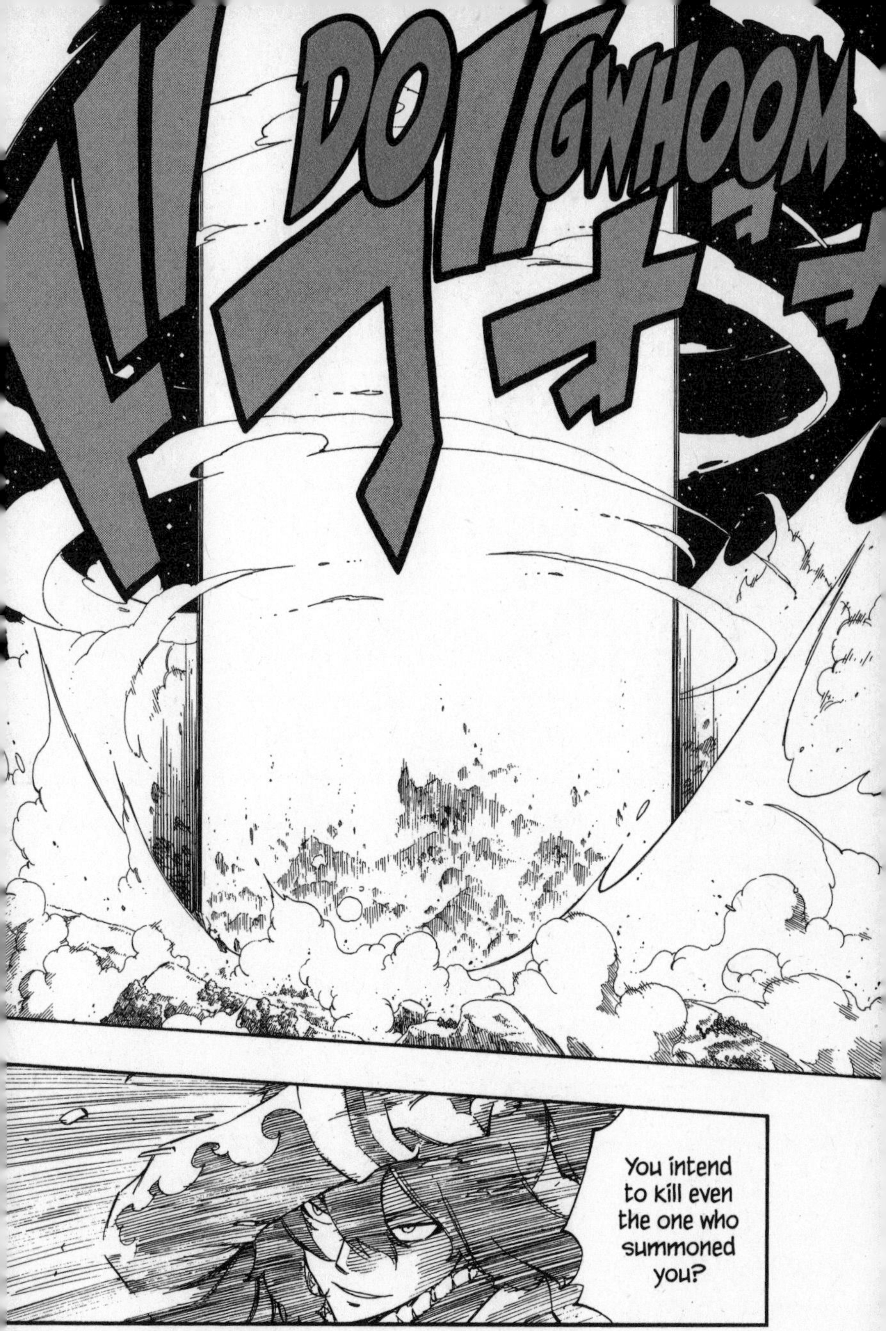
DOGWHOOM
You intend to kill even the one who summoned you?

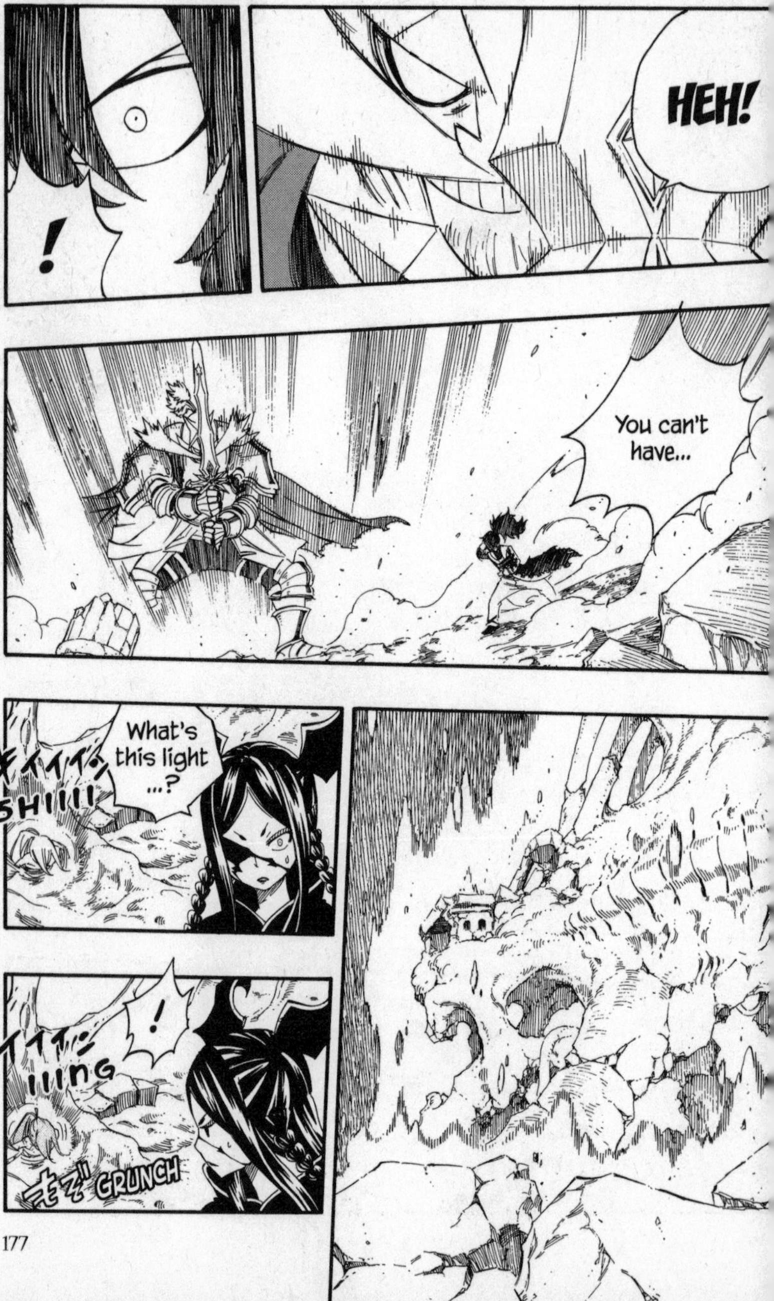
HEH!
!
You can't have...
キイイン
SHIIII
What's this light ...?
!
イイイン
IIING
もぞ
GRUNCH

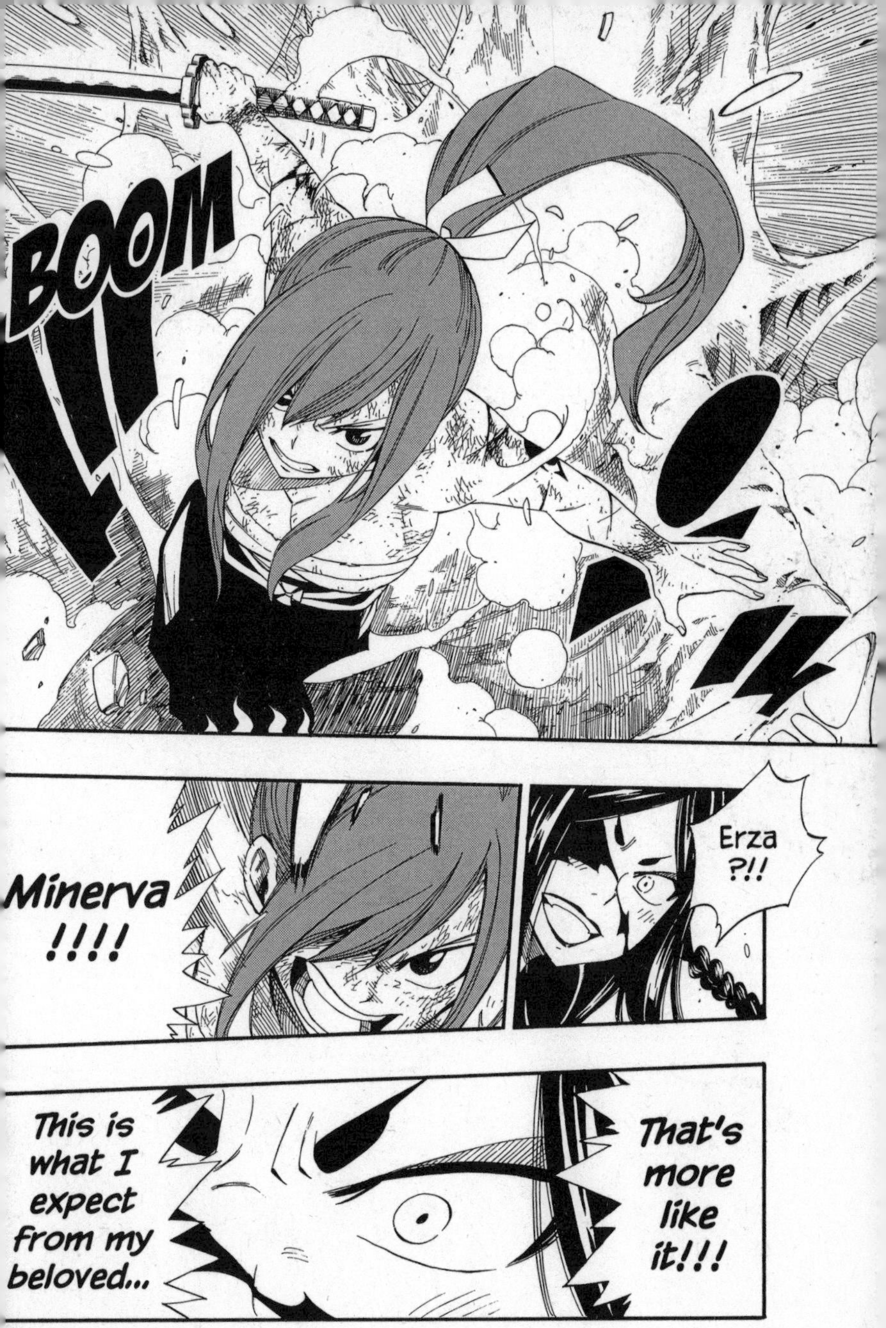
BOOM
Erza ?!!
Minerva !!!!
That's more like it!!!
This is what I expect from my beloved...

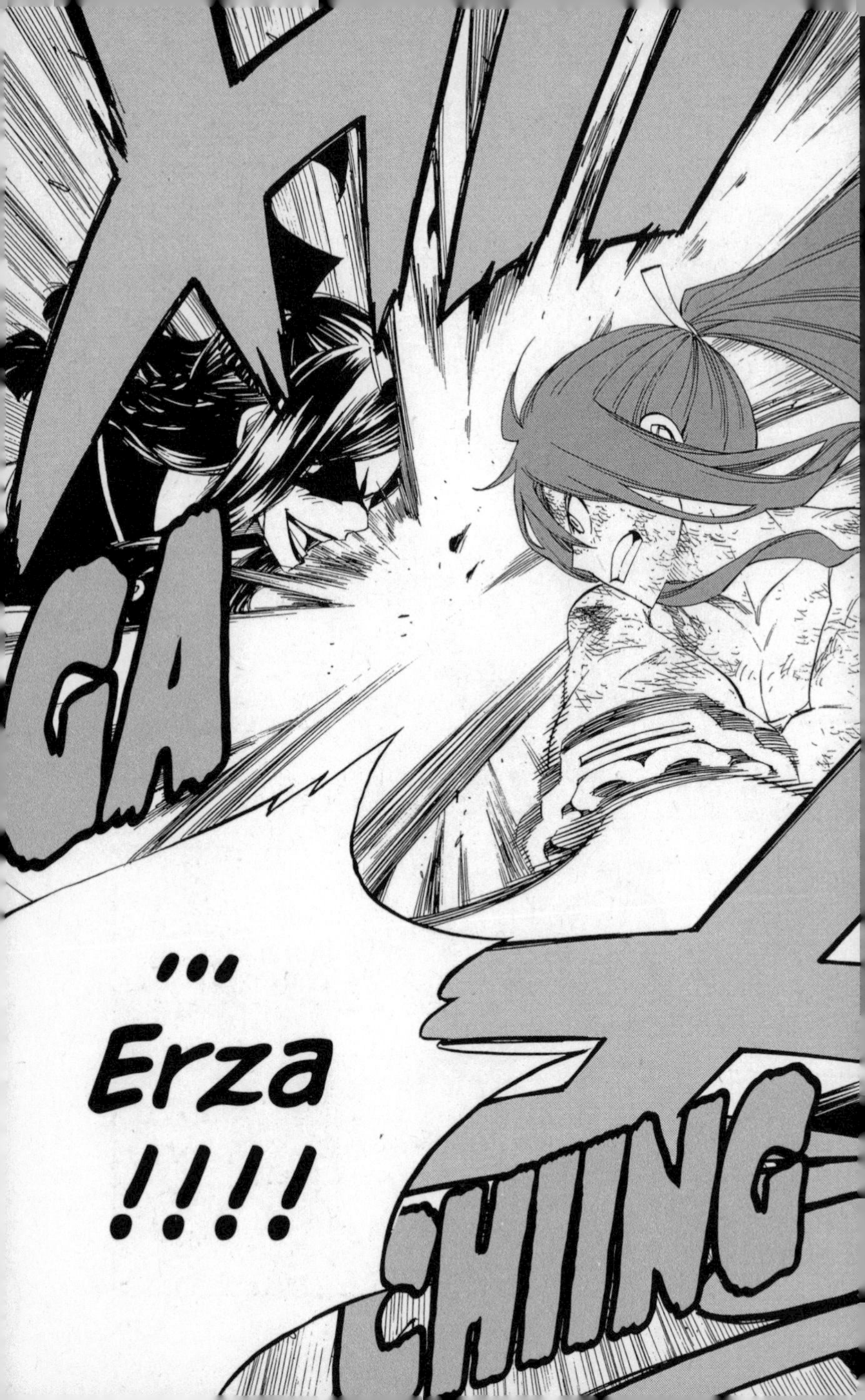
GA
CHING
...Erza!!!!

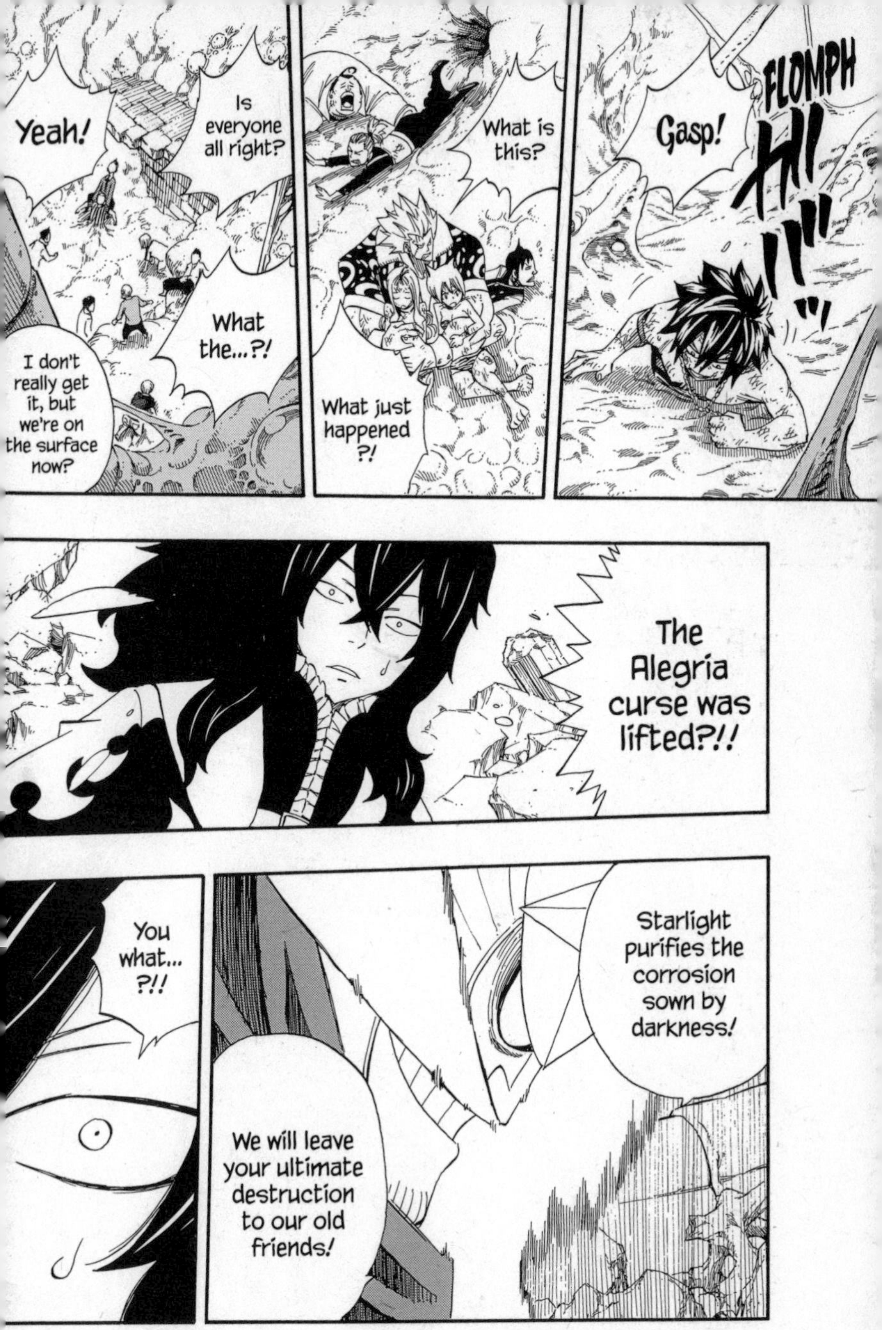
FLOMPH
Gasp!
What is this?
What just happened?!
Is everyone all right?
Yeah!
What the...?!
I don't really get it, but we're on the surface now?
The Alegria curse was lifted?!!
Starlight purifies the corrosion sown by darkness!
We will leave your ultimate destruction to our old friends!
You what...?!!

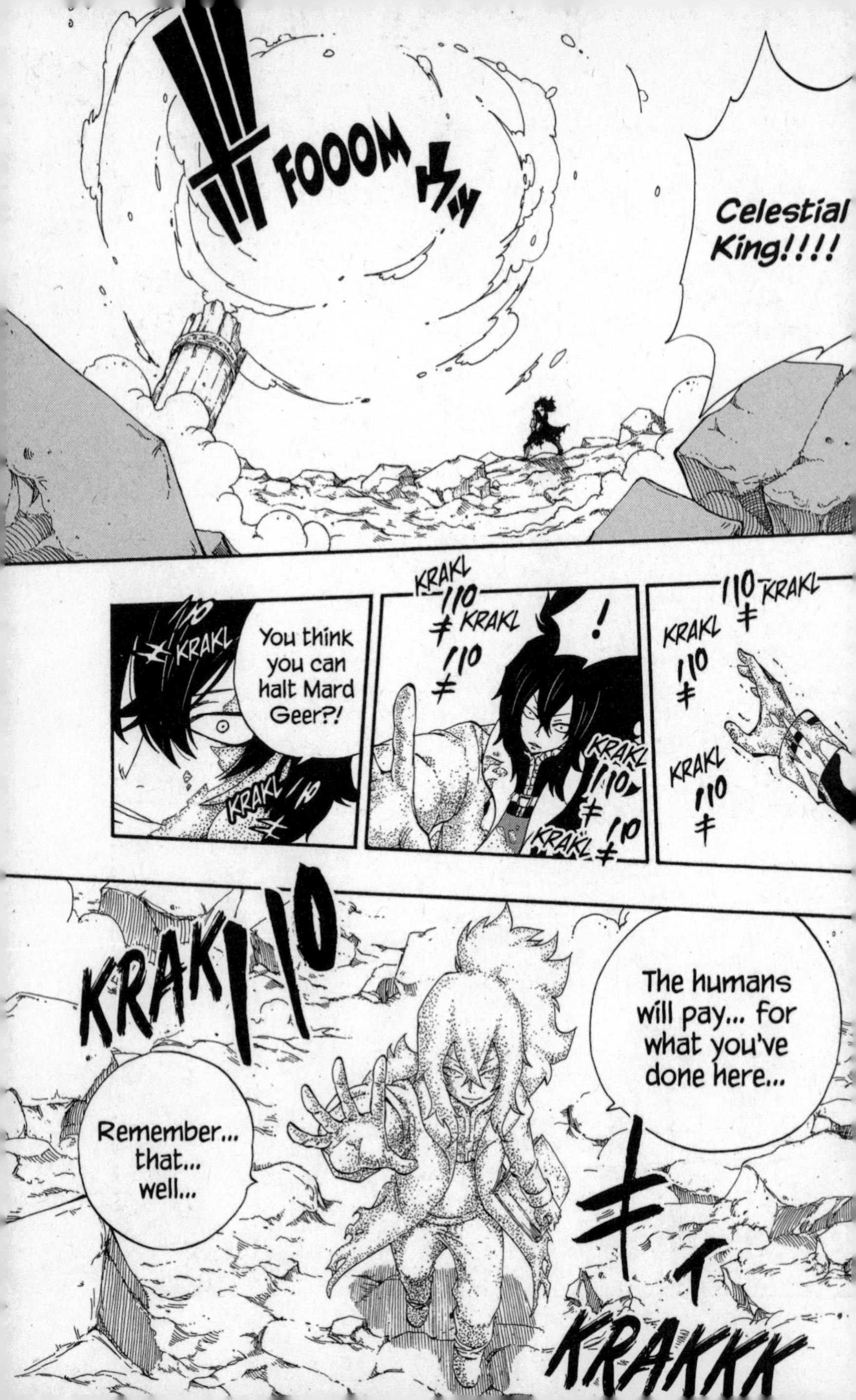
Celestial King!!!!
FOOOM
KRAKL
KRAKL
KRAKL
KRAKL
!
KRAKL
KRAKL
KRAKL
KRAKL
You think you can halt Mard Geer?!
KRAKL
The humans will pay... for what you've done here...
KRAKKK
KRAKL
Remember... that... well...

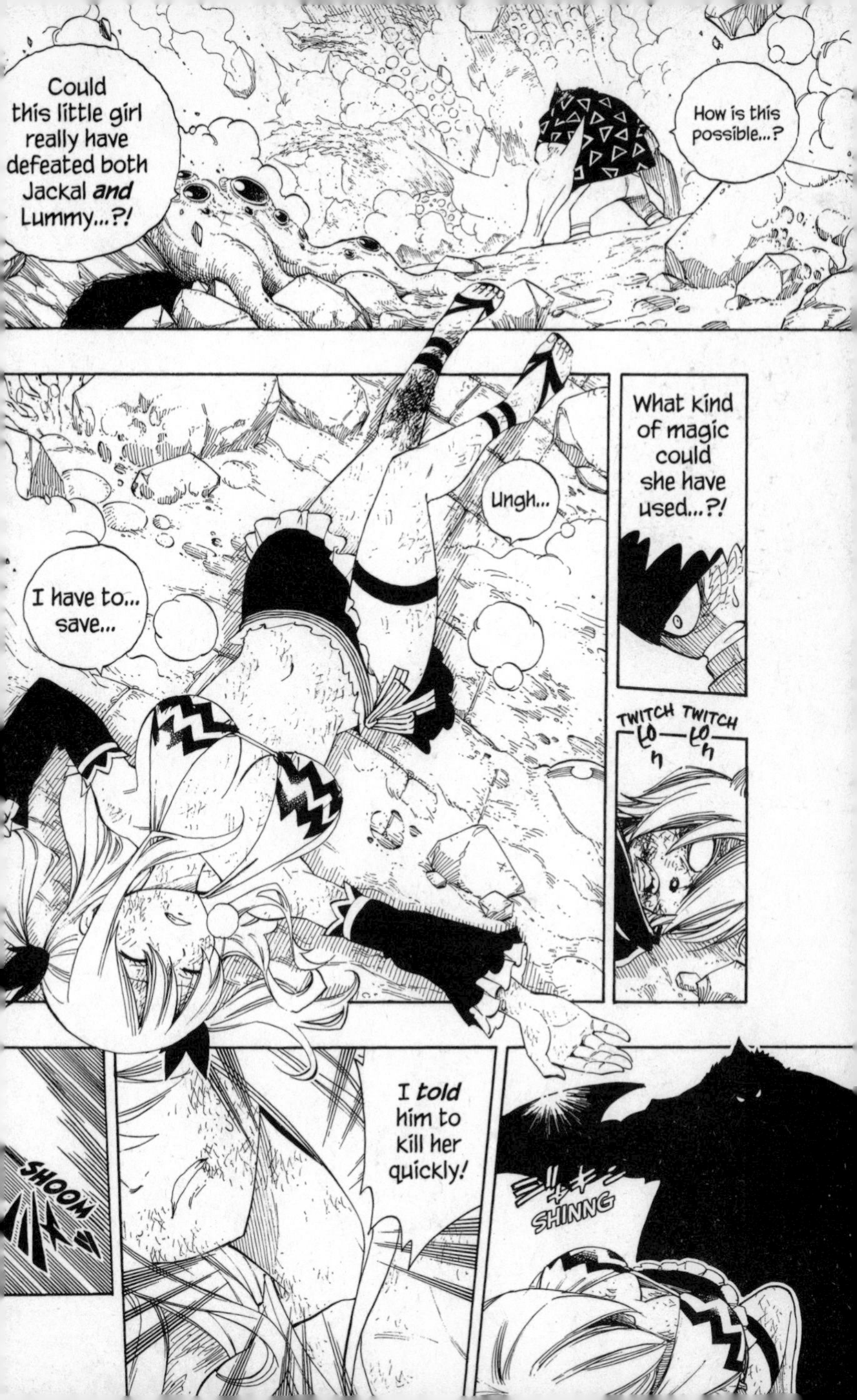
How is this possible...?
Could this little girl really have defeated both Jackal *and* Lummy...?!
What kind of magic could she have used...?!
TWITCH TWITCH
Ungh...
I have to... save...
SHINNG
I *told* him to kill her quickly!
SHOOM

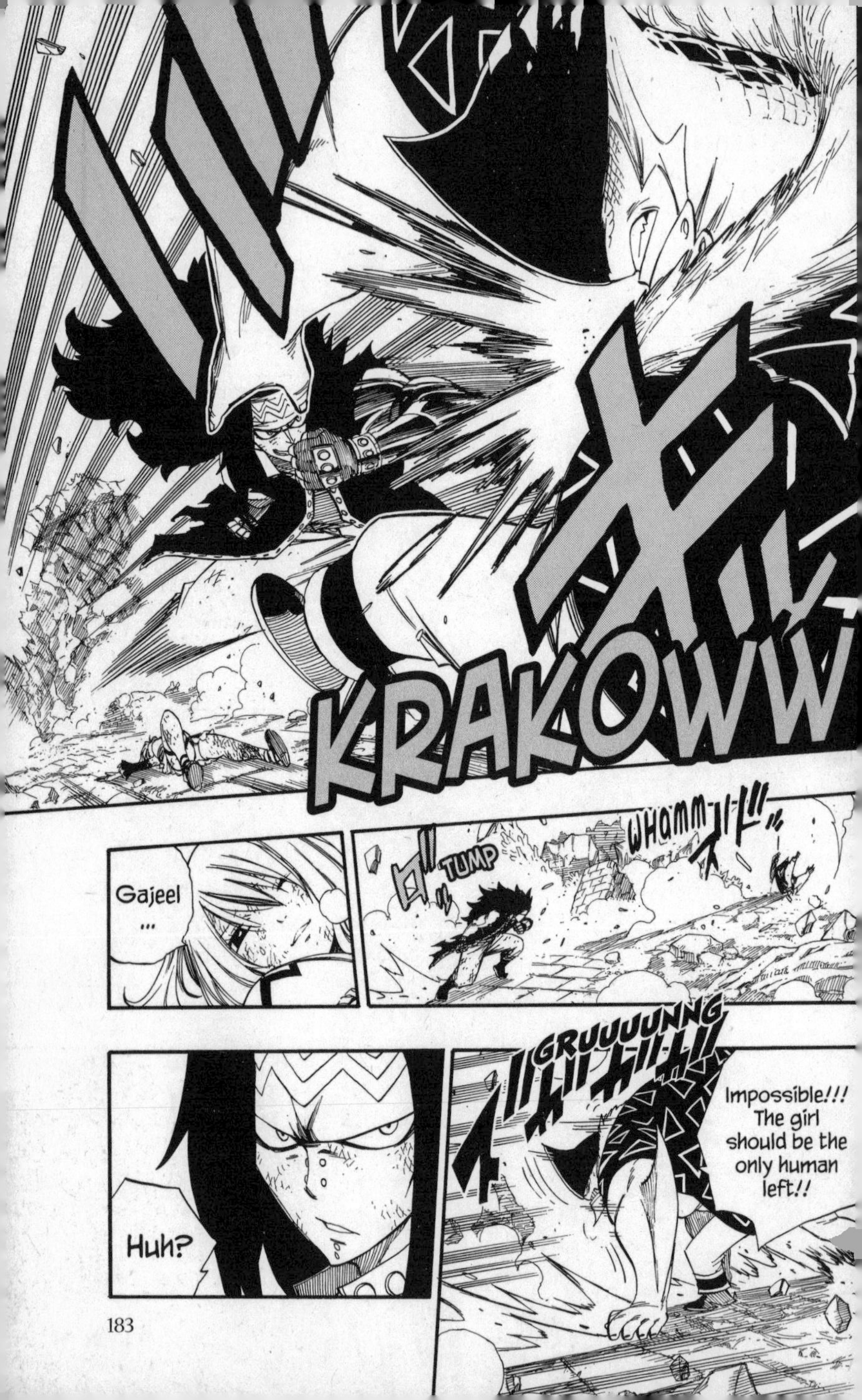
KRAKOWW
WHAMM
TUMP
Gajeel ...
GRUUUUNG
Impossible!!! The girl should be the only human left!!
Huh?

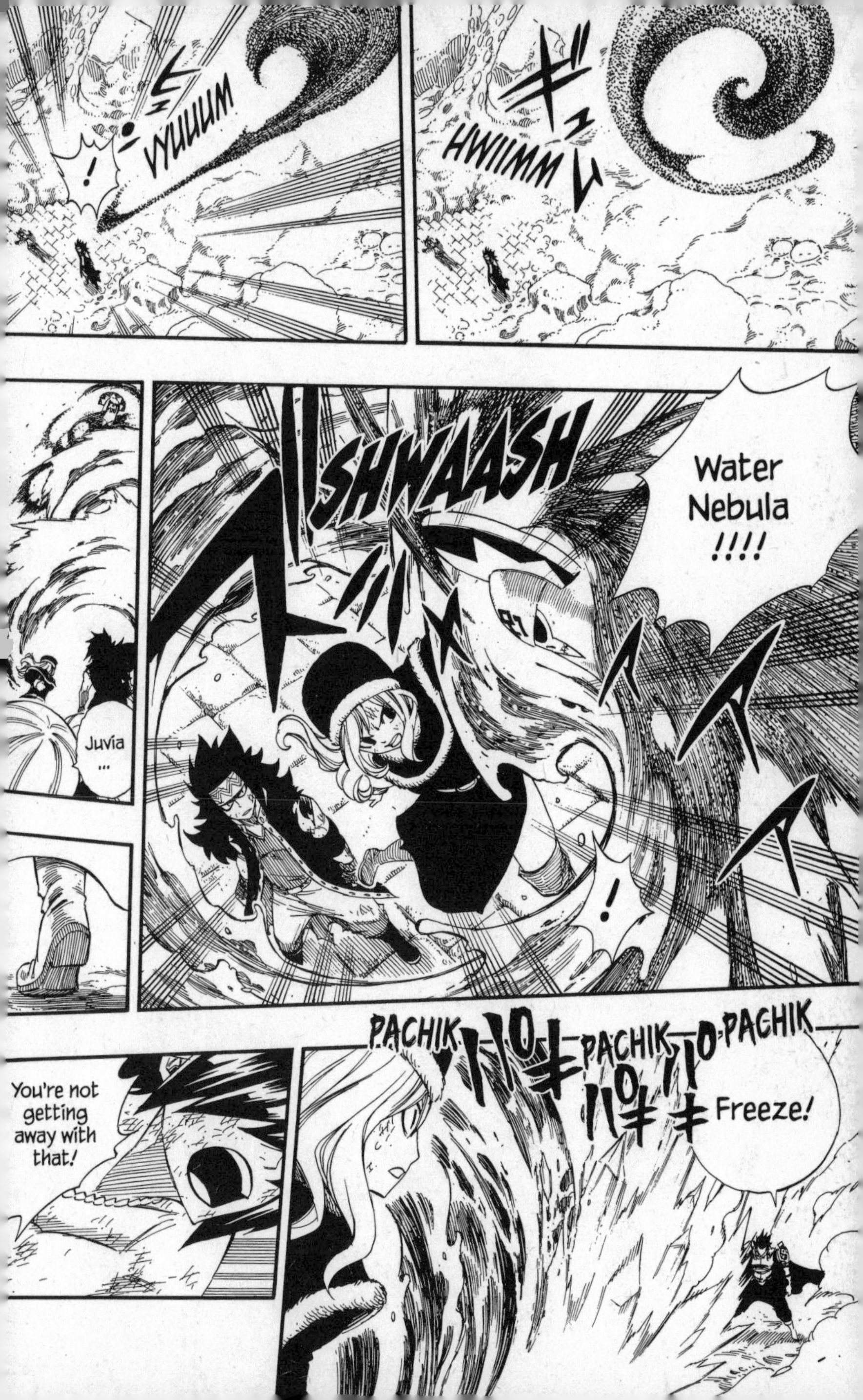

HWIIMM
!
VYUUUM
Water Nebula !!!!
SHWAASH
!
Juvia …
PACHIK PACHIK PACHIK
Freeze!
You're not getting away with that!

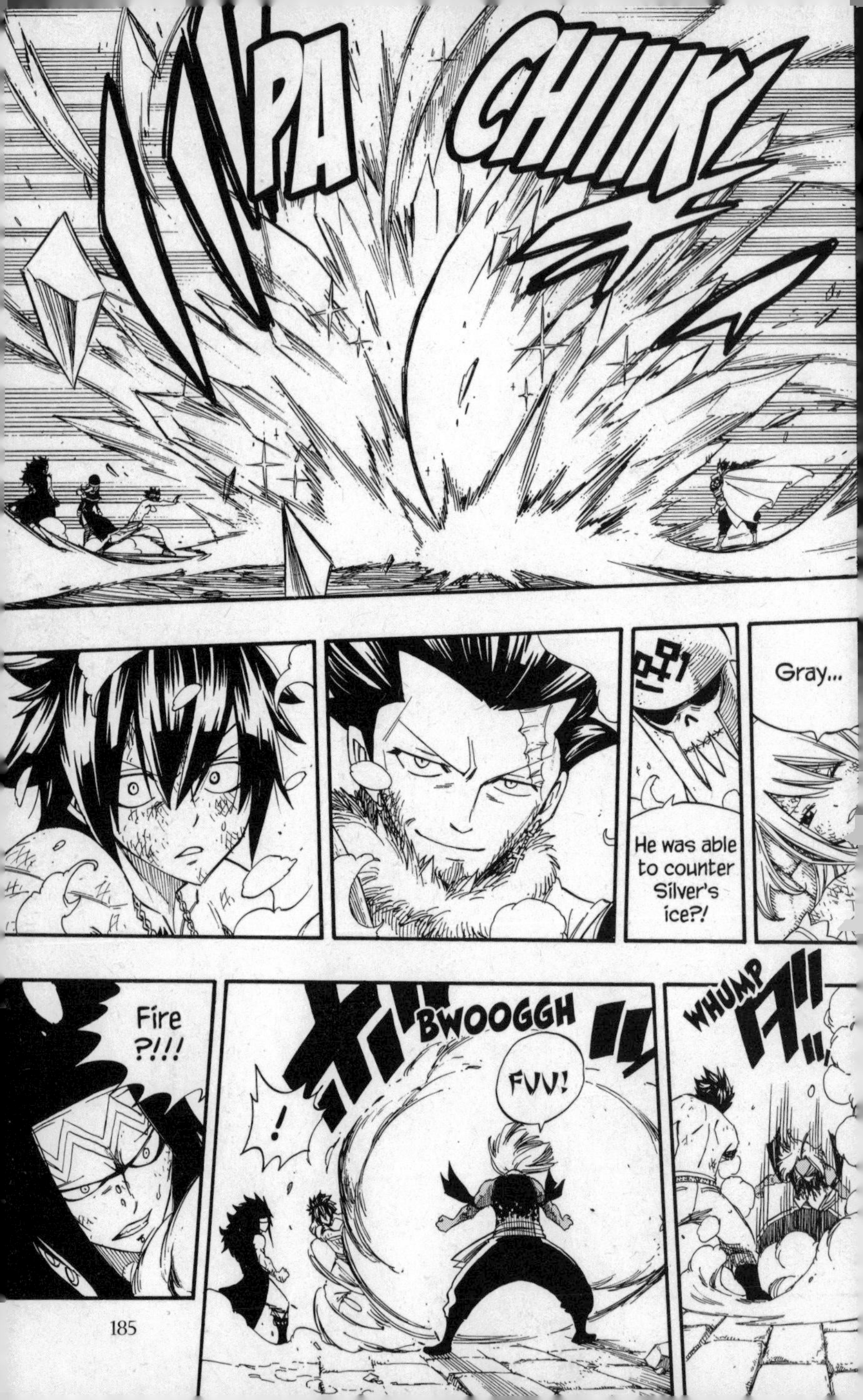
PA CHIIIN!
Gray...
He was able to counter Silver's ice?!
WHUMP
BWOOGGH
FUU!
!
Fire?!!!

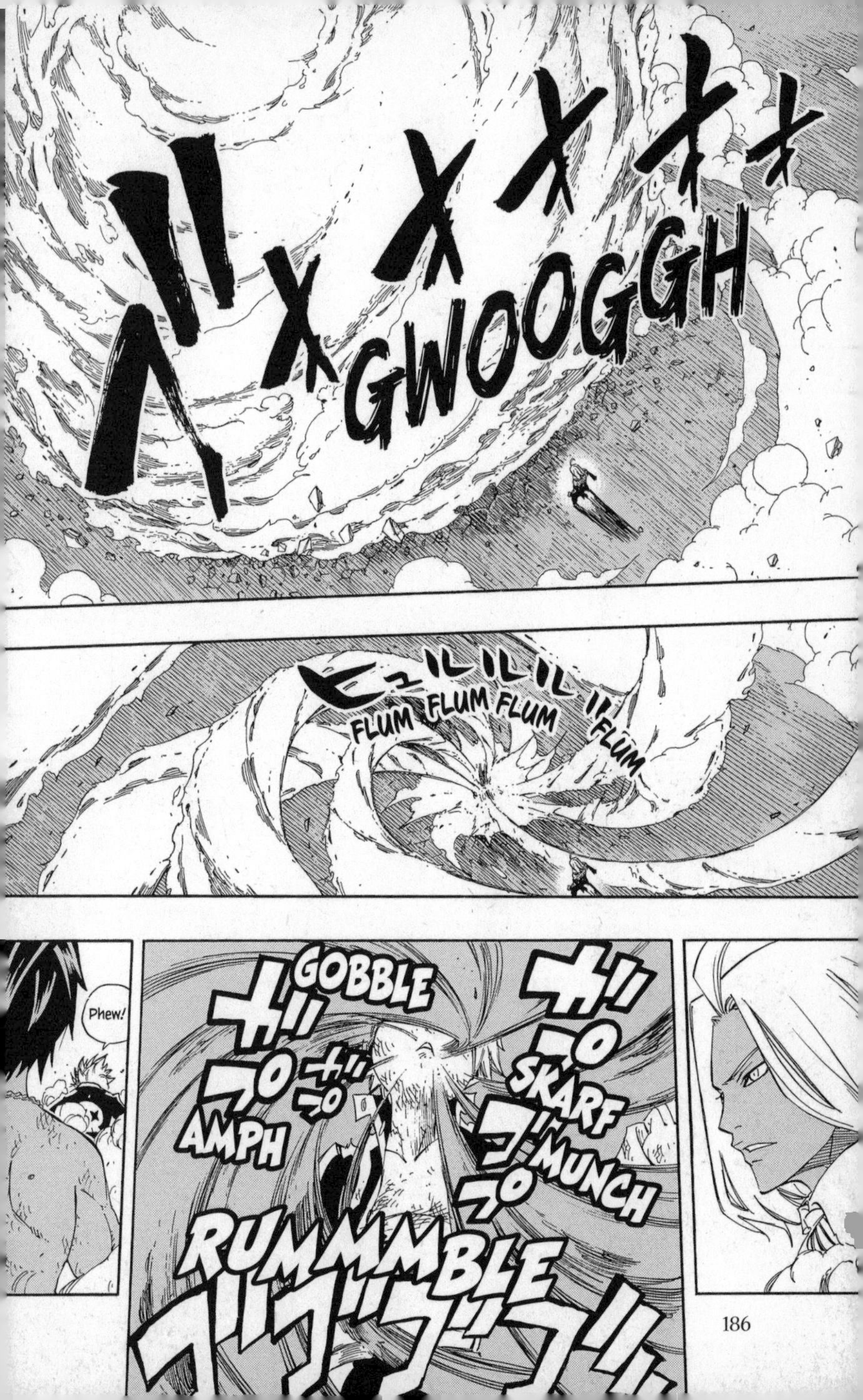
GWOOGGH
FLUM FLUM FLUM FLUM
SKARF
GOBBLE
MUNCH
AMPH
RUMMMBLE
Phew!

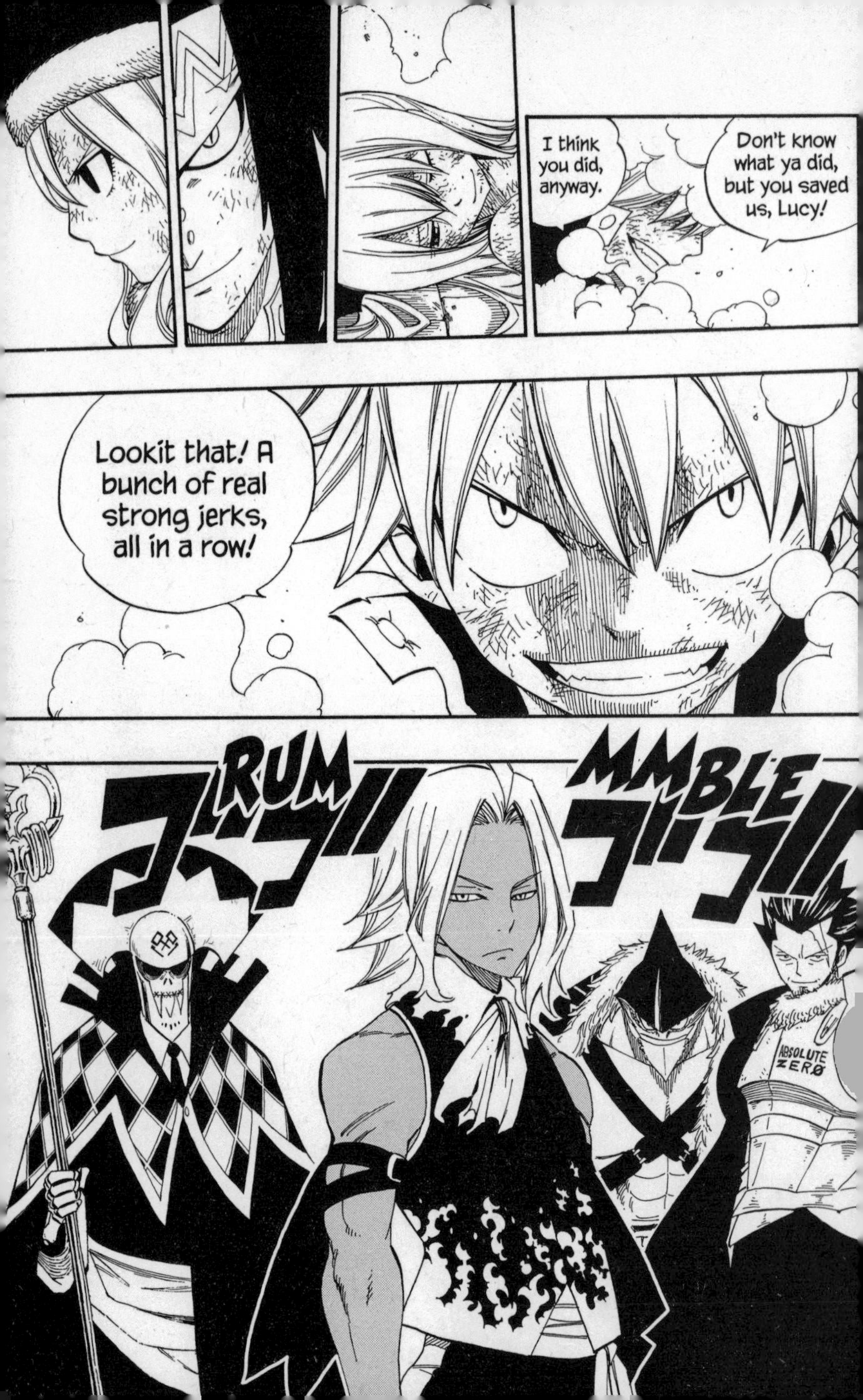
Don't know what ya did, but you saved us, Lucy!
I think you did, anyway.
Lookit that! A bunch of real strong jerks, all in a row!
RUMMMBLE
ABSOLUTE ZERØ

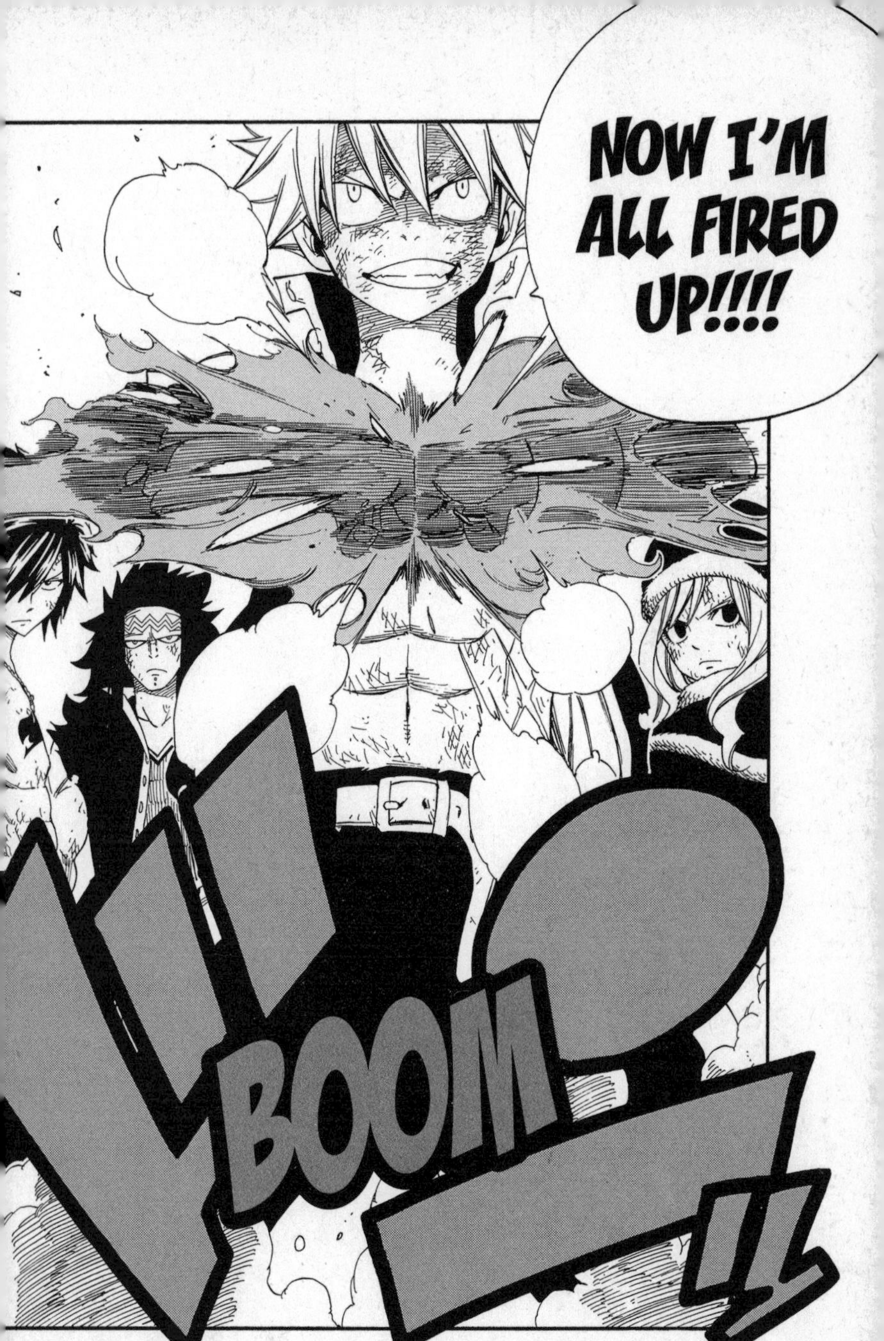
NOW I'M ALL FIRED UP!!!!
BOOM!!

TO BE CONTINUED

あとがき

Afterword

The method of summoning the Celestial King was a plot point I had been thinking about for a long time, and I kept wondering, "When can I use it?" "When can I use it?!" But the price that Lucy had to pay to summon him was an idea I had almost directly before I drew it. But when I consider whose key to sacrifice, it came down to only one choice. It was precisely because Lucy loves the character Aquarius so much that made it particularly sad. But I'd like to think that they aren't parted forever. Also the story of Mirajane, Elfman and Lisanna's past was something I thought up a very long time ago, but the chance to tell it just never seemed right. And when a perfect chance came along this time, I was so happy! I remember when Mira used the Macro on Elfman, and he suddenly appeared, my editor complained, "What is he, a robot?!!"

In the next volume is a story that I'm sure a lot of people are waiting for. The story of Silver. It's a sad story too, I'm afraid, but I hope you'll be anxiously awaiting it anyway.

By the way, it seems that one of the main villains of the story this time, Jackal, has unexpectedly become pretty popular. He's an awful guy though. (laughs) Also, Jackal's character calls for a half-baked Osaka-area accent, so I had a tough time trying to get the words he uses right. I'm not from the Osaka area myself, but it's a lot easier to write full-on Osaka-area accents. Hm…

Rejected
Rough Sketch

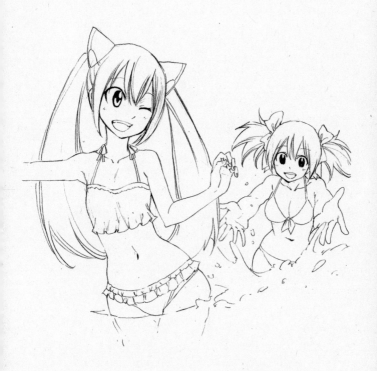

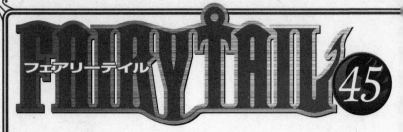

FAIRY TAIL
フェアリーテイル
45

Rejected Natsu

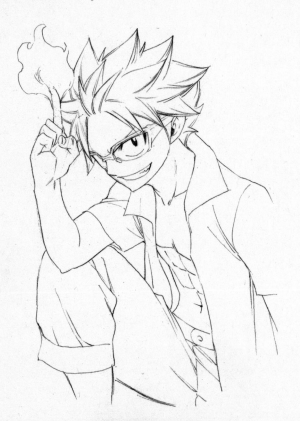

HIRO 真島ヒロ MASHIMA

FROM 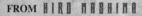 HIRO MASHINA

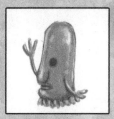

I went to a signing event in Hokkaido!!
It sure was a lot of fun. When a
Japanese guy thinks of Hokkaido, his
mind conjures up images of delicious
food, and although I was there only
a short time, I managed to eat some
sushi and ramen. The fans also gave
me lots of presents. Thank you so
much! I'll visit you again, Hokkaido!!

Original Jacket Design: Hisao Ogawa

Translation Notes:

Japanese is a tricky language for most Westerners, and translation is often more art than science. For your edification and reading pleasure, here are notes on some of the places where we could have gone in a different direction with our translation of the work, or where a Japanese cultural reference is used.

Page 41, Sytry

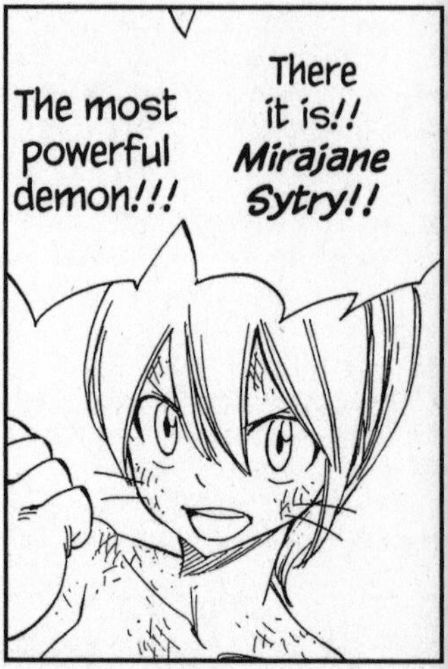
There it is!! Mirajane Sytry!!
The most powerful demon!!!

Sytry (or Prince Sitri) is a demon from the *Ars Goetia*, the first book of the spell book, *The Lesser Key of Solomon*, which is a book of sorcery compiled in the 1600s that allegedly gets its power by manipulating demons. The demon Sytry causes men to love women or vice versa and even strip themselves naked.

Page 47, Aetherious

There are a lot of meanings for this word, but the one that Hiro Mashima seems to be referencing the most is mythological idea of Aether, which means the "upper atmosphere" but also refers to air the Gods breathe. Aether is, in itself, a Greek God. As an avid game player, Mashima might have gotten his introduction to Aetherious from the action game, *The Elder Scrolls* (or some similar game) where Aetherious is the realm from which divine and powerful beings come.

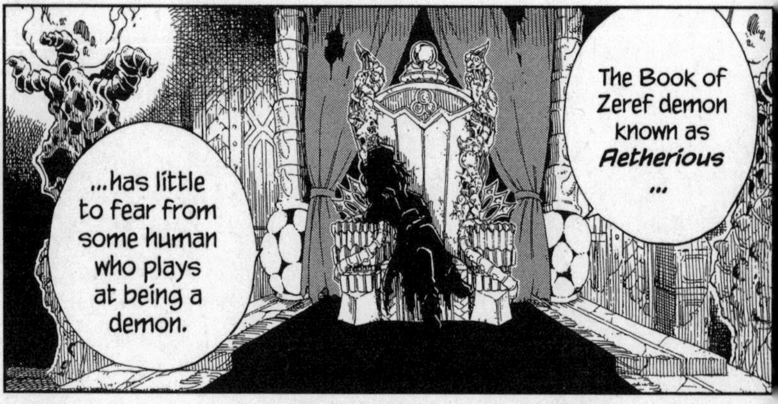
The Book of Zeref demon known as Aetherious ...
...has little to fear from some human who plays at being a demon.

Page 48, Mard Geer

The Mard Geer is a polearm weapon from India in the 16th-18th centuries. It had a regular spear-like spike, but it also had a hooked piece for use by infantry to use against cavalry. The infantryman would try to pull a cavalryman from his horse with the hook and then spear him with the spear section. Several games include a weapon called Mard Geer, although it seems to be a different weapon than the historical Indian polearm. Perhaps one of those games is where Hiro Mashima heard of it.

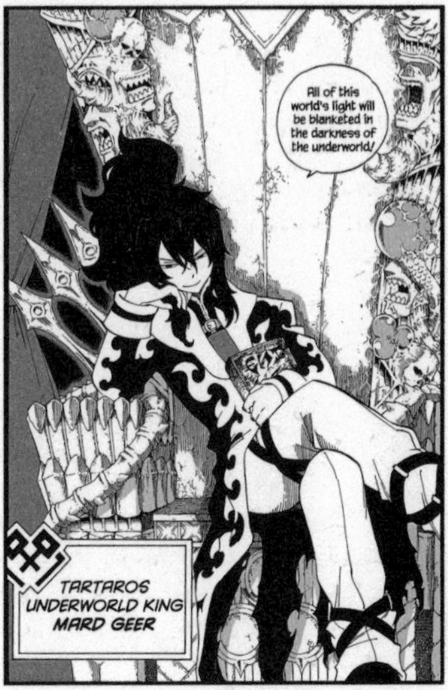
All of this world's light will be blanketed in the darkness of the underworld!
TARTAROS UNDERWORLD KING MARD GEER

Page 90, Pluto's Grim

Mard Geer calls himself the Underworld King, and in Greco-Roman mythology, there is also a god of the Underworld known as Hades in Greece and as Pluto in Rome. In Greco-Roman mythology, the underworld was not necessarily a place of torture, but rather simply a place where dead souls go. Note that Pluto, now a "dwarf planet," was named after the Roman God, and Mickey Mouse's dog, Pluto, who was created about the time the ex-planet Pluto was discovered, was named after the planet.

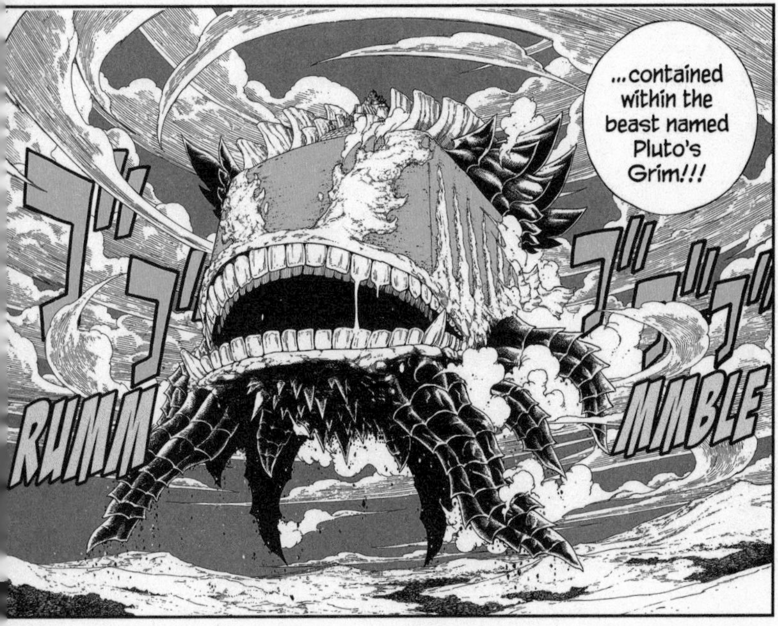
...contained within the beast named Pluto's Grim!!!
RUMMMMBLE

Page 165, Lucy's Incantation

As happens sometimes in the translation of a long series, later facts can prove an earlier translation wrong. In volume 18, Lucy says the same incantation, but to show that she is not doing it consciously, the far-right and far-left sides of the incantation were cut off by the word balloons. So I was translating from incomplete text. Now with the complete text, I can retranslate it so it says what it really means. I can only apologize to those with earlier printings of Volume 18, and hope you understand.

Page 165, Tetrabiblos

As mentioned in the notes for Volume 18, Claudius Ptolemy wrote a four-part series of books describing the heavens called the *Tetrabiblos*, The Four Books. One of the most important works of ancient astrology, the Tetrabiblos describes the constellations of the zodiac and their astrological influence on the world.

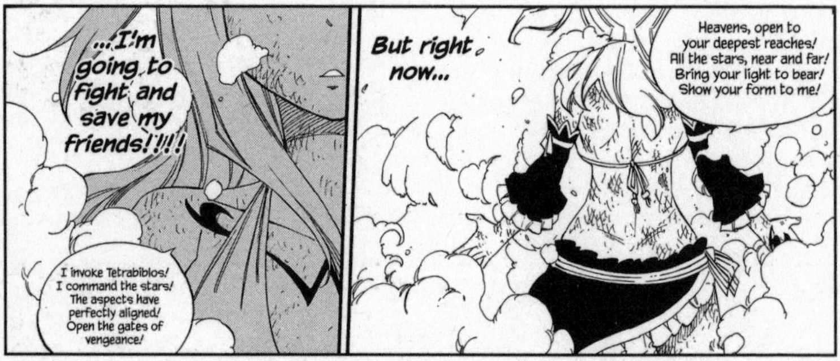
Heavens, open to your deepest reaches! All the stars, near and far! Bring your light to bear! Show your form to me!
But right now...
...I'm going to fight and save my friends!!!!
I invoke Tetrabiblos! I command the stars! The aspects have perfectly aligned! Open the gates of vengeance!

Preview of *Fairy Tail*, volume 46

We're pleased to present you with a preview from *Fairy Tail*, volume 46, now available digitally from Kodansha Comics and coming to print in January 2015. Check out our website (www.kodanshacomics.com) for details!

FAIRY TAIL

フェアリーテイル

Chapter 387: Tartaros Arc, Part Four: Father and Son

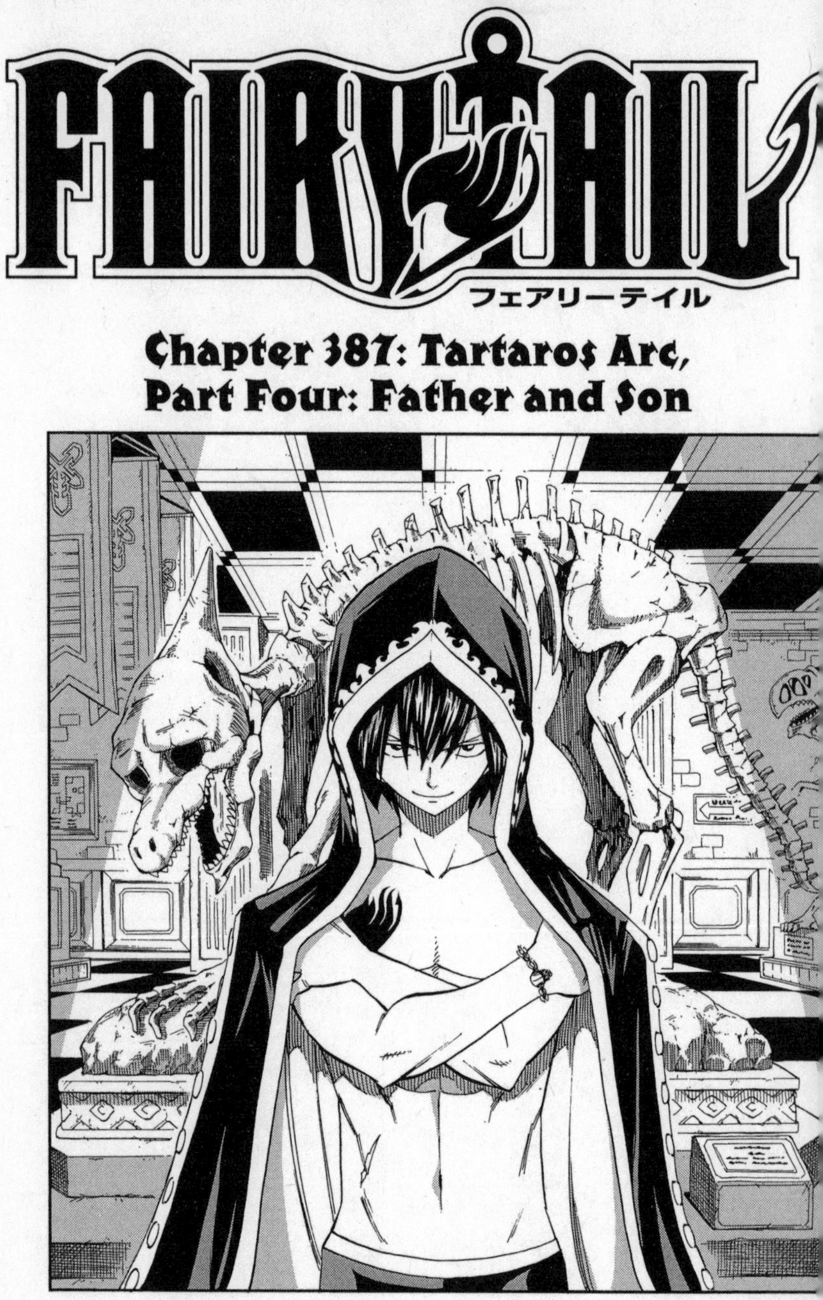

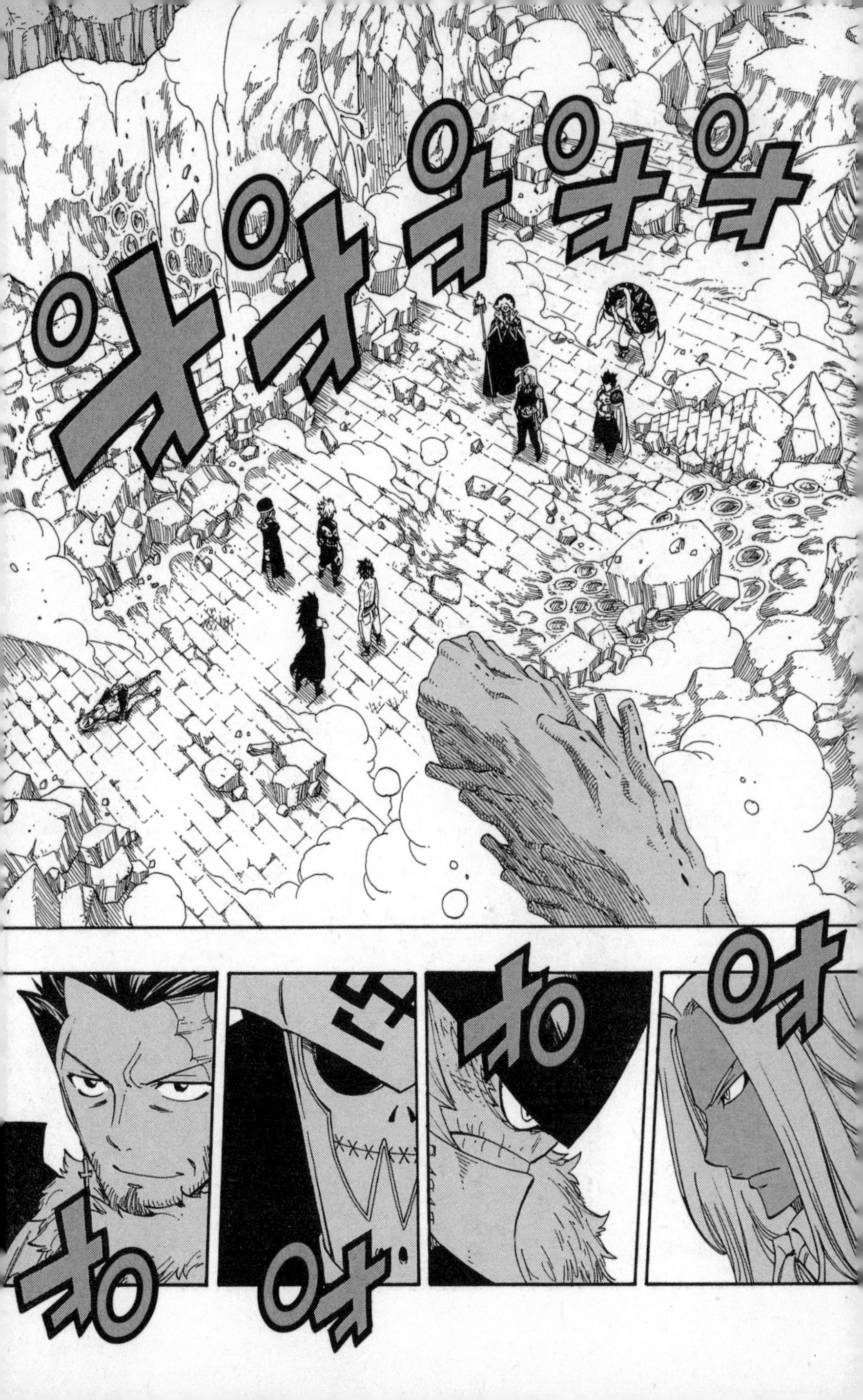
オオオオオ
オ
オ
オ
オ

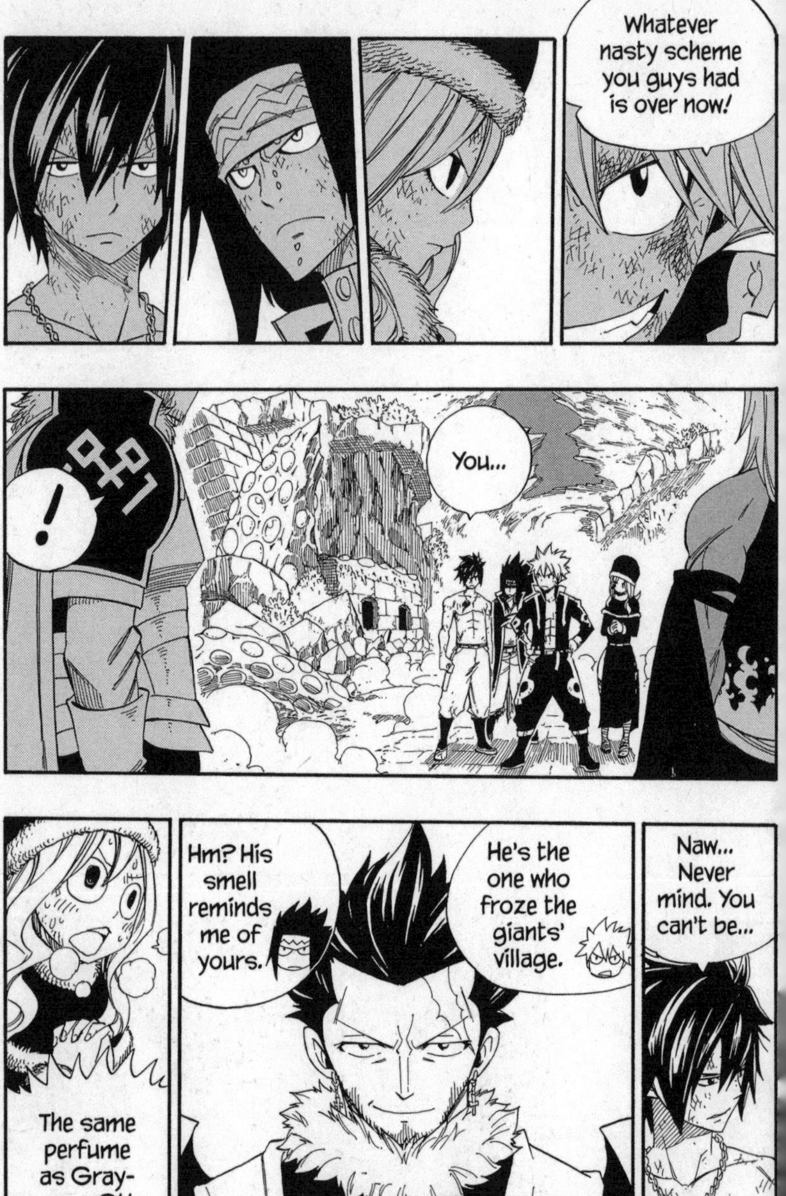
Whatever nasty scheme you guys had is over now!
You...
!
Naw... Never mind. You can't be...
He's the one who froze the giants' village.
Hm? His smell reminds me of yours.
The same perfume as Gray-sama?!!

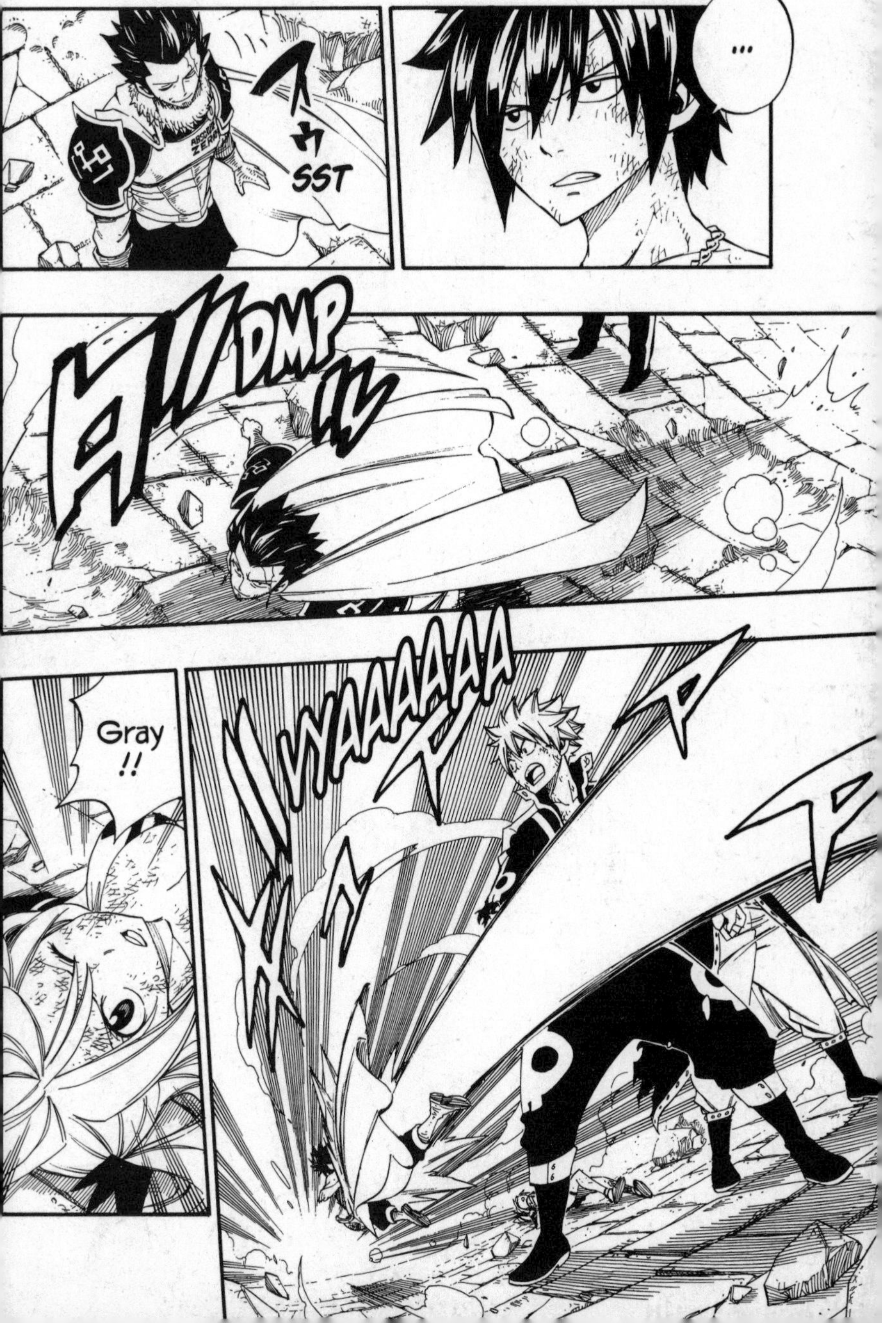
...
SST
DMP
WAAAAAA
Gray
!!

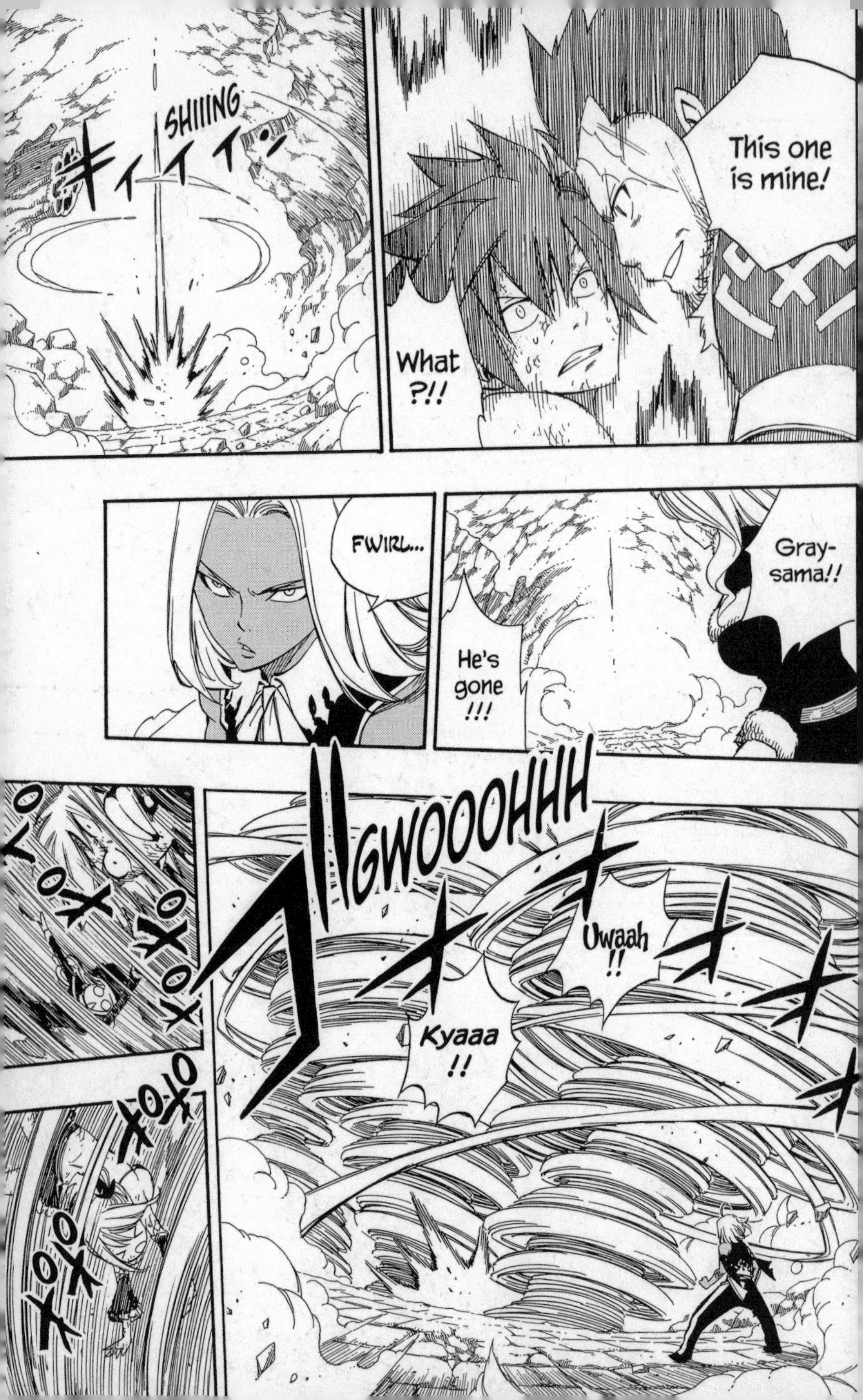

This one is mine!
What ?!!
SHIIING
Gray-sama!!
He's gone !!!
FWIRL...
GWOOOHHH
Uwaah !!
Kyaaa !!

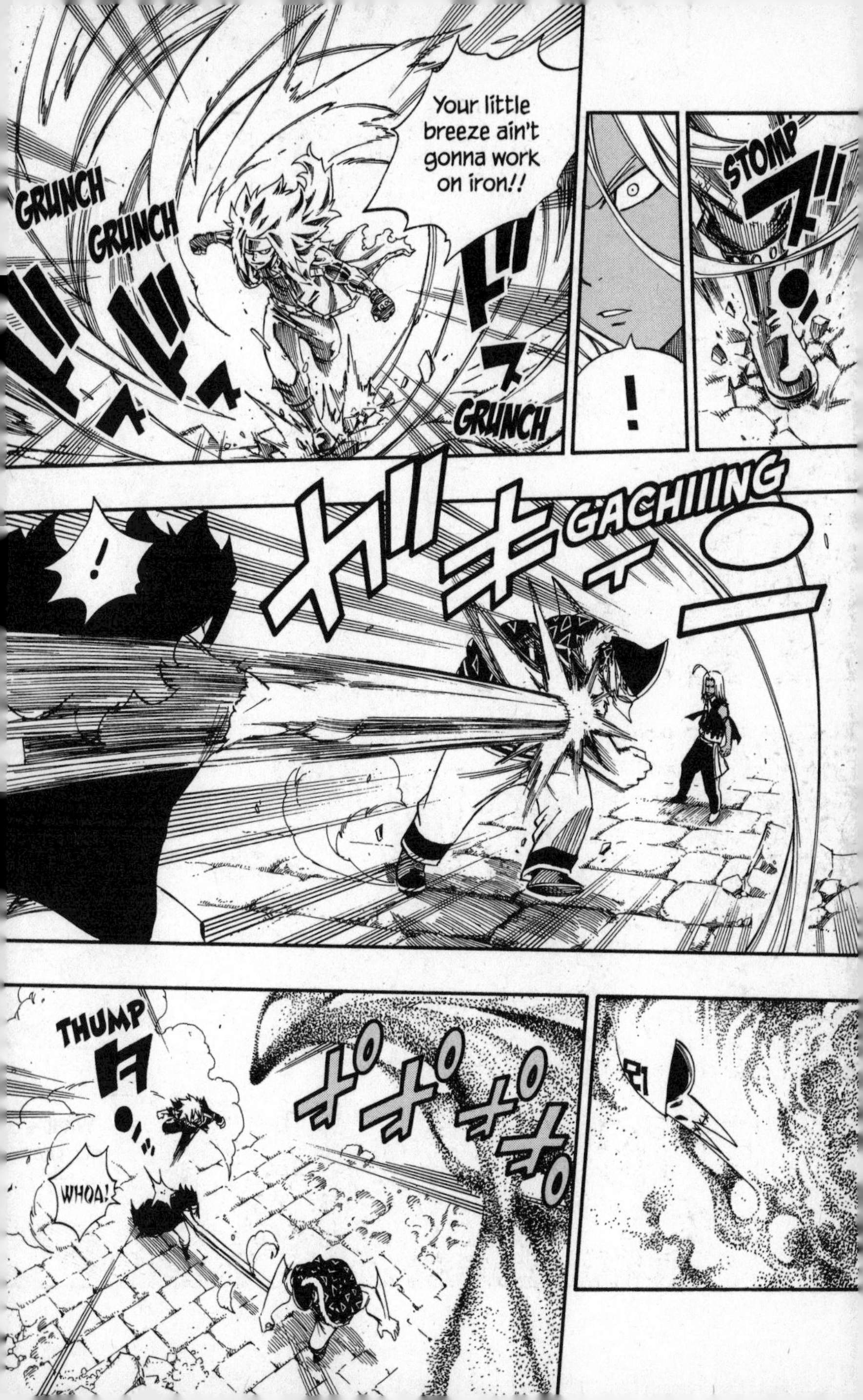
STOMP
!
Your little breeze ain't gonna work on iron!!
GRUNCH
GRUNCH
GRUNCH
GACHIIING
!
THUMP
WHOA!

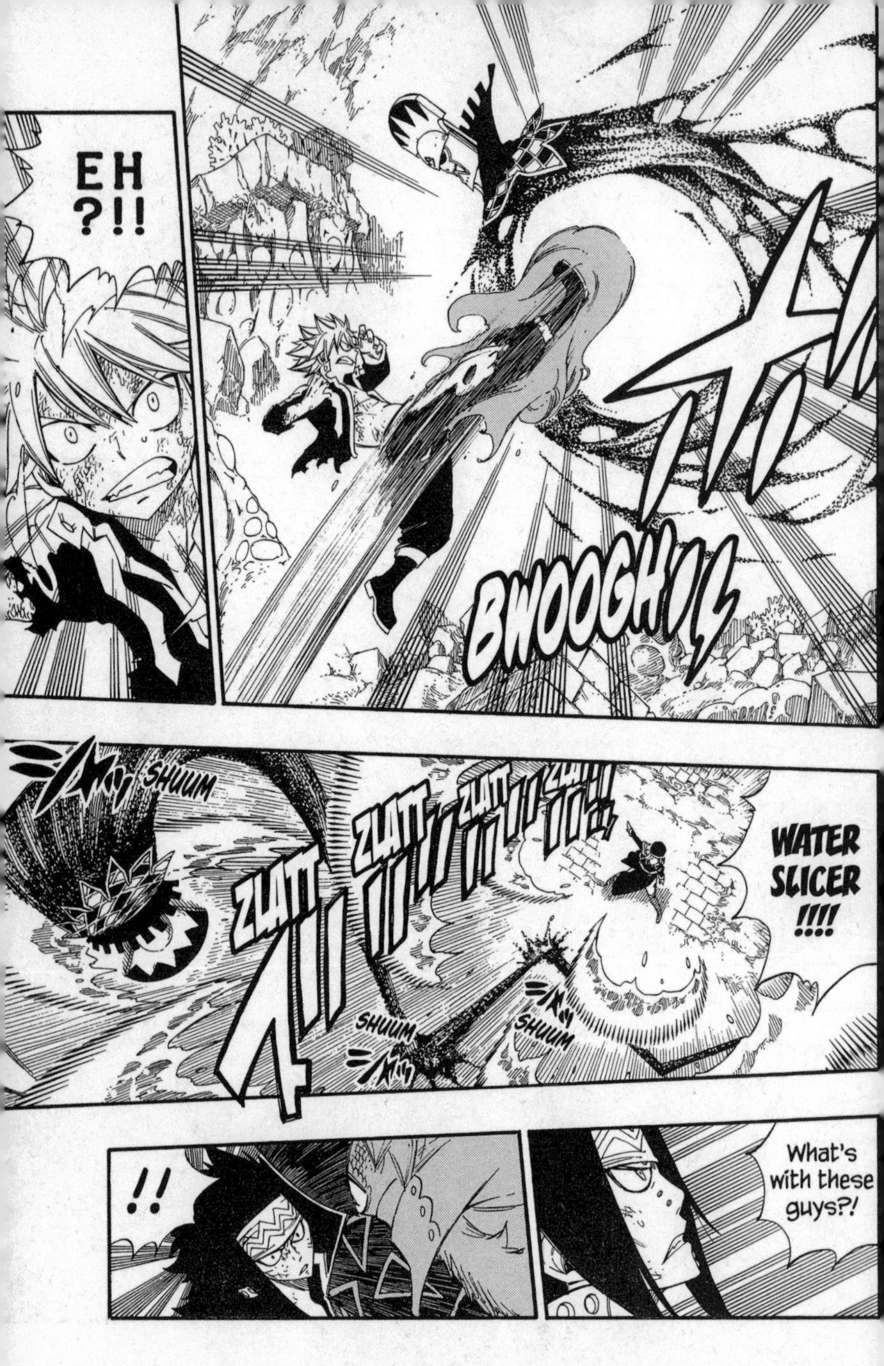
BWOOGH
EH?!!
WATER SLICER!!!!
ZLATT
ZLATT
ZLATT
SHUUM
SHUUM
SHUUM
What's with these guys?!
!!

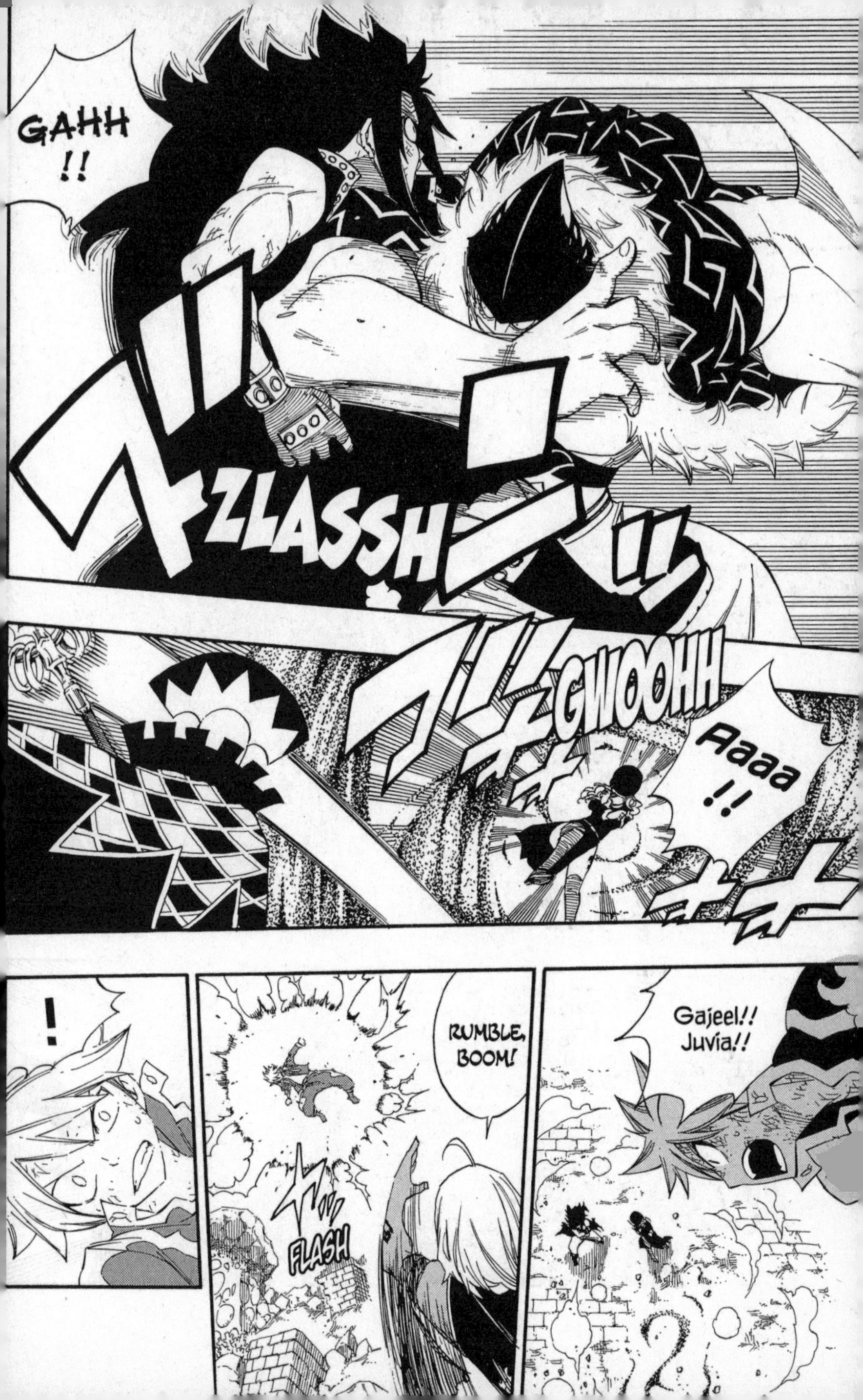
GAHH !!
ZLASSH !!
GWOOHH
Aaaa !!
Gajeel!! Juvia!!
RUMBLE, BOOM!
FLASH
!

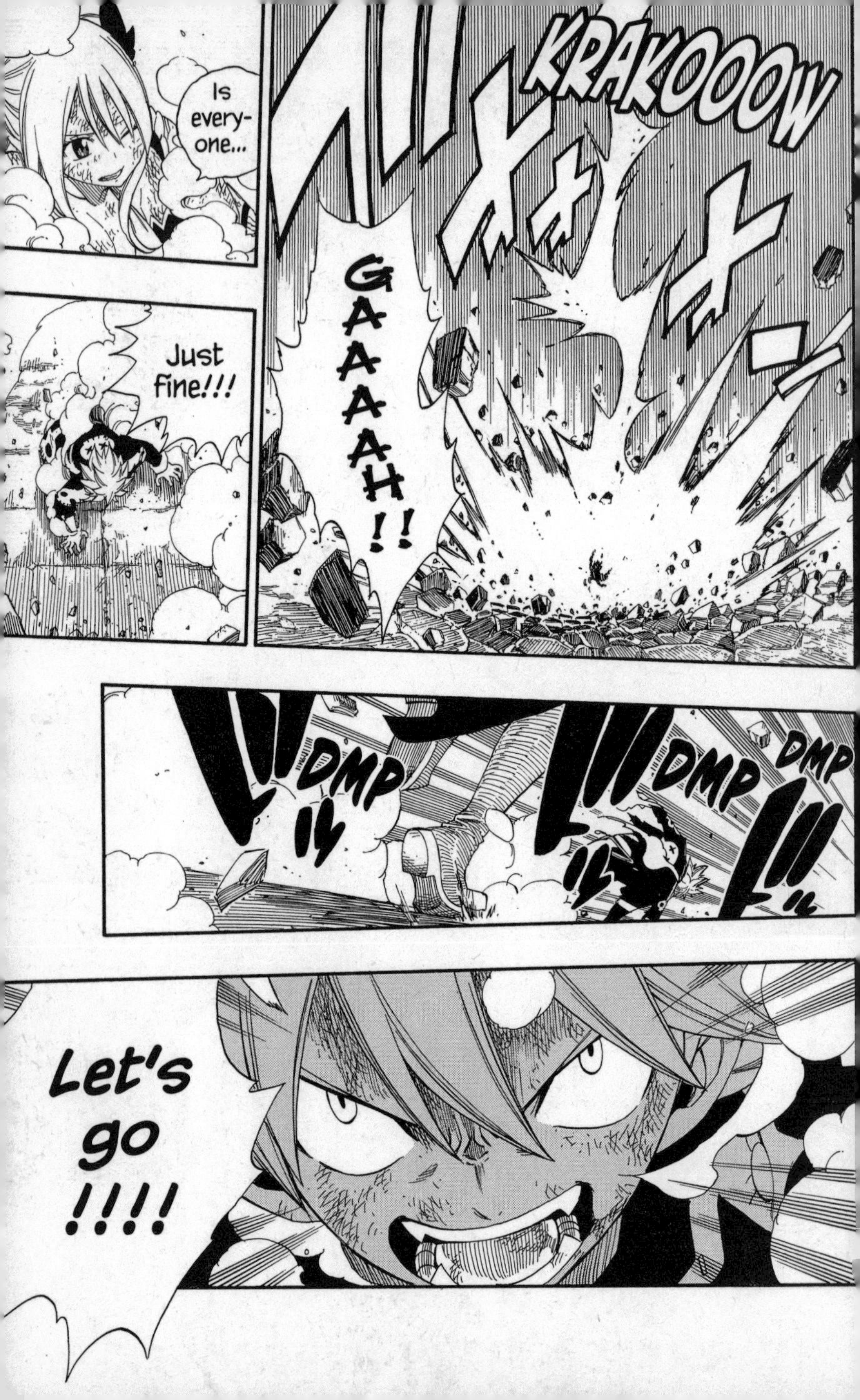

KRAKOOOW
GAAAAAH!!
Is every-one...
Just fine!!!
DMP
DMP
DMP
Let's go!!!!

Fairy Tail volume 45 is a work of fiction. Names, characters, places, and incidents are the products of the author's imagination or are used fictitiously. Any resemblance to actual events, locales, or persons, living or dead, is entirely coincidental.

A Kodansha Comics Trade Paperback Original.

Published in the United States by Kodansha Comics, an imprint of Kodansha USA Publishing, LLC, New York.

Publication rights for this English edition arranged through Kodansha Ltd., Tokyo.

First published in Japan in 2014 by Kodansha Ltd., Tokyo
ISBN 978-1-61262-564-5

Printed in the United States of America.

www.kodanshacomics.com

9 8 7 6 5 4 3 2 1

Translation: William Flanagan
Lettering: AndWorld Design
Editing: Ben Applegate
Kodansha Comics edition cover design by Phil Balsman

TOMARE!

止まれ

[STOP!]

You're going the wrong way!

Manga is a completely different type of reading experience.

To start at the *beginning*, go to the *end!*

hat's right! Authentic manga is read the traditional Japanese way—rom right to left, exactly the *opposite* of how American books are ead. It's easy to follow: Just go to the other end of the book and read ach page—and each panel—from right side to left side, starting at he top right. Now you're experiencing manga as it was meant to be!

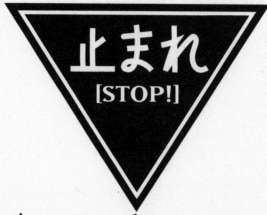